How to Find Out About Financial Aid and Funding 2003-2005

A Guide to Print, Electronic, and Internet Resources Listing
Scholarships •
Fellowships •
Loans •
Grants •
Awards •
Internships •

How to Find Out About Financial Aid and Funding 2003-2005

A Guide to Print, Electronic, and Internet Resources Listing
Scholarships •
Fellowships •
Loans •
Grants •
Awards •
Internships •

Gail Ann Schlachter

Reference Service Press • El Dorado Hills, California • 2003

© 2003 Gail Ann Schlachter

All rights reserved. No part of this publication may be reproduced, stored in a retrieval system, or transmitted, in any form or by any means, electronic, mechanical, photocopying, recording, or otherwise, except for the inclusion of brief quotations in a review, without the prior permission in writing from the publisher. Violation of copyright laws is a federal crime, punishable by fine and/or imprisonment *(Title 17, United States Code, Section 104)*

ISBN Number:
1-58841-093-5

10 9 8 7 6 5 4 3 2 1

Reference Service Press (RSP) began in 1977 with a single financial aid publication *(The Directory of Financial Aids for Women)* and now specializes in the development of financial aid resources in multiple formats, including books, large print books, disks, CD-ROMs, print-on-demand reports, eBooks, and online sources. Long recognized as a leader in the field, RSP has been called, by the *Simba Report on Directory Publishing,* "a true success in the world of independent directory publishers." Kaplan Educational Centers hailed RSP as "the leading authority on scholarships."

Reference Service Press
El Dorado Hills Business Park
5000 Windplay Drive, Suite 4
El Dorado Hills, CA 95762
    (916) 939-9620
    Fax: (916) 939-9626
    E-mail: findaid@aol.com
Visit our web site on the worldwide web:
http://www.rspfunding.com

Manufactured in the United States of America

Contents

Introduction i

Scholarships, Fellowships & Loans

General 5
   United States 5
   Arkansas 47
   Colorado 48
   Florida 49
   Idaho 49
   Illinois 50
   Indiana 50
   Kentucky 51
   Louisiana 52
   Maine 52
   Maryland 53
   Minnesota 54
   Missouri 55
   Montana 55
   New Hampshire 56
   North Carolina 57
   Oregon 56
   South Dakota 57
   Texas 58
   Vermont 58
   Washington 59
   Wyoming 60
   International 61

Social Sciences **70**
   General 70
   Business and Economics 73
   Education 74
   Librarianship 75
   Political Science and International Affairs 77
   Psychology 77

Humanities **78**
   General 78
   Communications and Mass Media 80
   History 83
   Literature 84
   Music 86
   Performing Arts 87
   Religion 88
   Visual Arts 89

Sciences **90**
   General 90
   Agricultural Sciences 92
   Aviation 93
   Biological Sciences 94
   Earth Sciences 95
   Engineering 95
   Health and Medical Sciences 96
   Mathematics 102
   Physical Sciences 102
   Technology 103

Special Population Groups **103**
   Athletes 104
   Ethnic Groups 106
   Foreign Students 113
   Gays, Lesbians, Etc. 114
   Military Personnel and Veterans 115
   Persons with Disabilities 118
   Reentry Students 120
   Religious Groups 122
   Union Members 124
   Women 124

Grants for Individuals

General **129**
   United States 129
   Hawaii 139
   Maryland 139
   Massachusetts 140
   New Hampshire 140
   Ohio 141
   International 141

Social Sciences **146**
   General 146
   Business and Economics 149
   Education 150

Humanities **151**
   General 151
   Applied Arts 154
   Architecture 154
   History 155
   Literature 156
   Music 159
   Performing Arts 161
   Religion 162
   Visual Arts 163

Sciences **164**
   General 164
   Biological Sciences 166
   Earth Sciences 167
   Health and Medical Sciences 167
   Physical Sciences 171

Special Population Groups **171**
   Ethnic Groups 172
   Military Personnel and Veterans 173
   Persons with Disabilities 176

Religious Groups 177
Women 178

Grants for Organizations

General **181**
   United States 181
   Alaska 208
   Arizona 209
   Arkansas 209
   California 210
   Colorado 211
   Connecticut 212
   District of Columbia 212
   Florida 213
   Georgia 215
   Hawaii 215
   Idaho 216
   Illinois 217
   Indiana 219
   Iowa 219
   Kansas 220
   Kentucky 221
   Louisiana 221
   Maine 222
   Maryland 223
   Massachusetts 225
   Michigan 225
   Minnesota 226
   Missouri 228
   Montana 229
   Nebraska 230
   Nevada 231
   New Hampshire 232
   New Jersey 232
   New Mexico 234
   New York 234
   North Carolina 235
   Ohio 236

Oklahoma 237
　　Oregon 238
　　Pennsylvania 239
　　Rhode Island 240
　　South Carolina 240
　　South Dakota 241
　　Tennessee 242
　　Texas 242
　　Utah 243
　　Vermont 243
　　Virginia 244
　　Washington 244
　　Wisconsin 246
　　Wyoming 247
　　International 248

Social Sciences 251
　　General 251
　　Business and Economics 253
　　Education 255
　　Librarianship 263
　　Sociology and Social Services 265

Humanities 267
　　General 267
　　Applied Arts 269
　　Religion 270

Sciences 272
　　General 272
　　Agricultural Sciences 273
　　Biological Sciences 274
　　Environmental Sciences 274
　　Health and Medical Sciences 276
　　Technology 279

Special Population Groups 281
　　Ethnic Groups 281
　　Gays, Lesbians, Etc. 283
　　Persons with Disabilities 284
　　Religious Groups 285
　　Women 285

Awards & Prizes

General ... **289**
   United States ... 289
   International ... 297

Social Sciences ... **299**
   General ... 299
   Law ... 300
   Librarianship ... 301

Humanities ... **301**
   General ... 301
   Applied Arts ... 303
   Communications and Mass Media ... 304
   History ... 306
   Literature ... 306
   Music ... 313
   Performing Arts ... 315
   Visual Arts ... 316

Sciences ... **316**
   General ... 316
   Biological Sciences ... 317
   Earth Sciences ... 317
   Health and Medical Sciences ... 318
   Physical Sciences ... 319

Special Population Groups ... **319**
   Ethnic Groups ... 319
   Military Personnel and Veterans ... 321
   Persons with Disabilities ... 322
   Religious Groups ... 322
   Women ... 323

Internships

General **327**
    United States 327
    New Jersey 338
    International 339

Social Sciences **344**
    General 344
    Political Sciences and International Affairs 345
    Psychology 346
    Sociology and Social Services 346

Humanities **347**
    General 347
    Communications and Mass Media 347
    History 350
    Music 351
    Performing Arts 351
    Religion 352
    Visual Arts 353

Sciences **353**
    General 353
    Aviation 354
    Biological Sciences 354
    Environmental Sciences 355
    Health and Medical Sciences 355
    Technology 358

Special Population Groups **358**
    Ethnic Groups 358
    Persons with Disabilities 361
    Religious Groups 362
    Women 362

Federal Government Bookmarks

Guides to Federal Sites 367

Web Sites 370

Indexes

Title Index 385

Name Index 397

Publisher and Producer Index 401

Geographic Index 405

Subject Index 409

Introduction

BACKGROUND

It's been 16 years since the first version of *How to Find Out About Financial Aid and Funding* was published. During that time there have been significant changes in the area of financial aid and funding. Federal funds for education have been reapportioned: the number of publicly-funded scholarships and fellowships has declined, while the number of publicly-funded loans has increased. Despite the steps taken by federal and state governments to curtail money for minorities and women, there are more funds than ever available to these groups. Similarly, the number of grantmaking organizations has climbed steadily, as has the total amount granted annually. Internship opportunities (most notably those that offer monetary support) are also on the upswing. In all, there is now more than $100 billion available each year in the form of publicly- or privately-funded scholarships, fellowships, loans, grants for individuals and organizations, awards, and internships.

Just as dramatic have been the changes in the way information about financial aid and funding has been made available. When the first version of *How to Find Out About Financial Aid* was issued in 1987, almost all of the directories identified were in print form; in fact, of the 900 resources covered in that edition, less than 25 involved searching online (as databases or search services). By the release of the next version, in 1999, the mix of resources had changed somewhat; while print was still the dominant medium, a full one third of the listings were available in electronic form and/or on the Internet. In the four years since then, that trend has only intensified, with the number of sources distributed electronically or made available on the Internet increasing at a dizzying pace (now making up more than half the entries in the 2003 edition).

Even more striking, when the two latest versions of *How to Find Out* are compared, is 1) the number of resources available in 1999 that have been discontinued or not updated since then and 2) the number of new sources included in the 2003 guide that were not available just four years ago. Of the 800+ funding sources described in the 1999 edition, a total of 256 (approximately one third of all the entries) were not reissued, revised, or updated between the end of 1998 and 2003: 115 directories listing scholarships and loans, 24 listing grants for individuals, 60 listing grants for organizations, 19 listing awards and prizes, and 38 listing internships. On the flip side, of the nearly 700 resources listed in the 2003 guide, more than half (55 percent, to be exact)

Introduction

did not exist prior to 1999; almost all of these are either electronic or Internet resources. Despite all this recent activity, the total number of resources available to student or professional grantseekers in any format continued to decline: from 904 in 1987, to 832 at the end of 1998, to 750 at the beginning of 2003.

One thing that has not changed over the years, however, is the complexity of tracking and maintaining control over the resources produced in this highly volatile field. Standard bibliographic sources have never proved particularly helpful. For example, *American Reference Books Annual,* which has offered professional reviews for decades, covered less than 170 different financial aid or funding titles in all of its annual editions issued since 1987. *Guide to Reference Books* has provided even less direction; fewer than 40 financial aid or funding resources were included in each edition or supplement. Similarly, *Choice's* Web Supplement has featured only a handful of the scores of financial aid and funding sites on the Internet. Even reference publications that focus solely on the appropriate format (directories) or subject (financial aid or funding) have offered less than comprehensive listings. Gale's *Guide to Directories,* while more inclusive than the general bibliographic guides, identifies less than 200 financial aid or funding directories in each edition. The Foundation Center's *Guide to Grantseeking on the Web* selectively covers government, foundation, and commercial Internet sites of potential value to grantseekers, but omits any discussion of resources in print (including print versions of the listed web databases). Likewise, the online lists (e.g., those found on search engines, or more focused sites like ask.com, or funding-related sites like finaid.com) tend to be selective, random, single-format focused (generally restricted to online resources), and/or out of date.

Without continuing and comprehensive bibliographic control, it would be difficult, if not impossible, for student and professional grantseekers to know what resources are available (particularly those outside the traditional print media), where to acquire or access those resources (even amazon.com lists only a portion of the available print materials and almost none in other formats), or how to identify the right resources before spending time and money identifying and perhaps buying them. That's why Reference Service Press has made an ongoing commitment to identify, classify, describe, evaluate, and provide ordering information for financial aid and funding resources, whatever their format. The 2003-2005 edition of *How to Find Out About Financial Aid and Funding* represents our latest attempt to help fundseekers navigate their way through the bewildering, continually changing, and potentially overwhelming sea of funding resources.

SCOPE

The 2003-2005 edition of *How to Find Out About Financial Aid and Funding* was compiled after an extensive search through a variety of resources: major bibliographic guides, review publications, and web gateways; acquisitions lists from such organizations as the Foundation Center; current publishers' catalogs and web sites; on-site visits to a number of major libraries, including the Library of Congress and the Foundation Center Library; extensive Internet exploration, and personal contact or correspon-

Introduction

dence with numerous individuals active in the area of financial aid. All sources identified in the guide's two predecessors were also considered for inclusion. Some of those publications had changed focus or had never been updated and were determined inappropriate for coverage. Others still deal with financial aid or funding but have changed names; those publications are included in the 2003-2005 edition and their title changes can be traced both in the entries and through the Title Index. Hundreds of new resources (primarily electronic and Internet) have also been added to the listing. Every item listed here has been personally examined and evaluated, subsequent editions have been compared, and web sites have been visited on numerous occasions, to determine product development. The result is an annotated listing of more than 700 pamphlets, books, newsletters, other print publications, software, CD-ROMs, online dial-up products, eBooks, and Internet resources—issued or updated during the past four years—that deal with financial aid or funding, focus on American recipients, and are readily available (i.e., still in print or available at a good-sized library). The compilation is intended to assist students, researchers, reference and collection development librarians, financial aid officers, career counselors, and anyone else interested in obtaining financial support for education, research, travel, training, projects, career development, or innovative effort.

A number of criteria were established to determine which resources to select for inclusion in the 2003-2005 edition of *How to Find Out About Financial Aid and Funding:*

> *Directory-type listings:* Only works that list scholarships, fellowships, grants, awards/prizes, loans, and/or internships (in print, electronic, or Internet format) are described in the guide. Sources that discuss financial aid or funding in general are omitted, as are bibliographies listing materials on financial aid or funding, web sites composed primarily of links, studies, reports, functional works, journals, and self-help manuals that describe financial aid or fundraising procedures.
>
> *Broad listings:* In general, the guide focuses on print, electronic, or Internet resources that identify funding opportunities offered by a variety of organizations. Web sites aimed at the students of a particular institution or small pamphlets promoting the programs of a single sponsor (e.g., American Chemical Society, Business and Professional Women's Foundation) are usually excluded. Exceptions are made, however, for representative publications issued by such organizations as the AFL-CIO and the National Science Foundation, since both the number and the diversity of the programs covered are substantial.
>
> *Current listings:* Because the information related to financial aid and funding rapidly becomes dated, only those sources published or produced during the past four years (1999 on) are covered in the guide. Resources with earlier imprints may be referred to in an annotation, when appropriate, but they are not separately listed.

Introduction

Materials of interest to American users: The guide is intended for an American audience. Resources are included here only if they are perceived to have value to an American user and/or would tend to be included in the collections of larger American libraries.

Readily-available materials: Only those resources that are still in print or, if not, are likely to be included in the collections of larger libraries are included in the guide. Processed materials (such as those issued by academic institutions for the benefit of their students), lists published solely as articles in journals, directories that are currently out of print (and not likely to be in a library collection), and defunct web sites are omitted.

ARRANGEMENT

The 2003-2005 edition of *How to Find Out About Financial Aid and Funding* consists of three parts. The first five chapters describe and, where appropriate, evaluate financial aid resources (print, electronic, or Internet) published or updated since the beginning of 1999. The last chapter focuses on 64 federal government web sites (or guides to federal government web sites) that fundseekers should be sure to bookmark. There is also a set of five indexes; these provide access to the nearly 700 entries by title, author or editor, publisher or producer, geographic coverage, and subject focus.

Financial Aid and Funding Resources. In order to permit quick and easy access to the information on particular types of financial aid, the first five chapters of the guide group nearly 700 entries by type of programs described. In the following order, the chapters cover:

Scholarships, Fellowships & Loans: Scholarships provide financial assistance to students pursuing undergraduate education in any type of postsecondary institution: vocational/technical schools, two-year colleges, four-year colleges, and universities. Fellowships provide financial assistance to students pursuing graduate, professional, or postgraduate education. Usually no return of service or repayment is required for either type of program. Loan programs represent the only type of financial assistance that eventually must be repaid, with or without interest.

Grants for Individuals: These programs provide funds directly to individuals to support research, innovative efforts, travel, or projects (some of which may be educational in nature) in the United States or abroad.

Grants for Organizations: These programs provide funding to (generally nonprofit) institutions or organizations for projects, construction or renovation, operating expenses, etc.; nonaffiliated individuals may not submit proposals directly.

Introduction

Awards & Prizes: These programs award money or other prizes on the local, state, regional, national, and international levels to recognize, reward, or support creative work, public service, or notable achievement.

Internships: These programs provide work experience opportunities and often monetary support for students (high school through postdoctoral), professionals, and other workers who are interested in short-term placements. Some internships can be held while pursuing other activities (e.g., school, job), but most of the programs listed in print, electronic, or online resources require a concentrated commitment for a limited time period (one month, a summer, an intersession, a semester, or a year). Many students find internships an excellent source of financial assistance.

Each of these five chapters is subdivided, first by discipline or group (General, Social Sciences, Humanities, Sciences, Special Population Groups) and then 1) by geographic coverage for the General sections (e.g., United States, California, International); 2) by topics for the Social Sciences, Humanities, and Sciences sections (e.g., Librarianship, Music, Technology); and 3) by intended audience in the Special Population Groups section (e.g., Ethnic Groups, Persons with Disabilities, Women). Within each of these subsections, the entries are arranged alphabetically by title.

Every attempt has been made to provide a complete bibliographic citation plus ordering information for each resource described in the guide. Included in each entry (where relevant) are: title, edition, author or editor, place, publisher, date, number of pages or frequency, series, International Standard Serial Number (ISSN) when available, International Standard Book Number (ISBN) when available, and price. Note: prices tend to change frequently and, therefore, the figures supplied in the citations should be taken as a guide rather than as definitive. To be sure you have the most up-to-date prices for the items of interest, it is best to contact the publishers directly; addresses, telephone numbers, fax numbers, and e-mail addresses—along with available toll-free numbers and web sites—are provided at the end of each entry.

Many of the resources listed in the guide are issued only in print form. But, in stark contrast to its two predecessors, more than half of the resources included in the 2003-2005 edition of *How to Find Out About Financial Aid and Funding* are now available in some type of computer-related format: on disk, CD-ROM, tape, dial-up service, or the Internet. To make it easy for fundseekers to spot resources issued in a particular format, the following icons are used throughout the guide:

The item is available as a book, pamphlet, newsletter, or other printed publication

The item is available on diskette, CD-ROM, tape, or a dial-up service

The item is available on the Internet, as a fee or free resource

Introduction

Both the icons and the annotations make it clear if a resource is available in multiple formats. In addition, the ¢ symbol has been used to indicate resources—whatever their format—that will be of interest to the bargain hunter. Any resource with this icon is either very inexpensive (no more than $10) or free (more than one third of the resources fall into this category!).

All of the nearly 700 entries in the first five chapters of the guide are annotated. The directory profiles are designed to provide information on purpose, scope, arrangement, limitations, and special features. In addition, whenever appropriate, publication history is traced (to identify previous editions and tricky name changes) and publication value is assessed. Expendable publications, standard sources, and best bets are indicated.

Because many of the directories included in *How to Find Out About Financial Aid and Funding* focus on more than one type of program or emphasize more than one subject area, titles are listed in all relevant chapters and sections/subsections. For example, the Journalism Awards and Fellowships' online database is covered under the "Humanities—Communications & Mass Media" section of both the Awards & Prizes chapter and the Scholarships, Fellowships & Loans chapter. *Directory of Indiana & Kentucky Grantmakers* is listed two times in the Grants for Organizations chapter, in the "General—Indiana" section, the "General—Kentucky" section. In all cases, however, a full description of the title is provided only once, in the section that seemed most appropriate. The reader is always directed to the entry with the fullest annotation.

Federal Government Bookmarks. Many government agencies describe their financial aid offerings or funding opportunities on their web sites. Most of these sites, however, would not be identified in the first five chapters of *How to Find Out About Financial Aid and Funding,* because listings from a single sponsor are generally excluded. Since billions of dollars in financial aid and funding are offered by the government to both individuals and organizations, Chapter 6 identifies the URLs of the federal web sites that would be of most interest to fundseekers. This listing is divided into two sections: guides to federal government sites and the web sites of individual government departments or agencies. Brief descriptions of the grant information provided at each site is given. The references in this section were verified at the time this book went to press (April, 2003). You can check for corrections, updates, or additions by visiting the publisher's web site: http://www.rspfunding.com/

Indexes. The guide provides five indexes to make it easy to search for appropriate financial aid and funding opportunities. Title, Name, Publisher and Producer, Geographic, and Subject Indexes follow a word-by-word arrangement and refer the user to the appropriate entry by number.

> *Title Index.* The current, previous, and variant names of all publications (print, electronic, and Internet) cited in the first five chapters of the guide (either as separate entries or as references in annotations describing other titles) are indexed here. Over 750 titles are included in this index.

Introduction

Name Index. This index provides an alphabetical listing of the authors, editors, and compilers listed on the title pages of the directories cited in the first five chapters of the guide. References are made only to the main entry (where the fullest annotation may be found). Since not all directories credit individual authors, a number of the publications (particularly those that are serial in nature, available on the Internet, or prepared by organizations) are not represented here.

Publisher and Producer Index. This index makes it easy to identify the specific publishers and producers who are responsible for the more than 750 resources covered in the guide. These organizations and companies constitute a virtual "who's who" in the area of financial aid publishing. They are listed here alphabetically, word by word. Use the numbers following each publisher/producer name to 1) identify the publications they've issued in the field, 2) read about the content of each of these publications, or 3) get their most recent contact information, including (when available) address, telephone number, toll-free number, fax number, e-mail address, and web site.

Geographic Index. This index enables the reader to identify by state, region, and country the geographic coverage of the financial aid and funding resources listed in the first five chapters of the guide. Since a directory can be cited in more than one place (e.g., a directory describing grant programs offered in New York, New Jersey, and Pennsylvania is listed in three sections), each of these entries is indexed.

Subject Index. This index allows the reader to identify by subject all of the financial aid and funding resources described in the first five chapters of the guide. Over 200 separate subject terms are used. Extensive "see" and "see also" references facilitate the search for appropriate resources. As in the Geographic Index, reference is generally made to all entries where the directory is cited. Thus, a directory describing grants available to both writers and musicians would be listed in two sections of the Grants for Individuals chapter, "Humanities—Literature" and "Humanities—Music," and indexed under both subject terms.

HOW TO USE THE GUIDE

To Identify Resources Listing a Particular Type of Financial Assistance. If you are looking for print, electronic, or Internet resources listing a particular type of financial aid (e.g., a scholarship for undergraduate courses, a grant for independent study, an award for outstanding achievement), turn to the appropriate chapter: Scholarships, Fellowships & Loans (for undergraduate, graduate, professional, and postgraduate study), Grants for Individuals (for research, study, travel, or creative efforts), Grants for Organizations (for projects, programs, operating expenses, building and renovation, etc.), Awards & Prizes (in recognition of outstanding achievement), or Internships (for work experience programs).

Introduction

To Identify Resources Listing Financial Aid or Funding in a Particular Subject Area. Each of the first five chapters (Scholarships, Fellowships & Loans; Grants for Individuals; Grants for Organizations; Awards & Prizes; and Internships) is divided into sections (an initial "General" section followed by sections arranged by discipline or target group) and then into topical subsections (following the same basic arrangement). Be sure to check the "General" section as well as the "General" and subject-oriented subsections in the discipline in which you are interested. For example, if you want to identify all the print, electronic, and Internet resources that list financial assistance for undergraduate study in the communications field in the United States, you would go to the Scholarships, Fellowships & Loans chapter, read all the entries in the "General—United States" section, and then all the entries in both the "Humanities—General" and the "Humanities—Communications and Mass Media" sections. Since directories covering multiple subjects are listed in every appropriate location (in the "General" sections/subsections, if there is broad coverage; in the specific subject subsections, if there is more focused coverage), you can browse through any of the sections or subsections in the guide without first consulting an index. However, if you are looking for resources dealing with a specific subject, it will be more efficient if you turn first to the Subject Index. To facilitate your search, the types of programs covered (e.g., grants for individuals, internships) are clearly indicated for each index subject term. Extensive cross-references are also provided.

To Identify Resources Listing Financial Aid and Funding Programs Open to Members of a Particular Group. In addition to listing directories by subject, this guide also groups resources by intended applicant pool: ethnic groups, foreign students, military personnel and veterans, reentry students, women, etc. To locate all resources listing programs for these groups, identify first the type of program in which you are interested, go to the appropriate chapter (e.g., Grants for Individuals, Internships), turn to the section focusing on "Special Population Groups" and read through the entries in the subsection covering the group in which you are interested. For example, if you are looking for resources that identify financial aid programs for Hispanic American graduate students, you would use the "Special Population Groups—Ethnic Groups" section in the Scholarships, Fellowships & Loans chapter. Remember, the "General" sections and subsections also will identify sources that may list programs for special population groups, so be sure to check there as well.

To Identify Resources by Format. To determine which resources are available in print, electronic, and/or Internet versions, just look for the icons that precede each entry. In addition, a ¢ symbol is used to highlight those resources that are either bargain priced ($10 and under) or free, whatever their format.

To Locate Financial Aid Resources Focusing on Particular Geographic Areas. The Geographic Index permits easy access to the resources listing financial aid and funding programs open to residents of or tenable in a particular country, state, region, or other location. "See" and "see also" references are used liberally, and index entries for a particular geographic area are subdivided by type of program: scholarships, fellowships & loans; grants for individuals; grants for organizations; awards; and internships. In addition, the "General" sections of each of the first five chapters in the guide

Introduction

are subdivided geographically (United States; names of specific states; international). You can browse through these sections quickly to identify the general resources that provide basic geographic coverage. For example, if you are interested in determining which sources list grants available to nonprofit agencies in California, turn to the Grants for Organizations chapter and read through the entries in the "General—California" section. Don't forget to check the "General—United States" section, as well, because resources identifying grants for organizations in any state (including California) are covered there.

To Locate the Description of a Particular Financial Aid or Funding Resource. If you know the name of a specific financial aid or funding resource and the type of assistance covered in the listing (e.g., scholarships, grants, internships), then go directly to the appropriate chapter and section/subsection. For example, the *Complete Guide to Literary Contests* is described in the Awards & Prizes chapter, under the "Humanities—Literature" heading. If you are looking for a specific source and do not find it in the subsection you have checked, be sure to refer to the Title Index to see if it is covered elsewhere in the guide. To save time, always check the Title Index first if you know the name of a specific resource and are not sure under which subsection it has been placed.

To Locate Resources Written by a Specific Author. The Name Index makes it easy to identify all the resources covered in the guide that were prepared by a specific individual. Authors, editors, and compilers are listed here. However, since many resources (particularly serial publications, electronic resources, and web sites) do not credit a specific individual on their title page, a number of the sources included in the guide are not referenced in this index.

To Identify Resources Prepared by a Specific Publisher or Producer. More than 250 publishers and producers are responsible for the 700 print, electronic, and Internet resources that have been issued since 1999 and are described in this guide. Use the numbers following each publisher/producer name to identify the publications they've issued in the field, read a summary about each of these publications, or get their most recent contact information.

To Purchase a Resource Listed in the Guide. Complete contact information is included in each entry: address, telephone number, toll-free number, fax number, TTY, TDD, e-mail address, and web site (when available). If an item is available for sale, current prices are given. Although all prices were verified just prior to printing (in March, 2003), some of the information is by its very nature outdated by the time the guide reaches the reader. Pricing figures, then, should be viewed as indicative rather than definitive. To obtain the most current prices, contact the publisher.

To Update the Listings in the Guide. All information included in the guide was verified through April, 2003. For corrections, modifications, or additions to the data included here, check Reference Service Press's web site: http://www.rspfunding.com/

Introduction

FUTURE EDITIONS OF THE GUIDE

The 2003-2005 edition of *How to Find Out About Financial Aid and Funding* focuses on resources issued or updated no earlier than the beginning of 1999. The bibliographic information, pricing, descriptions, and evaluations are current as of April, 2003. The guide will be issued biennially from now on. The next edition, covering resources issued or updated since 2003, will be released in mid-2005.

ABOUT THE AUTHOR

Dr. Gail Schlachter has worked for more than three decades as a library administrator, a library educator, and an administrator of library-related publishing companies. Active in the library community, Dr. Schlachter has been elected to the Councils of both the American Library Association and the California Library Association. In addition, she is the former editor of *Reference and User Services Quarterly,* was the reference book review editor of *RQ* for 10 years, and is a past president of the American Library Association's Reference and User Services Association. Well known for her lectures on the need to increase financial aid for special needs groups, Dr. Schlachter has written a series of directories on the topic, including the *Directory of Financial Aids for Women* (published biennially since 1978); the four-volume *Minority Funding Set* (for African Americans, Asian Americans, Hispanic Americans, and Native Americans published biennially since 1997), and *Financial Aid for the Disabled and Their Dependents* (published biennially since 1988). She is also the author of two award-winning bibliographic guides: *Minorities and Women: A Guide to Reference Literature in the Social Sciences,* which was chosen as an "Outstanding Reference Book of the Year" by *Choice;* and *Reference Sources in Library and Information Services,* which was selected to receive the first "Award for Outstanding Contribution to Library Literature." In recognition of her outstanding contributions to reference service, Dr. Schlachter has been awarded both the Isadore Gilbert Mudge Citation and the Louis Shores-Oryx Press Award.

ACKNOWLEDGEMENTS

A debt of gratitude is owed to the publishers that contributed review copies, the libraries that provided unlimited access to their collections of financial aid resources (particularly the Library of Congress, the Foundation Center, and the Grantsmanship Center in Los Angeles), and the numerous librarians who helped untangle difficult bibliographic problems. In addition, Martin Sklar at ACCI deserves special acknowledgement for his significant contributions, not only to the development of the database and the software used to format the content of this book, but to the design and layout of the finished product as well.

OTHER RELATED PUBLICATIONS

In addition to *How to Find Out About Financial Aid and Funding,* Reference Service Press publishes a number of award-winning directories identifying financial aid,

Introduction

including the *Directory of Financial Aids for Women,* which lists 1,600 scholarships, fellowships, grants, awards, loans, and internships set aside primarily or exclusively for women; the *College Student's Guide to Merit and Other No-Need Funding,* which identifies more than 1,200 funding opportunities that never consider income in the selection process, and *Financial Aid for the Disabled and Their Families,* which is the first directory to list and describe the hundreds of scholarships, fellowships, loans, awards, and grants-in-aid available specifically to persons with disabilities in America. For more information about these or other related publications, write to Reference Service Press' Marketing Department at 5000 Windplay Drive, Suite 4, El Dorado Hills, California, 95762 or visit Reference Service Press's web site: www.rspfunding.com/

Print, Electronic, & Internet Resources Listing:

- Scholarships, Fellowships, & Loans
- Grants for Organizations
- Grants for Individuals
- Awards & Prizes
- Internships

Scholarships, Fellowships & Loans

Scholarships provide financial assistance to students pursuing undergraduate education in any type of postsecondary institution: vocational/technical schools, two-year colleges, four-year colleges, and universities. Fellowships provide financial assistance to students pursuing graduate, professional, or postgraduate education. Usually no return of service or repayment is required for either scholarships or fellowships. Loan programs represent the only type of financial assistance that eventually must be repaid, with or without interest. Loans constitute one of the most important sources of financial aid for education, but because most of the money tends to come from a few large-scale public programs on the state or federal levels, there are just a couple of directories that list loan programs only. There are, however, a sizable number of titles that do include individual loans—along with scholarships and fellowships—in their listings. Identified in this chapter (the largest in the guide) are 234 print, electronic, and Internet resources that either focus solely on scholarships, fellowships, and/or loans or list substantial numbers of these types of programs on the state, national, or international level. Of these entries, 123 are general in nature, 15 focus on the social sciences, 28 concentrate on the humanities, 25 deal with the sciences, and the remainder (43 entries) are aimed at special population groups (especially ethnic groups). If you are looking for a specific resource and you do not find it in this chapter, be sure to check the Title Index to see if it is covered elsewhere in the guide.

GENERAL

United States

1 📖 ¢

The A's and B's of Academic Scholarships

Ed. by Anna Leider. Alexandria, VA: Octameron Associates, 1985- . Annual. ISSN 0227-1470. ISBN 1-57509-079-1. $10 (2003-2004 ed.). Paper.

Description: Do you have a B average or better? Are your SAT/ACT scores 900/21 or better? Are you in the upper one-third of your class? If so, you might be able to qualify for a college merit scholarship. This paperback identifies nearly 1,200 colleges and universities that offer no-need scholarships ranging from $200 to $25,000 to students who meet these criteria. In tabular form, information is given on some of the merit awards (number, value range, class standing, study fields, renewability, restrictions, and application date) at each of these schools. The table is organized by state and subdivided, alphabetically, by school. The information in the tables consists primarily of codes and abbreviations, so it is necessary to read the introductory materials carefully to figure out what is being presented. Although useful as a starting point, the listing is limited in several ways: no contact information is provided; selection criteria are not indicated; scholarship opportunities offered by the schools are not ranked or compared; and the summary information provided here is probably less than a student would get by contacting a school directly.

Available from: Octameron Associates, 1900 Mt. Vernon Avenue, P.O. Box 2748, Alexandria, VA 22301. *Telephone:* (703) 836-5480; *Fax:* (703) 836-5650; *E-mail:* info@octameron.com

Web site: www.octameron.com

2 📖

Annual Register of Grant Support: A Directory of Funding Sources

Medford, NJ: Information Today, 1969- . Annual. ISSN 0066-4049. ISBN 1-57387-145-1. $229 (2003 ed.). Hardcover.

Description: Despite its title, this annual covers scholarships, fellowships, and loans as well as grant opportunities. For more information about the publication, see entry 235 in the "Grants for Individuals—General—United States" section of this bibliography.

Available from: Information Today, Inc., 143 Old Marlton Pike, Medford, NJ 08055-8750. *Telephone:* (609) 654-6266; *Fax:* (609) 654-4309; *E-mail:* custserv@infotoday.com

Web site: www.infotoday.com

How to Find Out About Financial Aid and Funding

3

Best Buys in College Education

7th Ed. By Lucia Solórzano. Hauppauge, NY: Barron's, 2002. 784p. ISBN 0-7641-2018-2. $18.95. Paper.

Description: This popular directory shows where students can get a first-class education at a reasonable price. Approximately 300 colleges have been selected for inclusion (by students and administrators) because they represent both high quality and low cost. The information presented for each school is taken from Barron's authoritative college directory, *Profiles of American Colleges,* but almost nothing specifically about financial aid at those schools is included. A poor layout (small type, long lines, light print) makes the listing unnecessarily difficult to read.

Available from: Barron's Educational Series, Inc., 250 Wireless Boulevard, Hauppauge, NY 11788. *Telephone:* (631) 434-3311; *Toll-free:* (800) 645-3476, ext. 204; *Fax:* (631) 434-7682; *E-mail:* info@barronseduc.com

Web site: www.barronseduc.com

4

BrokeScholar

http://scholarships.brokescholar.com

Description: After filling out a lengthy registration form (be prepared to spend from 10 to 15 minutes) that includes such personal information as name, address, and family income—and wading through pages of advertisements—students will receive a list of scholarships ranked in order of relevance to their profile. Searchers can also locate funding programs by keyword. Once they find applicable scholarships, they can automatically create application letters and a personalized deadline calendar. Scholarship records tend to be quite brief and include information on applicable schools, applicable majors, number awarded and whether or not renewable, level of study, eligibility requirements, deadline, and contact information (with links directly to the provider's web site).

Available from: BrokeScholar, 44 School Street, 1st Floor, Suite 324, Boston, MA 02108. *E-mail:* bsfeedback@brokescholar.com

Web site: scholarships.brokescholar.com

5

The CARE Book: College Aid Resources for Education

By Herm Davis. Rockville, MD: National College Scholarship Foundation, 2002. 242p. ISBN 0-9656724-0-9. $23.95. Paper.

Scholarships, Etc.–General–United States

Description: Written by Davis, the founder of the National College Scholarship Foundation and a co-author of *College Financial Aid for Dummies* (see entry 13), the 2003-2005 edition of this book identifies (among other things) deadlines and types of college aid at more than 1,500 four-year colleges. It also incorporates information from the *Loan Forgiveness Directory* (which is no longer being separately published), including 200 ways to cancel or "forgive" loans, ways to reduce final loan debt, and a low-cost loan directory. Much of the data in the CARE book was provided by the Scholarship Resource Network (see entry 72).

Available from: National College Scholarship Foundation, 16728 Frontenac Terrace, Rockville, MD 20855. *Telephone:* (301) 548-9423; *Toll-free:* (800) 220-3919; *Fax:* (301) 548-9453; *E-mail:* ncsfdn@aol.com

Web site: www.ncsfdn.org

6

Cash for College: The Ultimate Guide to College Scholarships

Rev. ed. By Cynthia Ruiz McKee and Phillip C. McKee, Jr. New York: Quill/William Morrow (HarperCollins), 1999. 704p. ISBN 0-6881-6190-1. $19.95. Paper.

Description: Quantity does not always equal quality. Even though there are more than 6,000 entries and 700 pages in this reasonably-priced directory aimed at undergraduates (the McKees plan another directory, *Cash for Grad School,* for release late in 2003) this is far from "the ultimate guide to college scholarships" promised by the authors. Why? The descriptions of the individual financial aid programs are extremely brief. More than half the entries are random school-specific scholarships (and the rest are well covered in most of the general financial aid directories). No web sites or e-mail addresses are provided. And, the entries haven't been updated since 1999. There's little new or unique here. Modeled after this directory, a new listing for graduate students *(Cash for Grad School,* $21.95, paperback) is planned for late 2003.

Available from: HarperCollins Publishers, 10 East 53rd Street, New York, NY 10022. *Telephone:* (212) 207-7000

Web site: www.harpercollins.com

7

Catalog of Federal Domestic Assistance

Prep. by the U.S. General Services Administration. Washington, DC: G.P.O., 1965- . Annual. ISSN 0097-7799. $63 (2002 ed.), looseleaf; $85, CD-ROM; online, free.

Description: Nearly 1,500 domestic assistance programs and activities administered by federal agencies and departments are described in this annual publication, including loans, loan guarantees, shared revenue programs, and grants. For more information about the publication, see entry 339 in the "Grants for Organizations—General—United States" section of this bibliography.

Available from: U.S. Government Printing Office, Superintendent of Documents, P.O. Box 371954, Pittsburgh, PA 15250-7954. *Telephone:* (202) 512-1800, press 1; *Toll-free:* (800) 669-8331; *Fax:* (202) 512-2250; *E-mail:* gpoaccess@gpo.gov
   Web site: www.access.gpo.gov/su_docs

8

Chronicle Financial Aid Guide: Scholarships and Loans for High School Students, College Undergraduates, Graduates, and Adult Learners

Moravia, NY: Chronicle Guidance Publications, 1978- . Annual. ISSN 1063-7915. ISBN 1-55631-310-1. $24.98 (2002-2003 ed.). Paper.

Description: When it comes to general financial aid directories, this is one of the better ones. It provides detailed descriptions of nearly 1,800 well-known scholarships, loans, competitions, and essay contests offered nationally or regionally by approximately 700 private or public organizations for high school and undergraduate students (including adult learners). The financial aid opportunities listed here are sponsored by private organizations, clubs, foundations, sororities and fraternities, federal and state governments, and national and international labor unions. Entries provide information on: eligibility, number and amount of awards, selection criteria, application procedures, and deadlines. The programs are indexed by subject and sponsor. In the past, this information was available, as well, on CD-ROM, as part of *Chronicle Perspectives PLUS* and separately as the *Financial Aid Search*. However, those versions have now been discontinued. For summary information on financial aid offered by individual colleges, see Chronicle Guidance's companion volumes: *Chronicle Two-Year College Databook, Chronicle Vocational School Manual,* and *Chronicle Four-Year College Databook.*

Available from: Chronicle Guidance Publications, 66 Aurora Street, Moravia, NY 13118-3576. *Telephone:* (315) 497-0330; *Toll-free:* (800) 899-0454; *Fax:* (315) 497-3359; *E-mail:* customerservice@chronicleguidance.com
   Web site: www.chronicleguidance.com

9

The College Blue Book

New York: Macmillan, 1923- . Annual. 6v. ISSN 0069-5572. ISBN 0-02 865761-6. $300 (31st ed.). Hardcover.

Description: First issued in 1923 as a single-volume work, this reference publication has grown to a 2003 (31st) edition of six volumes. Each volume

Scholarships, Etc.–General–United States

provides information on a different area of higher education (e.g., tabular data on American colleges; degrees offered, by college and by subject). Volume 5 of the set, *Scholarships, Fellowships, Grants, and Loans,* identifies financial aid available to undergraduate and graduate students. It can be purchased separately from the set and describes more than 2,000 funding opportunities. Arranged by discipline and subdivided by specific subject, the volume is indexed by sponsor, title, interest field, and levels of awards (a cumbersome and time-consuming but feasible way of locating all of the programs scattered throughout the volume for undergraduate, graduate, professional, and/or seminary study). The six-volume set is also available as an eBook (ISBN 0-02-865994-1, $330) and can be accessed online at netLibrary's web site (www.netlibrary.com).

Available from: Macmillan Reference USA, 300 Park Avenue South, New York, NY 10010. *Toll-free:* (800) 877-4253; *Fax:* (800) 414-5043

Web site: www.galegroup.com/macmillan

10

The College Board College Cost & Financial Aid Handbook

New York: College Board, 1980- . Annual. ISSN 0270-8493. ISBN 0-87447-683-6. $22.95 (2003 ed.). Paper.

Description: In the latest edition (2003), the first section provides a number of informative articles that describe the types of financial aid available, how to apply for aid, how to estimate financial need and expected family contribution, and strategies for working your way through college. The main part of the book is organized by state and, for the 2,700 colleges and universities covered there, offers information on: college costs (e.g., tuition, room and board, books and supplies), need-based and non-need financial aid awarded by the institution, need-based aid offered to freshmen, merit scholarships, policies to reduce costs, available payment plans, and application procedures. A number of indexes are also included that make it easy to access general information on the academic, art, music/drama, ROTC, and athletic scholarships offered by each school. In the past, this publication was issued under various other titles: *Student Expenses at Postsecondary Institutions,* the *College Cost Book,* and *College Costs and Financial Aid Handbook.*

Available from: College Board Publications, Box 886, New York, NY 19191-0886. *Telephone:* (212) 713-8000; *Toll-free:* (800) 323-7155; *Fax:* (212) 713-8143

Web site: www.collegeboard.com

11

The College Board Scholarship Handbook

New York: College Board, 1998- . Annual. ISBN 0-87447-684-4. $25.95 (2003 ed.). Paper with CD-ROM.

Description: This is one of the best general financial aid directories, along with *Peterson's Scholarships, Grants & Prizes* (see entry 57) and Kaplan's *Scholarships* (entry 48). Covered here are more than 2,300 funding opportunities, including private, federal, and state scholarships, fellowships, grants, internships, and loans. The book also includes a "Real Stuff" CD-ROM (requires at least a Pentium processor, Windows 95, 64 MB of RAM, a 12X CD-ROM drive, 16 bit color, 800 x 600 screen resolution, a sound card, and an Internet browser); the CD-ROM allows users to link directly to the College Board's web site, perform customized scholarship searches, conduct college searches, and take a mini-SAT practice exam. Much of the information included in the directory (which is often cited as *The Scholarship Handbook)*, can also be accessed, without charge, on the College Board's web site (see entry 17).

Available from: College Board Publications, Box 886, New York, NY 19191-0886. *Telephone:* (212) 713-8000; *Toll-free:* (800) 323-7155; *Fax:* (212) 713-8143

Web site: www.collegeboard.com

12

College Dollars

http://www.statefarm.com/customer/customer.htm

Description: Nearly 2.5 million students will graduate from high school this year. Up to a third won't go on to college because they don't have the money. This is unfortunate, because billions of dollars are available—if students would only know where to look. To help them, State Farm is offering this free scholarship database to anyone that visits their site (you don't need to be a State Farm customer). Prepared by Systems Organization Services, College Dollars is a downloadable database (4.5 MB) describing nearly 1,800 local and national funding opportunities open to entering or continuing college students. While the directions provided to use the database aren't particularly helpful and there is no indication of when the information was last updated, this is still a source worth checking. It even comes with application request letters built in.

Available from: State Farm Insurance, One State Farm Plaza, Bloomington, IL 61710-0001. *Toll-free:* (800) 447-4930

Web site: www.statefarm.com

13

College Financial Aid for Dummies

2nd ed. By Herm Davis and Joyce Lain Kennedy. Hoboken, NJ: John Wiley, 1999. 409p. ISBN 0-7645-5165-5. $19.99. Paper.

Description: In typical "Dummies" style, most of this book provides basic information about financial aid: qualifying for aid, demonstrating need, filling out financial aid application forms, choosing a college financial aid planner, cut-

Scholarships, Etc.–General–United States

ting college costs, avoiding financial aid scams, etc. But one section succinctly describes about 200 funding opportunities for college, giving information on number of awards, award amounts, deadlines, and program features. The entries are grouped by focus (e.g., merit, athletics, minorities, teaching) and referenced in the index. The second edition of this directory is a much-expanded version of Davis and Kennedy's earlier *College Financial Aid Emergency Kit,* which is no longer being published. Davis, head of the National College Scholarship Foundation, was a founder of CASHE, a scholarship database previously offered on the SallieMae web site (see entry 77). He is also the author of *The CARE Book* (see entry 5).

Available from: John Wiley & Sons, Inc., 111 River Street, Hoboken, NJ 07030. *Telephone:* (201) 748-6000; *Toll-free:* (800) 225-5945; *Fax:* (201) 748-6088; *E-mail:* info@wiley.com

Web site: www.wiley.com

14

College: How to Get There & Go for Free!

5th ed. By Idalah D. Womack. Haverford, PA: Infinity, 2001. 162p. ISBN 0-7414-0524-5. $19.95. Paper.

Description: This is a poorly written and—despite being issued in 2001—dated guide to applying and paying for college. The briefest of information is given for a large portion of the 400 funding programs listed in the "Grants" chapter (partial title, sponsor and address, telephone number, and deadline), and many of those listed haven't been offered in years or, if they have, are listed with incorrect or superceded deadlines and addresses. The separate bibliography of financial aid directories cites a number of sources that haven't been updated since 1995 or ceased publication in the mid-1990s. Even the addresses given in the bibliography are dated; for example, both Gale Group's name and address changed years ago.

Available from: Infinity Publishing.com, 519 West Lancaster Avenue, Haverford, PA 19041-1413. *Telephone:* (610) 520-2500; *Toll-free:* (877) BUY-BOOK; *Fax:* (610) 519-0261

Web site: www.buybooksontheweb.com

15

College Spotlight

Ed. by Andrew Morkes. Chicago: College & Career Press. Bimonthly. ISSN 1525-4313. $30/yr. Paper.

Description: This newsletter, issued six times a year, is designed "to help those concerned with selecting, applying, evaluating, and entering college, as well as with other alternatives for today's high school graduates." Well written and informative, each issue of the newsletter is full of news, mini-reviews, and

How to Find Out About Financial Aid and Funding

(more to the point here) brief descriptions of 25 or so recently-announced school-based or portable scholarships and other financial aid opportunities. Until 2001, the newsletter was edited by Robert Calvert, Jr. and published by Garrett Park Press. It changed its name, from *Off to College,* in 1999. Prior to 1995, much of this information was included in another newsletter edited by Calvert, *Career Opportunity News* (now produced by Ferguson Publishing).

Available from: College & Career Press, P.O. Box 13103, Chicago, IL 60613-0103.

16

College Student's Guide to Merit and Other No-Need Funding

By Gail Ann Schlachter and R. David Weber. El Dorado Hills, CA: Reference Service Press, 1996- . Biennial. ISSN 1099-9086. ISBN 1-58841-041-2. $32 (2002-2004 ed.). Hardcover.

Description: It's a myth that only the neediest get financial aid. In fact, there are more than 1,200 funding programs, open only to college students and students returning to college, that never consider income in the selection process. To find out about those programs, use the latest edition of the *College Student's Guide to Merit and Other No-Need Funding.* This is the only directory to focus solely on no-need funding opportunities available to college students. Described here is money that's awarded not on the basis of need, but on academic record, career plans, creative activities, writing ability, research skills, religious or ethnic background, military or organizational activities, or just pure luck in random drawings. Plus, the listings in the directory can be accessed by discipline, specific subject, sponsor, program title, where you live, where your school of choice is located, and even deadline date. A companion volume, *High School Senior's Guide to Merit and Other No-Need Funding* (described in entry 45 in this section of the bibliography), provides similar coverage for high school seniors planning to go to college.

Available from: Reference Service Press, 5000 Windplay Drive, Suite 4, El Dorado Hills, CA 95762. *Telephone:* (916) 939-9620; *Fax:* (916) 939-9626; *E-mail:* findaid@aol.com

Web site: www.rspfunding.com

17

Collegeboard.com Scholarship Search

http://www.collegeboard.com

Description: The College Board is a national membership association of schools and colleges whose aim is to facilitate "the student transition to higher education." On its web site, the College Board offers a free web version of its scholarship database, ExPAN's FundFinder (see entry 26), which is marketed on a licensing basis. On the College Board's main screen, click on "Paying for

Scholarships, Etc.–General–United States

College." Then, by entering information about yourself and your educational goals, you can search without charge through the database's listing of 2,300 scholarships, loans, and other types of financial aid programs sponsored by national, state, and private sources. The listings here are similar to the information that's sold by the College Board for $25.95 in its print directory, *Scholarship Handbook* (see entry 11). The search interface on the web site is easy to complete, but the database's utility is limited by the relatively small number of programs (compared to other online search sites) and the fact that the information is updated only once a year. Further, unlike FastWeb (see entry 28), this site does not retain a student's personal information; this must be reentered each time a student searches for financial aid.

Available from: College Board Publications, Box 886, New York, NY 19191-0886. *Telephone:* (212) 713-8000; *Toll-free:* (800) 323-7155; *Fax:* (212) 713-8143; *E-mail:* expan@collegeboard.org

Web site: www.collegeboard.org

18

CollegeView's Scholarship Search

http://www.collegeview.com

Description: To access College View's Scholarship Search (a database of public, private, and college-specific scholarships awarded by 3,000 sources), click on "Financial Aid" on the site's main screen. Even though you must then fill out a four-page questionnaire to conduct your search, you may still be disappointed with the search results; frequently, many of the suggested funding programs are inappropriate or unavailable to you, given your personal characteristics (e.g., ethnicity, gender). Evidently, this happens so often that College View addresses the problem in its FAQs, explaining that "our scholarship search typically recommends scholarships that are not perfect matches, but rather scholarships that best reflect the criteria entered." Unlike most other scholarship search sites, it is possible to search this database by specific scholarship name and to browse the entire database alphabetically. In the past, visitors to the site were given the opportunity to purchase the database on a CD-ROM, the *Ultimate College Money Guide,* but that source is no longer offered.

Available from: Hobsons Publishing Company, 10200 Alliance Road, Suite 301, Cincinnati, OH 45242. *Telephone:* Toll-free (800) 927-VIEW; *Fax:* (800) 891-8531

Web site: www.collegeview.com

19

The Complete Scholarship Book

3rd ed. Prep. by Student Services, Inc. Naperville, IL: Sourcebooks, 2000. 576p. ISBN 1-57071-530-0. $22.99. Paper.

How to Find Out About Financial Aid and Funding

Description: Despite its title, this listing is far from complete. While the directory does identify more than 5,000 scholarships and grants, about half of these are college specific (recipients must attend a particular college to be eligible for the award). Further, only very brief information is provided for each program: amount awarded, deadline, majors/fields of study, and application process. The guide is cross-referenced by disability, ethnicity, gender, intercollegiate athletics, major/career objectives, marital status, military affiliation, and religion. It includes a major/special criteria index, but there is no index to sponsoring organizations. Nor is there a table of contents or an introduction to explain the scope, exclusions, or features of the publication. The directory was prepared by FastWeb.com, a free scholarship search site on the Internet (for more information on FastWeb, see entry 28). Since *The Complete Scholarship Book* has not been updated since 2000, it would make more sense (and cost less, as well) to check the free listings on the parent source: www.fastweb.com.

Available from: Sourcebooks, Inc., 1935 Brookdale Road, Suite 139, Naperville, IL 60563. *Telephone:* (630) 961-3900; *Toll-free:* (800) 432-7444; *Fax:* (630) 961-2168; *E-mail:* info@sourcebooks.com

Web site: www.sourcebooks.com

20

COS Funding Opportunities

http://www.cos.com

Description: COS Funding Opportunities is a web-based subscription database that is updated daily and contains descriptions of more than 23,000 funding opportunities from around the world that support training, research, collaborative activities, travel, curriculum development, conferences, postdoctoral positions, equipment acquisition, and operating or capital expenses. For more information about the database, see entry 237 in the "Grants for Individuals—General—United States" section of this bibliography.

Available from: Community of Science, Inc., 1629 Thames Street, Suite 200, Baltimore, MD 21231. *Telephone:* (410) 563-2378; *Fax:* (410) 563-5389; *E-mail:* evd@cos.com

Web site: www.cos.com

21

Dan Cassidy's Worldwide College Scholarship Directory

5th ed. By Daniel J. Cassidy. Franklin Lakes, NJ: Career Press, 2000. 608p. ISBN 1-56414-466-6. $23.99. Paper.

Description: The focus of this directory is unclear. It includes brief descriptions of 1,000 undergraduate scholarships, grants, and awards (most of which can be used only in the United States and Canada), plus 500 more programs from 75 countries around the globe. Since most of the U.S. and Canadian entries

Scholarships, Etc.–General–United States

are also included in Cassidy's *The Scholarship Book* (see entry 64 in this section of the bibliography) and there are more complete listings of funding to study abroad, there is little unique offered here. In the past, parts of this directory were published as the *International Scholarship Directory: The Complete Guide to Financial Aid for Study Anywhere in the World.* Currently, much of this information can also be obtained, without charge, at the FASTaid web site (see entry 27). Because Cassidy died in 2001, this may be last edition of this title.

Available from: Career Press, 3 Tice Road, P.O. Box 687, Franklin Lakes, NJ 07417. *Telephone:* (201) 848-0310; *Toll-free:* (800) CAREER-1; *Fax:* (201) 848-1727; *E-mail:* careerprs@aol.com

Web site: www.careerpress.com

22

Dan Cassidy's Worldwide Graduate Scholarship Directory

5th ed. By Daniel J. Cassidy. Franklin Lakes, NJ: Career Press, 2000. 600p. ISBN 1-56414-467-4. $26.99. Paper.

Description: The title of this publication might lead you to believe that this is either a 1) guide to funding for American graduate students to study abroad or 2) a guide to funding for foreign graduate students to study anywhere. That's not exactly the case. Most of the entries are aimed at American students (primarily for study in the United States); only some are for study abroad and less than 100 identify opportunities for international students. Organized by subject area, the directory contains more than 4,000 entries. But, this figure is misleading. The number of unique programs described in the book is actually considerably smaller than that, because awards that cover multiple subject areas are repeated in each and every field (for example, the entry for AWIS Predoctoral Awards is replicated more than 50 times in the book!). Further, many of the entries do not relate to graduate students at all (for example, postdoctorate fellowships are randomly included) or are tenable at a single institution only. While the book looks and feels authoritative, the contents leave much to be desired. Previously, this book was published as the *Graduate Scholarship Directory* and now includes some parts of the defunct *International Scholarship Directory.* Currently, much of this information can also be obtained, without charge, at the FASTaid web site (see entry 27). Because Cassidy died in 2001, this may be the last edition of this title.

Available from: Career Press, 3 Tice Road, P.O. Box 687, Franklin Lakes, NJ 07417. *Telephone:* (201) 848-0310; *Toll-free:* (800) CAREER-1; *Fax:* (201) 848-1727; *E-mail:* careerprs@aol.com

Web site: www.careerpress.com

23

Directory of Research Grants

Westport, CT: Oryx, 1975- . Annual. ISSN 0146-7336. ISBN 1-57356-570-9. $134.95 (2003 ed.). Paper.

Description: Scholarships, fellowships, and loans are described in this annual directory, in addition to research grants. For more information about the publication, see entry 238 in the "Grants for Individuals—General—United States" section of this bibliography.

Available from: Oryx Press, 88 Post Road West, Westport, CT 06881. *Telephone:* (602) 265-2651; *Toll-free:* (800) 279-6799; *Fax:* (800) 279-4663; *E-mail:* info@oryxpress.com

Web site: www.oryxpress.com

24

Discounts and Deals at the Nation's 360 Best Colleges: The Parent Soup Financial Aid and College Guide

By Bruce G. Hammond. New York: St. Martin's, 1999. 320p. ISBN 1-58238-030-9. $19.95. Paper.

Description: Wouldn't it be great if you could find out about deals and discounts at the "nation's best colleges?" Unfortunately, this book won't help you much. While there are thumbnail sketches for 360 colleges and universities, and summary information is given on their scholarship offerings, there are a number of things lacking. First of all, there is no explanation about how the 360 colleges were chosen and why Hammond views them as the nation's best. Many of the choices are surprising; for example: Albion College, with a 91 percent acceptance rate, and College of Santa Fe, with a 84 percent acceptance rate. Furthermore, the information presented for the school's financial aid is limited; it would have been helpful if he had included the average financial aid package per college. In addition, there's little discussion of actual discounts and deals offered by the individual schools. Plus, no contact information is given for the colleges listed. Finally, the deadlines listed for the colleges are seriously outdated. Overall, this is a book that promises more than it delivers.

Available from: St. Martin's Press, 175 Fifth Avenue, New York, NY 10616. *Telephone:* (212) 674-5151

Web site: www.stmartins.com

Scholarships, Etc.–General–United States

25

Don't Miss Out: The Ambitious Student's Guide to Financial Aid

By Anna Leider and Robert Leider. Alexandria, VA: Octameron Associates, 1976- . Annual. ISSN 0277-6987. ISBN 1-57509-078-3. $10 (2003-2004 ed.). Paper.

Description: Strategies for college students to use in searching for financial aid are outlined in this compact paperback (currently about 190 pages long). Each annual edition is divided into six parts, one of which identifies sample or representative programs: e.g., non-need, athletic, programs for particular careers, programs for minorities and women, programs for graduate students. Both scholarships and loans are covered. Very brief information is provided for these programs, generally address, purpose, eligibility, and stipend. Telephone numbers are given for some programs but not all. Another section covers in detail the major programs offered by the federal government. Although the lack of an index often makes the guide difficult to use, there is a lot of helpful information here for $10.

Available from: Octameron Associates, 1900 Mt. Vernon Avenue, P.O. Box 2748, Alexandria, VA 22301. *Telephone:* (703) 836-5480; *Fax:* (703) 836-5650; *E-mail:* info@octameron.com

Web site: www.octameron.com

26

ExPAN

New York: College Board. Annual. $595/yr., Widows and Macintosh versions.

Description: ExPAN is a comprehensive software resource produced by College Board that helps students in their college and career planning process. One of the sections, FundFinder, provides an annually-updated database of scholarships, fellowships, loans, awards, and other financial aid opportunities offered by thousands of national, state, and private sources. ExPAN can be licensed by educational institutions or education-related agencies/organizations in either a Widows or Mac version. The College Board's print directory, *Scholarship Handbook* (see entry 11), is based on data taken directly from the FundFinder section of ExPAN. The same information may also be be searched without charge on the College Board's web site (entry 17). In the past, the database was available in a personal version (ExPAN for the Home 1.0, $29.95. CD-ROM), but that product was discontinued in mid-2002.

Available from: College Board Publications, Box 886, New York, NY 19191-0886. *Telephone:* (212) 713-8000; *Toll-free:* (800) 323-7155; *Fax:* (212) 713-8143; *E-mail:* expan@collegeboard.org

Web site: www.collegeboard.org

27

FASTaid

http://www.fastaid.com
Description: Billing itself as the "World's largest FREE online scholarship database," this web site is a product of the National Scholarship Research Service (NSRS), a scholarship search service founded by Daniel J. Cassidy, the popular author of *The Scholarship Book* and other financial aid directories (see entries 21, 22, and 64). Thousands of financial aid programs, for undergraduates, graduate students, and beyond are briefly described in the database. Because Cassidy died in 2001, this site may not be available or kept up to date on the web in the future.
Available from: National Scholarship Research Service, 5577 Skyland Boulevard, Suite 6A, Santa Rosa, CA 95403. *Toll-free:* (800) 432-3782; *E-mail:* editor@www.fastaid.com
Web site: www.fastaid.com

28

FastWeb: Financial Aid Search Through the Web

http://www.fastweb.com
Description: FastWeb (Financial Aid Search Through the Web), previously provided by Student Services, Inc. and now owned by Monster.com, is probably the most visible financial aid service on the Internet; links to it are provided on numerous sites and it is featured on the popular FinAid! page (see entry 30). However, it is no longer an anchor tenant on America Online; now, only Peterson's scholarship search is there (see entry 56). FastWeb advertises itself as "the Internet's largest free scholarship search." It contains concise descriptions of approximately 8,000 scholarships, fellowships, and loans offered by 3,000 sponsoring organizations. About half of these, however, are single-school based (i.e., open only to students attending that school). To use FastWeb, a student must first register; FastWeb rents the names and addresses of students who use the service, but students are given the opportunity to be excluded from the mailing list when they register. Next, students fill out a six-page questionnaire online, providing information on personal characteristics, academic activities, and career goals; this can take up to 20 minutes, depending upon connection speed. This profile is then used to create a computer "match" with the financial aid opportunities described in the database. FastWeb sets up a mailbox for the student and within 15 minutes delivers a list of programs based on the information supplied. Each of the programs on the list is briefly described: eligibility requirements, contact information, award amount, and deadline. The database is updated on an ongoing basis. As new or revised programs are added to the database, they are compared with the existing student profiles. Information on matching programs is then sent to the student's mailbox and an e-mail

Scholarships, Etc.–General–United States

announcement is sent to the student. At this point, FastWeb is one of only a few Internet sites at which students can actually apply for a number of scholarships online (click on the E-Scholarships button). The data provided without charge at FastWeb is essentially the same as that sold in its print directories, especially the *Complete Scholarship Book* (see entry 19).

Available from: FastWeb Inc., 444 North Michigan Avenue, Suite 3100, Chicago, IL 60611. *Telephone:* (312) 467-0638; *Toll-free:* (800) FastWeb; *E-mail:* webmaster@fastweb.com

Web site: www.fastweb.com

29

FEDIX Opportunity Alert

http://www.sciencewise.com

Description: Currently suspended but promising a revival, this was a free, personalized e-mail service that delivered information about funding opportunities for study and research. For more information about the service, see entry 240 in the "Grants for Individuals—General—United States" section of this bibliography.

Available from: ScienceWise, 300 Professional Drive, Suite 200, Gaithersburg, MD 20879-3419. *Telephone:* (301) 975-0103; *Fax:* (301) 975-0109

Web site: www.sciencewise.com

30

FinAid! The SmartStudent Guide to Financial Aid

http://www.FinAid.com

Description: FinAid was established in the fall of 1994 and at one time was the premier source of financial aid information. Unfortunately, it is now appears to be suffering severely from benign neglect. Many of its sections have not been updated in years (see, for example, the "reference materials" section in "Answering Your Questions," where few of the cited items have been updated since 1996 and a large number of links do not work, e.g., MOLIS). While lists of financial aid opportunities available to specific groups are provided, (including women, minorities, international students, etc), these are so short, random, and outdated that they are not very useful. Previously, this site was known as FinAid: The Financial Aid Information Page. FinAid also maintains a parallel site for foreign students interested in studying in the United States: eduPASS: The SmartStudent Guide to Studying in the USA (www.edupass.org).

Available from: FinAid Page, LLC, P.O. Box 81620, Pittsburgh, PA 15217. *Fax:* (412) 422-6189; *E-mail:* feedback@FinAid.com

Web site: www.FinAid.com

31

The Financial Aid Book

3rd ed. Prep. by Student Financial Services. Seattle: Perpetual Press, 1999. 601p. ISBN 1-881199-01-0. $24.95. Paper.

Description: Looking at this directory, one has to wonder: does the world really need another general financial aid directory? It's not that this compilation is so bad. It's just that it doesn't offer anything new. Most of the programs listed here can be found in a number of other standard directories, generally with much more detailed descriptions. Plus, there are several unusual structural features in the book. Although the last numbered entry is 5,405, there are actually only about 3,300 program listings (there are many gaps in the numbering system). While there are no indexes in the back of the book, there are six "reference categories" in the front for each of the three main sections: scholarships; loans; and fellowships, internships, and research funding; these are awkward to use, but they do work. One particularly irritating feature: every entry ends with a variation on this imperative: "Write to the above address for more information." If more information is available, why wasn't it included in the entries? Although the price for the directory is reasonable, *Peterson's Scholarships, Grants & Prizes* (see entry 57) and the College Board's *Scholarship Handbook* (entry 11) are better buys—and more up to date, too. Perpetual Press, which at one time was owned by American Collegiate Media, is now an independent company. A trade version of the *The Financial Aid Book* has been sold under the title *Directory of Private Scholarships and Grants*.

Available from: Perpetual Press, P.O. Box 3956, Seattle, WA 98124. *Toll-free:* (800) 807-3030; *Fax:* (707) 221-1418; *E-mail:* sales@perpetualpress.com
Web site: www.FinancialAidFinder.com

32

For the People: 1,608 Ways to Get Your Share of the Little-Known Bargains the Government Offers

Ed. by Kevin Ireland. Emmaus, PA: Rodale, 2000. 480p. ISBN 1-57954-296-4. $19.95. Paper.

Description: *For the People* identifies ways you can get money (loans and grants) and help from the government: to buy a home, pay for college, start a business, get a government job, run for office, etc. For more information about the directory, see entry 241 in the "Grants for Individuals—General—United States" section of this bibliography.

Available from: Rodale, Inc., 33 East Minor Street, Emmaus, PA 18098-0099. *Telephone:* (610) 967-5171; *Fax:* (610) 967-8963
Web site: www.rodale.com

Scholarships, Etc.–General–United States

33

Foundation Grants to Individuals

12th ed. New York: Foundation Center, 2001. 1,117p. ISBN 0-87954-948-3, paper; 0-87954-997-1, CD-ROM. $65, paper; $75, CD-ROM; $9.95/month, online.

Description: Many of the opportunities for individual applicants identified in the 12th edition of this grants directory are, in fact, scholarship and loan programs. For more information about the various versions of this publication, see entry 243 in the "Grants for Individuals—General—United States" section of this bibliography.

Available from: Foundation Center, 79 Fifth Avenue, New York, NY 10003-3076. *Telephone:* (212) 807-3690; *Toll-free:* (800) 424-9836; *Fax:* (212) 807-3691

Web site: fdncenter.org

34

Free Money for College: A Guide to More Than 1,000 Grants and Scholarships for Undergraduate Study

5th ed. By Laurie Blum. New York: Facts On File, 1999. 225p. ISBN 0-8160-3947-X, hardcover; 0-8160-3948-8, paper. $30, hardcover; $14.95, paper.

Description: There are dozens of financial aid directories that identify funding opportunities for college students. Some do an excellent job, like *Peterson's Scholarships, Grants & Prizes* (see entry 57) and Kaplan's *Scholarships* (entry 48). Others are less than adequate. This title falls somewhere in between. Written by a professional fundraiser, it covers a sizable number of programs (about 1,000), has an attractive appearance, is organized well, and is not very expensive. On the other hand, many of the programs are too restrictive to be included in a general directory like this (the Foundation Center's *Foundation Grants to Individuals,* entry 243, does a better job of identifying this type of restrictive program), the program descriptions are too brief to get a good sense of the actual requirements, and many basic and important programs are not covered (especially in the chapters on women, which has only 6 entries, and minorities, which has less than 15 entries).

Available from: Facts On File, 132 West 31st Street, 17th Floor, New York, NY 10001. *Telephone:* (212) 683-2244; *Toll-free:* (800) 322-8755; *Fax:* (800) 678-3633; *E-mail:* CustServ@factsonfile.com

Web site: www.factsonfile.com

35

Free Money for Graduate School: A Guide to More Than 1,000 Grants and Scholarships for Graduate Study

4th ed. By Laurie Blum. New York: Facts On File, 2000. 298p. ISBN 0-8160-4278-0, hardcover; 0-8160-4279-9, paper. $38.50, hardcover; $16.95, paper.

Description: Of the many "free money" books written by Blum over the years, this is one of the better ones. It describes hundreds of funding programs available to graduate students. Entries are arranged by discipline (e.g., business, engineering) or student characteristic (e.g., foreign nationals, interested in studying abroad) and contain information on program focus, eligibility requirements, financial data, application process, and deadline. More comprehensive (but more expensive) is the four-volume *Money for Graduate Students* set (see entries 127, 143, 174, and 190).

Available from: Facts On File, 132 West 31st Street, 17th Floor, New York, NY 10001. *Telephone:* (212) 683-2244; *Toll-free:* (800) 322-8755; *Fax:* (800) 678-3633; *E-mail:* CustServ@factsonfile.com
    Web site: www.factsonfile.com

36

FreSch! The Free Scholarship Search Service

http://freschinfo.com
Description: FreSch! is the highly ambitious project of a single individual, Laura DiFiore, who started this site as an unemployed web designer. Much of the area is full of voluminous text; read through it and you'll end up knowing a great deal about DiFiore's views, philosophies, and personal life. However, don't be fooled by the chatty style; when it comes to the database section, this area is strictly professional. Thousands of scholarships (and other forms of financial aid) are described in detail, indicating contact address, telephone number, web site, deadline date, number awarded, amount awarded, school level of applicants, and eligibility requirements. Here's a plus: no registration is required to use the site; however, you do need a relatively modern modem browser and your Javascript turned on. It is possible to access the listings through the Scholarship Power Search (although it is still in Beta, there are a number of bug, and you can't save your search results). But, the Browse function (one of the unique features of this site in the past) has been unavailable for quite some time, and the schedule for availability has been repeatedly pushed back. In fact, the entire site seems strangely unattended; when checking the main screen on 1/10/03, this was the headline: "The next batch of updates to the scholarship database will be uploaded 10/15/02"!

Available from: FreSch! Information Services, LLC, 779 Denver Avenue, Calhan, CO 80808. *Telephone:* (719) 347-2602; *E-mail:* laura@freschinfo.com

Scholarships, Etc.–General–United States

Web site: www.freschinfo.com

37 ¢

Fundsnet

http://www.fundsnetservices.com
Description: On the Internet since 1996, this information-rich but difficult to navigate site provides information and links to scholarships for students as well as grants for individuals and grants for organizations. For more information on the site, see entry 367 in the "Grants for Organizations—General—United States" section of this bibliography.
Available from: Fundsnet Online Services, 419 Immaculada Street, San Juan, PR 00915. *E-mail:* info@fundsnetservices.com
Web site: www.fundsnetservices.com

38 ¢

Get Free Cash for College: Scholarship Secrets of Harvard Students

2nd ed. By Gen S. Tanabe and Kelly Y. Tanabe. Los Altos, CA: SuperCollege, 2003. 432p. ISBN 0-9657556-7-3. $26.95. Paper.
Description: The first third of this directory contains commonly-available information on the financial aid process, including tips on filling out applications, writing essays, and handling interviews; types of scholarships; calculating financial need; and using the Internet. The rest of the book contains very brief descriptions of less than 900 scholarships arranged by various categories: accounting, athletic ability, gender/marital status, multiple majors, voice, etc. The data were supplied by Wintergreen/Orchard House (see entry 48 for more information about the provider) and its utility is undermined by the preponderance of programs from random schools (e.g., Baruch College Incentive Grant; Mary Baldwin College Wilson Grant), by programs with restrictive geographic requirements (e.g., Van Wert County Foundation General Scholarship), and by listings that offer only minor amounts of money (e.g., $200 Amelia Student Award, $300 Volkwein Memorial Scholarship). Good news: you don't need to spend $26.95 for this erratic listing; the same information is available, for free, on the Tanabes' web site: http://www.supercollege.com. If you are really serious about your search for scholarships, however, your time (and money) will be better spent using the more comprehensive and current listings in *Peterson's Scholarships, Grants & Prizes* (see entry 57), *Kaplan Scholarships* (entry 48), or the College Board's *Scholarship Handbook* (entry 11).
Available from: SuperCollege, LLC, 4546 B10 El Camino Real, No. 281, Los Altos, CA 94022. *Telephone:* (650) 618-2221; *Toll-free:* (800) 852-4890; *Fax:* (650) 618-2221
Web site: www.supercollege.com

39

Getting Money for Graduate School: More than 1,000 Scholarships, Grants, Prizes, Forgivable Loans, and Fellowships

1st ed. Lawrenceville, NJ: Peterson's Guides, 2002. 404p. ISBN 0-7689-1294-6. $16.95. Paper.

Description: Organized somewhat like Peterson's undergraduate scholarship directory, *Scholarships, Grants & Prizes* (see entry 57), this new paperback describes in some detail approximately 1,100 grants, prizes, forgivable loans, and fellowships worth more than $250 million. Program descriptions are grouped by category (academic field and career goal, nonacademic and non-career criteria, and miscellaneous criteria); programs with multiple characteristics are described fully only once (in the category that represents the main feature of the program) and are cross-listed in the other appropriate sections or subsections. Each full description provides the following information: contact, address, program purpose, eligibility requirements, award type, number of awards, award amount, application procedures, and deadline. The entries are indexed 11 different ways: by award name, sponsor, academic fields and career goals, memberships, employment or volunteer experience, impairment, military service, nationality or ethnic heritage, religious affiliation, residency, and talents or areas of interest. Although the directory is aimed at graduate students, a number of the programs listed here are open, instead, only to postdoctorates (e.g., Pfizer Scholars Grant for Faculty Development in Clinical Epidemiology and the American Political Science Association's Small Research Grant Competition). Even so, the directory, overall, provides a useful introduction to graduate student funding at a reasonable price. But, if you are serious about searching for graduate funding, you'll need a more comprehensive listing (see entries 127, 143, 174, 190). While not a direct replacement, *Getting Money for Graduate School* at least partially expands the fellowship section in Peterson's *Financing Graduate School,* which was last published in 1996.

Available from: Peterson's Guides, Princeton Pike Corporate Center, 2000 Lenox Drive, P.O. Box 67005, Lawrenceville, NJ 08648. *Telephone:* (609) 896-1800; *Toll-free:* (800) 338-3282; *Fax:* (609) 896-4544; *E-mail:* sales@petersons.com

Web site: www.petersons.com

40

The Government Financial Aid Book: The Insider's Guide to State & Federal Government Grants and Loans

3rd ed. Prep. by Student Financial Services. Seattle: Perpetual Press, 1999. 204p. ISBN 1-881199-03-7. $14.95. Paper.

Description: The bulk of student financial aid comes from the federal and state governments. This guide, first published in 1994, is organized into ten sections, four of which provide directory-type information; the others contain worksheets and instructions for calculating expected family contributions, a worksheet to estimate a student's college budget, copies of the FAFSA and PROFILE forms, commonly-asked questions, and a glossary. The sections of direct interest to the fundseeker cover state and federal grants and loans, as well as information on ROTC, work-study, and other college financing options. While the directory is inexpensively priced, most of the information presented here is available either at no cost (e.g., in the federal government's *Student Guide*) or in a number of other commonly-available financial aid sources. Furthermore, the listing has not been updated since 1999 and is now seriously out of date (although a fourth edition is projected for 2003). Perpetual Press, which at one time was owned by American Collegiate Media, is now an independent company.

Available from: Perpetual Press, P.O. Box 3956, Seattle, WA 98124. *Toll-free:* (800) 807-3030; *Fax:* (707) 221-1418; *E-mail:* sales@perpetualpress.com
Web site: www.FinancialAidFinder.com

41

The Graduate School Funding Handbook

2nd ed. By April Vahle Hamel, with Mary Morris Heiberger and Julia Miller Vick. Philadelphia: University of Pennsylvania Press, 2002. 168p. ISBN 0-8122-1810-8. $17.95. Hardcover.

Description: Part handbook and part financial aid listing, this publication was "designed to guide students through the intricate process of applying for graduate school funding both in the United States and abroad." Each chapter focuses on a particular educational level, providing general information, application strategies, and a representative selection of specific funding opportunities. Program descriptions specify contact, deadline, award notification procedure, number of awards made, average number of applicants, award amounts, purpose, restrictions, award length, and applicant eligibility requirements. Although the handbook is reasonably priced, nothing new is presented here; most of the listings are basic (e.g., National Science Foundation Graduate Fellowships, Fulbright Grants, American Association of University Women Fellowships) and can be found in any fellowship directory. First published in 1994, the handbook was updated in 2002.

Available from: University of Pennsylvania Press, 4200 Pine Street, Philadelphia, PA 19104-4011. *Telephone:* (215) 898-6261; *Toll-free:* (800) 445-9880; *Fax:* (215) 898-0404; *E-mail:* custserv@pobox.upenn.edu
Web site: www.upenn.edu/pennpress

42

The Grants Register: The Complete Guide to Postgraduate Funding Worldwide

Ed. by Sara Hackwood. New York: Palgrave, 1969- . Annual. ISSN 0072-5471. ISBN 0-333-96474-8. $185 (2003 ed.). Hardcover.

Description: This annual directory describes fellowships, grants, and prizes open to nationals of the United States, Canada, the United Kingdom, Ireland, Australia, New Zealand, South Africa, and the developing countries. For more information about the publication, see entry 265 in the "Grants for Individuals—General—International" section of this bibliography.

Available from: Palgrave, 175 Fifth Avenue, New York, NY 10010. *Telephone:* (212) 982-3900; *Toll-free:* (800) 221-7945; *Fax:* (212) 777-6359

Web site: www.palgrave-usa.com

43

GrantSelect

http://www.grantselect.com

Description: Updated annually and used to generate Oryx Press's print funding directories, GrantSelect identifies more than 10,000 scholarships, fellowships, loans, and other funding opportunities sponsored by organizations and agencies in the United States and other countries. For more information about the database, see entry 247 in the "Grants for Individuals—General—United States" section of this bibliography.

Available from: Oryx Press, 88 Post Road West, Westport, CT 06881. *Telephone:* (602) 265-2651; *Toll-free:* (800) 279-6799; *Fax:* (800) 279-4663; *E-mail:* info@oryxpress.com

Web site: www.oryxpress.com

44

GrantsInfo.com: Student Funding Sources

http://www.arisnet.com/newstu.html

Description: Unlike the other sections offered in GrantsInfo.com (see entries 271, 282, and 316) this service (which was previously known as ARIS Funding Reports: Student Funding Sources) is free and provides both undergraduate and graduate students with information on scholarships, fellowships, grants, awards, internships, and traineeships in the arts and sciences, including creative arts, humanities, social sciences, natural sciences, and biomedical sciences. Both governmental and nongovernmental sources of funding are covered. While students can browse through program descriptions in each of these areas, the listing as a whole is not searchable. The detail provided for each program varies, from just contact information (including links to URLs) to 150-word descriptions. Most entries specify eligibility requirements, funding amounts, and deadline dates. While in the past this site was a "must see" for students looking for funding, in recent years it has been rather neglected; most of entries have not been updated since 2000.

Available from: Academic Research Information System, Inc., 2940 16th Street, Suite 314, San Francisco, CA 94103. *Telephone:* (415) 558-8133; *Fax:* (415) 558-8135; *E-mail:* arisnet@dnai.com

Web site: www.arisnet.com

45

High School Senior's Guide to Merit and Other No-Need Funding

By Gail Ann Schlachter and R. David Weber. El Dorado Hills, CA: Reference Service Press, 1996- . Biennial. ISBN 1-58841-044-7. $29.95 (2002-2004 ed.). Hardcover.

Description: The *High School Senior's Guide* is unique in several ways. First, the directory only lists programs open to high school seniors or recent graduates; most other directories mix together programs for a number of groups—high school students, college students, and even graduate students or postdoctorates. This focus will make a high school senior's search for funding much more efficient. Second, only merit and other no-need funding is covered. If a program requires financial need, it's not listed here. What is included? Programs that award money solely on the basis of academic record, writing or artistic ability, speech-making skills, athletic success, high school club membership, religious or ethnic background, parents' military or organizational activities, or just pure luck in random drawings. Third, many of the programs identified here are not covered in the other general financial aid directories. So, even students who can qualify for need-based programs will want to look at this listing for additional leads. In all, more than 1,100 funding opportunities for high school seniors are described; information is provided on purpose, eligibility, financial data, duration, special features, limitations, number awarded, and deadline date. These entries are organized by area of intended college study (humanities, social sciences, sciences, and any major) and indexed by program title, sponsor, residency, tenability, specific subject, and deadline. A companion volume, *College Student's Guide to Merit and Other No-Need Funding* (see entry 16), provides similar coverage for students currently enrolled or returning to college.

Available from: Reference Service Press, 5000 Windplay Drive, Suite 4, El Dorado Hills, CA 95762. *Telephone:* (916) 939-9620; *Fax:* (916) 939-9626; *E-mail:* findaid@aol.com

Web site: www.rspfunding.com

46

How to Find a Scholarship Online

By Shannon R. Turlington. New York: McGraw-Hill, 2001. 491p. ISBN 0-07-136511-7. $22.95. Paper or eBook.

Description: In recent years, college tuition has increased at an average rate of 8 percent. Finding out about scholarships that could help to pay these costs is often a time-consuming process. To make the process easier, Turlington has prepare this guide (available in paperback and as an eBook), which—in addition to providing information on financial aid, using the Internet to find scholarships, avoiding scholarships scams, and turning in a winning scholarship application—lists a couple of thousand scholarships that are posted by their sponsors online. Some of these may also have online applications; others do not. The scholarships covered in the book are grouped by applicant characteristics (e.g.,. minorities, persons with disabilities, military service) and indexed by sponsor and program title. Although the book was copyrighted in 2001, it was actually published in 2000. Given the volatile nature of the Internet, much of the information and URLs listed here are now out of date.

Available from: McGraw-Hill, Two Penn Plaza, 12th Floor, New York, NY 10121-2298. *Toll-free:* (800) 262-4729

Web site: books.mcgraw-hill.com

47

IRIS (Illinois Researcher Information Service)

Urbana: Illinois Researcher Information Service (IRIS). Updated daily. Annual Internet subscription fees range from $400 (for institutions with fewer than 3,000 students and faculty) to $2,000 (more than 15,000 students and faculty or more than $50 million annual research volume).

Description: This subscription database contains descriptions of nearly 8,000 funding opportunities open to graduate students, researchers, scholars, and faculty. For more information about the service, see entry 249 in the "Grants for Individuals—General—United States" section of this bibliography.

Available from: Illinois Researcher Information Service (IRIS), University of Illinois at Urbana-Champaign, 128 Observatory, 901 South Mathews Avenue, Urbana, IL 61801. *Telephone:* (217) 333-0284; *Fax:* (217) 333-7011; *E-mail:* a-trehub@uiuc.edu

Web site: www.library.uiuc.edu/iris

Scholarships, Etc.–General–United States

48

Kaplan Scholarships

Ed. by Gail A. Schlachter, R. David Weber, and the Staff of Reference Service Press. New York: Kaplan/Simon & Schuster, 2003. 638p. ISSN 1090-9052. ISBN 0-7432-3044-2. $27. Paper.

Description: Based on Reference Service Press's financial aid database (earlier editions used Wintergreen/Orchard House data), the latest edition of this directory (2003) identifies nearly 3,200 scholarships, grants, and awards (no loans) that can be used to support study in any discipline in junior and community colleges, vocational and technical institutes, four-year colleges, and universities in the United States. No information on research programs or money for study abroad is provided. What distinguishes this directory from most of the other general financial aid publications? The funding opportunities described here can be used at any number of schools (no single-school specific scholarships are included); only the biggest funding programs are covered (nothing under $1,000 per year); not one dollar of the programs listed here needs to be repaid; and the funding opportunities identified are not based just on need or academics—many of the sources award money because of career plans, writing ability, religious or ethnic background, military or organizational activities, athletic success, and personal characteristics. The programs are described in quite a bit of detail, are grouped by discipline (e.g., humanities, sciences), and are indexed by subject focus, geographic requirements, and sponsoring organization. This indepth coverage comes with a "price," however; the type size is quite small and can be tiring on the eyes.

Available from: Simon & Schuster, Attn: Order Department, 100 Front Street, Riverside, NJ 08075. *Toll-free:* (800) 223-2336; *Fax:* (800) 445-6991

Web site: www.simonsays.com

49

Loans and Grants from Uncle Sam: Am I Eligible and for How Much?

10th ed. By Anna Leider. Alexandria, VA: Octameron Associates, 2003. 64p. ISBN 1-57509-080-5. $7. Paper.

Description: Described in this booklet (2003-2004 edition is 64 pages) are the following federal grant and loan programs: Federal Pell Grants, Perkins Loans, Federal Family Educational Loans (Subsidized Stafford Loans, Unsubsidized Stafford Loans, PLUS Loans), Federal Direct Student Loans (Direct Subsidized Stafford Loan, Direct Unsubsidized Stafford Loans, and Direct PLUS Loans), Health Education Assistance Loans, Health Professions Student Loans, Nursing Student Loans, Loans for Disadvantaged Students, National Health Services Corps, Scholarships for Disadvantaged Students, Exceptional Need Scholarship Programs, and Loan Consolidation Programs. The text summarizes inter-

How to Find Out About Financial Aid and Funding

est rates, repayment provisions, grace periods, deferment conditions, and forbearance. There is a directory of guaranteeing agencies appended. This publication replaces two previous Octameron publications: *College Loans from Uncle Sam* and *College Grants from Uncle Sam*. Much of the information included in this guide can also be found in the Department of Education's free publication, *The Student Guide* (see entry 73 in this section of the bibliography).

Available from: Octameron Associates, 1900 Mt. Vernon Avenue, P.O. Box 2748, Alexandria, VA 22301. *Telephone:* (703) 836-5480; *Fax:* (703) 836-5650; *E-mail:* info@octameron.com

Web site: www.octameron.com

50

MACH25

http://www.collegenet.com/mach25

Description: The CollegeNET web site, which is hosted by a producer of administrative software for academic institutions, offers a guide to colleges and universities in the United States and selected other countries. Its scholarship search service, MACH25, is a free web version of the Wintergreen/Orchard House Scholarship Finder, which contains information on private and school-based financial aid programs offered by 1,600 sponsors (see entry 76). The database is similar to FastWeb, but not as precise. However, you don't have to register (a real plus). You either search by keyword (you type in the terms) or by profile (which restricts your search only by age, college level, and whether or not you want to see school-specific awards). The results of each search can be viewed in brief or detailed formats, although you have to click and wait, several times, to see the complete description. Individual awards can be saved and letters or e-mail messages generated to request additional information. Users may get more "hits" with a MACH25 search than with either FastWeb or SRN, but the search results will probably be less useful. However, expect changes in the future. Since MACH25 is currently based on Wintergreen/Orchard House financial aid data, and since Wintergreen/Orchard House is no longer updating or licensing its financial aid database, MACH25 will probably look and operate very differently before the end of 2003.

Available from: CollegeNET, Inc., 805 S.W. Broadway, Suite 1600, Portland, OR 97205. *Telephone:* (503) 973-5200; *Fax:* (503) 973-5252; *E-mail:* webadmin@collegenet.com

Web site: www.collegenet.com

51

MeritMoney.com

http://www.meritmoney.com

Scholarships, Etc.–General–United States

Description: MeritMoney differs in several substantial ways from the typical Internet scholarship search site. First of all, it's not free; subscribers must pay $39 for six months of unlimited searching. Second, it identifies only school-based (not portable) scholarships; merit scholarships from 1,100 colleges and universities are described here. Third, it never sells information about its subscribers. Fourth, it's not for everyone; only students with at least a 3.0 grade point average can qualified for the scholarships listed on the site. While this resource is far from comprehensive (less than one-third of U.S. colleges and universities are covered here) and doesn't offer the complete picture (only merit, not all, scholarships from the covered colleges and universities are identified), still the approach is unique—and motivational as well; students can see immediately how raising their SAT/ACT scores or GPA could qualify them for even more money. A similar, but less extensive listing of college-based scholarships can be found at www.guaranteed-scholarships.com. It's worth a look, though, because the free listing is not limited to solely to merit-based scholarships and may provide additional leads.

Available from: MeritMoney.com, 1742 West Katella Avenue, Suite 8, Orange, CA 92867. *Telephone:* (714) 288-4150; *Fax:* (714) 288-9544; *E-mail:* info@meritmoney.com

Web site: www.meritmoney.com

52 📖 ¢

Need a Lift? To Educational Opportunities, Careers, Loans, Scholarships & Employment

Prep. by the American Legion Educational and Scholarship Program. Indianapolis: American Legion, 1969- . Annual. $3 (2003 ed.). Paper.

Description: American Legion educational assistance (on the national and state level) is described here, along with information on private loans, some state educational benefits for veterans and their dependents, and other types of general financial aid. For more information about the publication, see entry 217 in the "Scholarships, Fellowships & Loans—Special Population Groups—Military Personnel and Veterans" section of this bibliography.

Available from: American Legion, Attn: Emblem Sales, P.O. Box 1050, Indianapolis, IN 46206-1050. *Telephone:* (317) 630-1207; *Toll-free:* (888) 453-4466; *Fax:* (317) 630-1223

Web site: www.legion.org

53 📖

Peterson's College Money Handbook

Lawrenceville, NJ: Peterson's Guides, 1983- . Annual. ISBN 0-7689-0932-5. $29.95 (2003 ed.). Paper.

Description: The cost of obtaining a four-year college degree can run as high as $60,000 or more. As a result, directories like *Peterson's College Money Handbook,* that detail college costs, are in great demand. Arranged alphabetically, profiles of more than 1,600 colleges and universities provide summary information on undergraduate financial aid, need-based awards, no-need awards, application deadlines, and other money-saving options available. Also included is a "sticker-price" chart that compares college costs and the amounts and types of financial aid awarded, showing what freshmen-year costs actually are. In addition, the major federal, state, and private financial aid programs are briefly described. The indexes provide access to colleges offering scholarships for athletic and academic ability, civic or religious services, and ethnic and religious background. Previous editions came with a Windows/Mac-formatted CD-ROM, called the Access Advisor, to make it possible for families to analyze their own financial need, compare their expected contributions with each college's costs, and compare various college loan options (but, no information on specific financial aid opportunities was provided on the CD-ROM); however, the current edition no longer includes the CD-ROM. Much of the information included here is also available in Peterson's newest financial aid directory, *Peterson's Complete Guide to Financial Aid* (see entry 54). Originally, this directory was issued under the title *Paying Less for College: The Complete Guide to $36 Billion in Financial Aid.*

Available from: Peterson's Guides, Princeton Pike Corporate Center, 2000 Lenox Drive, P.O. Box 67005, Lawrenceville, NJ 08648. *Telephone:* (609) 896-1800; *Toll-free:* (800) 338-3282; *Fax:* (609) 896-4544; *E-mail:* sales@petersons.com

Web site: www.petersons.com

54

Peterson's Complete Guide to Financial Aid

1st ed. Lawrenceville, NJ: Peterson's Guides, 2002. 1,525p. ISBN 0-7689-1115-X. $49.95. Hardcover.

Description: Despite its title, the first edition of this guide is not really "complete" or even new; rather, it simply combines two (albeit excellent) Peterson's publications: *Peterson's College Money Handbook* (see entry 53) and *Peterson's Scholarships, Grants & Prizes* (entry 57). If you already own or have used these two titles, you can safely skip this source. But, if you were considering buying both directories, you'll save $10 by purchasing the *Complete Guide* instead.

Available from: Peterson's Guides, Princeton Pike Corporate Center, 2000 Lenox Drive, P.O. Box 67005, Lawrenceville, NJ 08648. *Telephone:* (609) 896-1800; *Toll-free:* (800) 338-3282; *Fax:* (609) 896-4544; *E-mail:* sales@petersons.com

Web site: www.petersons.com

55

Peterson's Scholarship Almanac: A Compact Guide to Financial Aid

Lawrenceville, NJ: Peterson's Guides, 1997- . Annual. ISBN 0-7689-0943-0. $12.95 (2003 ed.). Paper.

Description: Extracted from the listings in *Peterson's Scholarships, Grants & Prizes* (see entry 57), this directory provides information on the 500 "largest" programs covered there. For the purposes of this directory, "largest" is defined by this formula: "1) The lowest number in the range representing the number of awards given in a year (never less than 1) is multiplied by the highest dollar figure reported. Any program with a result greater than $20,000 is selected; 2) Any program that reports giving 20 or more awards in a year is selected; 3) Any program whose lowest reported award is $2,500 or greater is selected." This means that scholarships worth $500 or less each (but given to a number of students) are viewed as "large" as scholarships worth $10,000 each (but given to only 1 recipient). The entries are grouped into two broad classes (academic fields/career areas and non-academic/career criteria); these classes, in turn, are divided into sections: 64 academic/career areas (e.g., agriculture, journalism, real estate) and 9 non-academic/career criteria (e.g., civic affiliation, impairment, talent). Cross-references (by name and sequential number) are made within sections, but not between the academic and non-academic classes. The following information is given for each listing: program description, academic/career areas, award number and amount, eligibility requirements, application requirements, contact, and address. No telephone numbers, faxes, e-mail addresses, or web sites are included. Paragraph descriptions of state-sponsored financial aid are provided in a separate section (not all entries have contact information). Four indexes complete the volume: award name, sponsor, academic/career areas, and non-academic/career criteria. The first edition of the guide was issued with a different subtitle: *Peterson's Scholarship Almanac: Key Facts You Need to Know about Scholarships*. While the *Almanac* is reasonably priced ($12.95 for the 2003 edition), it has little value to fundseekers who have or are going to check the more inclusive *Peterson's Scholarships, Grants & Prizes*. Further, much of this information is available, without charge, at Peterson's web site (see entry 56).

Available from: Peterson's Guides, Princeton Pike Corporate Center, 2000 Lenox Drive, P.O. Box 67005, Lawrenceville, NJ 08648. *Telephone:* (609) 896-1800; *Toll-free:* (800) 338-3282; *Fax:* (609) 896-4544; *E-mail:* sales@petersons.com
Web site: www.petersons.com

56

Peterson's Scholarship Search

http://www.petersons.com

Description: Click on "Financial Aid" on the main screen of Peterson's web site (in the past, this was also known as College Quest) to access the search service, which identifies scholarships, awards, and prizes available to support college study. This information is provided without charge and covers many of the same programs (although not always in the same detail) included in Peterson's print publications (for example, Peterson's *Scholarships, Grants & Awards,* described in entry 57). To conduct the free financial aid search, students must first register and, as part of that process, supply a password to enter or reenter the service. In case they forget their password, they must also supply a "challenge question" (e.g., mother's maiden name) that they must correctly answer if they need to check on their password with the toll-free support line. After registering, students answer a few simple questions (state of residence, date of birth, gender, etc.) and then wait for a minute or two for the results. Very brief information for each match is presented on a form, which covers sponsor, type of award, amount, deadline, number awarded, renewability, what's required in the application process, and contact. Some programs include award descriptions, but many others do not. Further, there is no way to browse the listings in the database and no way to identify new or updated entries. Peterson's is an anchor tenant on America Online, and this web site can also be accessed through AOL's Research and Learn Channel and through the U.S. Bank web site (usbank.com).

Available from: Peterson's Guides, Princeton Pike Corporate Center, 2000 Lenox Drive, P.O. Box 67005, Lawrenceville, NJ 08648. *Telephone:* (609) 896-1800; *Toll-free:* (800) 338-3282; *Fax:* (609) 896-4544; *E-mail:* sales@petersons.com

Web site: www.petersons.com

57

Peterson's Scholarships, Grants & Prizes: Sources of Financial Aid That Anyone Can Apply For

Lawrenceville, NJ: Peterson's Guides, 1996- . Annual. ISSN 1089-9898. ISBN 0-7689-0905-8. $29.95 (2003 ed.). Paper with CD-ROM.

Description: Published by the same company that produces the prestigious *Peterson's Guide to Four-Year Colleges, Peterson's Guide to Two-Year Colleges,* and other derivative college lists, this well-done annual directory describes in some detail approximately 2,000 scholarships, grants, awards, and prizes available to support college studies from civic, corporate, state, and other sources. Since these programs are frequently cross-listed but are not numbered, this creates the impression that there are far more opportunities than are actually listed. Program descriptions are grouped by category (e.g., academic field/career goal, civic affiliation, employment experience, military service, religious affiliation); programs with multiple characteristics are described fully only once (in the category that represents the main feature of the program) and are cross-listed in the other appropriate sections. Each full description provides the following information: contact, address, program purpose, eligibility requirements, award

Scholarships, Etc.–General–United States

type, number of awards, award amount, application procedures, and deadline. The entries are indexed by program name, sponsor, and eligibility requirements. Also included in the latest edition is an "Award Search" CD-ROM (earlier editions had a search disk) that permits users to search the profiled information in four or five categories and then print out a list of matching awards. Much of the information included here is also available in Peterson's newest financial aid directory, *Peterson's Complete Guide to Financial Aid* (see entry 54), and without charge at Peterson's web site (see entry 56). In the past, this directory was issued as *Peterson's Top 1000 Private Sources of Financial Aid* and *Peterson's Scholarships, Grants & Prizes: The Most Complete Guide to College Financial Aid from Private Sources.*

Available from: Peterson's Guides, Princeton Pike Corporate Center, 2000 Lenox Drive, P.O. Box 67005, Lawrenceville, NJ 08648. *Telephone:* (609) 896-1800; *Toll-free:* (800) 338-3282; *Fax:* (609) 896-4544; *E-mail:* sales@petersons.com
Web site: www.petersons.com

58

Princeton Review Scholarship Search

http://www.princetonreview.com

Description: In 2001, Princeton Review acquired Embark (formerly College Edge) and merged the contents of its web site (www.embark.com, formerly www.collegeedge.com) with Princeton Review's (review.com) to form a new, more comprehensive site: www.princetonreview.com. Most of the features on both sites remain, although Embark's Matchmaker has been modified and is now called Advanced School Search. The free scholarship search service is still available. Click on "Pay for School" on the site's main screen. To access this and the other areas, students have to fill out a one-page "member registration" form, which involves providing information for such questions as: gender, street address, telephone number, current status, college start date, and intended major. Unless the student requests otherwise, Princeton Review then sells or shares this information and the student can expect to receive unsolicited admissions information and special offers on products. To search the scholarship database (no browsing is permitted), students then fill out a relatively short questionnaire. These search questions, however, seem to do little to limit the results; in a recent search for an African American college woman, thousands of possible funding sources were listed—many of which either didn't relate or would be unavailable (wrong residency, ethnicity, etc.) to this particular student. However, expect changes in the future. Since Princeton Review Scholarship Search is currently based on Wintergreen/Orchard House financial aid data, and since Wintergreen/Orchard House is no longer planning to update or license its financial aid database, this site will probably look and operate very differently before the end of 2003.

Available from: Princeton Review, 2315 Broadway, New York, NY 10024. *Telephone:* (212) 874-8282; *Toll-free:* (800) REVIEW-6; *Fax:* (212) 874-0775

How to Find Out About Financial Aid and Funding

Web site: www.princetonreview.com

59

RSP Funding for Graduate Students

El Dorado Hills, CA: Reference Service Press (dist. by Ovid), 1996- . Annual, with semi-annual update. $695 and up. CD-ROM, disk, or online.

Description: *RSP Funding for Graduate Students* contains up-to-date information on more than 4,000 fellowships, loans, loan forgiveness programs, loan repayment programs, grants, and awards open to students entering, continuing, or returning to graduate school; the funds can be used to support work (study or research) on a master's degree, doctorate, advanced professional degree, or certificate. This provides more comprehensive coverage for graduate students than any other RSP product. The detailed program descriptions specify purpose, eligibility, financial data, duration, special features, limitations, number award, deadline date, heritage, special skills, student or parent affiliations, and many other applicant requirements, including student rank, gender, and ethnicity. Using Ovid's powerful search protocol, the data can be accessed by program title, sponsoring organizations, residency requirements, tenability, award amount, deadlines, keyword, and dozens of other ways. Updated every six months and available on subscription from Ovid (formerly SilverPlatter), the database can be used on the following platforms: Windows CD-ROM or hard disk, Macintosh CD-ROM or hard disk, UNIX, and the Internet.

Available from: Ovid Technologies, 100 River Ridge Drive, Norwood, MA 02062. *Telephone:* (781) 769-2599; *Toll-free:* (800) 343-0064; *Fax:* (781) 769-8763

Web site: www.ovid.com

60

RSP Funding for Undergraduates

El Dorado Hills, CA: Reference Service Press (dist. by Ovid), 1996- . Annual, with semi-annual update. $695 and up. CD-ROM, disk, or online.

Description: Updated every six months and available on subscription from Ovid (formerly SilverPlatter), *RSP Funding for Undergraduates* contains current information on more than 5,000 portable (not single-school based) financial aid programs open specifically to students entering, currently enrolled in, or returning to college. Both traditional and older students are covered. This provides more comprehensive coverage for undergraduate students than any other RSP product. The database identifies all types of aid: scholarships, loans, forgivable loans, loan repayments programs, awards, etc. The detailed program descriptions specify purpose, eligibility, financial data, duration, special features, limitations, number award, deadline date, heritage, special skills, student or parent affiliations, and many other applicant requirements, including student

Scholarships, Etc.–General–United States

rank, gender, and ethnicity. Using Ovid's powerful search protocol, the data can be accessed by program title, sponsoring organizations, residency requirements, tenability, award amount, deadlines, keyword, and dozens of other ways. The database is available on the following platforms: Windows CD-ROM or hard disk, Macintosh CD-ROM or hard disk, UNIX, and the Internet.

Available from: Ovid Technologies, 100 River Ridge Drive, Norwood, MA 02062. *Telephone:* (781) 769-2599; *Toll-free:* (800) 343-0064; *Fax:* (781) 769-8763

Web site: www.ovid.com

61

SavingforCollege

http://www.savingforcollege.com

Description: Currently, each of the 50 states has a 529 plan, which is a state-operated investment plan that gives families a federal tax-free way to save money for college. Authorized by Congress in 1996, these plans are officially known as qualified tuition programs (QTPs), although they are commonly referred to as "529 plans." These plans come in two varieties: prepaid tuition plans and college savings plans. Comprehensive information about these plans can be found at the SavingforCollege site, which was founded by accountant and 529 specialist Joseph Hurley (copies of his book, *The Best Way to Save for College,* can also be purchased there for $18.95). In addition to basic information and links to the web sites for each state 529 plan, the site provides a rating system that evaluates each plan based on investment return. Similar information (but not the ratings) can also be found on National Association of State Treasurers site, www.collegesavings.org, and in David Morton's *529 College Savings Plans,* published by Sourcebooks in 2002 (208p. ISBN 1-57248-238-9. $16.95, paperback).

Available from: Savingforcollege.com LLC, Corporate Crossings Office Park, 175 Sully's Trail, Suite 101, Pittsford, NY 14534. *Toll-free:* (800) 400-9113; *Fax:* (585) 419-7820

Web site: www.savingforcollege.com

62

Scholar$ite

http://www.scholarsite.com

Description: Produced by TIYM, publisher of the *Anuario Hispano-Hispanic Yearbook* and the *African-American Yearbook,* this site has been supported by the U.S. Department of Energy and provides information on scholarships, fellowships, and loans open to students at any level, from high school seniors through professionals and postdoctorates. The search screen makes it possible for students to access the listings by the following: institution offering

How to Find Out About Financial Aid and Funding

the funding, academic major, state of residence, academic level, citizenship requirements, and a few personal characteristics (minority group status, gender, military affiliation, financial need). Very brief information is provided for each program. Surprisingly, given that this is an online service, no URLs or links are provided for any of the programs in Scholar$ite's database. Registration is not required to use the service, but if you do register, you can enter the "Scholarship Giveaway" and compose personalized letters to send to sponsoring organizations and institutions. Previously, this site was known as Scholar$earch.

Available from: TIYM Publishing Company, Inc., 6718 Whittier Avenue, Suite 130, McLean, VA 22101-4531. *Telephone:* (703) 734-1632; *Fax:* (703) 356-0787

Web site: www.tiym.com

63

The Scholarship Advisor: Hundreds of Thousands of Scholarships Worth More Than $1 Billion

By Christopher Vuturo. New York: Princeton Review (dist. by Random House), 1998- . ISBN 0-375-76210-8. $26 (2002 ed.). Paper.

Description: This directory definitely challenges the adage that "bigger is better." There is no question that the 2002 edition of the *Scholarship Advisor* is bigger than most other scholarship directories. It numbers more than 900 pages, contains 5,000+ entries, weighs over 3 pounds, and has a spine that spans more than two inches. But, it is definitely not one of the best. The 5,000 entries are listed by sponsor, with no other access to the listings provided except for deadline date. In previous editions, several indexes had been included in the front of the book to help students find programs by title, major/academic interest, career interest, hobby/leisure, work experience, personal characteristics, residency, and single-school based scholarships. Now, without these indexes, users of the 2002 edition must read each and every entry to try to find any programs that might apply to them. Since much of the listing consists of random single school-based scholarships (open only to students who attend that college), readers may find that the results are just not worth the effort. A better approach might be to go directly to Princeton Review's web site (see entry 326) and search the listings (at no charge!) that have been posted there, since both the book and the web site are based on Wintergreen/Orchard House's financial aid data. While there is some useful supporting information in the book (e.g., advise on writing winning essays, sample letters, interview tips), students searching for specific financial aid opportunities are better served by a number of other general financial aid directories, including the College Board's *Scholarship Handbook* (see entry 11), Kaplan's *Scholarships* (entry 48), and Peterson's *Scholarships, Grants & Prizes* (entry 57).

Available from: Random House, Attn: Princeton Review Books, 280 Park Avenue, MD 10-4, New York, NY 10017. *Telephone:* (212) 874-8282; *Toll-free:* (800) 733-3000; *Fax:* (212) 874-0775

Web site: www.princetonreview.com

64

The Scholarship Book: The Complete Guide to Private-Sector Scholarships, Fellowships, Grants, and Loans for the Undergraduate

9th ed. By Daniel J. Cassidy. Englewood Cliffs, NJ: Prentice-Hall, 2002. 592p. ISSN 1528-9079. ISBN 0-7352-0276-1. $30. Paper with CD-ROM.

Description: Written by the president of National Scholarship Research Service, a computerized scholarship search service, this popular directory lists approximately 1,500 scholarships, awards, internships, and loans available to undergraduates that range from $100 to $20,000. Despite its subtitle, however, the source is neither "complete" (there are thousands of other opportunities open to this group that are not covered) nor restricted just to "private-sector" awards (state, federal, and college programs are covered as well). Nor are the program descriptions "complete;" only a brief summary is given and, sometimes, this lack of detail can be misleading. Furthermore, many of the entries describe scholarships offered by a single school rather than portable programs (where students can use the money at the college of their choice). Finally, a CD-ROM is included in the book, but it turns out to be just a .pdf copy of the book and the user must act as the "search engine" in order to use it. But, the indexing is extensive (providing access by field of study, geographic area, program title, and personal characteristics), the bibliography of other financial aid directories is handy, and the price is in line with other general financial aid directories. Much of this information can also be accessed without charge at FASTaid (National Scholarship Research Service's web site), described in entry 27 in this section of the bibliography. Because Cassidy died in 2001, the future of this title is not clear.

Available from: Prentice Hall, P.O. Box 11075, Des Moines, IA 50336-1075. *Toll-free:* (800) 947-7700; *Fax:* (515) 264-6719

Web site: www.phdirect.com

65

Scholarship & Grant Guide

http://scholarshipgrantguide.com

Description: Well, it probably was only a matter of time before someone figured out how to get students to pay for free scholarship searches. Here's the pitch: you pay $49.95 for the Scholarship & Grant Guide; in return, you receive direct links to the free scholarship search sites on the Internet that the Scholarship Group has determined to be the "Best of the Best," although they don't let you know what these are before you subscribe. And, you still have to fill out the profile submission forms on each of these sites. Your subscription also gives you access to several free electronic pamphlets and periodic reviews of search sites (using 10 specific rating fields that are chosen to test each site's ability to deliver pertinent information). The sample review posted at the site is for the scholarship database at: www.absolutelyscholarships.com; nothing is included in the review that can't be found in a number of free webographies or even on the sites themselves. While these features may not represent sufficient value added to justify the subscription price, there is one benefit that is worth noting: the guide's Top Site list includes only unique and "proprietary" databases (those that are the original property of the creators); this will save you from searching sites that look different but are just offering the same licensed data.

Available from: eFinancialAid.com, Inc., 2104 Valleydale Lane, Encinitas, CA 92024. *Telephone:* (760) 633-1773; *Fax:* (760) 633-1473; *E-mail:* info@eFinancialAid.com

Web site: www.scholarshipgrantguide.com

66

The Scholarship Scouting Report: An Insider's Guide to America's Best Scholarships

By Ben Kaplan. New York: HarperCollins, 2003. 384p. ISBN 0-0609-3654-1. $21.95. Paper.

Description: Prepared as a companion to Kaplan's popular *How to Go to College Almost for Free* (2nd ed. New York: HarperCollins, 2001. 400p. ISBN 0-0609-3765-3. $22, paperback), this nearly 400-page book provides details about a small number (100) of well-known scholarships, including information on entry requirements, application procedures, judging criteria, and actual experiences of the winners. Excerpts from winning scholarship entries are also included. As a bonus, readers receive access to the "Coach's Locker Room" on Kaplan's web site (www.scholarshipcoach.com), which provides updates to information in the *Scholarship Scouting Report* and other features.

Available from: HarperCollins Publishers, 10 East 53rd Street, New York, NY 10022. *Telephone:* (212) 207-7000

Web site: www.harpercollins.com

67

ScholarshipExperts

http://www.scholarshipexperts.com

Description: Unlike most of the other scholarship search sites on the Internet, ScholarshipExperts charges for its data: $29.95 per year to search the national and state awards; $49.95 per year to search all domestic awards (national, state, local, and institutional); funding to go abroad is not covered at any level. Members also receive access to an application request tool (common on most free sites) and one-on-one customer assistance in the scholarship search process—a feature missing from most of the other sites. Another unique

Scholarships, Etc.–General–United States

feature: ScholarshipExperts does not ever sell students' personal information to third parties. But how does its database compare to those that students can search at no charge, online or in a library? While the entries are quite detailed and the information is up to the minute, the way the information is presented sometimes makes it difficult to determine exactly what a program offers or requires. But, of more concern is not what's there, but what's missing from the database. Despite the site's claim that it has over 2.3 million awards worth more than $14 billion, students may be disappointed with their search results. For example, a sample search for an African American student returned only one record aimed specifically at Blacks; other resources (e.g., entry 198), however, have identified hundreds of programs open specifically to members of this group. Still, the site is relatively new (it was launched in January, 2001) and hopefully will expand; when that happens, students may in fact find their money well spent.

Available from: Scholarship Experts, 1120 Park Avenue, Suite G, Orange Park, FL 32073. *Telephone:* (904) 278-0877; *E-mail:* lori@scholarshipexperts.com

Web site: www.scholarshipexperts.com

68

Scholarships, Fellowships and Loans

Farmington Hills, MI: Gale, 1949- . Annual. ISSN 1058-5699. ISBN 0-7876-6166-X. $199 (2003 ed.). Hardcover.

Description: Although this directory is too expensive for most high school or college students (or their parents) to consider buying, it is available in the reference department of many larger libraries. Issued first irregularly and then biennially, this directory is now being released on an annual basis. The latest edition (2003) provides detailed information on more than 4,000 scholarships, fellowships, grants, and loans available to undergraduate and graduate students in the United States and Canada. It is arranged alphabetically by sponsoring agency and the information provided can be accessed through a set of indexes: vocational goals, field of study, residency, and place of study. Each entry identifies qualifications, funds, purpose, application process, and eligibility requirements. The Vocational Goals Index in the front of the volume pinpoints for whom the awards are geared: i.e., level of study, subject of study, geographic area, affiliation requirements, and citizenship. While *Scholarships, Fellowships and Loans* is clearly the most expensive of the financial aid directories, it is far from the best. Many of the entries are single-schools based, offer only limited funding, or are for employees of a particular company. Better bets, for considerably less money. are *Peterson's Scholarships, Grants & Prizes* (see entry 57) and Kaplan's *Scholarships* (entry 48). Before Gale took over *Scholarships, Fellowships, and Loans* in 1992, the directory was published by Bellman.

Available from: The Gale Group, P.O. Box 9187, Farmington Hills, MI 48333-9187. *Telephone:* (248) 699-GALE; *Toll-free:* (800) 877-GALE; *Fax:* (800) 414-5043; *E-mail:* galeord@gale.com

Web site: www.galegroup.com

69

Scholarships 101

http://www.scholarships101.com

Description: Prepared by Pinnacle Peak, this scholarship database describes approximately 10,000 scholarships, fellowships, and loans available to support undergraduate and graduate studies. The following information is provided for each program: eligibility requirements, due dates, number of awards, award amounts, and contact. To search the database, students must fill out a rather lengthy questionnaire (which includes such personal information as name, address, and family income) and, unless they opt out, they will be automatically mailed loan applications for the Stafford and PLUS loans. Exactly the same database is also available on a number of other sites on the web, including GoCollege (www.gocollege.com), the Wall Street Journal's CollegeJournal.com (www.collegejournal.com), and in the Education section of the U.S. News' site (www.usnews.com/usnews/home.htm). All of these versions are free. However, if students wish, they may order Scholarships 101 on CD-ROM for $19.95. In addition, Pinnacle Peak has an arrangement with Coca-Cola, similar to Tuition Funding Source's distribution agreement with Pepsi-Cola (see entry 74) and makes a customized version of Scholarships 101 available at modest or no charge to students at participating schools.

Available from: Pinnacle Peak Solutions, Inc., P.O. Box 11870, Glendale, AZ 85318-1870. *Telephone:* (623) 587-0217; *Toll-free:* (800) 762-7101; *Fax:* (623) 587-0235; *E-mail:* cokeschools@scholarships101.com

Web site: www.scholarships101.com

70

Scholarships.com

http://www.scholarships.com

Description: Yet another free scholarship database on the web! Like the others, it claims a huge database, requires students to fill out a registration form to use the service, interrupts the registration/search process with advertisements and promotions (in this case, for loans), and provides a custom application request letter for the users. However, the search results offer little detail about individual programs and the final selection often includes programs that are quite inappropriate (e.g., in sample searches, an African American student was informed about programs open only to Hispanics and a Baptist student was led to funding offered by the Presbyterian Church). One interesting feature: many of the programs lead the student directly to a sponsor's web site rather than to an editorial summary of the scholarship.

Scholarships, Etc.–General–United States

Available from: BrokeScholar, 44 School Street, 1st Floor, Suite 324, Boston, MA 02108. *E-mail:* bsfeedback@brokescholar.com
Web site: scholarships.brokescholar.com

71

SPIN (Sponsored Programs Information Network)

Guilderland, NY: InfoEd. Updated daily. Annual Internet subscription fees vary.

Description: SPIN (Sponsored Programs Information Network) is a subscription database that consists of information from 1,200 different sponsoring agencies around the world; together, these agencies offer more than 10,000 separate funding opportunities, including fellowships, travel grants, research grants, curriculum development grants, sabbatical support, publication support, international projects, collaborative programs, and academic exchange programs. For more information about the service, see entry 252 in the "Grants for Individuals—General—United States" section of this bibliography.

Available from: InfoEd International, Inc., 1873 Western Avenue, Suite 201, Albany, NY 12203. *Telephone:* (518) 464-0691; *Toll-free:* (800) 727-6427; *Fax:* (518) 464-0695; *E-mail:* office@infoed.org
Web site: www.infoed.org

72

SRN Express Scholarship Search

http://www.srnexpress.com

Description: SRN Express is a free scholarship database offered on the web. Students have to register (and give out their phone number), but in return they get a chance to search through SRN's scholarship database, which lists primarily private-sector aid offered by 1,500 sponsors. Single-school awards are not listed. Although the database is updated throughout the year, there is no way for users to save their profiles and SRN does not produce automatic updates the way that FastWeb does (see entry 28). One handy feature of the SRN Express site is the "State Programs" page, which provides online links to the agencies in each state that offer or administer student financial aid (many of which have searchable databases or lists of available financial aid). SRN Express is based on the Scholarship Resource Network/PC (SRN/PC) database, which contains information on 8,000 scholarships, fellowships, and educational loans; it can be licensed to educational institutions and education-related agencies/organizations. Alternatively, institutions can license an abbreviated and less-expensive version of SRN/PC, which asks fewer questions (uses fewer discriminators that SRN/PC) but has fewer records in the database. In both cases, licensees can customize the database by adding local programs. SRN was formed by employees who previously worked with CASHE (see entry 77), before it was sold to EdTech.

How to Find Out About Financial Aid and Funding

The SRN database can also be searched on SallieMae's Wiredscholar's site (see entry 77).

Available from: Scholarship Resource Network, Inc., 15 Beach Court, Saratoga Springs, NY 12866. *Telephone:* (518) 580-1022; *Fax:* (518) 584-7320; *E-mail:* srntech@srnexpress.com

Web site: www.srnexpress.com

73

The Student Guide: Financial Aid from the U.S. Department of Education

Washington, DC: U.S. Department of Education. Annual. Free (2003-2004 ed.). Paper or online.

Description: Of the $70 billion in student aid currently available, approximately one half of it will be supplied by the federal government. And, most of the federal funds will be channeled through a handful of programs: Federal Pell Grants, Direct and FFEL Stafford Loans, Direct and FFEL PLUS Loans, Federal Supplemental Educational Opportunity Grants, Federal Work-Study, and Federal Perkins Loans. Get information about these programs straight from the source, in this free booklet issued by the U.S. Department of Education. For each program, official information is provided on purpose, financial support offered, application procedures, eligibility requirements, recipient responsibilities, and notification process. The *Guide* is available in print (in English, Spanish, or Braille) or can be downloaded from the Department of Education's web site. This site also has a link to "FAFSA on the Web," which is an online Windows' version of the government's Free Application for Federal Student Aid. In the past, *The Student Guide* has been issued under several other titles, including *Five Federal Financial Aid Programs* and *Federal Financial Aid Programs*.

Available from: U.S. Department of Education, c/o Federal Student Information Aid Center, P.O. Box 84, Washington, DC 20044-0084. *Telephone:* (319) 337-5665; *Toll-free:* (800) 4-FED-AID; *E-mail:* sfamail@ncs.ed.gov

Web site: www.ed.gov/studentaid

74

Tuition Funding Sources (TFS)

Salt Lake City: Falcon Management, 1990- . Annual. CD-ROM and online.

Description: Like *Scholarships 101,* which has an arrangement with Coca-Cola (see entry 69), *Tuition Funding Sources (TFS)* is sponsored by Pepsi-Cola; it is sometimes referred to as *Pepsi-Cola Tuition Funding Sources* (or *Pepsi-Cola TFS).* However, unlike *Scholarships 101,* this database is available (to schools and colleges) only through the local bottler. Some of these Pepsi bottlers provide the database without restrictions; others require the recipients to commit

Scholarships, Etc.–General–United States

to sell only Pepsi products through campus vending machines. *TFS* is a CD-ROM software program that is designed to run on a school's computer system (Windows or Macintosh versions). Once students register at participating schools, they may use TFS there or use it on the Internet. The database is designed to help students locate scholarships and other financial aid for college tuition. It provides information on approximately 8,000 funding opportunities offered primarily by vocational schools, colleges, and universities; some private sources and most major federal programs are also included. Students can access the information by school or by the subject they are interested in studying. The product also contains a careers module, automatically generated personalized letters requesting applications for admissions and scholarships, selected college catalogs, and (on the CD-ROM version) actual college admissions and scholarship applications that can be completed by the student on the computer. The product is updated annually.

Available from: Falcon Management Group, Inc., 3690 East Fort Union Boulevard, Suite 103, Salt Lake City, UT 84121. *Telephone:* (801) 943-7676; *Toll-free:* (800) 232-4004; *Fax:* (801) 943-7668; *E-mail:* support@tuitions.com

Web site: www.tuitions.com

75

Winning Scholarships for College: An Insider's Guide

2nd ed. By Marianne Ragins. New York: Holt, 1999. 288p. ISBN 0-8050-5969-5. $12.95. Paper.

Description: The author, Marianne Ragins, made news several years ago because, as a high school senior, she received more than $400,000 in financial aid for college. In 1994, she wrote the first edition of this guide—in a student-to-student voice—to share with others her successful search strategies. The second edition was released in 1999. Despite what its title might imply, this is not a scholarship directory. While Ragins provides some helpful hints for getting organized, writing application essays, and searching for scholarships, she identifies less than 100 financial aid programs and only a few resource directories.

Available from: Henry Holt and Company, Inc., 115 West 18th Street, New York, NY 10011. *Telephone:* (212) 886-9200; *Toll-free:* (888) 330-8477; *Fax:* (800) 672-2054; *E-mail:* info@henryholt.com

Web site: www.henryholt.com

76

Wintergreen/Orchard House Scholarship Finder

Itasca, IL: Riverside Publishing, Annual. $259 (2001-2002 ed.). CD-ROM.

Description: Wintergreen/Orchard House is a database compiler and provider, specializing in the college, scholarship, and career fields. In the past, it has provided data for 33 different software products and online services, 23 different published guidebooks, and 3 national magazines: *U.S. News and World Report, Time,* and *Money Magazine.* One of software products compiled by Wintergreen/Orchard House was *Scholarship Finder,* a CD-ROM product for Windows. The last edition of *Scholarship Finder* (2001-2002) described 5,000+ scholarship sources that offer at least $500 per year (many of which are single-school based) and cost $259; program descriptions included the name, address, and phone number of the contact persons, average amount of each award given, number of annual awards offered, eligibility requirements, and application deadlines. The 2001-2002 edition is the last compilation of data produced by Wintergreen/Orchard House. As of mid-2002, the company has no plans to update or continue its financial aid database in any form. This decision will impact a number of sites that have been using Wintergreen/Orchard House data, including Princeton Review (see entry 326) and CollegeNET (entry 50).

Available from: Wintergreen/Orchard House, Riverside Publishing, 425 Spring Lake Drive, Itasca, IL 60143-2079. *Telephone:* (630) 467-7000; *Toll-free:* (800) 323-9540, option 4; *Fax:* (630) 467-6069; *E-mail:* rpcwebmaster@hmco.com

Web site: www.riverpub.com

77

Wiredscholar

http://salliemae.wiredscholar.com/paying/content/index.jsp

Description: Sallie Mae is the nation's largest source of funding and servicing support for educational loans. As part of its web offerings, Sallie Mae sponsors Wiredscholar, which provides information to students on preparing, selecting, applying, paying for, choosing, and financing a college education. In the "Paying" section, two types of free scholarship search services are offered: the "Express Search," which searches the database broadly and yields the largest number of scholarship leads, and the "Premier Search." which requires students to fill out more profile form fields—this could take up to 15 minutes—and returns a smaller but more targeted number of scholarship possibilities. Wiredscholar promises not to sell or rent any of this personal information Both of these searches use a scholarship database supplied by SRN (see entry 72), which replaces CASHE (College Aid Sources for Higher Education), the database previously offered on the site. Unlike the previous CASHE search, students can now view their results immediately online, save their search results to view or review later, and update their profile form at any time. However, they must have Javascript enabled on their browser to use this service.

Available from: Sallie Mae Servicing L.P., P.O. Box 9500, Wilkes Barre, PA 18773-9500. *Toll-free:* (800) 428-1039

Web site: www.salliemae.com

Scholarships, Etc.–General–Arkansas

78

Yale Daily News Guide to Fellowships and Grants

2nd ed. By Gail Schlachter, R. David Weber, and the Staff of Reference Service Press. New York: Kaplan/Simon & Schuster, 1999. 482p. ISBN 0-684-86281-6. $25. Paper.

Description: Kaplan combined the resources of Reference Service Press and the Yale Daily News to produce the second edition of this guide to fellowships and grants for graduate students. More than $1 billion in free money is described in detail here in 2,000 program entries grouped into two major sections: 1) fellowships and grants for study and training and 2) fellowships and grants for research and creative activities. The following information is provided for each program: purpose, eligibility, financial data, duration, special features, limitations, number awarded, deadline, and contacts (including e-mails and web sites). Because the directory focuses on the biggest and best funding opportunities (nothing less than $1,000) that can be used at any number of schools and don't need to be repaid, the listing provides a good overview of graduate funding, but it is now out of date. For more current and comprehensive information on graduate funding, check out Reference Service Press's biennially updated *Money for Graduate Students* directories (see entries 127, 143, 174, and 190).

Available from: Simon & Schuster, Attn: Order Department, 100 Front Street, Riverside, NJ 08075. *Toll-free:* (800) 223-2336; *Fax:* (800) 445-6991
Web site: www.simonsays.com

Arkansas

79

ASIS

http://scholarships-ar-us.org

Description: ASIS, an abbreviation for Arkansas Student Information Service, is a web site designed for students, parents, and financial aid counselors in the state of Arkansas. On the site, there is a searchable scholarship database which describes more than 900 Arkansas-based scholarships (along with some national programs). No registration is required to use the database. Students answer 14 questions (e.g., gender, high school district, major, ethnic background) and immediately retrieve their research results. One nice feature: the results can be displayed on one long form, rather than on separate screens. The following information for each entry is provided on a "preprinted" form (if no information is available, the categories are left blank): scholarship title, value, summary, additional requirements, sponsor name, contact name and address, telephone and fax numbers, and e-mail and web address. While many states have financial aid web pages, none of them offer a user-friendly state-wide searchable database like this one. Sponsored by the Arkansas Single Parent Scholarship Fund, the site is also known as Scholarships-Ar-Us.

Available from: Arkansas Single Parent Scholarship Fund, 614 East Emma Avenue, Suite 119, Springdale, AR 72764. *Telephone:* (479) 927-1402; *Fax:* (479) 751-1110; *E-mail:* aspsf@covern.uark.edu

Web site: scholarships-ar-us.org/aspsf.htm

Colorado

80

Colorado Collegiate Handbook

Durango: Colorado Council on High School/College Relations. Annual. ISSN 0898-4018. $5, members of the Colorado Council (this includes most high schools and colleges in Colorado, their students, parents, faculties, and staff); $7, others. Paper.

Description: The Colorado Council on High School/College Relations is an organization of colleges, universities, and high schools in Colorado. Its purpose is to foster cooperation and help students in the state plan their education. The council prepares and publishes this handbook each year (latest edition: 2002-03). It tells students about costs, educational programs, admission standards, and other features at each Colorado college and university that is a member of the council (other postsecondary schools in the state are not covered directly). Brief, general information about financial aid is provided in each school entry. More valuable, from a financial aid standpoint, are the sections in the front of the book that identify the major nationally-available and minority-focused scholarships; dozens of programs are listed and briefly described.

Available from: Colorado Council on High School/College Relations, c/o Bill Hathaway-Clark, Treasurer, P.O. Box 718, Denver, CO 80201-0718. *Telephone:* (970) 247-7190; *Fax:* (970) 247-7190

Web site: www.coloradocouncil.org

Florida

81

Florida Scholarships: Guide to Scholarships, Loans, Grants, and Other Financial Assistance Programs

5th ed. Ed. by Jose A. Cisneros. Miami: Florida Funding Publications, 2002. 120p. ISBN 1-879543-30-3. $24.95. Paper.

Description: This guide focuses on financial aid available to Florida students. It provides information on how, when, and where to apply for federal, state, and private scholarships (and other types of financial assistance) in Florida and throughout the United States; in all, approximately 500 programs are described. Separate chapters identify a limited number of graduate, minority, and women's programs. Program descriptions, in most cases, are so brief that it would be difficult to use this listing to search for funding. In the past, this guide was issued as *Your Guide to Florida Scholarships and Other Financial Assistance Programs.*

Available from: Florida Funding Publications, Inc., 8925 S.W. 148 Street, Suite 110, Miami, FL 33176. *Telephone:* (305) 251-2203; *Fax:* (305) 251-2773; *E-mail:* info@floridafunding.com

Web site: www.floridafunding.com

Idaho

82

Directory of Idaho Foundations

10th ed. Ed. by Elaine C. Leppert. Caldwell, ID: Caldwell Public Library, 2001. ISSN 1058-0689. Unpaged. $15. Comb binding

Description: The latest (2001) edition covers more than 200 foundations and corporations (including those offering scholarships) "either headquartered in Idaho or with a history of giving in Idaho." For more information about the publication, see entry 399 in the "Grants for Organizations—General—Idaho" section of this bibliography.

Available from: Caldwell Public Library, 1010 Dearborn Street, Caldwell, ID 83605-4195. *Telephone:* (208) 459-3242; *Fax:* (208) 459-7344; *E-mail:* caldwellpl@yahoo.com

How to Find Out About Financial Aid and Funding

Illinois

83 📖 ¢

Handbook of Illinois Postsecondary Institutions

Springfield: Illinois Student Assistance Commission. Annual. Free (2002-2003 ed.). Looseleaf.

Description: Issued annually, this 258-page publication (free to schools and educational institutions) lists and describes, in chart form, the postsecondary institutions in the state. The school profiles are grouped into five categories: four-year colleges and universities, two-year colleges, schools of nursing, proprietary schools, and professional schools/allied health programs. Both the financial aid contact person and the type of financial aid offered at each of these schools are noted. In addition, in a separate section in the front of the book, programs either sponsored or administered by the state or the Illinois Student Assistance Commission are described.

Available from: Illinois Student Assistance Commission, 1755 Lake Cook Road, Deerfield, IL 60015-5209. *Toll-free:* (800) 899-4722; *Fax:* (847) 948-8550

Web site: www.isac1.org

Indiana

84 📖 🖱

Directory of Indiana & Kentucky Grantmakers

Ed. by Susan R. Wilson. Indianapolis: Indiana Grantmakers Alliance, 2001. 1,300p. $80, members, paper; $100, nonmembers, paper; $100, members, CD-ROM; $125, nonmembers, CD-ROM.

Description: This directory profiles more than 2,000 active grantmaking foundations, trusts, and scholarship programs in Indiana and Kentucky, including a number that are located elsewhere but have a history of funding in the state. For more information about the listing, see entry 404 in the "Grants for Organizations—General—Indiana" section of this bibliography.

Available from: Indiana Grantmakers Alliance, Inc., 32 East Washington Street, Suite 1100, Indianapolis, IN 46204-3583. *Telephone:* (317) 630-5200; *Fax:* (317) 630-5210

Web site: www.ingrantmakers.org

Scholarships, Etc.–General–Kentucky

85

The Northwest Indiana Directory of Local Scholarships: A Guide for Lake, LaPorte, and Porter County Students

By Karen L. Williams. Lincoln, NE: iUniverse.com, 2001. 272p. ISBN 0-595-18607-6. $19.95. Paper.

Description: Self published by Karen Williams and available through iUniverse.com, this geographically-restricted directory identifies scholarships open to residents of three counties in northwestern Indiana: Lake, LaPorte, and Porter. These programs are sponsored by private foundations, trusts, civic organizations, businesses, and religious organizations. Local university and college scholarships are listed as well, but only if they are awarded to students from northwest Indiana. The entries are grouped into the following chapters: academic, geographic, need-based, organizational, returning students, school-based, vocational, and minority (which is defined to include "ethnic, gender, religion, etc."). Entries provide the following information: scholarship name, sponsor name and address as well as phone and e-mail, major, eligibility, amount awarded, frequency of award, and deadline. Incredibly, there are approximately 250 separate scholarships described here (more than in some national financial aid directories). You can browse the entire book at no charge and print out individual pages (subject, of course, to copyright restrictions) before you decide whether to buy it or not at iUniverse's web site.

Available from: iUniverse.com, Inc., 5220 South 16th, Suite 200, Lincoln, NE 68512. *E-mail:* klissell@yahoo.com
Web site: www.iuniverse.com

Kentucky

86

Directory of Indiana & Kentucky Grantmakers

Ed. by Susan R. Wilson. Indianapolis: Indiana Grantmakers Alliance, 2001. 1,300p. $80, members, paper; $100, nonmembers, paper; $100, members, CD-ROM; $125, nonmembers, CD-ROM.

Description: This directory profiles more than 2,000 active grantmaking foundations, trusts, and scholarship programs in Kentucky and Indiana, including a number that are located elsewhere but have a history of funding in the state. For more information about the listing, see entry 404 in the "Grants for Organizations—General—Indiana" section of this bibliography.

Available from: Indiana Grantmakers Alliance, Inc., 32 East Washington Street, Suite 1100, Indianapolis, IN 46204-3583. *Telephone:* (317) 630-5200; *Fax:* (317) 630-5210

Web site: www.ingrantmakers.org

Louisiana

87

Louisiana's Financial Aid Handbook

Baton Rouge: Louisiana Office of Student Financial Assistance. Annual. Free (2003-2004 ed.). Paper or online.

Description: Issued annually and without charge, this 80-page booklet (which is often referred to as the *"Blue Book"*) lists and briefly describes the federal and state scholarships, grants, savings programs, and outreach programs offered or administered by the Louisiana Office of Student Financial Assistance (LOFSA) for Louisiana residents. Information is also provided on need-based federal aid programs, merit-based aid programs, opportunities in the military, private and other sources of aid (including scholarship search web sites), community service opportunities, Pell Grants, and other campus-based aid programs. A particularly helpful feature is the checklist for high school students preparing for college. This booklet is also available as a .pdf file on the office's web site.

Available from: Louisiana Office of Student Financial Assistance, P.O. Box 91202, Baton Rouge, LA 70821-9202. *Toll-free:* (800) 259-5626, ext. 1012
Web site: www.osfa.state.la.us

Maine

88

Directory of Maine Grantmakers

Ed. by Priscilla Miller and Frances L. Rice. Portland: University of Southern Maine, 1973- . Irreg. $20 (2001 ed.). Paper or online.

Description: One section of this directory focuses on Maine foundations that award scholarships. For more information about the listing, see entry 410 in the "Grants for Organizations—General—Maine" section of this bibliography.

Available from: Maine Philanthropy Center, University of Southern Maine Library, P.O. Box 9301, Portland, ME 04104-9301. *Telephone:* (207) 780-5039; *Fax:* (207) 780-4649; *E-mail:* Jread@megrants.org
Web site: www.megrants.org

Scholarships, Etc.–General–Maryland

89

Financial Aid Tool Belt: A How-To Guide for Students

Augusta: Finance Authority of Maine, 2002. 32p. Free. Paper and online.

Description: Published annually by the Finance Authority of Maine (FAME) this free scholarship book briefly describes more than 150 privately-funded scholarships in Maine, plus a few random national programs. These scholarships generally range in size from $100 to $1,000 or more. Program descriptions are organized by title, coded for eligibility (e.g., A = adult students returning to school; H = high school students only), and include the following information: contact, eligibility, scholarship amount, selection process, application process, number awarded, and deadline. The information in this attractive, well-organized, and useful booklet is also reproduced at FAME's web site, where program entries can be accessed by deadline dates, eligibility codes, course codes, and specific listings. In the past, a similar publication was issued under the title *FAME/Fleet Bank Scholarship Book*.

Available from: Finance Authority of Maine, P.O. Box 949, Augusta, ME 04332-0949. *Telephone:* (207) 623-0095; *Toll-free:* (800) 228-3734; *TTY:* (207) 626-2717; *Fax:* (207) 626-8208; *E-mail:* info@famemaine.com

Web site: www.famemaine.com

Maryland

90

The Red Book: Catalog of State Assistance Programs

http://www.mdp.state.md.us/clhouse/redbook/redbook.html

Description: Over $2.25 billion in loans, scholarships, grants, technical assistance, and other services available from the state and federal government to public sector agencies and the general public in Maryland is identified in this source. For more information about the listing, see entry 255 in the "Grants for Individuals—General—Maryland" section of this bibliography.

Available from: Maryland Department of Planning, 301 West Preston Street, Room 1101, Baltimore, MD 21201-2365. *Telephone:* (410) 767-4500; *Toll-free:* (877) 767-6272; *Fax:* (410) 767-4480; *E-mail:* dczerwinski@mdp.state.md.us

Web site: www.op.state.md.us

How to Find Out About Financial Aid and Funding

91

Student Guide to Higher Education and Financial Aid in Maryland

Annapolis: Maryland Higher Education Commission. Annual. Free (2003-2004 ed.). Paper or online.

Description: More than 250,000 students go to college in Maryland. This 90-page guide is prepared annually to help them find the courses and the college they want, as well as to offer some information on scholarships and other forms of financial aid available to them. The following information is provided for each of the state-sponsored funding programs: purpose, qualifications, amount of money awarded, and application process. The same information is also provided on the Commission's web site.

Available from: Maryland Higher Education Commission, Attn: State Scholarship Administration, 839 Bestgate Road, Suite 400, Annapolis, MD 21401. *Telephone:* (410) 260-4565; *Toll-free:* (800) 974-1024; *TTY:* (800) 735-2258; *E-mail:* ssamail@mhec.state.md.us

Web site: www.mhec.state.md.us

Minnesota

92

Focus on Financial Aid

Saint Paul: Minnesota Higher Education Services Office, Annual. Free (2003-2004 ed.). Paper or online.

Description: Prepared for students living in Minnesota or interested in attending college there, this very attractive and useful free booklet (generally about 50 pages) is published annually by the Minnesota Higher Education Services Office (formerly the Minnesota Higher Education Coordinating Board). It not only provides descriptions of the major state and federal programs, but it also includes tips for applying for financial aid, a list of print and Internet resources, a short glossary, a list of colleges and universities in the state (with addresses and telephone numbers), a summary of financial aid tax provisions, and a student financial aid worksheet. The publication is also available as a .pdf file and can be downloaded, at no charge, from the Minnesota Higher Education Services Office's web site.

Available from: Minnesota Higher Education Services Office, 1450 Energy Park Drive, Suite 350, St. Paul, MN 55108-5227. *Telephone:* (651) 642-0567; *Toll-free:* (800) 657-3866; *TTY:* (800) 627-3529; *Fax:* (651) 642-0675; *E-mail:* info@heso.state.mn.us

Web site: www.mheso.state.mn.us

Missouri

93 📖

The Directory of Missouri Foundations

Ed. by Anne Borman. St. Louis: Directory of Missouri Foundations, 1985- . Biennial. ISSN 0884-7223. $62 (2001-2002 ed.). Paper.

Description: More than 400 private, corporate, and community foundations registered in Missouri are briefly described in the latest edition of this directory; one of the sections identifies foundations providing assistance to individuals (including scholarships and loans). For more information about the publication, see entry 420 in the "Grants for Organizations—General—Missouri" section of this bibliography.

Available from: Directory of Missouri Foundations, 8122 Edinburgh Drive, St. Louis, MO 63105. *Telephone:* (314) 725-6834; *Fax:* (314) 725-0211; *E-mail:* foundations@primary.net

Montana

94 📖

Montana Foundation Directory

14th ed. Ed. by Joan Bares. Billings: Montana State University at Billings, 2002. 155p. $25. Spiral bound.

Description: Foundations located in Montana (or funding within the state) that offer scholarships can be identified in the index of this annually-issued directory. For more information about the publication, see entry 94 in the "Grants for Organizations—General—Montana" section of this bibliography.

Available from: Montana State University at Billings, Grants Development Office, 1500 University Drive, Billings, Montana 59101-298. *Telephone:* (406) 657-1654; *Fax:* (406) 657-2264; *E-mail:* jbares@msubillings.edu
Web site: www.msubillings.edu/library/grants/index.html

New Hampshire

95 🕸 ¢

Directory of Charitable Funds in New Hampshire

http://www.state.nh.us/nhdoj/CHARITABLE/char.html
Description: More than half the listings in the latest online version (2002) of this directory describe scholarships offered to New Hampshire residents by organizations in the state. For more information about the directory, see entry 257 in the "Grants for Individuals—General—New Hampshire" section of this bibliography.
Available from: New Hampshire Department of Justice, Attn: Charitable Trusts Unit, 33 Capitol Street, Concord, NH 03301-6397. *Telephone:* (603) 271-3658; *Fax:* (603) 271-2110; *TDD:* (800) 735-2964
Web site: www.state.nh.us/nhdoj/CHARITABLE/char.html

North Carolina

96 📖 🕸 ¢

Student Financial Aid for North Carolinians

Prep. by Elizabeth McDuffie, Justin Greene, and Robbie Schultz. Chapel Hill: North Carolina State Education Assistance Authority, 2002. 56p. Free. Paper or online.
Description: Although the title indicates that this listing identifies funding just for North Carolina students, most of the 125 programs described in this annually-updated guide are actually open to students residing in any state. For each program, the following information is given: background, eligibility, number and value of the awards, and application procedure. The entries are grouped by type of recipients (e.g., high school seniors, military and their dependents, graduate and professional students) and indexed by program title or sponsor. Listings of community colleges and senior colleges/universities in North Carolina are included as appendices. The publication is also available without charge at the North Carolina State Education Assistance Authority's (NCSEAA) web site. In addition, the data included here can be searched (by program type and income requirements) on the College Foundation of North Carolina's web site, which is a service offered by NCSEAA, College Foundation Inc., and Pathways.
Available from: North Carolina State Education Assistance Authority, Attn: Education, Training and Outreach Division, P.O. Box 14103, Research Triangle, NC 27709. *Telephone:* (919) 549-8614; *Fax:* (919) 549-8481
Web site: www.cfnc.org

Scholarships, Etc.–General–Oregon

Oregon

97 📖 🕸 ¢

Pacific Northwest Scholarship Guide

8th ed. By Douglas J. Breithaupt. Seattle: College Planning Network, 2002. 200p. ISBN 1-880344-09-2. $29.95, paper; free, online.

Description: The *Pacific Northwest Scholarship Guide* was first published in 1989 by College Planning Network (CPN), a Seattle-based nonprofit organization assisting people seeking educational opportunities in the Pacific Northwest. The current (8th) edition was issued in 2002. Approximately $20 million in aid available to Pacific Northwest undergraduate and graduate students is identified. The following information is provided for each of the approximately 700 awards listed in the source: contact, address, phone and e-mail, web site, deadline, amount, renewability, number of awards, number of applications, eligibility requirements, and application procedures. The guide is also available at CPN's College Planning web site, which is sponsored by Boeing Employees' Credit Union; students can search the contents of the guide there, matching student characteristics with available scholarships using the search engine designed by Microsoft as a gift to CPN. The book and the free online database are designed to work together, so that students can sort a list of matching scholarships online, view or print the list there, and then review individual scholarship profiles in the book or on the web site. However, only students using the web version can link directly to the sponsoring organizations for further information and applications. Although the *Pacific Northwest Scholarship Guide* (in the print or online version) is aimed at students in the Pacific Northwest, few of the programs in the source are restricted solely to students living in that area; so students in any area could profit from using the free online version of this source.

Available from: College Planning Network, Campion Tower, 914 East Jefferson, Seattle, WA 98122-5366. *Telephone:* (206) 323-0624; *E-mail:* seacpn@collegeplan.org

Web site: www.collegeplan.org

South Dakota

98 🕸 ¢

South Dakota Grant Directory

http://www.sdstatelibrary.com/grants/index.cfm

How to Find Out About Financial Aid and Funding

Description: Included on this web site, which is "under construction," are foundations, trusts, and agencies in South Dakota that make scholarship awards. For more information about the site, see entry 442 in the "Grants for Organizations—General—South Dakota" section of this bibliography.

Available from: South Dakota State Library, Attn: Public Services Department, The MacKay Building, 800 Governors Drive, Pierre, SD 57501-2294. *Telephone:* (605) 773-3131; *Toll-free:* (800) 423-6665 (within SD); *Fax:* (605) 773-4950; *E-mail:* refrequest@stlib.state.sd.us

Web site: www.state.sd.us/lib

Texas

99

Financial Aid for Texas Students

Austin: Texas Higher Education Coordinating Board, 2000. 50p. Free. Paper.

Description: Prepared as a guide to help students and parents understand the "ins and outs" of acquiring financial aid, the latest edition of the booklet (available free from the Texas Higher Education Coordinating Board) briefly summarizes 60 scholarship and loan programs offered on the federal and state level to students in Texas. Also included is a short list of definitions, an introduction to the process of applying for scholarships, a list of colleges in Texas participating in the state-sponsored financial aid programs, and a program title index. The 2000 edition is the last edition of the booklet; it has been replaced by a fold-out chart titled "Just the Facts about Student Financial Aid." However, information about specific funding opportunities for students in Texas can now be found on the Coordinating Board's web site.

Available from: Texas Higher Education Coordinating Board, Capitol Station, P.O. Box 12788, Austin, TX 78711-2788. *Telephone:* (512) 427-6101; *Toll-free:* (800) 242-3062; *Fax:* (512) 427-6127; *E-mail:* grantino@thecb.state.tx.us

Web site: www.thecb.state.tx.us

Vermont

100

Scholarships Available to Vermonters

Winooski: Vermont Student Assistance Corporation, 2003. 46p. Free. Paper or online.

Scholarships, Etc.–General–Washington

Description: This very attractive booklet is distributed without charge by the Vermont Student Assistance Corporation (VSAC); it identifies scholarships, fellowships, and loans available to Vermont residents. Most of the programs included in the booklet are sponsored by private groups: Vermont businesses, charitable or service organizations, veterans groups, etc. This listing should be viewed as a supplement to other sources, since federal and national funding opportunities are not covered here. The booklet is divided into two sections: scholarships administered in part or in full by VSAC and scholarships administered by other agencies and organizations. The following information is generally provided for each entry: purpose, eligibility, selection process, amount of the award, documents required, application procedure, application deadline, and number of awards: One particularly nice feature: the average number of applicants for each award is usually indicated. The information in this booklet is also available as a .pdf file on VSAC's web site.

Available from: Vermont Student Assistance Corporation, Attn: Scholarship Programs, Champlain Mills, P.O. Box 2000, Winooski, VT 05404-2601. *Telephone:* (802) 655-9602; *Toll-free:* (800) 642-3177; *Fax:* (802) 654-3765; *TDD:* (800) 281-3341; *E-mail:* info@vsac.org

Web site: www.vsac.org

Washington

101

Pacific Northwest Scholarship Guide

8th ed. By Douglas J. Breithaupt. Seattle: College Planning Network, 2002. 200p. ISBN 1-880344-09-2. $29.95, paper; free, online.

Description: Approximately $20 million in aid available to Pacific Northwest undergraduate and graduate students is identified in this guide. For more information about the source, see entry 97 in the "Scholarships, Fellowships & Loans—General—Oregon" section of this bibliography.

Available from: College Planning Network, Campion Tower, 914 East Jefferson, Seattle, WA 98122-5366. *Telephone:* (206) 323-0624; *E-mail:* seacpn@collegeplan.org

Web site: www.collegeplan.org

Wyoming

102

Student Financial Aid and Scholarships at Wyoming Colleges

Laramie, WY: Student Financial Aid, University of Wyoming, 2003. 132p. Free. Paper or online.

Description: This very useful and well-done publication, distributed annually without charge by the University of Wyoming's Office of Student Financial Aid, identifies specific financial aid programs available at each of Wyoming's postsecondary institutions. Brief descriptions (purpose, amount awarded, number awarded) are provided in the latest edition (2003-2004). In addition, federal, state, and private-sector financial aid programs open to Wyoming residents are covered selectively. In the future, an electronic version of this book will be available at the Office's web site; currently, however, the page in under construction.

Available from: University of Wyoming, Office of Student Financial Aid, P.O. Box 3335, Laramie, WY 82071-3335. *Telephone:* (307) 766-2116; *Fax:* (307) 766-3960; *TDD:* (307) 766-3635; *E-mail:* finaid@uwyo.edu
Web site: siswww.uwyo.edu/sfa/schlbook/schlbook.htm

103

Wyoming Foundations Directory: A Guide to Private Foundations

8th ed. Ed. by M. Ann Miller. Cheyenne, WY: Laramie County Community College, 2001. Unpaged. $8. Paper.

Description: In the latest edition of this directory, entries are divided into two sections (multipurpose foundations and educational scholarships/loans) and indexed by foundation name. For more information about the publication, see entry 454 in the "Grants for Organizations—General—Wyoming" section of this bibliography.

Available from: Laramie County Community College, Instructional Resources Center, 1400 East College Drive, Cheyenne, WY 82007-3299. *Telephone:* (307) 778-1206; *Fax:* (307) 778-1309; *E-mail:* ktaylor@lccc.cc.wy.us
Web site: www.lccc.cc.wy.us/library/foundation/foundation.asp

Scholarships, Etc.–General–International

International

104

Annual Register of Grant Support: A Directory of Funding Sources

Medford, NJ: Information Today, 1969- . Annual. ISSN 0066-4049. ISBN 1-57387-145-1. $229 (2003 ed.). Hardcover.

Description: Although it focuses on North American programs, the *Annual Register* also describes a number of scholarships, fellowships, and loans available abroad. For more information about the publication, see entry 235 in the "Grants for Individuals—General—United States" section of this bibliography.

Available from: Information Today, Inc., 143 Old Marlton Pike, Medford, NJ 08055-8750. *Telephone:* (609) 654-6266; *Fax:* (609) 654-4309; *E-mail:* custserv@infotoday.com

Web site: www.infotoday.com

105

The College Blue Book

New York: Macmillan, 1923- . Annual. 6v. ISSN 0069-5572. ISBN 0-02-865761-6. $300 (31st ed.). Hardcover.

Description: A number of the scholarships described in Volume 5 of the *Blue Book* may be used to support study abroad. For more information about the publication, see the entry 9 in the "Scholarships, Fellowships & Loans—General—United States" section of this bibliography.

Available from: Macmillan Reference USA, 300 Park Avenue South, New York, NY 10010. *Toll-free:* (800) 877-4253; *Fax:* (800) 414-5043

Web site: www.galegroup.com/macmillan

106

COS Funding Opportunities

http://www.cos.com

Description: COS Funding Opportunities is a web-based subscription database that is updated daily and contains descriptions of more than 23,000 funding opportunities from around the world that support training, research, collaborative activities, travel, curriculum development, conferences, postdoctoral positions, equipment acquisition, and operating or capital expenses. For more information about the database, see entry 237 in the "Grants for Individuals—General—United States" section of this bibliography.

Available from: Community of Science, Inc., 1629 Thames Street, Suite 200, Baltimore, MD 21231. *Telephone:* (410) 563-2378; *Fax:* (410) 563-5389; *E-mail:* evd@cos.com
Web site: www.cos.com

107

Dan Cassidy's Worldwide College Scholarship Directory

5th ed. By Daniel J. Cassidy. Franklin Lakes, NJ: Career Press, 2000. 608p. ISBN 1-56414-466-6. $23.99. Paper.

Description: Included here are brief descriptions of 1,000 undergraduate scholarships, grants, and awards (most of which can be used only in the United States and Canada), plus 500 more programs from 75 countries around the globe. For more information about the publication, see entry 21 in the "Scholarships, Fellowships & Loans—United States—General" section of this bibliography.

Available from: Career Press, 3 Tice Road, P.O. Box 687, Franklin Lakes, NJ 07417. *Telephone:* (201) 848-0310; *Toll-free:* (800) CAREER-1; *Fax:* (201) 848-1727; *E-mail:* careerprs@aol.com
Web site: www.careerpress.com

108

Dan Cassidy's Worldwide Graduate Scholarship Directory

5th ed. By Daniel J. Cassidy. Franklin Lakes, NJ: Career Press, 2000. 600p. ISBN 1-56414-467-4. $26.99. Paper.

Description: While most of the entries in this directory are aimed at American students (primarily for study in the United States), some are for study abroad or for foreigners to study in the United States. For more information about the publication, see entry 22 in the "Scholarships, Fellowships & Loans—General—United States" section of this bibliography.

Available from: Career Press, 3 Tice Road, P.O. Box 687, Franklin Lakes, NJ 07417. *Telephone:* (201) 848-0310; *Toll-free:* (800) CAREER-1; *Fax:* (201) 848-1727; *E-mail:* careerprs@aol.com
Web site: www.careerpress.com

109

Directory of Research Grants

Westport, CT: Oryx, 1975- . Annual. ISSN 0146-7336. ISBN 1-57356-570-9. $134.95 (2003 ed.). Paper.

Scholarships, Etc.–General–International

Description: While the emphasis is on U.S. and Canadian programs, some scholarships, fellowships, loans, and research grants sponsored by other countries are also included in this directory. For more information about the publication, see entry 238 in the "Grants for Individuals—General—United States" section of this bibliography.

Available from: Oryx Press, 88 Post Road West, Westport, CT 06881. *Telephone:* (602) 265-2651; *Toll-free:* (800) 279-6799; *Fax:* (800) 279-4663; *E-mail:* info@oryxpress.com

Web site: www.oryxpress.com

110

FASTaid

http://www.fastaid.com

Description: Thousands of financial aid opportunities in the United States and abroad that are open to students from high school through postdoctorate are briefly described here. For more information about the service, see entry 27 in the "Scholarships, Fellowships & Loans—General—United States" section of this bibliography.

Available from: National Scholarship Research Service, 5577 Skyland Boulevard, Suite 6A, Santa Rosa, CA 95403. *Toll-free:* (800) 432-3782; *E-mail:* editor@www.fastaid.com

Web site: www.fastaid.com

111

Financial Aid for Research and Creative Activities Abroad

By Gail Ann Schlachter and R. David Weber. El Dorado Hills, CA: Reference Service Press, 1992- . Biennial. ISBN 1-58841-062-5. $45 (2002-2004 ed.). Paper.

Description: This directory will help Americans at any level (from high school students through professionals and postdoctorates) tap into the billions of dollars available to support research or creative activities abroad. For more information about the publication, see entry 262 in the "Grants for Individuals—General—International" section of this bibliography.

Available from: Reference Service Press, 5000 Windplay Drive, Suite 4, El Dorado Hills, CA 95762. *Telephone:* (916) 939-9620; *Fax:* (916) 939-9626; *E-mail:* findaid@aol.com

Web site: www.rspfunding.com

112

Financial Aid for Study and Training Abroad

By Gail Ann Schlachter and R. David Weber. El Dorado Hills, CA: Reference Service Press, 1992- . Biennial. ISBN 1-58841-031-5. $39.50. (2001-2003 ed.). Hardcover.

Description: If you want to go abroad to study and you need money to do so, check here. Described in the latest edition (2001-2003) of this biennially-issued directory are more than 1,000 scholarships, fellowships, and loans that Americans can use to support structured or unstructured study abroad, including money for formal academic classes, individual courses, degree-granting programs, independent study, seminars, workshops, and student internships. The entries are organized by recipient group (undergraduate students, graduate students, postdoctorates, and professionals or others) and indexed by program title, sponsoring organization, geographic coverage, subject coverage, and deadline date. Detailed information is provided for each program: address, telephone number (including fax and toll-free), e-mail, web site, purpose, eligibility, amount awarded, number awarded, duration, special features, limitations, and deadline date. A currency table and an annotated bibliography of other useful financial aid directories complete the volume. First issued in 1990 as part of *Financial Aid for Research, Study, Travel, and Other Activities Abroad,* the directory assumed its current title and focus in 1992.

Available from: Reference Service Press, 5000 Windplay Drive, Suite 4, El Dorado Hills, CA 95762. *Telephone:* (916) 939-9620; *Fax:* (916) 939-9626; *E-mail:* findaid@aol.com

Web site: www.rspfunding.com

113

Fulbright and Related Grants for Graduate Study and Research Abroad

New York: Institute of International Education. Annual. Free (2003-2004 ed.). Paper or online.

Description: This annual pamphlet, available without charge from the Institute of International Education, lists Institute-administered fellowships and grants available to U.S. graduate students for study and research abroad. For more information about the publication, see entry 263 in the "Grants for Individuals—General—International" section of this bibliography.

Available from: Institute of International Education, 809 United Nations Plaza, New York, NY 10017-3580. *Telephone:* (212) 883-8200; *Toll free:* (800) 445-0443; *Fax:* (212) 984-5452; *E-mail:* iiebooks@iie.org

Web site: www.iie.org/fulbright

Scholarships, Etc.–General–International

114

Fulbright Scholar Program: Grants for Faculty and Professionals

Washington, DC: Council for International Exchange of Scholars, 1994- . Annual. Free (2003-2004 ed.). Paper or online.

Description: This free pamphlet from the Council for International Exchange of Scholars identifies Fulbright fellowships and grants for university lecturing and research abroad (including research funding for advanced doctoral students). For more information about the publication, see entry 264 in the "Grants for Individuals—General—International" section of this bibliography.

Available from: Council for International Exchange of Scholars, 3007 Tilden Street, N.W., Suite 5L, Washington, DC 20008-3009. *Telephone:* (202) 686-4000; *Fax:* (202) 362-3442; *E-mail:* scholars@cies.iie.org

Web site: www.iie.org/cies

115

The Graduate School Funding Handbook

By April Vahle Hamel, with Mary Morris Heiberger and Julia Miller Vick. Philadelphia: University of Pennsylvania Press, 2002. 168p. ISBN 0-8122-1810-8. $17.95. Hardcover.

Description: Part handbook and part financial aid listing, this publication was "designed to guide students through the intricate process of applying for graduate school funding both in the United States and abroad." For more information about the publication, see entry 41 in the "Scholarships, Fellowships & Loans—General—United States" section of this bibliography.

Available from: University of Pennsylvania Press, 4200 Pine Street, Philadelphia, PA 19104-4011. *Telephone:* (215) 898-6261; *Toll-free:* (800) 445-9880; *Fax:* (215) 898-0404; *E-mail:* custserv@pobox.upenn.edu

Web site: www.upenn.edu/pennpress

116

The Grants Register: The Complete Guide to Postgraduate Funding Worldwide

Ed. by Sara Hackwood. New York: Palgrave, 1969- . Annual. ISSN 0072-5471. ISBN 0-333-96474-8. $185 (2003 ed.). Hardcover.

Description: This annual directory describes fellowships, grants, and prizes open to nationals of the United States, Canada, the United Kingdom, Ireland, Australia, New Zealand, South Africa, and the developing countries. For more information about the publication, see entry 265 in the "Grants for Individuals—General—International" section of this bibliography.

How to Find Out About Financial Aid and Funding

Available from: Palgrave, 175 Fifth Avenue, New York, NY 10010. *Telephone:* (212) 982-3900; *Toll-free:* (800) 221-7945; *Fax:* (212) 777-6359
Web site: www.palgrave-usa.com

117

GrantSelect

http://www.grantselect.com
Description: Updated annually and used to generate Oryx Press's print funding directories, GrantSelect identifies more than 10,000 scholarships, fellowships, loans, and other funding opportunities sponsored by organizations and agencies in the United States and Canada (some of which can be used abroad). For more information about the database, see entry 247 in the "Grants for Individuals—General—United States" section of this bibliography.
Available from: Oryx Press, 88 Post Road West, Westport, CT 06881. *Telephone:* (602) 265-2651; *Toll-free:* (800) 279-6799; *Fax:* (800) 279-4663; *E-mail:* info@oryxpress.com
Web site: www.oryxpress.com

118 ¢

IEFA's Scholarship Database

http://www.iefa.org/public/search.html
Description: This database is sponsored by the International Education Finance Corporation, a company that makes loans to students who wish to study in foreign countries. The database offered on this site is the same one you'll find at International Scholarships Online (www.internationalscholarships.com) and on Studyabroad.com's internship section (intern.studyabroad.com). It can be searched by host institution, field of study, and/or location of study. To browse through all awards, just leave the fields blank and hit the search button. Although the web site calls itself "the premier Internet resource listing financial aid information for students wishing to study in a foreign country," the database leaves much to be desired. There are numerous typos (see, for example, "J. Paul Ghetty, Ghetty Grant Program") and many of the 800 programs listed cannot be used to study abroad at all (for example, the Alvan T. and Viola D. Fuller Research Fellowships are sponsored by the American Cancer Society's Massachusetts Division for "Massachusetts (sic) residents pursuing studies in medical and veterinary sciences at a Massachusetts institution"). Plus, most programs are restricted to use at specific universities. A better Internet resource for students looking for money to go abroad is Online Study Abroad Directory (see entry 119).
Available from: International Education Finance Corporation, 222 Forbes Road, Suite 406, Braintree, MA 02184. *Telephone:* (781) 843-5334; *Toll-free:* (888) 296-IEFC; *Fax:* (781) 843-9034; *E-mail:* Inquiries@iefc.com

Web site: www.iefc.com

119

Online Study Abroad Directory

http://www.istc.umn.edu
Description: This site, maintained by the International Study and Travel Center at the University of Minnesota, contains three searchable databases that will be of interest to students looking for money to support activities abroad: the Work & Intern Database; the Volunteer Database, which identifies approximately 150 volunteer opportunities in developing countries and eastern Europe (some of which pay travel and/or per diem); and the Scholarships Database, which identifies 200 scholarships intended for American undergraduate students looking to study or conduct research abroad. Most of the programs included in the Scholarships Database are school bound (recipients must either register in a particular study abroad program or attend a specific school abroad); few are portable. The descriptions are detailed and the site is easy to use. Since the database is relatively small, you can browse through the entire listing. But, if you do conduct a search, it is best to limit the number of choices you enter (for region, program format, general subject, and/or eligibility categories), or you will not end up with any matches. In fact, if you select one of the eligibility categories (e.g., students of color, women students), it is generally best not to select any other option.
Available from: University of Minnesota, Attn: International Study and Travel Center, 94 Blegen Hall, 269 19th Avenue South, Minneapolis, MN 55455. *Telephone:* (612) 626-ISTC; *Toll-free:* (800) 770-ISTC; *Fax:* (612) 626-0979; *E-mail:* istc@umn.edu
Web site: www.istc.umn.edu

120

Scholarships for Foreign Students in Japan (Japanese & English)

Prep. by the Asian Students' Cultural Association. Tokyo: Asian Students' Cultural Association. Annual. Free. Paper.
Description: When the first edition of this directory was released in the 1980s (under the title *Gekkan Asia no Tomo*), there were fewer than 6,000 foreign students in all of Japan. Since then, the number of foreign students in Japan has grown, steadily approaching Japan's goal of 100,000 foreign students per year. Partly responsible for this increase is the funding offered by the Japanese Ministry of Education, Science, and Culture (since 1987), local governments, and private foundations. The most comprehensive and detailed listing of this funding can be found in *Scholarships for Foreign Students in Japan,* an annual paperback issued in both Japanese and English by the Asian Students' Cultural Association. The latest edition has more than 230 pages and describes nearly

500 funding opportunities available to undergraduate and graduate students from other countries who are currently enrolled in Japanese institutions (the majority of the programs) or who wish to study in Japan. The entries are grouped into four sections: Japanese government scholarships, tuition fee reduction and school-sponsored scholarships, local government scholarships, and scholarships from private organizations. For each entry, the following information is provided (in addition to contact information): residency requirements, application procedure, eligibility requirements, stipend awarded, duration, number of grantees (including a ratio of grantees to applicants), and deadline. Although there is no index, the "Scholarships at a Glance" section in the front of the book provides summary information (chart form) for each of the four sections; the entries here are arranged alphabetically by program title, but no page reference to the fuller descriptions is provided.

Available from: Asian Students' Cultural Association, 12-13 Honkomagome, 2-Chome Bunkyou-ku, Tokyo 113-8642, Japan. *Telephone:* 03-3946-4121; *Fax:* 03-3946-7599; *E-mail:* info@abk.or.jp

Web site: www.abk.or.jp

121

Scholarships for International Students in Japan

Prep. by the Information Center of the Association of International Education, Japan. Tokyo: Association of International Education, Japan. Annual. Free. Paper or online.

Description: This 50+ page free pamphlet is prepared by the Association of International Education's Information Center to make information available on funding for students from other countries who wish to study on the undergraduate or graduate school level in Japan. It is also available in a series of .pdf files on the association's web site. For some of the programs covered here, students must already be attending school in Japan; for others, students may apply from their own country. The listing is divided into three sections: funding provided from the Japanese government, funding from local governments, and funding from private foundations that responded to the association's request for information. Brief information on more than 200 funding opportunities is provided in chart form; sometimes, however, the presentation is so cryptic that it is hard to understand the exact scope or focus of a program. Furthermore, the lack of an index means that it is hard do anything but browse the listings. Nevertheless, this free pamphlet provides an helpful, quick overview of funding available to foreigners interested in studying in Japan. If more complete information is needed, see *Scholarships for Foreign Students in Japan* (described in entry 665).

Available from: Association of International Education, Japan, Attn: Information Center, 4-5-29 Komaba, Meguro-ku, Tokyo 153-8503, Japan. *Telephone:* 03-5454-5216; *Fax:* 03-5454-5236

Web site: www.aiej.or.jp

Scholarships, Etc.–General–International

122

SPIN (Sponsored Programs Information Network)

Guilderland, NY: InfoEd. Updated daily. Annual Internet subscription fees vary.

Description: SPIN (Sponsored Programs Information Network) is a subscription database that consists of information from 1,200 different sponsoring agencies around the world; together, these agencies offer more than 10,000 separate funding opportunities, including fellowships, travel grants, research grants, curriculum development grants, sabbatical support, publication support, international projects, collaborative programs, and academic exchange programs. For more information about the service, see entry 252 in the "Grants for Individuals—General—United States" section of this bibliography.

Available from: InfoEd International, Inc., 1873 Western Avenue, Suite 201, Albany, NY 12203. *Telephone:* (518) 464-0691; *Toll-free:* (800) 727-6427; *Fax:* (518) 464-0695; *E-mail:* office@infoed.org

Web site: www.infoed.org

123

Study Abroad: International Scholarships, International Courses

Paris: United Nations Educational, Scientific, and Cultural Organization (dist. by Bernan/UNIPUB), 1948- . Biennial. ISSN 0081-895X. ISBN 92-3-003606-4. $34.95 (2000-2001 ed.). Paper or CD-ROM.

Description: This directory of worldwide study opportunities at the university level has been issued since 1948. Over 2,900 opportunities to study in more than 129 countries and territories under the auspices of 1,000 national and 100 international organizations are described in two sections. The first section focuses on scholarships offered by international organizations and by national institutions. The entries are arranged by country and by discipline/profession. Each entry provides information on sponsoring agency, address, number of scholarships and type, subject's eligibility, amount, closing date, and address for application. The second section is arranged by country and lists areas of study by broad disciplinary headings. The following information is provided: sponsoring agency, address, type of course, eligibility, where held, duration, fees, scholarships offered, and application deadline and address. Detailed subject access is provided, as well as indexes by international organizations, national institutions, and countries. The text is in French, Spanish, and English. The work is complicated to use, but the value of the information makes the effort worthwhile. Note: Not all funding or educational opportunities listed here are available to Americans and many of the scholarships listed are single-school specific. Beginning with the 1998-1999 edition, the guide has also available on CD-ROM. The current edition (31st edition, 2000-2001) will be updated in mid-2003.

Available from: Bernan Associates/UNIPUB, 4611-F Assembly Drive, Lanham, MD 20706-4391. *Telephone:* (301) 459-2255; *Toll-free:* (800) 865-3457; *Fax:* (800) 865-3450; *E-mail:* info@bernan.com
Web site: www.bernan.com

SOCIAL SCIENCES
General

124

GrantFinder: The Complete Guide to Postgraduate Funding Worldwide: Social Sciences

New York: Palgrave, 2000. 516p. ISBN 0-312-22894-5. $50. Hardcover.

Description: This guide describes fellowships, prizes, and grants in the social sciences that are open to nationals of the United States, Canada, the United Kingdom, Ireland, Australia, New Zealand, South Africa, and the developing countries. For more information about the publication, see entry 269 in the "Grants for Individuals—Social Sciences—General" section of this bibliography.

Available from: Palgrave, 175 Fifth Avenue, New York, NY 10010. *Telephone:* (212) 982-3900; *Toll-free:* (800) 221-7945; *Fax:* (212) 777-6359
Web site: www.palgrave-usa.com

125

GrantsInfo.com: Social and Natural Sciences

http://www.arisnet.com/socnatu.html

Description: This inexpensive online searchable database provides information on hundreds of fellowship and grant opportunities in the social and natural sciences. For more information about the site, see entry 271 in the "Grants for Individuals—Social Sciences—General" section of this bibliography.

Available from: Academic Research Information System, Inc., 2940 16th Street, Suite 314, San Francisco, CA 94103. *Telephone:* (415) 558-8133; *Fax:* (415) 558-8135; *E-mail:* arisnet@dnai.com
Web site: www.arisnet.com

Scholarships, Etc.–Social Sciences–General

126

Making a Difference: Scholarships for a Better World

3rd ed. Ed. by Miriam Weinstein. Fairfax, CA: SageWorks, 2003. 240p. ISBN 0-9634618-7-7. $14.99. Paper.

Description: Here's an interesting twist: scholarships and fellowships for students who have made a difference. The financial aid listed here is awarded to undergraduate and graduate students. volunteers, activists, community organizers, and environmentalists who have an outstanding record of community service, are "social entrepreneurs" (run their own nonprofits), or are interested in working on a degree in such community-enhancing areas as labor, peace, and the environment. Many of these funding opportunities are sizeable—in the $5,000 to $10,000 range. And, if you're also interested in attending a college that can help you make a better world, be sure to check out Weinstein's companion title, *Making a Difference: College & Graduate Guide* (2002. 408p. ISBN 0-9634618-6-9. $18.50, paperback).

Available from: SageWorks Press, P.O. Box 441, Fairfax, CA 94978. *Toll-free:* (800) 218-4242; *E-mail:* info@sageworks.net

Web site: www.sageworks.net

127

Money for Graduate Students in the Social & Behavioral Sciences

By Gail Ann Schlachter and R. David Weber. El Dorado Hills, CA: Reference Service Press, 1996- . Biennial. (RSP Graduate Funding Set). ISBN 1-58841-078-1. $42.50 (2003-2005 ed.). Comb binding.

Description: Getting a graduate degree is definitely a smart move. According to the U.S. Census Bureau, the average salary for a college graduate is around $40,000. But, this figure rises to more than $65,000 for master's degree recipients and to nearly $90,000 for those with doctoral or professional degrees. However, graduate school is expensive. It can cost $20,000 or more to complete a master's degree and up to $100,000 to finish some doctoral or professional degrees. That's more than most students can afford to pay on their own. Fortunately, money is available. *Money for Graduate Students in the Social & Behavioral Sciences* identifies nearly 1,100 fellowships, grants, and awards, representing millions of dollars, which are available to support study or research (on the master's or doctoral level) in accounting, advertising, anthropology, business administration, economics, education, geography, international relations, law, library or information science, marketing, political science, psychology, sociology, or any other social or behavioral science. Each program is fully described: purpose, eligibility, financial data, duration, special features, limitations, number awarded, and deadline date. Entries are grouped by purpose (study or research) and indexed by program title, sponsoring organization, residency, tenability, subject, and deadline date. This title is part of the four-volume *RSP Graduate*

Funding Set; the other volumes cover graduate funding in the arts and humanities (see entry 143), in the biological and health sciences (see entry 174), and in the physical and earth sciences (see entry 190). Previously, this book was issued under a slightly different title: *Money for Graduate Students in the Social Sciences.*

Available from: Reference Service Press, 5000 Windplay Drive, Suite 4, El Dorado Hills, CA 95762. *Telephone:* (916) 939-9620; *Fax:* (916) 939-9626; *E-mail:* findaid@aol.com

Web site: www.rspfunding.com

128

Research and Funding: A German-American Guide for Historians and Social Scientists.

Ed. by Christof Mauch and Birgit Zischke. Washington, DC: German Historical Institute, 1999. Free. Paper or online.

Description: This directory focuses on exchanges between the United States and Germany and provides detailed information about institutions that offer financial support (fellowships and grants in history and the social sciences) and/or affiliations to non-native researchers. For more information about the paper and online versions of the publication, see entry 288 in the "Grants for Individuals—Humanities—History" section of this bibliography.

Available from: German Historical Institute, 1607 New Hampshire Avenue, N.W., Washington, DC 20009. *Telephone:* (202) 387-3355; *Fax:* (202) 483-3430; *E-mail:* ghiusa@ghi-dc.org

Web site: www.ghi-dc.org

129

Social Science Research Council Fellowships and Grants for Training and Research

New York: Social Science Research Council. Annual. Unpaged. Free (2002-2003 ed.). Paper.

Description: The Social Science Research Council is an autonomous, non-governmental, not-for-profit international association devoted to "the advancement of interdisciplinary research in the social sciences." This annual pamphlet, distributed without charge by the Social Science Research Council, provides a descriptive list of grants that the council sponsors either independently or with the American Council of Learned Societies. These programs (pre-dissertation and dissertation fellowships, postdoctoral fellowships, and research grants) focus on the social sciences and humanities in both the United States and, selectively, abroad. They are open to American and foreign citizens on the advanced graduate or postgraduate levels; applications are particularly invited from women and members of minority groups. The programs are listed alphabetically and the following information is provided for each: background, eligibility, duration, requirements, application deadline, financial data, and e-mail address. There are indexes by deadline and by tenability. Some of the information included here is also presented on the council's web site.

Available from: Social Science Research Council, 810 Seventh Avenue, New York, NY 10019. *Telephone:* (212) 377-2700; *Fax:* (212) 377-2727

Web site: www.ssrc.org

Business and Economics

130

How to Pay for Your Degree in Business & Related Fields

By Gail Ann Schlachter and R. David Weber. El Dorado Hills, CA: Reference Service Press, 2002- . Biennial. ISBN 1-58841-049-8, comb binding; 1-58841-090-0, eBook. $30 (2002-2004 ed.), comb binding or eBook.

Description: Billions of dollars are available to support students who are interested in working on a degree in finance, banking, accounting, industrial relations, sales, economics, marketing, personnel administration, management and other business-related fields. These financial aid programs are identified and described in detail in a new biennial directory from Reference Service Press: *How to Pay for Your Degree in Business & Related Fields.* Here, in one place, you'll find the following information for more than 600 scholarships, fellowships, grants, and other funding opportunities for undergraduate and graduate students in business-related fields: purpose, eligibility, monetary award, duration, special features, limitations, number awarded, and deadline date. Plus, the book is organized so you can search for aid by type of funding, program title, sponsoring organization, residency, tenability, business specialty, and date the applications are due. This directory is also available as an eBook on the netLibrary web site: www.netlibrary.com.

Available from: Reference Service Press, 5000 Windplay Drive, Suite 4, El Dorado Hills, CA 95762. *Telephone:* (916) 939-9620; *Fax:* (916) 939-9626; *E-mail:* findaid@aol.com

Web site: www.rspfunding.com

How to Find Out About Financial Aid and Funding

Education

131

Chronicle of Higher Education

Washington, DC: Chronicle of Higher Education, 1966- . Weekly. ISSN 0009-5982. $82.50. Paper.

Description: Included in each weekly print issue (and on the web site) are announcements of fellowships and grants of interest to academic faculty, researchers, graduate students, staff, and administrators. For more information about the *Chronicle,* see entry 277 in the "Grants for Individuals—Social Sciences—Education" section of this bibliography.

Available from: Chronicle of Higher Education, Attn: Circulation Department, 1255 23rd Street, N.W., Suite 700, Washington, DC 20037. *Telephone:* (202) 466-1000; *Toll-free:* (800) 728-2803; *E-mail:* circulation@chronicle.com
Web site: chronicle.com

132

Funding Sources for K-12 Education

Westport, CT: Oryx, 2002. 976p. ISBN 1-57356-566-0. $49.95. Paper.

Description: In addition to information about funding for K-12 schools, there is also some coverage of funding programs open to students interested in working on an education-related degree. For more information about the listing, see entry 473 in the "Scholarships, Fellowships & Loans" section of this bibliography.

Available from: Oryx Press, 88 Post Road West, Westport, CT 06881. *Telephone:* (602) 265-2651; *Toll-free:* (800) 279-6799; *Fax:* (800) 279-4663; *E-mail:* info@oryxpress.com
Web site: www.oryxpress.com

133

The Grant Advisor

Charlottesville, VA: The Grant Advisor, 1983- . Monthly, except July. ISSN 0740-5383. $198/yr., print; $398, online.

Description: *The Grant Advisor* newsletter provides information on fellowship and grant opportunities for U.S. institutions of higher education and their faculty. For more information about the publication and its online version, see entry 474 in the "Grants for Organizations—Social Sciences—Education" section of this bibliography.

Scholarships, Etc.–Social Sciences–Librarianship

Available from: The Grant Advisor, 1946 Lonicera Way, Charlottesville, VA 22911. *Telephone:* (434) 975-9098; *Fax:* (815) 361-2971; *E-mail:* info@grantadvisor.com
Web site: www.grantadvisor.com

134

How to Pay for Your Degree in Education & Related Fields

By Gail Ann Schlachter and R. David Weber. El Dorado Hills, CA: Reference Service Press, 2002- . Biennial. ISBN 1-58841-063-3, comb binding; 1-58841-91-9, eBook. $30 (2002-2004 ed.), comb binding or eBook.

Description: With the looming shortage of teachers, there has never been a better time to get a degree in education. An even bigger plus: there has never been as much financial aid available as there is today. Billions of dollars have been set aside just to support undergraduate and graduate students who want to prepare for a career in preschool education, K-12 education, adult education, special education educational administration, and the specialty fields of art education, music education, physical education, etc. These funding opportunities are described in detail in a new biennial publication, *How to Pay for Your Degree in Education & Related Fields*. The following information is provided for each: purpose, eligibility, monetary award, duration, special features, limitations, number awarded, and deadline date. Entries are indexed by sponsor, residency, tenability, educational specialty, and even deadline date. This directory is also available as an eBook on the netLibrary web site: www.netlibrary.com.

Available from: Reference Service Press, 5000 Windplay Drive, Suite 4, El Dorado Hills, CA 95762. *Telephone:* (916) 939-9620; *Fax:* (916) 939-9626; *E-mail:* findaid@aol.com
Web site: www.rspfunding.com

Librarianship

135

The Bowker Annual Library and Book Trade Almanac

Medford, NJ: Information Today, 1955- . Annual. ISSN 0068-0540. ISBN 1-57387-165-6. $199 (2003 ed.). Hardcover.

Description: Generally, each edition contains a list of library fellowships and up-to-date information on library legislation, funding, and grantmaking agencies. For more information about the publication, see entry 559 in the "Awards and Prizes—Social Sciences—Librarianship" section of this bibliography.

Available from: Information Today, Inc., 143 Old Marlton Pike, Medford, NJ 08055-8750. *Telephone:* (609) 654-6266; *Fax:* (609) 654-4309; *E-mail:* custserv@infotoday.com
Web site: www.infotoday.com

136

Financial Assistance for Library and Information Studies

Ed. by Maxine Moore. Chicago: American Library Association's Committee on Education, 1970- . Annual. ISSN 0569-6275. ISBN 0-8389-8220-4. $4 (2003-2004 ed.), paper; free, online.

Description: This summary of fellowships, scholarships, grants-in-aid, loans, and other financial aid programs for library education is available from the Office for Human Resource Development and Recruitment at the American Library Association (ALA) for $4 to cover postage. Even better, a .pdf file of the latest edition can be downloaded, at no charge, from ALA's web site. The 60-page booklet is revised annually and provides a list of awards from state library agencies, national and state library associations, local libraries, and academic institutions offering undergraduate or graduate programs in library education in the United States and Canada. Scholarships less than $200 are not listed. For each entry, the following information is given: granting body, level of program, type of assistance, number available, academic or other requirements, application deadline, and application address. The information is presented in table format and often is too brief or too generic to be helpful. The only other access provided is an index to sources of support for nonmaster's degree programs and for special groups of students (e.g., minority group applicants); master's degree awards (which make up the bulk of the listings in the booklet) are not indexed. In the past, this publication was issued under the title *Financial Assistance for Library Education*.

Available from: American Library Association, Attn: Office for Human Resource Development and Recruitment, 50 East Huron Street, Chicago, IL 60611. *Telephone:* (312) 836-9958; *Toll-free:* (800) 545-2433, ext. 4277; *Fax:* (312) 280-3256
Web site: www.ala.org/hrdr

Political Science and International Affairs

137

After Latin American Studies: A Guide to Graduate Study and Employment for Latin Americanists

By Shirley A. Kregar and Jorge Nallim. Pittsburgh: Center for Latin American Studies, University of Pittsburgh, 2000. 158p. $15. Spiral bound or online.

Description: This guide is aimed at students and recent graduates "interested in applying their Latin American background to employment or fellowship opportunities." It is organized into six sections: graduate study, embassies and chambers of commerce, opportunities in the private sector, opportunities in the U.S. government, opportunities in planning and research organizations, and opportunities with international organizations. In the previous (1995) edition, there was a separate section listing scholarships and fellowships, along with research grants and internships for students working on a degree in Latin American studies. That section has been eliminated in the 2000 edition and the information is now available in a 30-page pamphlet, *A Guide to Financial Assistance for Latin American Studies,* which is available without charge in print from the center or in downloadable form on the center's web site. A previous version of the pamphlet was published under the title *A Guide to Financial Assistance for Graduate Study, Dissertation Research and Internships for Students in Latin American Studies.*

Available from: University of Pittsburgh, Attn: Center for Latin American Studies, 4E04 Wesley W. Posvar Hall, Pittsburgh, PA 15260. *Telephone:* (412) 648-7392; *Fax:* (412) 648-2199; *E-mail:* clas+@pitt.edu
Web site: www.ucis.pitt.edu/clas

Psychology

138

Directory of Internships and Post-Doctoral Fellowships in Clinical Child/Pediatric Psychology

3rd ed. By Susan J. Simonian and Kenneth J. Tarnowski. Mahwah, NJ: Lawrence Erlbaum Associates, 1999. 129p. ISBN 0-8058-3595-4. $39.95. Paper.

Description: This directory identifies predoctoral internships and postdoctoral fellowships that offer training in clinical child psychology and pediatric psychology. For more information about the publication, see entry 645 in the "Internships—Social Sciences—Psychology" section of this bibliography.

How to Find Out About Financial Aid and Funding

Available from: Lawrence Erlbaum Associates, Inc., 10 Industrial Avenue, Mahwah, NJ 07430-2262. *Telephone:* (201) 236-9500; *Toll-free:* (800) 9-BOOKS-9; *Fax:* (201) 236-0072; *E-mail:* orders@erlbaum.com
Web site: www.erlbaum.com

HUMANITIES
General

139

Art Deadlines List

Ed. by Richard Gardner. Cambridge, MA: Art Deadlines List. Monthly. $36, paper; $18, e-mailed.
Description: Every month subscribers are mailed an international list of scholarships, competitions, contests (primarily), call for entries/papers, grants, fellowships, residencies, internships, and other opportunities for individuals involved in art or other creative activities (e.g., writing, photography, music). For more information about the service, see entry 560 in the "Awards and Prizes—Humanities—General" section of this bibliography.
Available from: Art Deadlines List, Box 381067, Harvard Square Station, Cambridge, MA 02238-1067. *E-mail:* contact@artdeadlineslist.com
Web site: www.artdeadlineslist.com

140

Directory of Grants in the Humanities

Westport, CT: Oryx, 1986- . Annual. ISSN 0877-0551. ISBN 1-57356-567-9. $84.95 (2002-2003 ed.). Paper.
Description: This annual directory identifies fellowships, awards, and grants in literature, languages, history, anthropology, philosophy, ethics, religion, the fine arts, and performing arts (including painting, dance, photography, sculpture, music, drama, crafts, folklore, and mime). For more information about the publication, see entry 280 in the "Grants for Individuals—Humanities—General" section of this bibliography.
Available from: Oryx Press, 88 Post Road West, Westport, CT 06881. *Telephone:* (602) 265-2651; *Toll-free:* (800) 279-6799; *Fax:* (800) 279-4663; *E-mail:* info@oryxpress.com
Web site: www.oryxpress.com

141

GrantFinder: The Complete Guide to Postgraduate Funding Worldwide: Arts and Humanities

New York: Palgrave, 2000. 476p. ISBN 0-312-22893-7. $50. Hardcover.

Description: This guide describes fellowships, prizes, and grants in the arts and humanities that are open to nationals of the United States, Canada, the United Kingdom, Ireland, Australia, New Zealand, South Africa, and the developing countries. For more information about the publication, see entry 281 in the "Grants for Individuals—Humanities—General" section of this bibliography.

Available from: Palgrave, 175 Fifth Avenue, New York, NY 10010. *Telephone:* (212) 982-3900; *Toll-free:* (800) 221-7945; *Fax:* (212) 777-6359

Web site: www.palgrave-usa.com

142

GrantsInfo.com: Creative Arts and Humanities

http://www.arisnet.com/arts.html

Description: This inexpensive online searchable database provides information on regional, national, and international fellowships, grants, and awards in the humanities, performing arts, and visual arts. For more information about the site, see entry 282 in the "Grants for Individuals—Humanities—General" section of this bibliography.

Available from: Academic Research Information System, Inc., 2940 16th Street, Suite 314, San Francisco, CA 94103. *Telephone:* (415) 558-8133; *Fax:* (415) 558-8135; *E-mail:* arisnet@dnai.com

Web site: www.arisnet.com

143

Money for Graduate Students in the Arts & Humanities

By Gail Ann Schlachter and R. David Weber. El Dorado Hills, CA: Reference Service Press, 1996- . Biennial. (RSP Graduate Funding Set). ISBN 1-58841-076-5. $40 (2003-2005 ed.). Comb binding.

Description: Millions of dollars are available to support graduate study and research in architecture, art, dance, design, filmmaking, history, languages, literature, music, performing arts, philosophy, religion, sculpture, and the rest of the humanities. *Money for Graduate Students in the Arts & Humanities* identifies nearly 1,000 fellowships, grants, and awards available to support graduate work in these fields. Full details are given for each program: contact, purpose, eligibility, money awarded, duration, special features, limitations, number offered, and deadline date. The entries are grouped by purpose (research or study) and indexed by subject, residency, tenability, sponsor, title, and deadline. This title is part of the four-volume *RSP Graduate Funding Set;* the other volumes cover graduate funding in the social and behavioral sciences (see entry 127), the biological and health sciences (entry 174), and the physical and earth sciences (entry 190). In the past, the directory was issued under a slightly different title: *Money for Graduate Students in the Humanities.*

Available from: Reference Service Press, 5000 Windplay Drive, Suite 4, El Dorado Hills, CA 95762. *Telephone:* (916) 939-9620; *Fax:* (916) 939-9626; *E-mail:* findaid@aol.com

Web site: www.rspfunding.com

144

Social Science Research Council Fellowships and Grants for Training and Research

New York: Social Science Research Council, 2002-2003. Unpaged. Free. Paper.

Description: This annual pamphlet describes national and international dissertation fellowships and research grants in both the humanities and social sciences that are open to American and foreign citizens on the advanced graduate or postgraduate levels. For more information about the publication, see entry 129 in the "Scholarships, Fellowships & Loans—Social Sciences—General" section of this bibliography.

Available from: Social Science Research Council, 810 Seventh Avenue, New York, NY 10019. *Telephone:* (212) 377-2700; *Fax:* (212) 377-2727

Web site: www.ssrc.org

Communications and Mass Media

145

Editor & Publisher Journalism Awards and Fellowships Directory

New York: Editor & Publisher Company. Annual. ISSN 0013-094X. $15 (2002 ed.). Paper.

Description: Published each year as a special pull-out section in the last issue of *Editor & Publisher* (the "only independent weekly journal of newspapering"), this directory describes over 500 scholarships, awards, and fellowships available in the field of journalism. For more information about the publication, see entry 568 in the "Awards and Prizes—Humanities—Communications and Mass Media" section of this bibliography.

Scholarships, Etc.–Humanities–Communications & Mass Media

Available from: Editor & Publisher, 770 Broadway, New York, NY 10003-9595. *Telephone:* (646) 654-5270; *Toll-free:* (800) 722-6658; *Fax:* (646) 654-5370; *E-mail:* edpub@mediainfo.com
Web site: www.mediainfo.com

146

How to Pay for Your Degree in Journalism & Related Fields

By Gail Ann Schlachter and R. David Weber. El Dorado Hills, CA: Reference Service Press, 2002- . Biennial. ISBN 1-58841-064-1, comb binding; 1-58841-092-7, eBook. $30 (2002-2004 ed.), comb binding or eBook.

Description: The latest Annual Survey of Journalism & Mass Communications Graduates reported that salaries paid to graduates of journalism and mass communications programs are at an all-time high. But, getting a journalism-related degree can be expensive. Fortunately, there are hundreds of financial aid programs, representing millions of dollars, currently available to help undergraduate or graduate students interested in preparing for a career in advertising, broadcasting, business reporting, graphic design, online journalism, photojournalism, public relations, science reporting, sports reporting, etc. These funding opportunities (nearly 600) are described in detail in *How to Pay for Your Degree in Journalism & Related Fields,* a new biennial directory from Reference Service Press; this is more than twice the number of opportunities for journalism students found in any other source. The following information is given for each entry: purpose, eligibility, monetary award, duration, special features, limitations, number awarded, and deadline date. Access to these entries is provided by type of funding, program title, sponsoring organization, residency, tenability, specialty, and date the applications are due. *How to Pay for Your Degree in Journalism & Related Fields* is also available as an eBook on the netLibrary web site: www.netlibrary.com.

Available from: Reference Service Press, 5000 Windplay Drive, Suite 4, El Dorado Hills, CA 95762. *Telephone:* (916) 939-9620; *Fax:* (916) 939-9626; *E-mail:* findaid@aol.com
Web site: www.rspfunding.com

147

Journalism Awards and Fellowships

http://ajr.org
Description: Described on the American Journalism Review's web site are nearly 100 scholarships, awards, and fellowships available to students and practicing journalists interested in careers in broadcast, radio, online, and print journalism. For more information about the listing, see entry 569 in the "Awards and Prizes—Humanities—Communications and Mass Media" section of this bibliography.

Available from: American Journalism Review, Attn: Awards Issue, University of Maryland, 1117 Journalism Building, College Park, MD 20742-7111. *Telephone:* (301) 405-8803; *Toll-free:* (800) 827-0771; *Fax:* (301) 405-8323
  Web site: ajr.org

148

The Journalist's Road to Success: A Career and Scholarship Guide

Princeton: Dow Jones Newspaper Fund, 1979-1999. Annual. $3 (1999 ed.). Paper.

Description: Published until 1993 under the title *Journalism Career and Scholarship Guide,* this paperback identifies financial aid for students majoring in journalism or communications offered by news organizations, professional societies, journalism-related groups, colleges, and universities. First, the guide provides valuable information on what to study in college, where to study journalism and mass communications, where the jobs are, and how to find them. Then, over $8 million in financial aid for more than 3,000 journalism students is described. The financial aid listings are arranged into two main sections. Part 1 deals with aid offered through schools and departments of journalism in American and Canadian colleges and universities, as well as by newspapers and professional societies. Part 2 lists miscellaneous sources of scholarships and programs that target minority students. The entries are arranged by state and indexed by sponsor. The last edition of the guide was published in 1999. Beginning in 2002, much of the information that was in the guide, along with the information formerly included in *Newspapers, Diversity and You* (see entry 149) was posted on the Newspaper Fund's web site. To access the information, click on the High School Seniors tab on the site's main screen.

Available from: Dow Jones Newspaper Fund, P.O. Box 300, Princeton, NJ 08543-0300. *Telephone:* (609) 452-2820; *Fax:* (609) 520-5804; *E-mail:* newsfund@wsj.dowjones.com
  Web site: djnewspaperfund.dowjones.com/fund/default.asp

149

Newspapers, Diversity, & You

Princeton, NJ: Dow Jones Newspaper Fund, 1993-1999. Annual. Free (1999 ed.). Paper.

Description: The American Society of Newspaper Editors has adopted a goal of employing minorities in newsrooms at the same level as the nation's minority population. In an attempt to help meet the American Society of Newspaper Editors' goal, the Dow Jones Newspaper Fund began issuing this free 48-page guide in 1993. The last print version was released in 1999. The guide was designed "to guide minority professionals in pursuing careers as newspaper journalists." One section dealt with scholarships, fellowships, internships, and spe-

Scholarships, Etc.–Humanities–History

cial training programs for minorities. Most of that material was taken directly from the *Journalist's Road to Success* (see entry 148). Prior to 1993, this booklet was issued under the title *Journalism Career Guide for Minorities.* Since 2002, the directory, along with the information formerly included in *The Journalist's Road to Success,* has been available only in the High School Seniors section of the Newspaper Fund's web site.

Available from: Dow Jones Newspaper Fund, P.O. Box 300, Princeton, NJ 08543-0300. *Telephone:* (609) 452-2820; *Fax:* (609) 520-5804; *E-mail:* newsfund@wsf.dowjones.com

Web site: djnewspaperfund.dowjones.com/fund/default.asp

History

150

Grants, Fellowships, and Prizes of Interest to Historians

Ed. by Pillarisetti Sudhir, with Kim Foote and Jesse Erdheim. Washington, DC: American Historical Association, 1978-2000. Annual. ISSN 0275-830X. $10, members; $12, nonmembers (2000-2001 ed.). Paper.

Description: Last issued in 2000, this directory identifies and describes more than 450 fellowships, awards, prizes, and travel grants of interest to graduate students, postdoctoral researchers, and scholars in history. For more information about the listing and its online replacement, see entry 287 in the "Grants for Individuals—Humanities—History" section of this bibliography.

Available from: American Historical Association, 400 A Street, S.E., Washington, DC 20003-3889. *Telephone:* (202) 544-2422; *Fax:* (202) 544-8307; *E-mail:* pubsales@theaha.org

Web site: www.theaha.org

151

Research and Funding: A German-American Guide for Historians and Social Scientists.

Ed. by Christof Mauch and Birgit Zischke. Washington, DC: German Historical Institute, 1999. Free. Paper or online.

Description: This directory focuses on exchanges between the United States and Germany and provides detailed information about institutions that offer financial support (fellowships and grants in history and the social sciences) and/or affiliations to non-native researchers. For more information about the paper and online versions of the publication, see entry 288 in the "Grants for Individuals—Humanities—History" section of this bibliography.

Available from: German Historical Institute, 1607 New Hampshire Avenue, N.W., Washington, DC 20009. *Telephone:* (202) 387-3355; *Fax:* (202) 483-3430; *E-mail:* ghiusa@ghi-dc.org
Web site: www.ghi-dc.org

Literature

152

Artists and Writers Colonies: Retreats, Residencies, and Respites for the Creative Mind

2nd ed. By Robyn Middleton, et. al. Hillsboro, OR: Blue Heron Publishers, 2000. 352p. ISBN 0-936085-62-2. $19.95. Paper.

Description: Described here are approximately 200 residencies, retreats, and fellowships available to writers and artists. For more information about the publication, see entry 289 in the "Grants for Individuals—Humanities—Literature" section of this bibliography.

Available from: Blue Heron Publishers, 1234 S.W. Stark Street, Portland, OR 97205. *Telephone:* (503) 223-8098; *Fax:* (503) 223-9474; *E-mail:* info@blueheronpublishing.com
Web site: www.greatnorthwestbooks.com

153

Artists' Communities: A Directory of Residencies in the United States That Offer Time and Space for Creativity

2nd ed. By the Alliance of Artists' Communities. New York: Allworth Press, 2000. 224p. ISBN 1-58115-044-X. $18.95. Paper.

Description: This is a guide to fellowships and residencies in the United States for writers, visual and performing artists, and composers. For more information about the publication, see entry 303 in the "Grants for Individuals—Humanities—Visual Arts" section of this bibliography.

Available from: Allworth Press, 10 East 23rd Street, Suite 510, New York, NY 10010. *Telephone:* (212) 777-8395; *Toll-free:* (800) 491-2808; *Fax:* (212) 777-8395; *E-mail:* pub@allworth.com
Web site: www.allworth.com

154

Dramatists Sourcebook: Complete Opportunities for Playwrights, Translators, Composers, Lyricists, and Librettists

Ed. by Kathy Sova, Samantha R. Healy, and Jennifer Sokolov. New York: Theatre Communications Group, 1982- . Annual. ISSN 0733-1606. ISBN 1-55936-217-0. $21.95 (2002-2003 ed.). Paper.

Description: There are a number of sections in this sourcebook that describe various financial aid programs for dramatists, including fellowships, grants, awards and prizes, colonies and residencies, and emergency funds. For more information about the publication, see entry 574 in the "Awards and Prizes—Humanities—Literature" section of this bibliography.

Available from: Theatre Communications Group, 355 Lexington Avenue, New York, NY 10017-6603. *Telephone:* (212) 697-5230; *Fax:* (212) 983-4847; *E-mail:* tcg@tcg.org
Web site: www.tcg.org

155

Literary Market Place: The Directory of the American Book Publishing Industry

Medford, NJ: Information Today, 1972- . Annual. ISSN 0000-1155. ISBN 1-57387-148-6. $299 (2003 ed.), paper; $389, online.

Description: Originally designed as a register of personnel in publishing and allied fields, over the years this annual has been expanded to include 16,000 entries in a dozen major sections. One of these sections focuses on scholarships, awards, fellowships, and grants-in-aid of interest to the American writer. For more information about the publication and its Internet version, see entry 577 in the "Awards and Prizes—Humanities—Literature" section of this bibliography.

Available from: Information Today, Inc., 143 Old Marlton Pike, Medford, NJ 08055-8750. *Telephone:* (609) 654-6266; *Fax:* (609) 654-4309; *E-mail:* custserv@infotoday.com
Web site: www.literarymarketplace.com

156

The Playwright's Companion: A Practical Guide to Script Opportunities in the U.S.A.

Ed. by Mollie Ann Meserve. Brooklin, ME: Feedback Theatrebooks, 1983-1999. Annual. ISSN 0887-1507. ISBN 0937657-47-6. $20.95 (1999 ed.). Paper.

Description: Provided in the final edition of this annual guide is brief information on fellowships, grants, writers' colonies, and residencies of interest to American playwrights. For more information about the publication, see entry 294 in the "Grants for Individuals—Humanities—Literature" section of this bibliography.

Available from: Feedback Theatrebooks, P.O. Box 220, Brooklin, ME 04616. *Telephone:* (207) 359-2781; *Fax:* (207) 359-5532; *E-mail:* feedback@hypernet.com

157

Poets & Writers Magazine

New York: Poets & Writers Magazine, 1972- . Bimonthly. ISSN 0891-6136. $19.95/yr. Paper.

Description: Published six times a year, this is an excellent source of information on fellowships, grants, and awards for poets and other writers. For more information about the magazine and its online bimonthly issues, see entry 295 in the "Grants for Individuals—Humanities—Literature" section of this bibliography.

Available from: Poets & Writers Inc., 72 Spring Street, Suite 301, New York, NY 10012. *Telephone:* (212) 226-3586; *Fax:* (212) 226-3963
Web site: www.pw.org

Music

158

Artists' Communities: A Directory of Residencies in the United States That Offer Time and Space for Creativity

2nd ed. By the Alliance of Artists' Communities. New York: Allworth Press, 2000. 224p. ISBN 1-58115-044-X. $18.95. Paper.

Description: This is a guide to fellowships and residencies in the United States for composers, visual and performing artists, and writers. For more information about the publication, see entry 303 in the "Grants for Individuals—Humanities—Visual Arts" section of this bibliography.

Available from: Allworth Press, 10 East 23rd Street, Suite 510, New York, NY 10010. *Telephone:* (212) 777-8395; *Toll-free:* (800) 491-2808; *Fax:* (212) 777-8395; *E-mail:* pub@allworth.com
Web site: www.allworth.com

159

Dramatists Sourcebook: Complete Opportunities for Playwrights, Translators, Composers, Lyricists, and Librettists

Ed. by Kathy Sova, Samantha R. Healy, and Jennifer Sokolov. New York: Theatre Communications Group, 1982- . Annual. ISSN 0733-1606. ISBN 1-55936-217-0. $21.95 (2002-2003 ed.). Paper.

Description: There are a number of sections in this sourcebook that describe various financial aid programs for composers, lyricists, and librettists, including fellowships, grants, awards and prizes, colonies and residencies, and emergency funds. For more information about the publication, see entry 574 in the "Awards and Prizes—Humanities—Literature" section of this bibliography.

Available from: Theatre Communications Group, 355 Lexington Avenue, New York, NY 10017-6603. *Telephone:* (212) 697-5230; *Fax:* (212) 983-4847; *E-mail:* tcg@tcg.org
Web site: www.tcg.org

Performing Arts

160

Artists' Communities: A Directory of Residencies in the United States That Offer Time and Space for Creativity

2nd ed. By the Alliance of Artists' Communities. New York: Allworth Press, 2000. 224p. ISBN 1-58115-044-X. $18.95. Paper.

Description: This is a guide to fellowships and residencies in the United States for performing and visual artists, composers, and writers. For more information about the publication, see entry 303 in the "Grants for Individuals—Humanities—Visual Arts" section of this bibliography.

Available from: Allworth Press, 10 East 23rd Street, Suite 510, New York, NY 10010. *Telephone:* (212) 777-8395; *Toll-free:* (800) 491-2808; *Fax:* (212) 777-8395; *E-mail:* pub@allworth.com
Web site: www.allworth.com

161

National Directory of Arts Internships

Ed. by Warren Christensen and Ron Clawges. Los Angeles: National Network for Artist Placement, 1989- . Annual. ISSN 1043-092X. ISBN 0-945941-13-7. $85 (2003-2004 ed.). Paper.

How to Find Out About Financial Aid and Funding

Description: More than 3,000 fellowships and internships open to undergraduates, graduate students, and others in the performing and fine arts are described here. For more information about the publication, see entry 660 in the "Internships—Humanities—Visual Arts" section of this bibliography.

Available from: National Network for Artist Placement, 935 West Avenue 37, Los Angeles, CA 90065. *Telephone:* (323) 222-4035; *Fax:* (323) 222-4035; *E-mail:* NNAPnow@aol.com
Web site: www.artistplacement.com

Religion

162

Fellowship Plus

http://www.thefund.org/programs/fellowships

Description: In an attempt to help meet the financial needs of theological students (of any denomination), the Fund for Theological Education has prepared this online database. Described here are approximately 200 "outside" (not single-school based) funding opportunities, available to supplement funding offered at a student's school (some programs are aimed specifically at women, minorities, international students, or postdoctorates). Entries contain the following information: eligibility requirements, application deadline, program description, award amount, and address. Telephone numbers, e-mail addresses, and web site locations are also specified. The database can be searched alphabetically, by keyword, and by selected categories (e.g., religious denomination, gender, ethnicity, educational level). Loaded in May, 2000, this online service replaces the six earlier printed *Catalogs: Outside Financial Resources for Theological Students* that were prepared by the Presbyterian Church (U.S.A.) and the Association of Theological Schools in the United States and Canada (the last *Catalog* was printed in 1999).

Available from: Fund for Theological Education, Inc., 825 Houston Mill Road, Suite 250, Atlanta, GA 30329. *Telephone:* (404) 727-1450; *Fax:* (404) 727-1490; *E-mail:* fte@thefund.org
Web site: www.thefund.org

Scholarships, Etc.–Humanities–Visual Arts

Visual Arts

163

American Art Directory

New Providence, NJ: National Register, 1898- . Biennial. ISSN 0065-6968. ISBN 0-8721-7849-8. $275 (2001-2002 ed.). Hardcover.

Description: Revised biennially in odd-numbered years, this directory lists art museums, associations, and schools in the United States and Canada, along with art museums and schools abroad. A separate section in each volume focuses on art-related agencies and activities, including scholarships and fellowships.

Available from: National Register Publishing, 121 Chanlon Road, New Providence, NJ 07974. *Telephone:* (908) 464-6800; *Toll-free:* (800) 473-7020; *Fax:* (800) 836-7766

Web site: www.nationalregisterpub.com

164

Artists and Writers Colonies: Retreats, Residencies, and Respites for the Creative Mind

2nd ed. By Robyn Middleton, et. al. Hillsboro, OR: Blue Heron Publishers, 2000. 352p. ISBN 0-936085-62-2. $19.95. Paper.

Description: Described here are approximately 200 residencies, retreats, and fellowships available to artists and writers. For more information about the publication, see entry 289 in the "Grants for Individuals—Humanities—Literature" section of this bibliography.

Available from: Blue Heron Publishers, 1234 S.W. Stark Street, Portland, OR 97205. *Telephone:* (503) 223-8098; *Fax:* (503) 223-9474; *E-mail:* info@blueheronpublishing.com

Web site: www.greatnorthwestbooks.com

165

Artists' Communities: A Directory of Residencies in the United States That Offer Time and Space for Creativity

2nd ed. By the Alliance of Artists' Communities. New York: Allworth Press, 2000. 224p. ISBN 1-58115-044-X. $18.95. Paper.

Description: This is a guide to fellowships and residencies in the United States for performing and visual artists, composers, and writers. For more infor-

How to Find Out About Financial Aid and Funding

mation about the publication, see entry 303 in the "Grants for Individuals—Humanities—Visual Arts" section of this bibliography.
Available from: Allworth Press, 10 East 23rd Street, Suite 510, New York, NY 10010. *Telephone:* (212) 777-8395; *Toll-free:* (800) 491-2808; *Fax:* (212) 777-8395; *E-mail:* pub@allworth.com
Web site: www.allworth.com

166

National Directory of Arts Internships

Ed. by Warren Christensen and Ron Clawges. Los Angeles: National Network for Artist Placement, 1989- . Annual. ISSN 1043-092X. ISBN 0-945941-13-7. $85 (2003-2004 ed.). Paper.
Description: More than 3,000 fellowships and internships open to undergraduates, graduate students, and others in the arts are described here. For more information about the publication, see entry 660 in the "Internships—Humanities—Visual Arts" section of this bibliography.
Available from: National Network for Artist Placement, 935 West Avenue 37, Los Angeles, CA 90065. *Telephone:* (323) 222-4035; *Fax:* (323) 222-4035; *E-mail:* NNAPnow@aol.com
Web site: www.artistplacement.com

SCIENCES
General

167

GrantFinder: The Complete Guide to Postgraduate Funding Worldwide: Sciences

New York: Palgrave, 2000. 468p. ISBN 0-312-22895-3. $50. Hardcover.
Description: This guide describes fellowships, prizes, and grants in the sciences that are open to nationals of the United States, Canada, the United Kingdom, Ireland, Australia, New Zealand, South Africa, and the developing countries. For more information about the publication, see entry 306 in the "Grants for Individuals—Sciences—General" section of this bibliography.
Available from: Palgrave, 175 Fifth Avenue, New York, NY 10010. *Telephone:* (212) 982-3900; *Toll-free:* (800) 221-7945; *Fax:* (212) 777-6359
Web site: www.palgrave-usa.com

Scholarships, Etc.–Sciences–General

168 🕸 ¢

GrantsInfo.com: Social and Natural Sciences

http://www.arisnet.com/socnatu.html
Description: This inexpensive online searchable database provides information on hundreds of fellowship and grant opportunities in the natural and social sciences. For more information about the site, see entry 271 in the "Grants for Individuals—Social Sciences—General" section of this bibliography.

Available from: Academic Research Information System, Inc., 2940 16th Street, Suite 314, San Francisco, CA 94103. *Telephone:* (415) 558-8133; *Fax:* (415) 558-8135; *E-mail:* arisnet@dnai.com
Web site: www.arisnet.com

169 🕸 ¢

GrantsNet

http://www.grantsnet.org
Description: Because American scientists-in-training (undergraduates, graduate students, postdoctorates, and junior faculty members) are especially vulnerable in the area of competitive funding, the American Association for the Advancement of Science and the Howard Hughes Medical Institute created this continuously updated searchable database of approximately 1,000 biomedical and scientific funding options from nonprofit organizations and federal agencies. Comprehensive information is provided on about 70 percent of them: eligible research areas, program type, program description, amount awarded in most recent competition year, application requirements, deadlines, activities allowed by the award, average length of award, renewability, application procedures, and contact (links, when appropriate, are included). A password is required to search the database, but membership in GrantsNet is free. Fundseekers can also sign up for a free electronic newsletter at the site. In addition, the site also offers interviews with application reviewers, program officers, and recent award recipients; discussion forums; and lists of resources. This is the only funding database tailored to scientists in the early stage of their career.

Available from: American Association for the Advancement of Science, 1200 New York Avenue, N.W., Washington, DC 20005-3920. *Telephone:* (202) 326-6636; *Fax:* (202) 789-2008
Web site: www.grantsnet.org

How to Find Out About Financial Aid and Funding

170 🕸 ¢

National Science Foundation Guide to Programs: A Compilation of NSF Funding Opportunities

http://www.nsf.gov
Description: Described in this free annual guide (available on NSF's web site) are fellowships and grants sponsored by the National Science Foundation or administered in cooperation with foreign countries. For more information about the listing, see entry 309 in the "Grants for Individuals—Sciences—General" section of this bibliography.
Available from: National Science Foundation, 4201 Wilson Boulevard, Arlington, VA 22230. *Telephone:* (703) 292-5111; *TDD:* (703) 292-5090; *E-mail:* pubs@nsf.gov
Web site: www.nsf.gov

Agricultural Sciences

171 📖🕸

How to Pay for Your Degree in Agriculture & Related Fields

By Gail Ann Schlachter and R. David Weber. El Dorado Hills, CA: Reference Service Press, 2002- . Biennial. ISBN 1-58841-065-X, comb binding; 1-58841-089-7, eBook. $30 (2002-2004 ed.), comb binding or eBook.
Description: According to the *Occupational Outlook Handbook,* "employment of agricultural scientists is expected to grow faster than the average" and "the need to replace agricultural scientists who retire or otherwise leave the occupation permanently will account for many more job openings than projected growth." Getting an agricultural-related degree, however, can be expensive. It can cost $100,000 or more. That's why it's good to know that *How to Pay for Your Degree in Agriculture & Related Fields* identifies millions of dollars in financial aid available to undergraduate and graduate students interested in working on a degree in agribusiness, agricultural communications, agricultural economics, agricultural education, agricultural engineering, agronomy, animal or veterinary sciences, dairy science, enology, horticulture, soils science, and related fields. The following information is given for each program: purpose, eligibility, monetary award, duration, special features, limitations, number awarded, and deadline date. This directory is also available as an eBook on the netLibrary web site: www.netlibrary.com.
Available from: Reference Service Press, 5000 Windplay Drive, Suite 4, El Dorado Hills, CA 95762. *Telephone:* (916) 939-9620; *Fax:* (916) 939-9626; *E-mail:* findaid@aol.com
Web site: www.rspfunding.com

Aviation

172

AvScholars.com Free Scholarship Database

http://www.avscholars.com
Description: The AvScholars Network Foundation is a nonprofit educational and career network that targets the needs of high school, college, and graduate students interested in pursuing and/or continuing a career within the field of aviation, aerospace, and space exploration. It was created by Sedgwick Hines, the author of *Aviation Scholarships* (2nd ed. Chicago: Flight Time, 1997. ISBN 0-965738-42-6. 148p. $24.95, paperback). On March 1, 2000, the foundation launched AvScholars.com, a free online service that provides information on financial aid, college admissions, flight training, and career advancement. Both portable and school-specific scholarships and fellowships are covered in 12 separate sections: all majors, aeronautics and astronautics, aerospace science and technology, administration/management, aviation/maintenance, avionics/aircraft electronics, fellowships, flight training, military affiliation, school sponsored, special interest and affiliation, and women. There are also separate sections for loans and internships. Detailed descriptions are provided for each program, including sponsor, contact information, deadline, purpose/description, eligibility, notes, and awards and amounts.
Available from: AvScholars Network Foundation, 8526 South Drexel Avenue, Chicago, IL 60619. *Telephone:* (708) 493-0324; *Fax:* (708) 493-0324; *E-mail:* info@avscholars.com
Web site: www.avscholars.com

173

Collegiate Aviation Scholarship Listing

6th ed. Auburn, AL: University Aviation Association, 2002. 42p. $12.95, members; $19.95, nonmembers. Paper or CD-ROM.
Description: If you've dreamed about being in the aviation field but don't have enough money to pay for your education, you will be very interested in the listings in this booklet. Described in the 2002-2003 edition are 125 undergraduate scholarships and other funding opportunities, totaling more than $650,000, open to students who are majoring in aviation or flight, are working on an Airframe and Powerplant (A&P) license, are involved in sports aviation endeavors, or are pursuing other aviation-related activities. Each entry provides information on contact name and address, eligibility requirements, financial data, and deadlines. Most of the listings describe portable programs (only a few are institution specific). The directory is also available on CD-ROM at the same

price. For a more comprehensive listing (and free, too!), see AvScholars.com (entry 172).

Available from: University Aviation Association, 3410 Skyway Drive, Auburn, AL 36830-6444. *Telephone:* (334) 844-2434; *Fax:* (334) 844-2432
Web site: uaa.auburn.edu/casl.htm

Biological Sciences

174

Money for Graduate Students in the Biological & Health Sciences

By Gail Ann Schlachter and R. David Weber. El Dorado Hills, CA: Reference Service Press, 2001- . Biennial. (RSP Graduate Funding Set). ISBN 1-58841-075-7. $42.50 (2003-2005 ed.). Comb binding.

Description: This directory is aimed at graduate students looking for funding in the biological and health sciences. Described here are more than 1,100 fellowships, loans, grants, and awards set aside just for students interested in working on a master's or doctoral degree in botany, dentistry, genetics, horticulture, medicine, nutrition, pharmacology, rehabilitation, veterinary sciences, zoology, and the rest of the biological and health sciences. The directory is easy to use. Each funding program is clearly described, with detailed information given on purpose, eligibility requirements, financial data, duration, special features, limitations, number awarded, and deadline date. Entries are grouped by purpose (research or study) and indexed by program title, sponsoring organization, geographic coverage, subject, and deadline. This title, along with *Money for Graduate Students in the Physical & Earth Sciences* (see entry 190), replaces the previously published *Money for Graduate Students in the Sciences* (1996-2000); the huge number of funding opportunities now available to graduate students in the sciences made it necessary to split the listing into these two separate titles. Both *Money for Graduate Students in the Biological & Health Sciences* and *Money for Graduate Students in the Physical & Earth Sciences* are issued as part of the four-volume *RSP Graduate Funding Set;* the other volumes cover graduate funding in the arts and humanities (see entry 143) and in the social and behavioral sciences (entry 127).

Available from: Reference Service Press, 5000 Windplay Drive, Suite 4, El Dorado Hills, CA 95762. *Telephone:* (916) 939-9620; *Fax:* (916) 939-9626; *E-mail:* findaid@aol.com
Web site: www.rspfunding.com

Earth Sciences

175 📖

Money for Graduate Students in the Physical & Earth Sciences

By Gail Ann Schlachter and R. David Weber. El Dorado Hills, CA: Reference Service Press, 2001- . Biennial. (RSP Graduate Funding Set). ISBN 1-58841-077-3. $35 (2003-2005 ed.). Comb binding.

Description: Described here are 800 fellowships, grants, loans, and awards set aside just for students interested in working on a master's or doctoral degree in the earth or physical sciences. For more information about the publication, see entry 190 in the "Scholarships, Fellowships & Loans—Sciences—Physical Sciences" section of this bibliography.

Available from: Reference Service Press, 5000 Windplay Drive, Suite 4, El Dorado Hills, CA 95762. *Telephone:* (916) 939-9620; *Fax:* (916) 939-9626; *E-mail:* findaid@aol.com

Web site: www.rspfunding.com

Engineering

176 📖🕸

RSP Funding for Engineering Students

By Gail Ann Schlachter and R. David Weber. El Dorado Hills, CA: Reference Service Press, 1999- . Biennial. ISBN 1-58841-045-5, comb binding; 1-58841-080-3, eBook. $30 (2002-2004 ed.), comb binding or eBook.

Description: This is the most comprehensive listing of scholarships, fellowships, and loans available to undergraduate and graduate students majoring in engineering. In all, nearly 800 funding opportunities are described, twice the number of engineering-related programs covered in any other financial aid source. Each of the program profiles is prepared from current material supplied by the sponsoring organization. Entries are grouped alphabetically by program title in two sections: undergraduate students and graduate students. Using the indexes, you can search for funding opportunities by title, sponsor, residency, tenability, subject, and deadline date. The following information is given for each program: purpose, eligibility, monetary award, duration, special features, limitations, number awarded, and deadline date. This directory is also available as an eBook on the netLibrary web site: www.netlibrary.com.

Available from: Reference Service Press, 5000 Windplay Drive, Suite 4, El Dorado Hills, CA 95762. *Telephone:* (916) 939-9620; *Fax:* (916) 939-9626; *E-mail:* findaid@aol.com

Web site: www.rspfunding.com

Health and Medical Sciences

177

Directory of Biomedical and Health Care Grants

Westport, CT: Oryx, 1985- . Annual. ISSN 0883-5330. ISBN 1-57356-569-5. $84.50 (2003 ed.). Paper.

Description: The current edition of this directory identifies 3,000 fellowships, grants, and awards in the biomedical and health areas. For more information about the publication, see entry 313 in the "Grants for Individuals—Sciences—Health and Medical Sciences" section of this bibliography.

Available from: Oryx Press, 88 Post Road West, Westport, CT 06881. *Telephone:* (602) 265-2651; *Toll-free:* (800) 279-6799; *Fax:* (800) 279-4663; *E-mail:* info@oryxpress.com

Web site: www.oryxpress.com

178

Directory of International Grants and Fellowships in the Health Sciences

Bethesda, MD: Fogarty International Center, 2002. 108p. Free. Paper or online.

Description: About 175 programs that support doctoral or postdoctoral research in the health sciences in the United States or abroad are described here. For more information about the publication, see entry 314 in the "Grants for Individuals—Sciences—Health and Medical Sciences" section of this bibliography.

Available from: John E. Fogarty International Center for Advanced Study in the Health, Sciences, National Institutes of Health, Building 31, Room B2C29, 31 Center Drive, MSC 2220, Bethesda, MD 20892-2220. *Telephone:* (301) 496-2075; *Fax:* (301) 594-1211; *E-mail:* ficinfo@nih.gov

Web site: www.nih.gov/fic

Scholarships, Etc.–Sciences–Health & Medical Sciences

179

Directory of Pathology Training Programs (Residencies and Fellowships) in the United States and Canada

Bethesda, MD: Intersociety Committee on Pathology Information, 1970- . Annual. ISSN 0070-6086. $5, medical students and residents; $25, all others. Paper.

Description: This annually-issued directory identifies anatomic, clinical, and specialized pathology training programs (residencies and fellowships) in the United States and Canada. The listing overlaps to a great extent with the American Medical Association's *Graduate Medical Education Directory* (described in entry 181). More detail, however, is provided here. Entries are arranged geographically and specify facilities, methods, staff, application procedures, and stipends. Also included, in separate sections, are detailed descriptions of approximately 350 fellowships in specialized areas of pathology and 70 post-sophomore pathology fellowships. Descriptions in the directory are paid for and provided by the participating institutions. This information, and more, is also available on the Committee's web site, where listings can be searched by geographic location.

Available from: Intersociety Committee on Pathology Information, Inc., 9650 Rockville Pike, Bethesda, MD 20814-3993. *Telephone:* (301) 571-1880; *Fax:* (301) 571-1879; *E-mail:* ICPI@pathol.faseb.org

Web site: www.pathologytraining.org

180

Financial Assistance Resource Guide

Alexandria, VA: American Physical Therapy Association, 2002. ISBN 1-887759-27-1. 44p. $10, members; $17, nonmembers. Paper.

Description: The stated purpose of this guide is to list "scholarships, awards, fellowships, and grants available to students and physical therapists." A separate section lists financial aid open specifically to minorities. However, few of programs covered here have anything to do with physical therapy. And, some of them (e.g., Levi Strauss Foundation Special Emphasis Grants) are not even open to individuals in any field (only nonprofit organizations). Nothing is listed here that you wouldn't have already found in a general financial aid directory—and there are many programs that could have been included that are not. Even if you are majoring in physical therapy, you can safely skip this source; there are many other publications that will give you a better return on your $17 investment.

Available from: American Physical Therapy Association, 1111 North Fairfax Street, Alexandria, VA 22314. *Telephone:* (703) 684-2782; *Toll-free:* (800) 999-APTA; *Fax:* (703) 684-7343

Web site: www.apta.org

181

Graduate Medical Education Directory

Chicago: American Medical Association, 1981- . Annual. $55 (2002-2003 ed.), members, paper; $75, nonmembers, paper; $80, members, CD-ROM; $105, nonmembers, CD-ROM.

Description: Issued previously as the *Directory of Residency Training Programs Accredited by the Accreditation Council for Graduate Medical Education,* this annual directory lists nearly 8,000 residency programs at more than 1,600 teaching institutions accredited by the Accreditation Council for Graduate Medical Education. It is also known, affectionately, as the *Green Book.* Entries specify program name, name and address of director, specialties available, teaching hospitals' names, requirements, remuneration, and length of program. The latest edition of the directory is also available on CD-ROM; *Graduate Medical Education Directory on CD-ROM* provides the convenience of on-screen navigation and extensive indexes to search the residency program information. Even, better, this same information is available without charge at the association's web site; FREIDA Online (Fellowship and Residency Electronic Interactive Database Access) can be searched by numerous variables, from specialty and state to program size. Similar directories have been prepared for residencies in medical subspecialties; for example, the Association for the Care of Children's Health publishes the *Directory of Student Placements in Health Care Settings in North America* and the American Academy of Family Physicians issues the *Directory of Family Practice Residency Programs.*

Available from: American Medical Association, 515 North State Street, Chicago, IL 60610. *Telephone:* (312) 464-5000; *Toll-free:* (800) AMA-3211; *Fax:* (312) 464-5837

Web site: www.ama-assn.org

182

GrantFinder: The Complete Guide to Postgraduate Funding Worldwide: Medicine

New York: Palgrave, 2000. 394p. ISBN 0-312-22896-1. $50. Hardcover.

Description: This guide describes fellowships, prizes, and grants in the medical sciences that are open to nationals of the United States, Canada, the United Kingdom, Ireland, Australia, New Zealand, South Africa, and the developing countries. For more information about the publication, see entry 315 in the "Grants for Individuals—Sciences—Health and Medical Sciences" section of this bibliography.

Available from: Palgrave, 175 Fifth Avenue, New York, NY 10010. *Telephone:* (212) 982-3900; *Toll-free:* (800) 221-7945; *Fax:* (212) 777-6359

Web site: www.palgrave-usa.com

183 🕸 ¢

GrantsInfo.com: Biomedical Sciences

http://www.arisnet.com/biomed.html
Description: This inexpensive online searchable database offers information on hundreds of fellowships and grants in the biomedical sciences. For more information about the site, see entry 316 in the "Grants for Individuals—Sciences—Health and Medical Sciences" section of this bibliography.
Available from: Academic Research Information System, Inc., 2940 16th Street, Suite 314, San Francisco, CA 94103. *Telephone:* (415) 558-8133; *Fax:* (415) 558-8135; *E-mail:* arisnet@dnai.com
Web site: www.arisnet.com

184 📖 🕸 ¢

Interorganizational Financial & Experiential Information Document: "If I'd" Only Known about That Scholarship

Prep. by the member organizations of the Interorganizational Council on Student Affairs. Washington, DC: Interorganizational Council on Student Affairs, 1999. Unpaged. Free. Paper or online.
Description: The Interorganizational Council on Student Affairs (ICSA) is made up of the following member groups: Academy of Managed Care Pharmacy, American Association of Colleges of Pharmacy, American College of Apothecaries, American College of Clinical Pharmacy, American Pharmaceutical Association, American Society of Consultant Pharmacists, National Community Pharmacists Association, National Association of Chain Drug Stores, and National Council of State Pharmacy Association Executives. These member organizations compiled this selected list of scholarships and fellowships open to pharmacy students. Entries are grouped into the following sections: scholarships, loans, awards, grants, experiential programs, residencies, research, and meetings of ICSA member organizations. Brief information for these programs is presented in tabular format and includes eligibility/description, award amount and number, deadline, and contact (address, phone number, and fax number). There is no index. Further, because there is no introduction, it is difficult to determine the intended scope of the listing (e.g., what is included and excluded). Even so, this is quite an extensive listing of funding opportunities available specifically to pharmacy students. Best of all, it's free. The same information included in the print edition can also be found on the web site listed below. Two other members of ICSA have also prepared listings of residencies and/or fellowships that would be of interest to the pharmacy students: *Directory of Residencies and Fellowships* (see entry 665) and *Residency Directory* (entry 668).
Available from: Interorganizational Council on Student Affairs, 2215 Constitution Avenue, N.W., Washington, DC 20037-2985. *Telephone:* (202) 429-7595; *Toll-free:* (800) 237-AphA, ext. 7595; *E-mail:* edt@mail.aphanet.org

Web site: www.aphanet.org/students/ifeid.html

185

Medical Research Funding Bulletin

New York: Science Support Center, 1972- . Bi-weekly. $75/yr. E-mail.

Description: Each bi-weekly issue identifies between 50 and 100 research fellowships and grants in the medical sciences offered by federal agencies and private organizations. For more information about the service, see entry 318 in the "Grants for Individuals—Sciences—Health and Medical Sciences" section of this bibliography.

Available from: Science Support Center, P.O. Box 7507, FDR Station, New York, NY 10150-7507. *Telephone:* (212) 371-3398; *E-mail:* grants1@ATTglobal.net

186

Money for Graduate Students in the Biological & Health Sciences

By Gail Ann Schlachter and R. David Weber. El Dorado Hills, CA: Reference Service Press, 2001- . Biennial. (RSP Graduate Funding Set). ISBN 1-58841-075-7. $42.50 (2003-2005 ed.). Comb binding.

Description: Described here are more than 1,100 fellowships, grants, loans, and awards set aside just for students interested in working on a master's or doctoral degree in the health or biological sciences. For more information about the publication, see entry 174 in the "Scholarships, Fellowships & Loans—Sciences—Biological Sciences" section of this bibliography.

Available from: Reference Service Press, 5000 Windplay Drive, Suite 4, El Dorado Hills, CA 95762. *Telephone:* (916) 939-9620; *Fax:* (916) 939-9626; *E-mail:* findaid@aol.com

Web site: www.rspfunding.com

187

Postgraduate Orthopaedic Fellowships

Rosemont, IL: American Academy of Orthopaedic Surgeons, 2002. 400p. ISBN 0-89203-272-3. $40, residents; $45, members; $50, others. Paper or online.

Description: Published annually by the American Academy of Orthopaedic Surgeons in collaboration with the Academic Orthopaedic Society, this directory lists orthopedic fellowships in the United States and abroad. In the latest edition, 400 fellowship opportunities are described in 12 subspecialty groups. Each list-

Scholarships, Etc.–Sciences–Health & Medical Sciences

ing indicates: director's name, address, phone and fax numbers; participating hospitals, stipend, and fellowship goals and characteristics. Also included is ACGME accreditation and match program participation information. This information is also available on the Academy's web site; click first on "Library & Archives" and then on "Postgraduate Orthopaedic Fellowships." Access is provided free to purchasers of the print guide, or users can subscribe to the online version only: $35 for residents, $40 for members, and $45 for all others.

Available from: American Academy of Orthopaedic Surgeons, 6300 North River Road, Rosemont, IL 60018-4262. *Telephone:* (847) 823-7186; *Toll-free:* (800) 626-6726; *Fax:* (800) 823-8025; *E-mail:* custserv@aaos.org
   Web site: www.aaos.org

188

RSP Funding for Nursing Students and Nurses

By Gail Ann Schlachter and R. David Weber. El Dorado Hills, CA: Reference Service Press, 1998- . Biennial. ISBN 1-58841-046-3, comb binding; 1-58841-081-1, eBook. $30 (2002-2004 ed.), comb binding or eBook.

Description: The U.S. Department of Labor estimates that nearly 2.5 million nurses will be needed in the first part of the 21st century. Hundreds of financial aid programs, representing millions of dollars, are available to help students prepare for those jobs, as well as to help nurses already in the field fund their professional or research activities. These scholarships, fellowships, loans, and grants are described in detail here. Each program description is prepared from current material supplied by the sponsoring organization. Entries are grouped purpose (study and training or research and creative activities). Using the indexes, you can search for these funding opportunities by title, sponsor, residency, tenability, subject, and deadline date. The following information is given for each program: purpose, eligibility, monetary award, duration, special features, limitations, number awarded, and deadline date. In all, more than 600 funding opportunities are covered; this is nearly three times the number of nursing-related funding programs covered in any other source. This directory is also available as an eBook on the netLibrary web site: www.netlibrary.com.

Available from: Reference Service Press, 5000 Windplay Drive, Suite 4, El Dorado Hills, CA 95762. *Telephone:* (916) 939-9620; *Fax:* (916) 939-9626; *E-mail:* findaid@aol.com
   Web site: www.rspfunding.com

Mathematics

189

Assistantships and Graduate Fellowships in the Mathematical Sciences

Providence, RI: American Mathematical Society, 1953- . Annual. ISSN 1040-7650. ISBN 0-8218-3230-1. $13 (2003 ed.), members; $22, nonmembers. Paper.

Description: Originally published as part of the December issue of *Notices of the AMS,* this separately-issued directory lists graduate assistantships and fellowships in mathematics available at about 280 U.S. and Canadian universities. Entries for the nearly 400 departments of math, applied math, statistics, and computer science at these schools contain the following information: address, type of assistantship, number to be awarded, amount of stipend, tuition and fees, services required, and degrees awarded. The annual also includes information on approximately 50 financial aid programs available to support 1) study and travel abroad by U.S. students and 2) study in the United States by foreign students. To update these listings, see the following columns in *Notices of the AMS:* "Stipends for Study and Travel" in the October issue and "Funding Information for Mathematical Sciences" in each monthly issue.

Available from: American Mathematical Society, P.O. Box 6248, Providence, RI 02940-6248. *Telephone:* (401) 455-4000; *Toll-free:* (800) 321-4267; *Fax:* (401) 455-4046; *E-mail:* cust-serv@ams.org

Web site: www.ams.org

Physical Sciences

190

Money for Graduate Students in the Physical & Earth Sciences

By Gail Ann Schlachter and R. David Weber. El Dorado Hills, CA: Reference Service Press, 2001- . Biennial. (RSP Graduate Funding Set). ISBN 1-58841-077-3. $35 (2003-2005 ed.). Comb binding.

Description: Now you only need to check in one place to learn about the 800 biggest and best fellowships, grants, awards, and forgivable loans that support graduate study, training, research, and creative activities in the physical and earth sciences. All areas are covered, including atmospheric sciences, aviation, chemistry, computer sciences, geology, mathematics, physics, space sciences, technology, and many more. The funding opportunities described here are sponsored by more than 400 federal and state government agencies, professional societies, foundations, educational associations, social groups, and corporations. Each program description is prepared from current material supplied by the sponsoring organization. In seconds, you can read about purpose, eligibility, monetary award, duration, special features, limitations, number awarded, and deadline date for any program that interests you. Plus, the book is organized so you can search for aid by purpose, program title, sponsor, residency, tenability, subject coverage, and even deadline date. This title, along with *Money for Graduate Students in the Biological & Health Sciences* (see entry 174) replaces the previously published *Money for Graduate Students in the Sciences* (1996-2000); the huge number of funding opportunities now available to graduate students in the sciences made it necessary to split the listing into these two separate titles. Both *Money for Graduate Students in the Physical & Earth Sciences* and *Money for Graduate Students in the Biological & Health Sciences* are issued as part of the four-volume *RSP Graduate Funding Set;* the other volumes cover graduate funding in the arts and humanities (see entry 143) and in the social and behavioral sciences (entry 127).

Available from: Reference Service Press, 5000 Windplay Drive, Suite 4, El Dorado Hills, CA 95762. *Telephone:* (916) 939-9620; *Fax:* (916) 939-9626; *E-mail:* findaid@aol.com

Web site: www.rspfunding.com

Technology

191

Graduate Assistantship Directory in Computing

http://info.acm.org/gad

Description: Originally available in print form, this information is now offered without charge as a searchable, annually-updated database on the Association for Computing Machinery (ACM) web site. The online directory contains information on existing graduate programs in computing (including degrees offered and specialties, numbers of computing faculty and students, faculty interest areas, and computer equipment available), admission requirements and application deadlines, and types and amounts of financial aid available to qualified students at each institution. Over 100 graduate programs are described. This information is supplied by the various university departments and computing centers; the publisher makes no attempt to verify its accuracy.

Available from: Association for Computing Machinery, 1515 Broadway, New York, NY 10036-5701. *Telephone:* (212) 869-7440; *Toll-free:* (800) 342-6626; *Fax:* (212) 944-1318; *E-mail:* acmhelp@acm.org

Web site: www.acm.org

SPECIAL POPULATION GROUPS
Athletes

192

Athletic Scholarships: Thousands of Grants—and over $400 Million—for College-Bound Athletes

4th ed. By Andy Clark and Amy Clark. New York: Facts On File, 2000. 352p. ISBN 0-8160-4308-6, hardcover; 0-8160-4309-4, paper. $38.50, hardcover; $16.95, paper.

Description: It's not only the star athletes who receive college scholarships. There are millions of dollars available to college-bound students who have participated in a whole range of sports—ranging from baseball and football to the less common sports of badminton, racquetball, and skiing. But don't be misled. This is not a guide to portable athletic scholarships (the kind that student-athletes can use at any school); rather this is a state-by-state listing of 2-year and 4-year colleges which identifies the type of athletic scholarships offered by the schools solely to their own students. Profiles for each school include address, phone number, contact persons, number of grants, amount of aid available at the school, and sports offered for men and women. Similar information, but in greater detail, can be found in *Peterson's Sports Scholarships & College Athletic Programs* (see entry 195).

Available from: Facts On File, 132 West 31st Street, 17th Floor, New York, NY 10001. *Telephone:* (212) 683-2244; *Toll-free:* (800) 322-8755; *Fax:* (800) 678-3633; *E-mail:* CustServ@factsonfile.com
Web site: www.factsonfile.com

193

College Athletic Scholarships Database

http://www.womenssportsfoundation.org

Description: In the past, the Women's Sports Foundation issued information about women's sports scholarships in a pamphlet, first entitled *College Athletic Scholarship Guide* and then *Women's Collegiate Sports Scholarship Guide*. The last edition of the pamphlet was printed in 1998. Since then, the Foundation has moved information about women's sports scholarships to its web site. Use the College Athletic Scholarships Database there to access general information about sports scholarships offered to women by individual colleges (no information about portable scholarships is provided). The site also contains information about the various sports-related scholarships offered by the Foundation.

Scholarships, Etc.–Special Population Groups–Athletes

Available from: Women's Sports Foundation, Eisenhower Park, East Meadow, NY 11554. *Telephone:* (516) 542-4700; *Toll-free:* (800) 227-3988; *Fax:* (516) 542-4716; *E-mail:* wosport@aol.com
Web site: www.womenssportsfoundation.org

194

How to Win a Sports Scholarship

2nd ed. By Penny Hastings and Todd D. Caven. Manhattan Beach, First Base Sports, 1999. 250p. ISBN 1-884309-10-0. $19.95. Paper.

Description: There is little to distinguish this from many of the other so-called guides to sports scholarships. Like the others, the focus here is on strategy rather than individual financial aid opportunities for athletes. Only Chapter 3 ("Athletic Scholarships") and Chapter 12 ("College Scholarships and Other Financial Aid") deal specifically with financial aid for student athletes.

Available from: First Base Sports, Inc., P.O. Box 1731, Manhattan Beach, CA 90267-1731. *Toll-free:* (800) 247-8228; *Fax:* (413) 751-8774; *E-mail:* sales@firstbasesports.com
Web site: www.firstbasesports.com

195

Peterson's Sports Scholarships & College Athletic Programs

4th ed. Ed. by Ronald E. Walker. Lawrenceville, NJ: Peterson's Guides, 1999. 880p. ISSN 1069-1383. ISBN 0-7689-0273-8. $26.95. Paper.

Description: The world of college athletic scholarships doesn't begin and end with football and basketball. In fact, each year hundreds of American colleges award more than $80 million to freshman athletes in 32 sports—ranging from Alpine skiing to wrestling. This volume provides details on athletic programs at over 1,700 two-year and four-year schools, organized by division of play—from the community college level to the NCAA. Information is provided on the number of students participating in the sport, the number and dollar amount of the scholarships awarded; the number of athletes who applied the year before, eligibility requirements, terms of the typical scholarship (number of years, possibility of renewal) and contact person. In addition, there is a master sports index that lists more than 30 women's and men's sports and each school that offers them. Rounding out this guide is a special section in which college coaches and former college athletes present advice on how to select a college, what to look for in a sports program, and how to make college athletics work for the student-athlete. It should be noted that only campus-based aid is summarized; information is not presented on "portable" sports scholarships. Another limitation: the directory was last published in 1999 and has not been updated since then.

Available from: Peterson's Guides, Princeton Pike Corporate Center, 2000 Lenox Drive, P.O. Box 67005, Lawrenceville, NJ 08648. *Telephone:* (609) 896-1800; *Toll-free:* (800) 338-3282; *Fax:* (609) 896-4544; *E-mail:* sales@petersons.com
Web site: www.petersons.com

Ethnic Groups

196

Black Excel African American Student's College Guide: Your One-Stop Resource for Choosing the Right College, Getting in, and Paying the Bill

Ed. by Issac Black. New York: John Wiley, 2000. 384p. ISBN 0-471-29552-3. $19.95. Paper.

Description: Although the primary focus of this guide is on choosing the right college for African Americans (profiles of 100 top colleges are provided), there is a separate section prepared by Black Excel that lists hundreds of private and school-based scholarship sources. Brief information is provided on each, although some of the information is quite out of date. This same information can be found, at no charge, on Black Excel's web site: www.blackexcel.org. However, African American students will find more leads, and more information for each lead, in *Financial Aid for African Americans* (see entry 198).

Available from: John Wiley & Sons, Inc., 111 River Street, Hoboken, NJ 07030. *Telephone:* (201) 748-6000; *Toll-free:* (800) 225-5945; *Fax:* (201) 748-6088; *E-mail:* info@wiley.com
Web site: www.wiley.com

197

The Black Student's Guide to Scholarships: 700+ Private Money Sources for Black and Minority Students

5th ed. Ed. by Barry Beckham. Lanham, MD: Madison Books, 1999. 243p. ISBN 1-56833-117-7. $17.95. Paper.

Description: What began as a pamphlet called *75 Scholarships Every Black High School Student Should Know About* has now become a 243-page paperback with brief descriptions (generally one or two sentences) of approximately 700 funding opportunities for African American and other minority students. Although the subtitle indicates these scholarships come from the private sector, a large number of entries describe programs offered by colleges and universities only for their own students. The entries are arranged by sponsor and indexed

Scholarships, Etc.–Special Population Groups–Ethnic Groups

by institution, discipline, and state. There is also a glossary of terms and a brief, unannotated, and very out-of-date bibliography (most citations date back to 1993 and 1994). *The Black Student's Guide* is far from comprehensive; many programs available to Black students are not covered here. Further, the listings that are included are now quite out of date.

Available from: Madison Books, 4720 Boston Way, Lanham, MD 20706. *Telephone:* (301) 459-3366; *Toll-free:* (800) 462-6420; *E-mail:* beckham@erols.com

198

Financial Aid for African Americans

By Gail Ann Schlachter and R. David Weber. El Dorado Hills, CA: Reference Service Press, 1997- . Biennial. (Minority Funding Set). ISBN 1-58841-068-4. $40 (2003-2005 ed.). Hardcover.

Description: If you are a Black or African American looking for financial aid, you will be interested in this directory. Described here are 1,500 scholarships, fellowships, grants, loans, awards, prizes, and internships—representing billions of dollars—open specifically to Black/African Americans. This money can be used to support a whole range of activities, including study, training, research, creative endeavors, future projects, professional development, and work experience. The listings cover every major subject area and are sponsored by hundreds of private and public agencies and organizations. The following information is provided: contact, address, telephone number, e-mail and web sites, purpose, eligibility, financial data, duration, special features, limitations, number awarded and deadline date. Users can access this information by program title, sponsoring organizations, residency, tenability, subject coverage, type of funding, and even deadline date. The directory is part of Reference Service Press's four-volume *Minority Funding Set,* which replaced the *Directory of Financial Aids for Minorities* in 1997.

Available from: Reference Service Press, 5000 Windplay Drive, Suite 4, El Dorado Hills, CA 95762. *Telephone:* (916) 939-9620; *Fax:* (916) 939-9626; *E-mail:* findaid@aol.com

Web site: www.rspfunding.com

199

Financial Aid for Asian Americans

By Gail Ann Schlachter and R. David Weber. El Dorado Hills, CA: Reference Service Press, 1997- . Biennial. (Minority Funding Set). ISBN 1-58841-069-2. $37.50 (2003-2005 ed.). Hardcover.

Description: This directory is aimed at Americans of Chinese, Japanese, Korean, Vietnamese, Filipino, or other Asian ancestry. The book has been designed so that users can quickly identify available funding by specific subject,

How to Find Out About Financial Aid and Funding

sponsor, title, residency requirements, where the money can be spent, type of funding, and deadline date. More than 1,000 scholarships, fellowships, loans, grants, awards, and internships set aside for Asian Americans are described here. Full information is provided for each of these programs: purpose, eligibility, financial data, duration, special features, limitations, number awarded, and deadline date. This directory is part of Reference Service Press's four-volume *Minority Funding Set,* which replaced the *Directory of Financial Aids for Minorities* in 1997.

Available from: Reference Service Press, 5000 Windplay Drive, Suite 4, El Dorado Hills, CA 95762. *Telephone:* (916) 939-9620; *Fax:* (916) 939-9626; *E-mail:* findaid@aol.com

Web site: www.rspfunding.com

200

Financial Aid for Hispanic Americans

By Gail Ann Schlachter and R. David Weber. El Dorado Hills, CA: Reference Service Press, 1997- . Biennial. (Minority Funding Set). ISBN 1-58841-070-6. $40 (2003-2005 ed.). Hardcover.

Description: One of the four titles in Reference Service Press's *Minority Funding Set* (which replaced the *Directory of Financial Aids for Minorities* in 1997), this directory identifies nearly 1,400 scholarships, fellowships, loans, grants, awards, and internships available to Hispanic Americans, including Mexican Americans, Puerto Ricans, Cuban Americans, and others of Latin American origin. The directory is organized by program type and indexed by sponsoring organization, program title, geographic coverage, subject focus, and deadline date. Detailed program entries provide information on purpose, eligibility, financial data, duration, special features, number awarded, limitations, and deadline date.

Available from: Reference Service Press, 5000 Windplay Drive, Suite 4, El Dorado Hills, CA 95762. *Telephone:* (916) 939-9620; *Fax:* (916) 939-9626; *E-mail:* findaid@aol.com

Web site: www.rspfunding.com

201

Financial Aid for Native Americans

By Gail Ann Schlachter and R. David Weber. El Dorado Hills, CA: Reference Service Press, 1997- . Biennial. (Minority Funding Set). ISBN 1-58841-071-4. $40 (2003-2005 ed.). Hardcover.

Description: Detailed information on nearly 1,500 funding opportunities open to American Indians, Native Alaskans, and Native Pacific Islanders (including Native Hawaiians and Samoans) is presented in this directory. Program entries are arranged by type of funding; additional access is provided by

Scholarships, Etc.–Special Population Groups–Ethnic Groups

the subject, title, sponsor, residency, tenability, and deadline date indexes. The following information is given for each program: sponsor address and telephone numbers (including toll-free and fax), e-mail and web addresses, purpose, eligibility, financial data, duration, special features, limitations, number awarded, and deadline. Plus, the directory contains an annotated bibliography of key resources that identify even more financial aid opportunities. This directory is part of Reference Service Press's four-volume *Minority Funding Set,* which replaced the *Directory of Financial Aids for Minorities* in 1997.

Available from: Reference Service Press, 5000 Windplay Drive, Suite 4, El Dorado Hills, CA 95762. *Telephone:* (916) 939-9620; *Fax:* (916) 939-9626; *E-mail:* findaid@aol.com
Web site: www.rspfunding.com

202

The Hispanic Scholarship Directory: Over 1,000 Ways to Finance Your Education

5th ed. Carlsbad, CA: WPR Publishing, 2002. 241p. ISBN 1-889379-24-7. $19.95. Paper.

Description: Although the cover of this paper is very attractive, the inside leaves much to be desired. First of all, the organization is confusing. The entries are "sorted" by state. But what this really means is not the state where applicants must reside or even where recipients may go, but where the sponsoring organization is located. Therefore, unless you browsed through the Pennsylvania chapter, you would not run across the National Association for Campus Activities' Multicultural Scholarship Program, which is open to students residing in any state. The indexes are of some help (there is an index to national programs, for example), but because only the state chapter is indicated, rather than a page or entry reference, the process is cumbersome. Many of the entries are not aimed at Hispanic Americans specifically. For example, the Black Cultural Heritage Scholarship is open to African Americans and the Colonel Arthur L. Bakewell Veterans Scholarships is for *any* honorably discharged veteran. Further, about half the entries are single-school based, open only to students at that particular institution. Finally, the page layout isn't very easy to use or efficient. Each entry appears to be a form that's been filled in; as a result, many categories that don't apply (e.g., web site) or for which information wasn't supplied (e.g., deadline, number of scholarships) are left blank.

Available from: WPR Publishing, 1207 Carlsbad Village Drive, Suite D, Carlsbad, CA 92008-2856. *Telephone:* (760) 434-7474; *Fax:* (760) 434-7476; *E-mail:* kirk@whisler.com

203

MOLIS (Minority On-Line Information Service)

http://www.sciencewise.com/molis/index.htm
Description: In 1988, the U.S. Department of Energy's (DOE) Industry/University Program Office commissioned a study to evaluate the quality of the agency's relationship with colleges and universities. The study revealed that DOE was viewed as a "closed organization," not making its funding opportunities readily available. To correct this, the Federal Information Exchange (FIE) was created. In 1990, FIE developed the Minority On-Line Information System to provide free information of interest to Hispanic Serving Institutions, Historically Black Colleges and Universities, Predominantly Black Colleges and Universities, Tribally Controlled Colleges and Universities, and other minority institutions. One section of MOLIS was a searchable database of selected financial aid opportunities available to minority undergraduate and graduate students; to develop a searchable profile, students entered information on residency, gender, race, heritage, degree level, course of study, and grade point average. The utility of the database was limited; a test search (conducted by GrantsNet) for graduate funding in the natural sciences "came up with only nine programs (a small fraction of the programs that target minorities in science)." The MOLIS database was extracted primarily from the Scholarship Resource Network (SRN) database (see entry 72). Originally sponsored by RAMS-FIE, MOLIS next became part of ScienceWise (see entry 217), a division of TheScientificWorld. However, in mid-2002, ScienceWise suspended operations. Although the web site promised that "the combination of free and paid-for services" would resume as of December 2002, the site was still not operating in April of 2003 and e-mails sent to the posted contact were returned as undeliverable.

Available from: ScienceWise, 300 Professional Drive, Suite 200, Gaithersburg, MD 20879-3419. *Telephone:* (301) 975-0103; *Fax:* (301) 975-0109
Web site: www.sciencewise.com

204

National Directory of Scholarships, Internships, and Fellowships for Latino Youth

2nd ed. Washington, DC: Congressional Hispanic Caucus Institute, 2002. 136p. Free. Paper or online.
Description: Aimed at "Latino students and young professionals wishing to finance their higher education and/or enhance their educational and professional experience with leadership development opportunities," this slickly-produced directory provides brief information (2 short descriptions per page) on approximately 150 scholarship, internship, and fellowship programs available to them. While a number of the listings are not restricted just to Hispanics or even minorities (e.g., AFL-CIO Union Summer) and a number of programs open specifi-

Scholarships, Etc.–Special Population Groups–Ethnic Groups

cally to underrepresented minorities are not covered here, still this pamphlet is helpful. Best of all, it's free. An abbreviated 41-page .pdf version of the publication is also available, at no charge, on the Congressional Hispanic Caucus Institute's web site. But, keep in mind the editors' warning: "this directory should not be viewed the definitive source on fellowships, internships, and scholarships for Latino students." For a more comprehensive listing (1,300+ funding opportunities), see *Financial Aid for Hispanic Americans* (entry 200).

Available from: Congressional Hispanic Caucus Institute, 504 C Street N.E., Washington, DC 20002. *Telephone:* (202) 543-1771; *Toll-free:* (800) EXCEL-DC; *Fax:* (202) 546-2143
Web site: www.chci.org

205

Newspapers, Diversity, & You

Princeton, NJ: Dow Jones Newspaper Fund, 1993-1999. Annual. Free (1999 ed.). Paper.

Description: One section of this free booklet deals with scholarships, fellowships, internships, and special training programs for minorities interested in journalism. For more information about the publication, see entry 149 in the "Scholarships, Fellowships & Loans—Humanities—Communications and Mass Media" section of this bibliography.

Available from: Dow Jones Newspaper Fund, P.O. Box 300, Princeton, NJ 08543-0300. *Telephone:* (609) 452-2820; *Fax:* (609) 520-5804; *E-mail:* newsfund@wsf.dowjones.com
Web site: djnewspaperfund.dowjones.com/fund/default.asp

206

On the Road to Higher Education: Guide to Hispanic Financial Aid Opportunities

Prep. by Hispanic Association of Colleges and Universities. Highland Park, MI: DaimlerChrysler. Annual. 146p. Free (2001-2002 ed.). Paper or online.

Description: Prepared by the Hispanic Association of Colleges and Universities, this free publication identifies and describes 300+ random private and institution-based financial aid programs. Despite its title, however, the listing does not focus solely on opportunities for Hispanics. A number of the programs are open to minorities in general (e.g., Student Opportunities Scholarships for Ethnic Minority Groups) and a few more are not restricted to minorities at all (e.g., programs sponsored by the Texas Electric Cooperative). Entries are grouped by topic (arts and humanities, communications, education, social and behavioral sciences, etc.). There is no index. Funding to underwrite the publication of this booklet was provided by the DaimlerChrysler Corporation; thanks to Daimler-

Chrysler, this guide is distributed without change to any interested fundseeker. Similar guides have been funded by Chrysler in the past, including the *VISTA Scholarship Guide for Hispanics*. The information included in the latest annual is also available on DaimlerChrysler's dedicated web site: HispanicScholarship.com, where you can automatically generate a request letter for any scholarship that interests you.

Available from: DaimlerChrysler Corporation, Attn: Hispanic Scholarships, P.O. Box 3189, Highland Park, MI 48203. *Toll-free:* (800) 521-0953; *Fax:* (800) 883-8338

Web site: HispanicScholarship.com

207

Pathways to Career Success for Minorities: A Resource Guide to Colleges, Financial Aid, and Work

Ed. by Tim Schaffert. Chicago: Ferguson, 2000. 386p. ISBN 0-89434-303-3. $29.95. Paper.

Description: Similar to Ferguson's *Pathways to Career Success for Women* (see entry 234), this directory briefly describes approximately 400 funding opportunities open to minorities or offered by minority organizations; these include scholarships, fellowships, grants, awards, loans, and internships. This listing is hardly comprehensive, but it is useful. Although not organized in quite the same way, the directory supercedes Ferguson's *Big Book of Minority Opportunities: The Directory of Special Programs for Minority Group Members*, which was last published in 1997, and its 1997 series of pamphlets on *Financial Aid for Minorities*.

Available from: Ferguson Publishing Company, 200 West Jackson Boulevard, Chicago, IL 60606. *Toll-free:* (800) 306-9941; *Fax:* (800) 306-9942

Web site: www.fergpubco.com

208

Sources of Financial Aid Available to American Indian Students

Ed. by Jan Merchant. Las Cruces, NM: Indian Resource Development, New Mexico State University, 2003. 110p. Free, New Mexico residents; $4, all others. Spiral bound.

Description: This booklet is intended as a "beginning point" for American Indian undergraduate and graduate students looking for aid. Only some of the sources of financial aid established exclusively for American Indian students are identified here. The rest of the pamphlet is concerned with general information (e.g., federal aid programs, tips), descriptions of additional financial aid programs that are open to all minorities (and some that are open to all segments of society), and a listing of job opportunities (particularly internships and co-op programs) for college students. Some program entries are well annotated and others contain only contact information. Still, there's quite a bit of information for the price. The listing is funded by the state of New Mexico and is updated annually. In the past, it was issued under the title *Student Financial Aid for American Indians.*

Available from: Indian Resource Development, New Mexico State University, Box 30001, MSC 3IRD, Las Cruces, NM 88003-8001. *Telephone:* (505) 646-1347; *Fax:* (505) 646-7740; *E-mail:* ird@nmsu.edu

Web site: www.nmsu.edu/~ird

209

Where's the Money?

Highland Park, MI: DaimlerChrysler. 2001. Free (2001-2002 ed.). Paper or online.

Description: Similar to DaimlerChrysler's guide to financial aid opportunities for Hispanic Americans (see entry 206), but aimed at African Americans rather than Hispanic Americans, *Where's the Money?* provides detailed information on approximately 225 scholarships, grants, and awards. The listing is available both in print (in an attractive booklet) and online (where programs can be browsed or searched by state, academic field, and academic level). There is no charge for either. Many of the entries in *Where's the Money?* were prepared in the year 2000 by Reference Service Press. Because DaimlerChrysler has not updated the database since 2001, much of the information is now out of date. For a more current (and comprehensive) listing of funding available to African Americans, see the 2003-2005 edition of *Financial Aid for African Americans,* described in entry 198.

Available from: DaimlerChrysler Corporation, Attn: African American Scholarships, P.O. Box 3189, Highland Park, MI 48203. *Toll-free:* (800) 521-0953; *Fax:* (800) 883-8338

Web site: www.africanamericanscholarship.com

Foreign Students

210

Directory of Grants for Study and Research in the U.S.A.

By Susan Offerman. Ocean Grove, NJ: Overseas Academic Opportunities, 2000. 285p. ISBN 1-930459-00-9. $42. Paper.

Description: This book is aimed at students from countries outside the United States who are interested in attending an undergraduate or graduate school in the United States. The directory describes available scholarships, fellowships, and grants. The author has been involved in international education for more than 15 years; she has also compiled another funding directory aimed at foreign students interested in study in the United States, *Directory of Grants for Medical Study and Research in the U.S.A.* (2000. 165p. ISBN 1-930459-01-7. $52, paperback), as well as one for American students interested in study abroad, *Directory of Grants for Study and Research Overseas* (2000. 305p. ISBN 1-930459-02-5. $29, paperback). All three of these titles are scheduled to be updated in 2003.

Available from: Overseas Academic Opportunities, 71 Mount Hermon Way, P.O. Box 102, Ocean Grove, NJ 07756. *Telephone:* (732) 294-2410; *Fax:* (732) 866-8383

211

Peterson's Scholarships for Study in the USA & Canada: The Money You Need for the Education You Want

3rd ed. Lawrenceville, NJ: Peterson's Guides, 1999. 376p. ISBN 0-7689-0266-5. $21.95. Paper.

Description: The latest edition of this directory (1999) identifies scholarships and other funding opportunities for foreign students interested in pursuing an undergraduate or graduate degree in the United States or Canada. Many of the programs described here are open to Americans as well as foreign students, and a large number are for small amounts ($500 or less) or have very restricted eligibility requirements. Still, this listing has value; it is one of only a few sources that provide information on financial aid available to foreigners interested in studying in North America.

Available from: Peterson's Guides, Princeton Pike Corporate Center, 2000 Lenox Drive, P.O. Box 67005, Lawrenceville, NJ 08648. *Telephone:* (609) 896-1800;   *Toll-free:*   (800)   338-3282;   *Fax:*   (609)   896-4544;   *E-mail:* sales@petersons.com

Web site: www.petersons.com

Gays, Lesbians, Etc.

212

Funders of Lesbian, Gay, Bisexual and Transgender Programs: A Directory for Grantseekers

New York: Funders for Lesbian and Gay Issues, 2002. $15, paper; free, online.

Scholarships, Etc.–Special Population Groups–Military, Etc.

Description: A limited number of scholarship funds and fellowships available for lesbian and gay students, as well as for those pursuing gay and lesbian studies, are described in a separate section in this directory. For more information about the paper and web versions of this directory, see entry 523 in the "Grants for Organizations—Special Populations—Gays, Lesbians, Etc." section of this bibliography.

Available from: Funders for Lesbian and Gay Issues, 116 East 16th Street, 7th Floor, New York, NY 10003. *Telephone:* (212) 475-2930; *Fax:* (212) 982-3321; *E-mail:* info@lgbtfunders.org

Web site: www.lgbtfunders.org

213

Minnesota's List of Gay, Lesbian, Bisexual, & Transgender Scholarships

http://scc.net/~t-bonham/EDLINKS.HTM

Description: Despite its name, this site is not restricted to Minnesota residents or programs. Instead, it lists approximately 150 national, regional, and state/provincial scholarships, fellowships, and loans set aside for gay, lesbian, bisexual, and transgender students in the United States and Canada, as well as funding for students with GLBT parents. Most entries are a paragraph in length and indicate purpose, eligibility, financial award, deadline, and contact (including web links). The listing is far more inclusive than others that can be found on the web, including Queertheory.com's Financial Aid Resources (www.queertheory.com), Delta Lambda Phi's GLBT Student Scholarship Resource Guide (www.dlp.org), and the California Association of Student Financial Aid Administrators Task Force on Lesbian, Gay and Bisexual Issues' Financial Aid for Lesbian, Gay and Bisexual Students on FinAid's site (www.finaid.org/otheraid/gay.phtml).

Available from: Minnesota Gay/Lesbian/Bisexual/Transgender Education Fund, 1409 Willow Street, Suite 305, Minneapolis, MN 55403-3251. *Telephone:* (612) 870-1806; *E-mail:* philanth@scc.net

Web site: scc.net/~t-bonham/EDFUND.HTM

Military Personnel and Veterans

214

Code of Federal Regulations, Title 38: Pensions, Bonuses, and Veterans Relief

Washington, DC: G.P.O. 2v. Annual. Vol. 1 (2002), $57; vol. 2, $58. Paper.

Description: Title 38 of the *Code* contains the exact text of laws relating to veterans' benefits (including the financial aid programs established by the federal government). For more information about the publication, see entry 326 in the "Grants for Individuals—Special Population Groups—Military Personnel and Veterans" section of this bibliography.

Available from: U.S. Government Printing Office, Superintendent of Documents, P.O. Box 371954, Pittsburgh, PA 15250-7954. *Telephone:* (202) 512-1800, press 1; *Toll-free:* (800) 669-8331; *Fax:* (202) 512-2250; *E-mail:* gpoaccess@gpo.gov

Web site: www.access.gpo.gov/su_docs

215

Federal Benefits for Veterans and Dependents

Prep. by the U.S. Department of Veterans Affairs. Washington, DC: G.P.O., 1969- . Annual. ISSN 0883-3370. ISBN 0-16-051085-6. $5 (2002 ed.), paper; free, online.

Description: This annual booklet provides a comprehensive summary of federal benefits (including scholarships and loans) available to veterans and their dependents. For more information about the publication and its online version, see entry 327 in the "Grants for Individuals—Special Population Groups—Military Personnel and Veterans" section of this bibliography.

Available from: U.S. Government Printing Office, Superintendent of Documents, P.O. Box 371954, Pittsburgh, PA 15250-7954. *Telephone:* (202) 512-1800, press 1; *Toll-free:* (800) 669-8331; *Fax:* (202) 512-2250; *E-mail:* gpoaccess@gpo.gov

Web site: www.access.gpo.gov/su_docs

216

Financial Aid for Veterans, Military Personnel, and Their Dependents

By Gail Ann Schlachter and R. David Weber. El Dorado Hills, CA: Reference Service Press, 1988- . Biennial. ISSN 0896-7792. ISBN 1-58841-043-9. $40 (2002-2004 ed.). Hardcover.

Description: Veterans, military personnel, and their dependents (spouses, children, grandchildren, and dependent parents) make up more than one third of America's population today. Each year, public and private agencies set aside billions of dollars in financial aid for these groups. This is the only directory to identify the full spectrum of available funding from the federal government, state agencies, professional organizations, foundations, educational associations, and military/veterans organizations. In all, more than 1,100 scholarships, fellowships, loans, grants/grants-in-aid, and awards are described in the latest edition

Scholarships, Etc.–Special Population Groups–Military , Etc.

(2002-2004). These opportunities are open to applicants at all levels (from high school through postdoctorate) for education, research, travel, training, career development, or emergency situations. The following information is provided for each: contact information (including fax numbers, e-mail addresses, and web sites), purpose, eligibility, financial data, duration, special features, limitations, number awarded, and deadline date. The detailed entries are indexed by program title, sponsoring organization, residency, tenability, subject, and deadline dates.

Available from: Reference Service Press, 5000 Windplay Drive, Suite 4, El Dorado Hills, CA 95762. *Telephone:* (916) 939-9620; *Fax:* (916) 939-9626; *E-mail:* findaid@aol.com

Web site: www.rspfunding.com

217

Need a Lift? To Educational Opportunities, Careers, Loans, Scholarships & Employment

Prep. by the American Legion Educational and Scholarship Program. Indianapolis: American Legion, 1969- . Annual. $3 (2003 ed.). Paper.

Description: What started as just a listing of financial aid offered by American Legion affiliates around the country has grown to become a 150+ page general financial aid handbook, with data compiled previously by EdTech and now by SRN (see entry 72). While American Legion educational assistance (on the national and state level) is still covered, much more is now presented in each annual issue: information on calculating financial need, a chart describing the major federal programs, a section on private loans, a list of some of the state educational benefits for veterans and their dependents, short descriptions of other types of financial aid, and a general index. There is even a list of postsecondary schools nationwide, which gives phone number, enrollment by gender, costs for tuition as well as room and board, deadlines for admissions and financial aid, majors offered, and the college's web site. All this for $3. Quite a bargain.

Available from: American Legion, Attn: Emblem Sales, P.O. Box 1050, Indianapolis, IN 46206-1050. *Telephone:* (317) 630-1207; *Toll-free:* (888) 453-4466; *Fax:* (317) 630-1223

Web site: www.legion.org

218

Uniformed Services Almanac

Falls Church, VA: Uniformed Services Almanac, 1959- . Annual. $7.95 (2002 ed). Paper.

Description: In addition to summary information on pay, retirement, travel and transportation, and military health care for active-duty military personnel,

How to Find Out About Financial Aid and Funding

this annual also covers educational benefits, tax benefits, survivor benefits, and other monetary and nonmonetary benefits for them. For more information about the publication, see entry 329 in the "Grants for Individuals—Special Population Groups—Military Personnel and Veterans" section of this bibliography.

Available from: Uniformed Services Almanac, Inc., P.O. Box 4144, Falls Church, VA 22044. *Telephone:* (703) 532-1631; *Toll-free:* (888) 872-9698; *Fax:* (703) 532-1635

Web site: www.militaryalmanac.com

219

Veterans' Benefits: A Guide to State Programs

By R.E. Armstrong and Terry P. Rizzauti. Westport, CT: Greenwood, 2001. 344p. ISBN 0-313-31905-7. $59.95. Paper.

Description: Written by two former members of the armed forces, this guide describes the benefits programs (some monetary, some not) offered to veterans by each of the 50 states. The guide is organized by state (there is also an index) and federal benefits are briefly described in an appendix. For more comprehensive coverage (and at less cost), use the biennially-updated *Financial Aid for Veterans, Military Personnel, and Their Dependents* (see entry 216).

Available from: Greenwood Publishing Group, Inc., 88 Post Road West, P.O. Box 5007, Westport, CT 06881-5007. *Telephone:* (203) 226-3571; *Toll-free:* (800) 225-5800; *Fax:* (203) 222-1502

Web site: www.greenwood.com

Persons with Disabilities

220

The Complete Directory for People with Disabilities

Millerton, NY: Sedgwick/Grey House, 2003. 1,139p. ISBN 1-930956-69-X. $165, paper with CD-ROM; $215, online.

Description: Despite the fact that this listing (which is available in paper with CD-ROM or online) is intended to be a "complete directory for people with disabilities," there are only a few, random financial aid programs identified here. For a comprehensive list of funding available to persons with disabilities, see *Financial Aid for the Disabled and Their Families* (entry 222); for information on funding available to organizations serving the disabled, see entry 524. in this source

Available from: Sedgwick Press/Grey House Publishing, 185 Millerton Road, P.O. Box 860, Millerton, NY 12546. *Telephone:* (518) 789-8700; *Toll-free:* (800) 562-2139; *Fax:* (518) 789-0556

Scholarships, Etc.–Special Population Groups–Disabilities

Web site: www.greyhouse.com

221

Creating Options: A Resource on Financial Aid for Students with Disabilities

By Daniel Gardner and Tanya Scott. Washington, DC: HEATH, 2002. 18p. Free. Paper, audiocassette, disk, or online.

Description: The HEATH Resource Center operates a national clearinghouse on postsecondary education for persons with disabilities. As of October 1, 2001, HEATH's long affiliation with the American Council on Education ended, and all clearinghouse operations moved to George Washington University's Graduate School of Education and Human Development. As in the past, HEATH continues to publish a number of useful pamphlets. In *Creating Options,* which is updated annually, approximately 35 sponsors of scholarships open to students with disabilities are identified and their funding opportunities briefly described. Information on federal student aid programs is also provided. The publication is available without charge in print, on audiocassette, and on computer disk. In addition, the document can be downloaded at HEATH's web site. In the past, this booklet was issued under the title *Financial Aid for Students with Disabilities.*

Available from: HEATH Resource Center, Graduate School of Education and Human Development, George Washington University, 2121 K Street, N.W., Suite 220, Washington, DC 20037. *Telephone:* (202) 973-0904; *Toll-free:* (800) 54-HEATH; *Fax:* (202) 973-0908; *E-mail:* askheath@heath.gwu.edu

Web site: www.heath.gwu.edu

222

Financial Aid for the Disabled and Their Families

By Gail Ann Schlachter and R. David Weber. El Dorado Hills, CA: Reference Service Press, 1988- . Biennial. ISSN 0898-9222. ISBN 1-58841-042-0. $40 (2002-2004 ed.). Hardcover.

Description: There are nearly 1,100 funding opportunities available to meet the individual needs of America's largest minority: 44 million persons with disabilities and their children or parents. These programs, open to individuals at any level from high school through professional and postdoctorate, are described in detail in this biennially-issued directory. The funding listed here may be used for study, research, travel, training, career development, emergencies, assistive technology, specially-adapted housing, and other expenses. All disabilities are covered, including visual impairments, hearing impairments, orthopedic disabilities, learning disabilities, and multiple disabilities. The following information is provided for each of the entries: program title, sponsoring organization, address, telephone number, e-mail address and web site, purpose of program, eligibility, financial data, duration, special features, limitations, number awarded, and deadline date. The volume also identifies state educational offices, state agencies concerned with the disabled, and the key directories that any individual (disabled or not) can use to locate additional information. Entries are extensively indexed by program title, sponsoring organization, geographic coverage, subject, and deadline date. Excluded from the compilation are funding programs open only to organizations involved in helping the disabled; for information on those programs, see *Directory of Grants for Organizations Serving People with Disabilities* (entry 524) and *Directory of Biomedical and Health Care Grants* (entry 238). To meet the needs of the visually impaired, portions of *Financial Aid for the Disabled and Their Families* are updated annually in a large print edition (*Funding for Persons with Visual Impairments,* ISBN 1-58841-073-0, $30) and an IBM- or Mac-compatible disk (*Funding for Persons with Visual Impairments, PLUS Edition,* ISBN 1-58841-074-9, $50).

Available from: Reference Service Press, 5000 Windplay Drive, Suite 4, El Dorado Hills, CA 95762. *Telephone:* (916) 939-9620; *Fax:* (916) 939-9626; *E-mail:* findaid@aol.com

Web site: www.rspfunding.com

223

Resources for People with Disabilities: A National Directory

2nd ed. Chicago: Ferguson Publishing, 2001. ISBN 0-89434-309-2, hardcover; 0-89434-256-8, CD-ROM. $89.95, 2-volume hardcover or CD-ROM single-user; $199, CD-ROM network.

Description: One of the sections in this directory provides information on funding sources available for education, technology, and research. For more information about the publication, see entry 333 in the "Grants for Individuals—Special Population Groups—Persons with Disabilities" section of this bibliography.

Available from: Ferguson Publishing Company, 200 West Jackson Boulevard, Chicago, IL 60606. *Toll-free:* (800) 306-9941; *Fax:* (800) 306-9942

Web site: www.fergpubco.com

Reentry Students

224

Peterson's Scholarships and Loans for Adult Students

1st ed. Lawrenceville, NJ: Peterson's Guides, 2000. 398p. ISBN 0-7689-0296-7. $19.95. Paper.

Scholarships, Etc.–Special Population Groups–Reentry Students

Description: Peterson's is known for producing excellent directories. But, this is not one of them. Presenting itself as "the only guide to college financing for students 25 and over," this directory provides descriptions of 549 awards, scholarships, fellowships, loans, and other gift aid worth in the aggregate more than $40 million. These entries are grouped into 10 broad categories (association affiliation, impairment, religious affiliation, talent, etc.) and accessed through 24 indexes (12 each for undergraduate and graduate awards, including name index, sponsor index, military service index, and state of residence index). The following information is provided for each program: contact information (including e-mail addresses and web sites), award description, academic/career areas, eligibility requirements, and application requirements. Despite its title and stated purpose, however, few of the entries focus specifically on adult students; many entries are neither age specific (e.g., Rhode Island Advertising Scholarship is open to college sophomores) nor specifically for students over the age of 25 (e.g., American Guild of Organists Regional Competitions for Young Organists is "open to organists under the age of 23" and the Fort Collins Symphony Association's Young Artist Competition is open to competitors "between 12 and 18 years of age."). Worse, hundreds of programs that are actually open only to older students are not covered here.

Available from: Peterson's Guides, Princeton Pike Corporate Center, 2000 Lenox Drive, P.O. Box 67005, Lawrenceville, NJ 08648. *Telephone:* (609) 896-1800; *Toll-free:* (800) 338-3282; *Fax:* (609) 896-4544; *E-mail:* sales@petersons.com
Web site: www.petersons.com

225

Scholarships for Re-entry Students: Grants and Retraining Assistance for Adults Returning to College

Fullerton, CA: WD Communications, 2000. 37p. $14.95. eBook.

Description: From the picture on the web site, this eBook looks substantial, with a lovely colored cover and a hefty spine. How misleading! The guide, when you print it out, is only 37 pages long (at $14.95, that's $.41 per page, plus your paper and ink). There's not much value in the information, either. While the listing is more consistently focused on adult students than *Peterson's Scholarships and Loans for Adult Students* (see entry 224), there are less than 100 portable programs (plus a smattering of random single school-based scholarships) covered here. Even more serious: some of them were discontinued years ago (e.g., Orville Redenbachers Second Start Scholarship, Project Cambrio Scholarship) and others are so restrictive that you have to wonder why they were listed at all (e.g., Zonta Club of Santa Clarita Valley scholarships, George and Gertrude Schiff Charitable Endowment Scholarship Fund for adult students in Kosciusko County, Indiana). None of them are described in any depth. This is a source you can safely skip.

Available from: WD Communications LLC, P.O. Box 2001, Fullerton, CA 92837. *Telephone:* (714) 447-0734; *E-mail:* admin@wd-communications.com

Web site: www.back2college.com

Religious Groups

226

Fellowship Plus

http://www.thefund.org/programs/fellowships
Description: This online database was compiled to help meet the financial needs of theology students (e.g., Episcopal, Presbyterian). For more information about the site, see entry 162 in the "Scholarships, Fellowships & Loans—Humanities—Religion" section of this bibliography.
Available from: Fund for Theological Education, Inc., 825 Houston Mill Road, Suite 250, Atlanta, GA 30329. *Telephone:* (404) 727-1450; *Fax:* (404) 727-1490; *E-mail:* fte@thefund.org
Web site: www.thefund.org

227

Financial Support for Jewish College Students

http://www.thebagel.org/financial_aid/matcher.php
Description: Hillel has compiled this online searchable database of more than 100 awards, loans, scholarships, fellowships, and internships available to Jewish students for study, research, or other activities in the United States or abroad (particularly in Israel). Some of these programs are campus-based; others are portable. You can search for opportunities by type of aid (scholarships, awards, internships), level of study (high school, undergraduate, etc.), geographic origin or destination, special criteria (for example, Sephardic, female, need-based), and areas of study, occupational interest, or personal interest. Or, don't check any of the choices and hit the "Submit Query" button to browse the entire listing. Since there is no indication of posting date, it's impossible to tell how up to date the listing is. The online database replaces an earlier print version, *Hillel/FACETS National Guide to Scholarships, Fellowships, and Financial Support for Jewish Students* (which was also known as *Scholarships, Fellowships, and Financial Support for Jewish Students*).
Available from: Los Angeles Hillel Council, 6505 Wilshire Boulevard, Suite 450, Los Angeles, CA 90048. *Telephone:* (323) 761-8555; *Fax:* (323) 761-8566; *E-mail:* mail@lahillel.org
Web site: www.lahillel.org

Scholarships, Etc.–Special Population Groups–Religious Groups

228

Handbook of United Methodist-Related Schools, Colleges, Universities, and Theological Schools, with a Guide to United Methodist Loans and Scholarships

3rd ed. Nashville: United Methodist Church, 2000. 344p. $5. Paper.

Description: Since its inception, the United Methodist Church has established more than 1,200 schools, colleges, and universities—of which 123 remain today. Nearly 250,000 students are currently enrolled at those schools. This handbook, published last in 2000, provides directory-type and descriptive information on each of these schools. Financial aid is not covered in the school profiles, but a separate section identifies the nearly two dozen national scholarships offered by the United Methodist Church. Since the Church generally does not share information about its programs with the standard financial aid directories, this section is very useful. Most of this information is also available, at no charge, on the Church's web site. Previous editions of the *Handbook* were published in 1992 and 1996.

Available from: United Methodist Church, General Board of Higher Education and Ministry, Division of Higher Education, P.O. Box 3440007, Nashville, TN 37203-0007. *Telephone:* (615) 340-7406; *Fax:* (615) 340-7379

Web site: www.gbhem.org

229

Princeton Theological Seminary Scholarship Guide

http://www.ptsem.edu/open/scholarships

Description: Although this directory of 130 scholarships is aimed at Princeton Theological Seminary students, almost all of the opportunities described here could be used by seminary students at any school. The scholarships are divided into the following categories: Baptist, Episcopal, fellowships, focused areas of study, general scholarships, grants, loans, Methodist, minority, Ph.D., Presbyterian, Reformed Church, regional Roman Catholic, Society of Friends, travel, and United Church of Christ. Some programs are described in more than one category. Descriptions are clearly written and are generally a paragraph in length. Many include links to the sponsor's web site. Specific deadline date is always indicated, but use with care; none of the listings have been updated since April, 2002.

Available from: Princeton Theological Seminary, 64 Mercer Street, P.O. Box 821, Princeton, NJ 08542. *Telephone:* (609) 921-8300

Web site: www.ptsem.edu

Union Members

230 🕸 ¢

Union-Sponsored Scholarships and Aid

http://www.aflcio.org/scholarships/scholar.htm

Description: Unions have an outstanding record of providing assistance to members and their families. Prior to the year 2000, the AFL-CIO described selected union-sponsored funding opportunities in an annual directory, *AFL-CIO Scholarship Guide: A Source for Union Sponsored Scholarships, Awards, and Student Financial Aid.* In 2000, the print version was discontinued, and since then the information has been posted annually on the AFL-CIO web site, in a section called "Help with College Costs." The programs listed there are sponsored by international and national unions, local unions, and AFL-CIO state and local central bodies. They are intended to aid union members, their dependents, and certain nonunion students in their search for financial assistance to cover the cost of attending colleges and other postsecondary institutions. The information presented was obtained from questionnaires, union newspaper articles, and a limited survey of AFL-CIO state federations and other affiliates. There are three ways to look for funding on the site: 1) search for financial aid from a specific national or international union; 2) search for funding from unions in a particular state; and 3) search for other union-related scholarships. In all, more than $4 million in funding is described. It should be noted, however, that these listings just scratch the surface of scholarships offered by many of the 60,000 international, national, regional, state, and local unions. So, fundseekers should be sure to check what unions in their area offer as well. They should do this even if they are not a union member; not all awards require applicants to belong to a union.

Available from: AFL-CIO, 815 16th Street, N.W., Room 209, Washington, DC 20006. *Telephone:* (202) 637-5000; *Toll-free:* (800) 342-1235; *Fax:* (202) 637-5058

Web site: www.aflcio.org

Women

231 🕸 ¢

College Athletic Scholarships Database

http://www.womenssportsfoundation.org

Description: This database identifies women's collegiate sports programs (and sports scholarships) at hundreds of American colleges and universities. For

Scholarships, Etc.–Special Population Groups–Women

more information about the database, see entry 193 in the "Scholarships, Fellowships & Loans—Special Population Groups—Athletes" section of this bibliography.

Available from: Women's Sports Foundation, Eisenhower Park, East Meadow, NY 11554. *Telephone:* (516) 542-4700; *Toll-free:* (800) 227-3988; *Fax:* (516) 542-4716; *E-mail:* wosport@aol.com
    Web site: www.womenssportsfoundation.org

232

Directory of Financial Aids for Women

By Gail Ann Schlachter and R. David Weber. El Dorado Hills, CA: Reference Service Press, 1978- . Biennial. ISSN 0732-5215. ISBN 1-58841-067-6. $45 (2003-2005 ed.). Hardcover.

Description: Billions of dollars in financial aid are set aside for women and women's organizations each year. Some examples: up to $5,000 for high school women athletes to go to college; thousands of dollars for women to study engineering or chemistry, up to $5,000 annually for older women to start or go back to college; $18,000 for women to work on a Ph.D. dissertation, $14,000 per year for women interested in graduate study in the biological sciences, up to $50,000 in venture capital, and $4,000 annually for women who want to major in accounting. Detailed information about these funding opportunities is available in this directory, which has been coming out biennially since 1978. It is divided into three separate sections: a descriptive list of 1,600 scholarships, fellowships, loans, grants, awards, and internships set aside for women, an annotated bibliography of key directories listing general financial aid programs, and a set of indexes that provide access by program title, sponsoring organization, geographic coverage, deadline date, and subject. This is the only comprehensive and regularly updated list of funding opportunities available to women and women's organizations.

Available from: Reference Service Press, 5000 Windplay Drive, Suite 4, El Dorado Hills, CA 95762. *Telephone:* (916) 939-9620; *Fax:* (916) 939-9626; *E-mail:* findaid@aol.com
    Web site: www.rspfunding.com

233

Free College and Training Money for Women

1st ed. By Matthew Lesko and Mary Ann Martello. Kensington, MD: Information USA, 2000. 767p. ISBN 0-878346-52-0. $24.95. Paper.

Description: This is a large book (nearly 800 pages), but only about 300 random programs offering college money are described (a small percentage of the total number of programs available), and many of the listings are not even specifically for women (for example, the Cascade Policy Essay Competition and the American Dietetic Technicians scholarships are available to men and women equally). The rest of the book identifies federal aid, lists (but does not describe) state financial aid programs, lists federal and state job training agencies/programs, and describes career and employment sites on the web. Overall, there is little new here. And, the book promises much more than it delivers. Bottom line: this is more hype than help. For individuals not in college, Lesko, along with Andrew Naprawa and Mary Ann Martello, has written a number of similar publications issued by Information USA, including *Free Money for Your Retirement* (2000. ISBN 1-878346-60-1. $24.95, paperback), *Free Money and Help for Women Entrepreneurs* (2000. ISBN 1-878346-51-2. $31.90, paperback; $24.95, electronic), *Government Giveaways for Entrepreneurs IV* (2000. ISBN 1-878346-59-8. $37.95, paperback), and *Free Money to Change Your Life* in print (2001. ISBN 10878346-40-7. $37.95, paperback), audio ($19.95), or on CD-ROM ($69.95).

Available from: Information USA, Inc., 12079 Nebel Street, Rockville, MD 20852. *Toll-free:* (800) 955-POWER

Web site: www.lesko.com

234

Pathways to Career Success for Women: A Resource Guide to Colleges, Financial Aid, and Work

Ed. by Laurie Sabol. Chicago: Ferguson, 2000. 368p. ISBN 0-89434-281-9. $29.95. Paper.

Description: This directory offers tools "to help women get started or take their career to the next level." The first section in the directory, "Financial Aid," lists and briefly describes a random selection of 300+ scholarships, fellowships, grants, awards, and loans set aside for women (for more complete coverage of women's funding opportunities, see the *Directory of Financial Aids for Women,* described in entry 232). Some of the programs are open to women in Canada or other foreign countries, but most focus on opportunities for American women. Not all programs covered in *Pathways* provide monetary stipends. Further, financial aid that requires membership in an organization is not listed (although membership-based financial aid is referred to generally in the section on "Professional Organizations"). Another, smaller section in the directory briefly describes internships either available to women or offered by women's organizations. Although not organized in quite the same way, this directory supercedes Ferguson's *Big Book of Opportunities for Women: The Directory of Women's Organizations,* which was last published in 1997.

Available from: Ferguson Publishing Company, 200 West Jackson Boulevard, Chicago, IL 60606. *Toll-free:* (800) 306-9941; *Fax:* (800) 306-9942

Web site: www.fergpubco.com

Grants for Individuals

Grants for individuals provide funds to support research, innovative efforts, travel, or projects (some of which may be educational in nature). Many are restricted by geographic location, purpose of the proposed program, or type of applicant. Described in this section of the guide are 102 print, electronic, and Internet resources listing grants available to individuals on the international, national, and/or state levels. Of these directories, 33 are general in their subject coverage, 11 focus on grants in the social sciences, 27 cover the humanities, 16 deal with the sciences, and 15 are aimed at special population groups. If you are looking for a specific grants source and you do not find it in this chapter, be sure to check the Title Index to see if it is covered elsewhere in the guide.

GENERAL
United States

235

Annual Register of Grant Support: A Directory of Funding Sources

Medford, NJ: Information Today, 1969- . Annual. ISSN 0066-4049. ISBN 1-57387-145-1. $229 (2003 ed.). Hardcover.

Description: More than 3,500 programs (representing $130 billion in aid) sponsored by government agencies, private foundations, corporations, unions, church groups, and educational and professional associations are described in the latest edition of this directory. Although it focuses on North American programs, the *Annual Register* also describes a number of opportunities offered abroad. The programs included provide grant and other types of support in 11 different categories, including the humanities, international affairs, race and minority concerns, education, environmental and urban affairs, social sciences, physical sciences, life sciences, technology, and other areas. Each entry contains the following information: organization name; address and telephone number; major field(s) of organizational interest; name(s) of grant program(s); purpose; nature of support available; amount of support per award; number of applicants and recipients for the most recent years; legal basis for program; eligibility requirements; application instructions; and deadline. The work is indexed by subject, sponsor, geographic requirements, and personnel. Over the years, the publisher of this directory has changed (from Academic Media, to National Register, to R.R. Bowker, to Information Today).

Available from: Information Today, Inc., 143 Old Marlton Pike, Medford, NJ 08055-8750. *Telephone:* (609) 654-6266; *Fax:* (609) 654-4309; *E-mail:* custserv@infotoday.com

Web site: www.infotoday.com

236

Catalog of Federal Domestic Assistance

Prep. by the U.S. General Services Administration. Washington, DC: G.P.O., 1965- . Annual. ISSN 0097-7799. $63 (2002 ed.), looseleaf; $85, CD-ROM; online, free.

Description: Nearly 1,500 domestic assistance programs and activities administered by 60 different federal agencies and departments are described in this annual publication, including grants, loans, loan guarantees, and shared revenue programs. For more information about the publication, see entry 339 in the "Grants for Organizations—General—United States" section of this bibliography.

How to Find Out About Financial Aid and Funding

Available from: U.S. Government Printing Office, Superintendent of Documents, P.O. Box 371954, Pittsburgh, PA 15250-7954. *Telephone:* (202) 512-1800, press 1; *Toll-free:* (800) 669-8331; *Fax:* (202) 512-2250; *E-mail:* gpoaccess@gpo.gov
Web site: www.access.gpo.gov/su_docs

237

COS Funding Opportunities

http://www.cos.com

Description: Community of Science (COS) was founded in 1989 by The Johns Hopkins University. It is a collaborative network of scientists, scholars, and their institutions. Its purpose is to "promote the visibility and funding of scientific and scholarly research." The heart of this service is COS Funding Opportunities, a web-based subscription database ($500 to $1,500/yr.) that is updated daily and contains descriptions of more than 23,000 funding opportunities from around the world, worth more than $33 billion and sponsored by federal and regional governments, foundations, professional societies, associations, and corporations. These funds support research, collaborative activities, travel, curriculum development, conferences, training, postdoctoral positions, equipment acquisition, and operating or capital expenses. Excluded are loans, refinancing, and employment opportunities, as well as single school-based aid. Records in the database contain the following information: contact, summary, deadline, amount, eligibility, keywords, activity location, citizenship requirements, funding type, and sponsor type. Although the title of the database indicates a scientific focus, the scope is actually wider than that; there are programs in the database that support the arts, humanities, cultural activities, education, law, management, and commerce. The database can be searched in several ways: keyword, country, sponsor, deadline, and free text. Subscribers are also entitled to receive COS Funding Alert, which is a weekly e-mail update service. There are no print equivalents to these two services. Nonsubscribers may sign up at the web site for the COS Funding News, a free weekly update sent electronically that lists the highlights of COS funding opportunities.

Available from: Community of Science, Inc., 1629 Thames Street, Suite 200, Baltimore, MD 21231. *Telephone:* (410) 563-2378; *Fax:* (410) 563-5389; *E-mail:* evd@cos.com
Web site: www.cos.com

238

Directory of Research Grants

Westport, CT: Oryx, 1975- . Annual. ISSN 0146-7336. ISBN 1-57356-570-9. $134.95 (2003 ed.). Paper.

Grants for Individuals–General–United States

Description: For more than two decades, Oryx Press's *Directory of Research Grants* has provided current information on research-related grants, fellowships, scholarships, loans, conferences, and internships in medicine, physical sciences, social sciences, the arts, humanities, and education. The emphasis is on U.S. and Canadian programs, although some sponsored by other countries are also included. In the latest edition, nearly 6,000 funding opportunities are described; information is provided on purpose, eligibility requirements, restrictions, funding amount, application or renewal date, contact, and sponsor. The entries are arranged by program title and indexed by subject and sponsoring organization. Although the *Annual Register of Grant Support* (see entry 235) is broader in scope—and more expensive—the *Directory of Research Grants* provides better coverage of academic, public, and private sources. The information presented here is also included in Oryx Press's GrantSelect database (see entry 247) and in several derivative publications: e.g., *Directory of Grants in the Humanities* and *Directory of Biomedical and Health Care Grants* (see entries 280 and 313). Oryx Press is now an imprint of Greenwood.

Available from: Oryx Press, 88 Post Road West, Westport, CT 06881. *Telephone:* (602) 265-2651; *Toll-free:* (800) 279-6799; *Fax:* (800) 279-4663; *E-mail:* info@oryxpress.com

Web site: www.oryxpress.com

239

Federal Register

Prep. by the U.S. Office of the Federal Register. Washington, DC: G.P.O., 1936- . Daily (Monday through Friday, except legal holidays). $674/yr., paper; $264/yr., microfiche.

Description: This is an excellent place to check for the latest information (including deadline date) on federally funded programs. For more information about the publication, see entry 357 in the "Grants for Organizations—General—United States" section of this bibliography.

Available from: U.S. Government Printing Office, Superintendent of Documents, P.O. Box 371954, Pittsburgh, PA 15250-7954. *Telephone:* (202) 512-1800, press 1; *Fax:* (202) 512-2250; *E-mail:* gpoaccess@gpo.gov

Web site: www.access.gpo.gov/su_docs

240

FEDIX Opportunity Alert

http://www.sciencewise.com

Description: FEDIX, a free service offered by ScienceWise (see entry 217), was formerly known first as Federal Information Exchange & Research and Management Systems (FIE-RAMS) and later as Federal Information Exchange (FEDIX). Listed on this site were funding opportunities for research and education organizations sponsored by seven federal agencies: Department of Defense, Air Force Office of Scientific Research, Agency for International Development, Department of Agriculture, National Aeronautics & Space Administration, National Institutes of Health, and Department of Transportation. These listings were taken primarily from FedBizOpps (see entry 467) and the *Federal Register* (entry 357). Users could also subscribe ($99/yr.) to ScienceWise's *fundingA-LERT,* which was a personalized e-mail service that delivered information about targeted research and education funding opportunities from these agencies. However, in mid-2002, ScienceWise's operations were suspended. Although the web site promised that "the combination of free and paid-for services" would resume as of December, 2002, the site was still not operating in April of 2003 and e-mails sent to the posted contact were returned as undeliverable.

Available from: ScienceWise, 300 Professional Drive, Suite 200, Gaithersburg, MD 20879-3419. *Telephone:* (301) 975-0103; *Fax:* (301) 975-0109

Web site: www.sciencewise.com

241

For the People: 1,608 Ways to Get Your Share of the Little-Known Bargains the Government Offers

Ed. by Kevin Ireland. Emmaus, PA: Rodale, 2000. 480p. ISBN 1-57954-296-4. $19.95. Paper.

Description: Similar but somewhat better than Matthew Lesko's "government giveaway" books (see entry 233), *For the People* identifies ways you can get money and help from the government: to buy a home, pay for college, start a business, get a government job, run for office, etc. Grants, loans, and assistance programs offered by federal and state sources are described. The directory provides addresses, phone numbers, web sites, and information about various resources and agencies. Appendices cover benefits for residents of individual states, tax advantages for retirees, support for college tuition, costs and incentives for small businesses, and consumer taxes.

Available from: Rodale, Inc., 33 East Minor Street, Emmaus, PA 18098-0099. *Telephone:* (610) 967-5171; *Fax:* (610) 967-8963

Web site: www.rodale.com

242

The Foundation Center's Guide to Grantseeking on the Web

2nd ed. Ed. by Kief Schladweiler. New York: Foundation Center, 2001. 764p. ISBN 0-87954-966-1, paper; 0-87954-967-X, CD-ROM. $29.95, paper or CD-ROM.

Description: This excellent guide will be useful to both individuals and organizations interested in searching for grants on the web. For more information about the publication, see entry 358 in the "Grants for Organizations—General—United States" section of this bibliography.

Available from: Foundation Center, 79 Fifth Avenue, New York, NY 10003-3076. *Telephone:* (212) 807-3690; *Toll-free:* (800) 424-9836; *Fax:* (212) 807-3691

Web site: fdncenter.org

243

Foundation Grants to Individuals

12th ed. New York: Foundation Center, 2001. 1,117p. ISBN 0-87954-948-3, paper; 0-87954-997-1, CD-ROM. $65, paper; $75, CD-ROM; $9.95/month, online.

Description: This is the only national publication devoted entirely to foundation grant opportunities (including some scholarships and loans) for individual applicants. The current biennial print edition (over 1,000 pages) provides full descriptions of more than 4,300 foundations annually making grants of at least $2,000 to individuals. Approximately 250 foundations appear in this edition for the first time. All information from the earlier editions has been fully revised: addresses, program descriptions, interview and deadline requirements, and financial data. The work is organized by type of grant awarded (e.g., scholarships, general welfare, awards and prizes), subdivided by eligibility requirements and means of access (including "Grants to Foreign Individuals" and "Grants to Employees of Specific Companies"). Multiple avenues of access are provided through the following indexes: subject, geographic restrictions, educational institutions, company-related grants, type of support, and foundations. In addition to foundation listings, there are articles on approaching foundations and a bibliography of information sources for individuals. Collectively, the grants described in this directory total more than $100 million each year. Even so, financial aid seekers may find this directory to be of limited utility; most of the programs sponsored by foundations for individuals are extremely restrictive and will relate to only small segments of the population. Since 1999, the information in this source has also been available on CD-ROM (originally called *FC Scholar: The Foundation Center's Database of Education Funding for Individuals),* which allows users to select multiple criteria and generate lists of potential funders using nine different search fields: grantmaker name, grantmaker state, grantmaker city, geographic focus, types of support, fields of interest, school name, company name, and text search. An online, searchable database of 5,000+ foundations that award grants to individuals became available in 2003; the database is updated quarterly, provides links to 500 foundation web sites, and can be subscribed to on a monthly basis ($9.95/month); users can search the database by foundation name, foundation state, foundation city, geographic focus, field of interest, type of support, company name, school name, and full text.

Available from: Foundation Center, 79 Fifth Avenue, New York, NY 10003-3076. *Telephone:* (212) 807-3690; *Toll-free:* (800) 424-9836; *Fax:* (212) 807-3691

Web site: fdncenter.org

244

Fundsnet

http://www.fundsnetservices.com

Description: On the Internet since 1996, this information-rich but difficult to navigate site provides information and links to grants for individuals as well as grants for organizations and scholarships for students. For more information on the site, see entry 367 in the "Grants for Organizations—General—United States" section of this bibliography.

Available from: Fundsnet Online Services, 419 Immaculada Street, San Juan, PR 00915. *E-mail:* info@fundsnetservices.com

Web site: www.fundsnetservices.com

245

Getting Money for Graduate School: More than 1,000 Scholarships, Grants, Prizes, Forgivable Loans, and Fellowships

1st ed. Lawrenceville, NJ: Peterson's Guides, 2002. 404p. ISBN 0-7689-1294-6. $16.95. Paper.

Description: Described here are 1,100 grants, prizes, forgivable loans, and fellowships, not all of which are open to graduate students (despite the title). For more information about the publication, see entry 39 in the "Scholarships, Fellowships & Loans—General—United States" section of this bibliography.

Available from: Peterson's Guides, Princeton Pike Corporate Center, 2000 Lenox Drive, P.O. Box 67005, Lawrenceville, NJ 08648. *Telephone:* (609) 896-1800; *Toll-free:* (800) 338-3282; *Fax:* (609) 896-4544; *E-mail:* sales@petersons.com

Web site: www.petersons.com

246

The Grants Register: The Complete Guide to Postgraduate Funding Worldwide

Ed. by Sara Hackwood. New York: Palgrave, 1969- . Annual. ISSN 0072-5471. ISBN 0-333-96474-8. $185 (2003 ed.). Hardcover.

Grants for Individuals–General–United States

Description: This annual directory describes grants, fellowships, and prizes open to nationals of the United States, Canada, the United Kingdom, Ireland, Australia, New Zealand, South Africa, and the developing countries. For more information about the publication, see entry 265 in the "Grants for Individuals—General—International" section of this bibliography.
Available from: Palgrave, 175 Fifth Avenue, New York, NY 10010. *Telephone:* (212) 982-3900; *Toll-free:* (800) 221-7945; *Fax:* (212) 777-6359
Web site: www.palgrave-usa.com

247

GrantSelect

http://www.grantselect.com
Description: Updated daily, the GrantSelect database provides information on more than 10,000 funding programs (representing more than $7 billion) offered by 4,000 nonprofit organizations, foundations, private sector sources, and government agencies located in the United States and Canada (and some foreign countries as well). These programs are open to both individuals and organizations and represent all areas of research, with a special emphasis placed on corporate and foundation sponsors as well as federal and state programs. The database can be searched by type, subject, geographic area, sponsor, population groups, and more. The subscription price for the full database is $1,000 per year. Or, for $350 each per year, subscriptions are available for the following database segments: Biomedical & Health Care Grants, Grants in the Arts & Humanities, Community & Economic Development Grants, Grants for Children & Youth Program, Grants for K-12 Schools & Adult Basic Education, International Programs, and Operating Grants for Nonprofit Organizations. For less expensive—but less up-to-date—print versions of many of these segments, see entries 280, 313, 382, 468, and 473. A useful feature of GrantSelect is an e-mail alert subscription option, which notifies subscribers immediately of any new funding opportunities within their area of interest; the subscription price for the e-mail alert is $1,000 per year, $1,500 for a subscription to the e-mail alert and the full database, and $500 for a subscription to the e-mail alert and any one of the database segments. The GrantSelect database is also used to generate Oryx Press's comprehensive annual print directory: *Directory of Research Grants* (see entry 238). In the past, GrantSelect was distributed in CD-ROM, electronic, and online versions under the title GRANTS Database.
Available from: Oryx Press, 88 Post Road West, Westport, CT 06881. *Telephone:* (602) 265-2651; *Toll-free:* (800) 279-6799; *Fax:* (800) 279-4663; *E-mail:* info@oryxpress.com
Web site: www.oryxpress.com

How to Find Out About Financial Aid and Funding

248 🕸 ¢

GrantsInfo.com: Student Funding Sources

http://www.arisnet.com/newstu.html
Description: This site provides both undergraduate and graduate students with information on grants, scholarships, fellowships, awards, and internships in the arts and sciences, including creative arts, humanities, social sciences, natural sciences, and biomedical sciences. For more information about the site, see entry 44 in the "Scholarships, Fellowships & Loans—General—United States" section of this bibliography.
Available from: Academic Research Information System, Inc., 2940 16th Street, Suite 314, San Francisco, CA 94103. *Telephone:* (415) 558-8133; *Fax:* (415) 558-8135; *E-mail:* arisnet@dnai.com
Web site: www.arisnet.com

249 🕸

IRIS (Illinois Researcher Information Service)

Urbana: Illinois Researcher Information Service (IRIS). Updated daily. Annual Internet subscription fees range from $400 (for institutions with fewer than 3,000 students and faculty) to $2,000 (for institutions with more than 15,000 students and faculty or more than $50 million annual research volume).
Description: The Illinois Researcher Information Service (IRIS) is a unit of the University of Illinois Library at Urbana-Champaign. Since 1979, the IRIS office has compiled the IRIS database of funding opportunities, which currently contains descriptions of nearly 8,000 federal and non-federal funding programs in the sciences, social sciences, arts, and humanities. Users can search IRIS by sponsor, deadline date, keyword, and other criteria. Most IRIS records link directly to sponsor web sites. While the funding programs described in the IRIS database are aimed at researchers, scholars, faculty, and graduate students, subscriptions to the service are not available to individuals. Only colleges and universities can subscribe. The database, which is updated daily, is searchable by subject, type of support, population group, sponsor type, citizenship, application deadlines, and more. In addition to the IRIS database, the IRIS office also maintains the IRIS Alert Service, which allows users at subscribing institutions to create personal IRIS search profiles and receive funding updates automatically. There is no print equivalent for either of these services.
Available from: Illinois Researcher Information Service (IRIS), University of Illinois at Urbana-Champaign, 128 Observatory, 901 South Mathews Avenue, Urbana, IL 61801. *Telephone:* (217) 333-0284; *Fax:* (217) 333-7811; *E-mail:* a-trehub@uiuc.edu
Web site: www.library.uiuc.edu/iris

Grants for Individuals–General–United States

250

RSP Funding for Graduate Students

El Dorado Hills, CA: Reference Service Press (dist. by Ovid), 1996- . Annual, with semi-annual update. $695 and up. CD-ROM, disk, or online.

Description: *RSP Funding for Graduate Students* contains up-to-date information on more than 4,000 grants, awards, fellowships, loans, loan forgiveness programs, and loan repayment programs open to students entering, continuing, or returning to graduate school. For more information about the product, see entry 59 in the "Scholarships, Fellowships & Loans—General—United States" section of this bibliography.

Available from: Ovid Technologies, 100 River Ridge Drive, Norwood, MA 02062. *Telephone:* (781) 769-2599; *Toll-free:* (800) 343-0064; *Fax:* (781) 769-8763

Web site: www.ovid.com

251

RSP Funding for Postdoctorates and Professionals

El Dorado Hills, CA: Reference Service Press (dist. by Ovid), 1996- . Annual, with semi-annual update. $695 and up. CD-ROM, disk, or online.

Description: Updated every six months and available on subscription from Ovid (formerly SilverPlatter), *RSP Funding for Postdoctorates and Professionals* contains current information on more than 5,000 funding programs available to postdoctorates and professionals (e.g., architects, artists, engineers, librarians, nurses, lawyers, school teachers, writers) for research, study, training, creative activities, conference attendance, travel, etc. This provides more comprehensive coverage for professionals and postdoctorates than any other RSP product. The database identifies all types of aid: grants, awards, residencies, and more. The detailed program descriptions specify purpose, eligibility, financial data, duration, special features, limitations, number award, deadline date, heritage, special skills, professional or social affiliations, and many other applicant requirements, including gender, ethnicity, and residency. Using Ovid's powerful search protocol, the data can be accessed by program title, sponsoring organizations, residency requirements, tenability, award amount, deadlines, keyword, and dozens of other ways. The database is available on the following platforms: Windows CD-ROM or hard disk, Macintosh CD-ROM or hard disk, UNIX, and the Internet.

Available from: Ovid Technologies, 100 River Ridge Drive, Norwood, MA 02062. *Telephone:* (781) 769-2599; *Toll-free:* (800) 343-0064; *Fax:* (781) 769-8763

Web site: www.ovid.com

252

SPIN (Sponsored Programs Information Network)

Guilderland, NY: InfoEd. Updated daily. Annual Internet subscription fees vary.

Description: SPIN (Sponsored Programs Information Network) is a subscription database that consists of information from 1,200 different sponsoring agencies around the world (unlike IRIS, described in entry 249, which focuses on the United States). Together, these agencies offer more than 10,000 separate funding opportunities, including fellowships, travel grants, research grants, curriculum development grants, sabbatical support, publication support, international projects, collaborative programs, academic exchange programs, and more. Information can be accessed by applicant type, recipient type, geographic restrictions, sponsor name, sponsor type, and deadlines. The funding opportunity profiles on SPIN are quite detailed and provide information on contact person, address, telephone, deadline dates, program title, *Catalog of Federal Domestic Assistance* number (for U.S. programs), purpose, eligibility requirements, award amounts, duration, allowable costs, indirect costs, policies, and application procedures. SPIN subscribers are also offered SMARTS (SPIN Matching and Researcher Transmittal System), a daily notification system that provides investigators with a direct and targeted electronic link to funding programs that match their profile. There is no print equivalent for either of these services.

Available from: InfoEd International, Inc., 1873 Western Avenue, Suite 201, Albany, NY 12203. *Telephone:* (518) 464-0691; *Toll-free:* (800) 727-6427; *Fax:* (518) 464-0695; *E-mail:* office@infoed.org

Web site: www.infoed.org

253

Yale Daily News Guide to Fellowships and Grants

2nd ed. By Gail Schlachter, R. David Weber, and the Staff of Reference Service Press. New York: Kaplan/Simon & Schuster, 1999. 482p. ISBN 0-684-86281-6. $25. Paper.

Description: Approximately 2,000 grants and fellowships open to graduate students in any field are described in detail in the second edition of this directory. For more information about the publication, see entry 78 in the "Scholarships, Fellowships & Loans—General—United States" section of this bibliography.

Available from: Simon & Schuster, Attn: Order Department, 100 Front Street, Riverside, NJ 08075. *Toll-free:* (800) 223-2336; *Fax:* (800) 445-6991

Web site: www.simonsays.com

Hawaii

254

Directory of Charitable Trusts and Foundations: A Guide for Hawai'i's Nonprofit Organizations

Comp. by Alberta Freidus-Flagg. Honolulu: Helping Hands Hawai'i, 1999. 227p. $30. Spiral bound.

Description: The latest edition of this directory provides information on local trusts and foundations that give grants to individuals and organizations in Hawaii. For more information about the publication, see entry 398 in the "Grants for Organizations—General—Hawaii" section of this bibliography.

Available from: Helping Hands Hawai'i, 2100 North Nimitz Highway, Honolulu, HI 96819. *Telephone:* (808) 536-7234; *Fax:* (808) 536-7235

Web site: www.helpinghandshawaii.org

Maryland

255

The Red Book: Catalog of State Assistance Programs

http://www.mdp.state.md.us/clhouse/redbook/redbook.html

Description: Annually, the Maryland Department of Planning collects information from 70 state agencies on grants, loans, federal funds passed through state agencies, direct and indirect subsidies, and nonfinancial assistance offered (e.g., technical, regulatory, or advisory information). This information, the most comprehensive available about state assistance programs in Maryland, is then posted on the Department's web site, as the Red Book, which can be searched by subject or by agency. The following information is given for each entry: official name, contact, purpose and use of the assistance, eligible applicants, application procedures and deadlines, matching requirements, amount and number of awards, source of funds, type of funds, and *Catalog of Federal Domestic Assistance* (CFDA) number. Links are provided to the agencies' web sites. Until 1996, the *Red Book* was issued in print and cost $75; since then, annual revisions of the listing have been available at no charge, but only online. Also available at this site is the Maryland Grants Searchable Database, where a general search by keyword or CFDA number can be performed simultaneously on the Red Book and the following online databases: the Catalog of Federal Domestic Assistance (see entry 339), the State Attorney General's Records of Private Foundations (see entry 411), and FAADS (the Federal Awards Assistance Data System).

Available from: Maryland Department of Planning, 301 West Preston Street, Room 1101, Baltimore, MD 21201-2365. *Telephone:* (410) 767-4500; *Toll-free:* (877) 767-6272; *Fax:* (410) 767-4480; *E-mail:* dczerwinski@mdp.state.md.us
Web site: www.op.state.md.us

Massachusetts

256

Massachusetts Grantmakers Directory

Boston: Associated Grantmakers of Massachusetts, 1999. 339p. ISSN 0898-7025. ISBN 0-912427-06-X. $50. Paper.

Description: Nearly 500 foundations making grants to individuals or organizations in Massachusetts are covered in this directory. For more information about the publication, see entry 415 in the "Grants for Organizations—General—Massachusetts" section of this bibliography.

Available from: Associated Grantmakers of Massachusetts, 55 Court Street, Suite 520, Boston, MA 02108. *Telephone:* (617) 426-2606; *Fax:* (617) 426-2849; *E-mail:* agm@agmconnect.org
Web site: www.agmconnect.org

New Hampshire

257

Directory of Charitable Funds in New Hampshire

http://www.state.nh.us/nhdoj/CHARITABLE/char.html

Description: Previously issued in print, this directory is now available only as a .pdf file on the New Hampshire Department of Justice's web site. The current edition (2002) is not searchable, but there are plans to make the online directory "more user friendly in future updates." As in the previous edition, the current version indexes all the charitable funds in New Hampshire registered with the state's Attorney General that provide scholarship assistance or make grants to residents and organizations in New Hampshire. For the purposes of the directory, "charitable purposes" are defined as "the aid of the needy, the relief of sickness and adversity, the advancement of education and religion, specialized programs which are of benefit to the general public and the community and individual scholarship aid." Omitted are trusts that fund specific charitable organizations and operating charities that use their funds to provide services directly to the public. The 400 entries are arranged alphabetically by sponsoring

Grants for Individuals–General–Ohio

organization and indexed by geographic restrictions and subject interests. Each entry specifies sponsoring organization, founding date, purposes, assets, contact person, and address.

Available from: New Hampshire Department of Justice, Attn: Charitable Trusts Unit, 33 Capitol Street, Concord, NH 03301-6397. *Telephone:* (603) 271-3658; *Fax:* (603) 271-2110; *TDD:* (800) 735-2964

Web site: www.state.nh.us/nhdoj/CHARITABLE/char.html

Ohio

258

Charitable Foundations Directory of Ohio

Columbus, OH: Office of the Attorney General, 1973- . Biennial. $7.50 (13th ed.). Paper.

Description: Prepared by the Ohio State Attorney General's Office, this biennial directory is intended to benefit individuals and organizations seeking grants and other types of assistance from charitable foundations in Ohio. For more information about the publication, see entry 433 in the "Grants for Organizations—General—Ohio" section of this bibliography.

Available from: Ohio Attorney General's Office, Attn: Charitable Law Section, 101 East Town Street, 4th Floor, Columbus, OH 43215-5148. *Telephone:* (614) 466-3180; *Fax:* (614) 466-9788

Web site: www.ag.state.oh.us

International

259

Annual Register of Grant Support: A Directory of Funding Sources

Medford, NJ: Information Today, 1969- . Annual. ISSN 0066-4049. ISBN 1-57387-145-1. $229 (2003 ed.). Hardcover.

Description: Although it focuses on North American programs, the *Annual Register* also describes a number of grants for individuals available abroad. For more information about the publication, see entry 235 in the "Grants for Individuals—General—United States" section of this bibliography.

Available from: Information Today, Inc., 143 Old Marlton Pike, Medford, NJ 08055-8750. *Telephone:* (609) 654-6266; *Fax:* (609) 654-4309; *E-mail:* custserv@infotoday.com

Web site: www.infotoday.com

260

COS Funding Opportunities

http://www.cos.com

Description: COS Funding Opportunities is a web-based subscription database that is updated daily and contains descriptions of more than 23,000 funding opportunities from around the world that support research, collaborative activities, travel, training, curriculum development, conferences, postdoctoral positions, equipment acquisition, and operating or capital expenses. For more information about the database, see entry 237 in the "Grants for Individuals—General—United States" section of this bibliography.

Available from: Community of Science, Inc., 1629 Thames Street, Suite 200, Baltimore, MD 21231. *Telephone:* (410) 563-2378; *Fax:* (410) 563-5389; *E-mail:* evd@cos.com
Web site: www.cos.com

261

Directory of Research Grants

Westport, CT: Oryx, 1975- . Annual. ISSN 0146-7336. ISBN 1-57356-570-9. $134.95 (2003 ed.). Paper.

Description: Although the emphasis is on U.S. and Canadian programs, some grants, scholarships, fellowships, and loans sponsored by other countries are also included in this directory. For more information about the publication, see entry 238 in the "Grants for Individuals—General—United States" section of this bibliography.

Available from: Oryx Press, 88 Post Road West, Westport, CT 06881. *Telephone:* (602) 265-2651; *Toll-free:* (800) 279-6799; *Fax:* (800) 279-4663; *E-mail:* info@oryxpress.com
Web site: www.oryxpress.com

262

Financial Aid for Research and Creative Activities Abroad

By Gail Ann Schlachter and R. David Weber. El Dorado Hills, CA: Reference Service Press, 1992- . Biennial. ISBN 1-58841-062-5. $45 (2002-2004 ed.). Paper.

Description: This directory will help Americans tap into the billions of dollars available for research, lectureships, exchange programs, work assignments, conference attendance, professional development, and creative projects (e.g., writing, artistic work) abroad. The listings cover every major subject area, are tenable in practically every country and region of the world (from the Aegean

Grants for Individuals–General–International

Islands to Zimbabwe), are sponsored by more than 500 different private and public agencies and organizations, and are open to all segments of the population—from high school students through postdoctorates and professionals. Entries specify purpose, eligibility, amount awarded, duration, special features, limitations, number awarded, and deadline date. Indexing is by title, sponsoring organization, geographic coverage, subject coverage, and deadline date. First issued (in 1990) as part of *Financial Aid for Research, Study, Travel, and Other Activities Abroad,* the directory assumed its current title and focus in 1992.

Available from: Reference Service Press, 5000 Windplay Drive, Suite 4, El Dorado Hills, CA 95762. *Telephone:* (916) 939-9620; *Fax:* (916) 939-9626; *E-mail:* findaid@aol.com
Web site: www.rspfunding.com

263

Fulbright and Related Grants for Graduate Study and Research Abroad

New York: Institute of International Education. Annual. Free (2003-2004 ed.). Paper or online.

Description: The Fulbright student program is designed to give recent B.S./B.A. graduates, master's degree and doctoral candidates, young professionals, and artists opportunities for personal development and international experience. This 100-page pamphlet, available annually without charge from the Institute of International Education, lists Institute-administered Fulbright and other fellowships and grants available to U.S. graduate students for study and research abroad. The arrangement is by country in which the recipient will study or conduct research. Entries specify recommended fields of study or investigation, language requirements, duration, selection procedures, financial data, application process, special features, and limitations. Much of this information is also available at the Institute's web site. Previously, this publication was issued as *Fulbright and Other Grants for Graduate Study Abroad* and *U.S. Student Fulbright Grants & Other Grants for Graduate Study and Research Abroad.* A similar publication for more advanced scholars is *Fulbright Scholar Program* (see entry 264).

Available from: Institute of International Education, 809 United Nations Plaza, New York, NY 10017-3580. *Telephone:* (212) 883-8200; *Toll-free:* (800) 445-0443; *Fax:* (212) 984-5452; *E-mail:* iiebooks@iie.org
Web site: www.iie.org/fulbright

264

Fulbright Scholar Program: Grants for Faculty and Professionals

Washington, DC: Council for International Exchange of Scholars, 1994- . Annual. Free (2003-2004 ed.). Paper or online.

Description: Issued as a complement to *Fulbright and Related Grants for Graduate Study and Research Abroad* (see entry 263), this free 184-page pamphlet from the Council for International Exchange of Scholars identifies Fulbright grants and fellowships for university lecturing and advanced research abroad. The programs covered are open to U.S. citizens who are recent Ph.D.s, advanced Ph.D. candidates, and teachers of English. Entries are arranged by world area and indexed by discipline. Also included are a stipend and benefits table as well as a professional index that identifies opportunities specifically targeted for professionals outside academe. This information is also available on the Council for International Exchange of Scholars' web site. In prior years, this pamphlet was published under the titles *Fulbright Lecturing and Research Abroad, Fulbright Awards Abroad,* and *Fulbright Senior Scholars Awards Abroad.* Information on the Fulbright Teacher Exchange Program is available in a separate, free pamphlet from the USIA (600 Maryland Avenue, S.W., Room 140, Washington, DC 20024-2520).

Available from: Council for International Exchange of Scholars, 3007 Tilden Street, N.W., Suite 5L, Washington, DC 20008-3009. *Telephone:* (202) 686-4000; *Fax:* (202) 362-3442; *E-mail:* scholars@cies.iie.org

Web site: www.iie.org/cies

265

The Grants Register: The Complete Guide to Postgraduate Funding Worldwide

Ed. by Sara Hackwood. New York: Palgrave, 1969- . Annual. ISSN 0072-5471. ISBN 0-333-96474-8. $185 (2003 ed.). Hardcover.

Description: Despite its title, this directory is not restricted just to grants; it also includes fellowships, exchanges, grants-in-aid, competitions, prizes, and other awards (including awards for refugees, war veterans, minority groups, and students in unexpected financial difficulties). Originally published as a biennial (until the 15th edition, 1995-1997) and now issued every year, the *Grants Register* provides up-to-date information on 3,500 awards (from more than 60 countries) sponsored by government agencies, international agencies, national organizations, and private agencies. Emphasis is on awards for nationals of the United States, Canada, the United Kingdom, Ireland, Australia, New Zealand, South Africa, and the developing countries. The programs included are open to graduate students, young professionals, academics, scholars, vocational trainees, the disabled, etc. The following information is provided for each program: remuneration, eligibility, deadline, application procedures, subject areas cov-

Grants for Individuals–General–International

ered, purpose, number offered, where tenable, awarding organizations, and address for application and/or further information. The *Register* is divided into five sections: a subject and eligibility guide, the grants register, an index of awards, an index of awarding bodies, and an index of discontinued awards. Previously, the directory was published by St. Martin's Press (Palgrave is now an imprint of St. Martin's). While the directory complements the information included in other standard grants directories (e.g., *Annual Register of Grant Support* and the *Directory of Research Grants* (see entries 235 and 238), it is not the "complete guide" promised by its subtitle. Some of the content in *The Grants Register* is extracted and published in several *GrantFinder* publications, which focus on medicine, (see entry 315), the arts and humanities (entry 281), the social sciences (entry 269), and the sciences (entry 306).

Available from: Palgrave, 175 Fifth Avenue, New York, NY 10010. *Telephone:* (212) 982-3900; *Toll-free:* (800) 221-7945; *Fax:* (212) 777-6359

Web site: www.palgrave-usa.com

266

GrantSelect

http://www.grantselect.com

Description: Updated daily and used to generate Oryx Press's print funding directories, GrantSelect identifies more than 10,000 grants and other funding opportunities for individuals and organizations sponsored by organizations and agencies in the United States and Canada (some of which can be used abroad). For more information about the database, see entry 247 in the "Grants for Individuals—General—United States" section of this bibliography.

Available from: Oryx Press, 88 Post Road West, Westport, CT 06881. *Telephone:* (602) 265-2651; *Toll-free:* (800) 279-6799; *Fax:* (800) 279-4663; *E-mail:* info@oryxpress.com

Web site: www.oryxpress.com

267

SPIN (Sponsored Programs Information Network)

Guilderland, NY: InfoEd. Updated daily. Annual Internet subscription fees vary.

Description: SPIN (Sponsored Programs Information Network) is a subscription database that consists of information from 1,200 different sponsoring agencies around the world; together, these agencies offer more than 10,000 separate funding opportunities, including travel grants, research grants, curriculum development grants, sabbatical support, publication support, international projects, collaborative programs, academic exchange programs, and fellowships. For more information about the service, see entry 252 in the "Grants for Individuals—General—United States" section of this bibliography.

Available from: InfoEd International, Inc., 1873 Western Avenue, Suite 201, Albany, NY 12203. *Telephone:* (518) 464-0691; *Toll-free:* (800) 727-6427; *Fax:* (518) 464-0695; *E-mail:* office@infoed.org
 Web site: www.infoed.org

SOCIAL SCIENCES
General

268

FundSource

http://www.decadeofbehavior.org/fundsource
Description: FundSource was initiated by the National Science Foundation and developed by the American Psychological Association as a service to the "Decade of Behavior." This site is designed to help behavioral and social scientists who are interested in finding research funding. There is no charge to search the database, which provides short descriptions, contact information, and web links to research funding in the behavioral and social sciences offered by federal agencies, foundations, and international organizations. There are three ways to access the information in FundSource: 1) use the List Search to generate a complete list of FundSource organizations and then click on those that interest you to get contact information and a brief description; 2) use the Database Search to generate a tailored list of FundSource organizations (select by name, discipline, and/or topic) and then click on the selected organizations to see contact information and a brief description; and 3) use keywords in the Web Search to navigate directly to the web sites of organizations offering research funding.
 Available from: American Psychological Association, 750 First Street, N.E., Washington, DC 20002-4242. *Telephone:* (202) 336-5500; *Toll-free:* (800) 374-2721; *Fax:* (202) 336-5502; *E-mail:* order@apa.org
 Web site: www.apa.org/books

269

GrantFinder: The Complete Guide to Postgraduate Funding Worldwide: Social Sciences

New York: Palgrave, 2000. 516p. ISBN 0-312-22894-5. $50. Hardcover.
 Description: This guide to worldwide postgraduate funding in the social sciences is one of a four-volume set extracted directly from the listings in the 2000 edition of the *Grants Register* (see entry 265). The other volumes in the set focus on arts and humanities, sciences, and medicine (see entries 281, 306, and

Grants for Individuals–Social Sciences–General

315). Like the parent volume, this directory describes grants, prizes, and fellowships open to nationals of the United States, Canada, the United Kingdom, Ireland, Australia, New Zealand, South Africa, and the developing countries—but only those that relate to the social sciences. There's nothing in here that you can't find in the *Grants Register,* which is more up to date as well.

Available from: Palgrave, 175 Fifth Avenue, New York, NY 10010. *Telephone:* (212) 982-3900; *Toll-free:* (800) 221-7945; *Fax:* (212) 777-6359

Web site: www.palgrave-usa.com

270

GrantLink

http://www.grantlink.org

Description: This online subscription source is updated weekly ($150/yr.) and provides funding information of interest to social science and public policy researchers. This includes, but is not limited to, funding offered by federal or private sponsors for research, research training, and professional development in the following fields: anthropology, business, economics, demography, geography, health sciences, history, international affairs, law, management, political science, psychology, public administration, public finance, sociology, and statistics. Weekly updates are e-mailed to subscribers; the information is also posted in a members-only section on the web site.

Available from: Carolyn Looff & Associates, P.O. Box 22258, Lexington, KY 40522-2258. *Telephone:* (859) 266-8274

Web site: www.grantlink.org

271

GrantsInfo.com: Social and Natural Sciences

http://www.arisnet.com/socnatu.html

Description: For the past 20 years, ARIS (Academic Research Information System) has been providing information to individuals and organizations interested in federal and private grants, fellowships, scholarships, contracts, and awards in the social and natural sciences—previously in the printed *ARIS Funding Messenger: Social and Natural Sciences Report* (ISSN 0747-9921) and now only on the Internet at GrantsInfo.com. The programs included in the online database cover the fields of 1) social sciences research, including business, education, law, and the behavioral sciences; and 2) natural sciences research, including agriculture, computer sciences, engineering, environmental sciences, mathematics, and space sciences. Each entry provides address, telephone number, concise guidelines, and deadline dates. Although subscriptions for the now-defunct *Social and Natural Sciences Report* used to run as high as $240 a year, the Internet version may be searched on an unlimited basis for the seemingly bargain price of $10. But beware, this "savings" comes at a price—much of the material in the database has not been updated since 2000.

Available from: Academic Research Information System, Inc., 2940 16th Street, Suite 314, San Francisco, CA 94103. *Telephone:* (415) 558-8133; *Fax:* (415) 558-8135; *E-mail:* arisnet@dnai.com

Web site: www.arisnet.com

272

Money for Graduate Students in the Social & Behavioral Sciences

By Gail Ann Schlachter and R. David Weber. El Dorado Hills, CA: Reference Service Press, 1996- . Biennial. (RSP Graduate Funding Set). ISBN 1-58841-078-1. $42.50 (2003-2005 ed.). Comb binding.

Description: *Money for Graduate Students in the Social & Behavioral Sciences* identifies nearly 1,100 grants, fellowships, and awards—representing millions of dollars—available to support study or research on the master's or doctoral level in those fields. For more information about the publication, see entry 127 in the "Scholarships, Fellowships & Loans—Social Sciences—General" section of this bibliography.

Available from: Reference Service Press, 5000 Windplay Drive, Suite 4, El Dorado Hills, CA 95762. *Telephone:* (916) 939-9620; *Fax:* (916) 939-9626; *E-mail:* findaid@aol.com

Web site: www.rspfunding.com

273

Research and Funding: A German-American Guide for Historians and Social Scientists.

Ed. by Christof Mauch and Birgit Zischke. Washington, DC: German Historical Institute, 1999. Free. Paper or online.

Description: This directory focuses on exchanges between the United States and Germany and provides detailed information about institutions that offer financial support (grants and fellowships in history and the social sciences) and/or affiliations to non-native researchers. For more information about the paper and online versions of the publication, see entry 288 in the "Grants for Individuals—Humanities—History" section of this bibliography.

Available from: German Historical Institute, 1607 New Hampshire Avenue, N.W., Washington, DC 20009. *Telephone:* (202) 387-3355; *Fax:* (202) 483-3430; *E-mail:* ghiusa@ghi-dc.org

Web site: www.ghi-dc.org

274

Social Science Research Council Fellowships and Grants for Training and Research

New York: Social Science Research Council, 2002-2003. Unpaged. Free. Paper.

Description: This annual pamphlet describes national and international research grants and fellowships in both the humanities and social sciences that are open to American and foreign citizens on the advanced graduate or postgraduate levels. For more information about the publication, see entry 129 in the "Scholarships, Fellowships & Loans—Social Sciences—General" section of this bibliography.

Available from: Social Science Research Council, 810 Seventh Avenue, New York, NY 10019. *Telephone:* (212) 377-2700; *Fax:* (212) 377-2727

Web site: www.ssrc.org

Business and Economics

275

Free Help from Uncle Sam to Start Your Own Business (Or Expand the One You Have)

5th ed. By William Alarid. Santa Maria, CA: Puma Publishing, 2000. 234p. ISBN 0-940673-75-4. $17.95. Paper.

Description: Approximately 750,000 entrepreneurs start a business each year. This book, which also contains case histories and success stories, identifies information services, counseling services, and funds available from the federal and individual state governments. About 200 loan programs, loan guarantees, direct payment program, and grant programs are informally described. Entries are grouped by category (e.g., financial help, international trade, women and minorities). Contact information, including telephone number, is provided. Additional, related information can be found on the publisher's web site, including a list of and links to state financing programs, a list of Internet business resources, and free business planning software.

Available from: Puma Publishing, 1670 Coral Drive, Santa Maria, CA 93454. *Telephone:* (805) 925-3216; *Toll-free:* (800) 255-5730, ext. 110; *Fax:* (805) 925-2656; *E-mail:* publications@pumapublishing.com

Web site: www.pumapublishing.com

276

Lesko Business Money Finder for Maryland

By Matthew Lesko. Rockville, MD: Information USA, 2002. $295. Paper with CD-ROM.

Description: Unlike other Lesko titles (see entry 233), this one bundles a printed volume (that describes 530 sources of money just for Maryland business) with a CD-ROM that stores 3,000 pages of applications that can be printed, filled out, and sent in. So, after you search for funding opportunities for Maryland businesses and find those that meet your needs, you'll be able to fill out and print out actual applications for each of those programs. That's the plus. The minus is that many funding programs available to businesses in Maryland are not covered here, and a number of the applications provided on the CD-ROM are not the current versions.

Available from: Information USA, Inc., 12079 Nebel Street, Rockville, MD 20852. *Toll-free:* (800) 955-POWER

Web site: www.lesko.com

Education

277

Chronicle of Higher Education

Washington, DC: Chronicle of Higher Education, 1966- . Weekly. ISSN 0009-5982. $82.50. Paper.

Description: This newspaper is published weekly (except the third week in August and the last two weeks in December). It contains news stories, articles, editorials, job announcements, and other types of information of interest to academic faculty, researchers, staff, and administrators. One section announces new fellowship and grant competitions. In addition, subscribers are given access to this information on the *Chronicle's* web site (which is also known by the name Academe Today). Using the link to the Chronicle Guide to Grants online database (see entry 341), subscribers can search by keyword, grantmaker, and recipient characteristics for grant and fellowship announcements (during the past two years) and grant awards (since April, 1992) that were included in the *Chronicle of Higher Education* and its companion newsletter, the *Chronicle of Philanthropy* (entry 342).

Available from: Chronicle of Higher Education, Attn: Circulation Department, 1255 23rd Street, N.W., Suite 700, Washington, DC 20037. *Telephone:* (202) 466-1000; *Toll-free:* (800) 728-2803; *E-mail:* circulation@chronicle.com

Web site: chronicle.com

Grants for Individuals–Humanities–General

278

The Grant Advisor

Charlottesville, VA: The Grant Advisor, 1983- . Monthly, except July. ISSN 0740-5383. $198/yr., print; $398, online.

Description: *The Grant Advisor* newsletter provides information on grant and fellowship opportunities for U.S. institutions of higher education and their faculty. For more information about the publication and its online version, see entry 474 in the "Grants for Organizations—Social Sciences—Education" section of this bibliography.

Available from: The Grant Advisor, 1946 Lonicera Way, Charlottesville, VA 22911. *Telephone:* (434) 975-9098; *Fax:* (815) 361-2971; *E-mail:* info@grantadvisor.com

Web site: www.grantadvisor.com

HUMANITIES

General

279

Art Deadlines List

Ed. by Richard Gardner. Cambridge, MA: Art Deadlines List. Monthly. $36, paper; $18, e-mailed.

Description: Every month subscribers are mailed an international list of grants, fellowships, competitions, contests (primarily), call for entries/papers, scholarships, residencies, internships, and other opportunities for individuals involved in art or other creative activities (e.g., writing, photography, music). For more information about the service, see entry 560 in the "Awards and Prizes—Humanities—General" section of this bibliography.

Available from: Art Deadlines List, Box 381067, Harvard Square Station, Cambridge, MA 02238-1067. *E-mail:* contact@artdeadlineslist.com

Web site: www.artdeadlineslist.com

280

Directory of Grants in the Humanities

Westport, CT: Oryx, 1986- . Annual. ISSN 0877-0551. ISBN 1-57356-567-9. $84.95 (2002-2003 ed.). Paper.

Description: This annually-issued compilation (released in mid-year) identifies funding sources in literature, languages, history, anthropology, philosophy, ethics, religion, fine arts, and performing arts (including painting, dance, photography, sculpture, music, drama, crafts, folklore, and mime). The latest edition contains more than 3,600 entries, each of which includes information on restrictions and requirements, amount of money available, application deadline, renewability, sponsoring organization name and address, and *Catalog of Federal Domestic Assistance* number. Listed programs fund research, travel, internships, fellowships, dissertation support, conferences, exhibitions, and performances in the United States and Canada. About half of the listing focuses on federal programs; the remainder is devoted to state government programs, university-sponsored programs, and corporate or foundation funding sources. Entries are indexed by subject, sponsoring organization, program type, and geographic coverage. The information is taken directly from Oryx's comprehensive GrantSelect database (see entry 247). Most of the programs described here are also covered in Oryx Press' more inclusive *Directory of Research Grants* (see entry 238).

Available from: Oryx Press, 88 Post Road West, Westport, CT 06881. *Telephone:* (602) 265-2651; *Toll-free:* (800) 279-6799; *Fax:* (800) 279-4663; *E-mail:* info@oryxpress.com

Web site: www.oryxpress.com

281

GrantFinder: The Complete Guide to Postgraduate Funding Worldwide: Arts and Humanities

New York: Palgrave, 2000. 476p. ISBN 0-312-22893-7. $50. Hardcover.

Description: This guide to worldwide postgraduate funding in the arts and humanities is one of several titles extracted directly from the listings in the 2000 edition of the *Grants Register* (see entry 265). The other volumes in the set focus on the social sciences, sciences, and medicine (see entries 269, 306, and 315). Like the parent volume, this directory describes grants, prizes, and fellowships open to nationals of the United States, Canada, the United Kingdom, Ireland, Australia, New Zealand, South Africa, and the developing countries—but only those that relate to the arts and humanities. There's nothing in here that you can't find in the *Grants Register*, which is more up to date as well.

Available from: Palgrave, 175 Fifth Avenue, New York, NY 10010. *Telephone:* (212) 982-3900; *Toll-free:* (800) 221-7945; *Fax:* (212) 777-6359

Web site: www.palgrave-usa.com

282

GrantsInfo.com: Creative Arts and Humanities

http://www.arisnet.com/arts.html

Grants for Individuals–Humanities–General

Description: For the past 20 years, ARIS (Academic Research Information System) has been providing information to individuals and organizations interested in federal and private grants, fellowships, scholarships, contracts, and awards in the humanities and creative arts—previously in the printed *ARIS Funding Messenger: Creative Arts and Humanities Report* (ISSN 0747-993X) and now only on the Internet at GrantsInfo.com. The programs included in the online database cover the performing arts, visual arts, and humanities (including the traditional humanistic disciplines as well as broad social and community applications). Regional, national, and international competitions are highlighted. Each entry provides address, telephone numbers, concise guidelines, and deadline dates. Although subscriptions for the now-defunct *Creative Arts and Humanities Report* used to run as high as $145 a year, the Internet version may be searched on an unlimited basis for the seemingly bargain price of $10. But beware, this "savings" comes at a price—much of the material in the database has not been updated since 2000.

Available from: Academic Research Information System, Inc., 2940 16th Street, Suite 314, San Francisco, CA 94103. *Telephone:* (415) 558-8133; *Fax:* (415) 558-8135; *E-mail:* arisnet@dnai.com

Web site: www.arisnet.com

283

Money for Graduate Students in the Arts & Humanities

By Gail Ann Schlachter and R. David Weber. El Dorado Hills, CA: Reference Service Press, 1996- . Biennial. (RSP Graduate Funding Set). ISBN 1-58841-076-5. $40 (2003-2005 ed.). Comb binding.

Description: This biennially-issued directory identifies 1,000 grants, fellowships, and awards available to support graduate work in the arts and humanities. For more information about the publication, see entry 143 in the "Scholarships, Fellowships & Loans—Humanities—General" section of this bibliography.

Available from: Reference Service Press, 5000 Windplay Drive, Suite 4, El Dorado Hills, CA 95762. *Telephone:* (916) 939-9620; *Fax:* (916) 939-9626; *E-mail:* findaid@aol.com

Web site: www.rspfunding.com

284

Social Science Research Council Fellowships and Grants for Training and Research

New York: Social Science Research Council, 2002-2003. Unpaged. Free. Paper.

Description: This annual pamphlet describes national and international research grants and fellowships in both the humanities and social sciences that

How to Find Out About Financial Aid and Funding

are open to American and foreign citizens on the advanced graduate or postgraduate levels. For more information about the publication, see entry 129 in the "Scholarships, Fellowships & Loans—Social Sciences—General" section of this bibliography.

Available from: Social Science Research Council, 810 Seventh Avenue, New York, NY 10019. *Telephone:* (212) 377-2700; *Fax:* (212) 377-2727
Web site: www.ssrc.org

Applied Arts

285

Directory of Grants for Crafts: How to Write a Winning Proposal

By James Dillehay. Torreon, NM: Warm Snow, 2000. 216p. ISBN 0-9629923-4-8. $19.95. Paper.

Description: In addition to discussing how to win grants for crafts, this publication identifies, in 140 pages of appendices, hundreds of foundations, government agencies, public arts programs, residency programs, arts agencies, and other related sources that offer grants to crafters. Contact information is given for each but, with the exception of selected government grants, few entries contain additional information or detail.

Available from: Warm Snow Publishers, P.O. Box 75, Torreon, NM 87061. *Telephone:* (505) 384-1195; *Toll-free:* (800) 235-6570; *E-mail:* info@craftmarketer.com
Web site: www.craftmarketer.com/warm_snow_publishers.htm

Architecture

286

Energywi$e Construction Funding Directory for Green Buildings

By Jan McAdams. Las Vegas, McAdams, 2003. 150p. $295. Looseleaf.

Description: There is no other funding directory quite like this one. Described here are the major (150+) grants, loans, and creative partnership strategies for commercial "green" buildings. Also included are funding sources for projects that incorporate solar/PV. In addition, the book features a "how to" section, which contains sample grant proposals and proven fundraising strategies for capital campaigns (new construction, renovation, and retrofits). This listing will be helpful to architects, contractors, building owners, sustainability advocates, and civil leaders interested in promoting energy efficiency for commercial buildings. While the price is high, it should be noted that it covers not only the directory, but also a monthly funding newsletter, access to a private online funding area, fundraising technical assistance, and free admission to "Funding Green Buildings" workshops.

Available from: McAdams Group, 1350 East Flamingo Road, No. 362, Las Vegas. NV 89119. *Telephone:* (702) 456-5827; *Fax:* (702) 456-9940; *E-mail:* janmcadams@aol.com

Web site: www.fundinggreenbuildings.com

History

287

Grants, Fellowships, and Prizes of Interest to Historians

Ed. by Pillarisetti Sudhir, with Kim Foote and Jesse Erdheim. Washington, DC: American Historical Association, 1978-2000. Annual. ISSN 0275-830X. $10, members; $12, nonmembers (2000-2001 ed.). Paper.

Description: Begun as a 46-page pamphlet, *Grants, Fellowships, and Prizes* has expanded over the years; the 2000-2001 edition consists of more than 200 pages and describes more than 450 sources of funding for graduate students, postdoctoral researchers, and scholars in the history profession tenable in the United State or abroad. Covered here are fellowships, internships, awards, prizes, and travel grants. The entries are arranged in three sections: fellowships and grants for individuals; support for organizations and groups working in the fields of historical education, study, or preservation; prizes and awards given for books, publications, or manuscripts already completed. A bibliography, which lists books and pamphlets that contain additional information about funding prizes, and a program title index complete the work. The 2000-2001 edition was the last print edition. Now, information on grants, fellowships, and prizes is available only online (in a regularly-updated and searchable format), but only to association members.

Available from: American Historical Association, 400 A Street, S.E., Washington, DC 20003-3889. *Telephone:* (202) 544-2422; *Fax:* (202) 544-8307; *E-mail:* pubsales@theaha.org

Web site: www.theaha.org

288

Research and Funding: A German-American Guide for Historians and Social Scientists

Ed. by Christof Mauch and Birgit Zischke. Washington, DC: German Historical Institute, 1999. Free. Paper or online.

Description: One of the tasks of the German Historical Institute (GHI) has been to "promote the exchange of ideas between historians and political scientists from Germany and the United States and to provide information and assistance to and facilitate the research of American and German scholars." Because there was no comprehensive guide to academic exchange programs between the United States and Germany, the institute began this directory (in 1989). Listed in the latest print edition (1999) are grants and fellowships of interest to graduate students and scholars. Focusing on exchanges between the United States and Germany, the guide provides detailed information about institutions that offer financial support and/or affiliations to non-native researchers. It is divided into two sections: funding available for study and research in the United States and funding available for study and research in Germany (excluding funding from German state governments). Entries are listed alphabetically by sponsoring organization. The following information is provided for each: scope, eligibility, scholarship provisions, and applications. Entries are indexed by purpose (e.g., graduate studies, postdoctoral research, travel). The information in the guide was updated in 2001 by Michael Wala and the updated information is available on GHI's web site. Previously, the guide was issued under the title *German-American Scholarship Guide: Exchange Opportunities for Historians and Social Scientists* (1989 and 1994).

Available from: German Historical Institute, 1607 New Hampshire Avenue, N.W., Washington, DC 20009. *Telephone:* (202) 387-3355; *Fax:* (202) 483-3430; *E-mail:* ghiusa@ghi-dc.org
Web site: www.ghi-dc.org

Literature

289

Artists and Writers Colonies: Retreats, Residencies, and Respites for the Creative Mind

2nd ed. By Robyn Middleton, et. al. Hillsboro, OR: Blue Heron Publishers, 2000. 352p. ISBN 0-936085-62-2. $19.95. Paper.

Description: This is the making of writer's dreams. Described here are approximately 200 residencies, retreats, and fellowships available to writers and artists. All offer a place to read, write, and create. Some have extensive facilities

Grants for Individuals–Humanities–Literature

and others are much more primitive. Entries describing these opportunities are grouped geographically (in the U.S. and abroad) and indexed by subject and discipline. The following information is provided for each colony: who may apply, how to apply, locations, deadlines, and what is offered to the residents. An appendix lists colonies by the type of artist they host.

Available from: Blue Heron Publishers, 1234 S.W. Stark Street, Portland, OR 97205. *Telephone:* (503) 223-8098; *Fax:* (503) 223-9474; *E-mail:* info@blueheronpublishing.com

Web site: www.greatnorthwestbooks.com

290

Artists' Communities: A Directory of Residencies in the United States That Offer Time and Space for Creativity

2nd ed. By the Alliance of Artists' Communities. New York: Allworth Press, 2000. 224p. ISBN 1-58115-044-X. $18.95. Paper.

Description: This is a guide to residencies and fellowships in the United States for writers, visual and performing artists, and composers. For more information about the publication, see entry 303 in the "Grants for Individuals—Humanities—Visual Arts" section of this bibliography.

Available from: Allworth Press, 10 East 23rd Street, Suite 510, New York, NY 10010. *Telephone:* (212) 777-8395; *Toll-free:* (800) 491-2808; *Fax:* (212) 777-8395; *E-mail:* pub@allworth.com

Web site: www.allworth.com

291

Dramatists Sourcebook: Complete Opportunities for Playwrights, Translators, Composers, Lyricists, and Librettists

Ed. by Kathy Sova, Samantha R. Healy, and Jennifer Sokolov. New York: Theatre Communications Group, 1982- . Annual. ISSN 0733-1606. ISBN 1-55936-217-0. $21.95 (2002-2003 ed.). Paper.

Description: There are a number of sections in this sourcebook that describe various financial aid programs for dramatists, including grants, fellowships, awards and prizes, colonies and residencies, and emergency funds. For more information about the publication, see entry 574 in the "Awards and Prizes—Humanities—Literature" section of this bibliography.

Available from: Theatre Communications Group, 355 Lexington Avenue, New York, NY 10017-6603. *Telephone:* (212) 697-5230; *Fax:* (212) 983-4847; *E-mail:* tcg@tcg.org

Web site: www.tcg.org

292

Grants and Awards Available to American Writers

New York: P.E.N. American Center, 1969- . Biennial. ISSN 0092-5268. ISBN 0-934638-20-9. $15 (2002-2003 ed.), individuals; $18, libraries and institutions. Paper.

Description: Grants and awards in excess of $500, available to American writers for use in the United States and abroad, are described in this directory. For more information about the publication, see entry 575 in the "Awards and Prizes—Humanities—Literature" section of this bibliography.

Available from: P.E.N. American Center, 568 Broadway, Suite 401, New York, NY 10012-3225. *Telephone:* (212) 334-1660; *Fax:* (212) 334-2181; *E-mail:* pen@pen.org

Web site: www.pen.org

293

Literary Market Place: The Directory of the American Book Publishing Industry

Medford, NJ: Information Today, 1972- . Annual. ISSN 0000-1155. ISBN 1-57387-148-6. $299 (2003 ed.), paper; $389, online.

Description: Originally designed as a register of personnel in publishing and allied fields, over the years this annual has been expanded to include 16,000 entries in a dozen major sections. One of these sections focuses on grants, grants-in-aid, awards, scholarships, and fellowships of interest to the American writer. For more information about the publication and its Internet version, see entry 577 in the "Awards and Prizes—Humanities—Literature" section of this bibliography.

Available from: Information Today, Inc., 143 Old Marlton Pike, Medford, NJ 08055-8750. *Telephone:* (609) 654-6266; *Fax:* (609) 654-4309; *E-mail:* custserv@infotoday.com

Web site: www.literarymarketplace.com

294

The Playwright's Companion: A Practical Guide to Script Opportunities in the U.S.A.

Ed. by Mollie Ann Meserve. Brooklin, ME: Feedback Theatrebooks, 1983-1999. Annual. ISSN 0887-1507. ISBN 0937657-47-6. $20.95 (1999 ed.). Paper.

Description: The final edition of this popular guide for dramatic writers in America was issued in 1999 and provided up-to-date information on more than 1,400 marketing opportunities, including Broadway producers, regional theaters,

Grants for Individuals–Humanities–Music

community playhouses, and college theaters. Also covered in the last annual were grants, fellowships, writers' colonies, and residencies of interest to American playwrights.

Available from: Feedback Theatrebooks, P.O. Box 220, Brooklin, ME 04616. *Telephone:* (207) 359-2781; *Toll-free:* (800) 800-8671; *Fax:* (207) 359-5532; *E-mail:* feedback@hypernet.com

295

Poets & Writers Magazine

New York: Poets & Writers Magazine, 1972- . Bimonthly. ISSN 0891-6136. $19.95/yr. Paper.

Description: Published six times a year, this is an excellent source of information on grants, awards, and fellowships for poets and other writers. In each issue, the "Grants & Awards" section announces the recent winners of poetry and fiction prizes of $500 or more and of prestigious nonmonetary awards in these two genres; since the awards are described and contact information is provided, this section can also be used to identify available opportunities. Two other sections are geared even more to those looking for literary funds: the "Deadlines" and "State Grants" sections identify and describe more than 140 upcoming funding opportunities (fellowships, grants, awards, residencies, etc.) in each issue. Even the "Classifieds" section is a source of information on numerous poetry and other literary competitions. Taken together, these listings provide an unrivaled source of current information on money for poets and other writers. This information is also offered without charge on the publisher's web site, issue by issue, with links to available online applications or guidelines.

Available from: Poets & Writers Inc., 72 Spring Street, Suite 301, New York, NY 10012. *Telephone:* (212) 226-3586; *Fax:* (212) 226-3963

Web site: www.pw.org

Music

296

Artists' Communities: A Directory of Residencies in the United States That Offer Time and Space for Creativity

2nd ed. By the Alliance of Artists' Communities. New York: Allworth Press, 2000. 224p. ISBN 1-58115-044-X. $18.95. Paper.

Description: This is a guide to residencies and fellowships in the United States for composers, visual and performing artists, and writers. For more infor-

mation about the publication, see entry 303 in the "Grants for Individuals—Humanities—Visual Arts" section of this bibliography.
Available from: Allworth Press, 10 East 23rd Street, Suite 510, New York, NY 10010. *Telephone:* (212) 777-8395; *Toll-free:* (800) 491-2808; *Fax:* (212) 777-8395; *E-mail:* pub@allworth.com
Web site: www.allworth.com

297

Career Guide for Singers

6th ed. Washington, DC: Opera America, 2003. 294p. ISBN 0-885131-03-8. $40, members; $70, nonmembers. Paper.
Description: This guide identifies nearly 1,000 opportunities for aspiring opera singers, including grants and competitions open to singers within the United States, Canada, and abroad. For more information about the publication, see entry 584 in the "Awards and Prizes—Humanities—Music" section of this bibliography.
Available from: Opera America, 1156 15th Street, Suite 810, Washington, DC 20005-1704. *Telephone:* (202) 293-4466; *Fax:* (202) 393-0735; *E-mail:* frontdesk@operaam.org
Web site: www.operaam.org

298

Dramatists Sourcebook: Complete Opportunities for Playwrights, Translators, Composers, Lyricists, and Librettists

Ed. by Kathy Sova, Samantha R. Healy, and Jennifer Sokolov. New York: Theatre Communications Group, 1982- . Annual. ISSN 0733-1606. ISBN 1-55936-217-0. $21.95 (2002-2003 ed.). Paper.
Description: There are a number of sections in this sourcebook that describe various financial aid programs for composers, lyricists, and librettists, including grants, fellowships, awards and prizes, colonies and residencies, and emergency funds. For more information about the publication, see entry 574 in the "Awards and Prizes—Humanities—Literature" section of this bibliography.
Available from: Theatre Communications Group, 355 Lexington Avenue, New York, NY 10017-6603. *Telephone:* (212) 697-5230; *Fax:* (212) 983-4847; *E-mail:* tcg@tcg.org
Web site: www.tcg.org

Grants for Individuals–Humanities–Performing Arts

299

Opportunities in New Music

10th ed. New York: American Music Center, 2002. 49p. $15, members; $30, nonmembers. Spiral bound.

Description: This is a listing of ongoing American and foreign grants, competitions, awards, commissioning programs, workshops, calls for scores, and residencies in the fields of jazz and contemporary concert music. For more information about the publication, see entry 587 in the "Awards and Prizes—Humanities—Music" section of this bibliography.

Available from: American Music Center, 30 West 26th Street, Suite 1001, New York, NY 10010-2011. *Telephone:* (212) 366-5260; *Fax:* (212) 366-5265; *E-mail:* center@amc.net

Web site: www.amc.net

Performing Arts

300

Artists' Communities: A Directory of Residencies in the United States That Offer Time and Space for Creativity

2nd ed. By the Alliance of Artists' Communities. New York: Allworth Press, 2000. 224p. ISBN 1-58115-044-X. $18.95. Paper.

Description: This is a guide to residencies and fellowships in the United States for performing and visual artists, composers, and writers. For more information about the publication, see entry 303 in the "Grants for Individuals—Humanities—Visual Arts" section of this bibliography.

Available from: Allworth Press, 10 East 23rd Street, Suite 510, New York, NY 10010. *Telephone:* (212) 777-8395; *Toll-free:* (800) 491-2808; *Fax:* (212) 777-8395; *E-mail:* pub@allworth.com

Web site: www.allworth.com

301

NYFA Source

http://www.nyfa.org

Description: NYFA Source is the nation's most extensive free databank of grants, residencies, publications, and sources of information and assistance for artists of all disciplines. The site was created by the New York Foundation for the Arts (NYFA) in collaboration with the Washington, D.C.-based Urban Insti-

How to Find Out About Financial Aid and Funding

tute in 2001-2. Identified here are more than 2,800 awards programs, 2,600 services, and 900 publications for artists in the dance, music, folk/traditional, theater, performance art, visual, design, and media—from the Conrad Cantzen Shoe Fund of the Actors Fund of America (granting a new pair of shoes to unemployed actors going on auditions) to the MacArthur Fellowship Program (multiyear awards reaching $500,000). The search function on the site allows users to narrow queries by discipline, location, gender, age group, application deadline, and more. In addition to the web site, artists may receive personal assistance by calling toll-free at (800) 232-2789 or by e-mailing their requests to sourcevisual@nyfa.org.

Available from: New York Foundation for the Arts, 155 Avenue of the Americas, 14th Floor, New York, NY 10013-1507. *Telephone:* (212) 366-6900; *Fax:* (212) 366-1778; *E-mail:* nyfaweb@nyfa.org
Web site: www.nyfa.org

Religion

302

Faculty Grants Directory

http://www.ats.edu/faculty/fgdirtoc.htm

Description: The online Faculty Grants Directory is sponsored by the Association of Theological Schools and provides information, at no charge, on more than 750 grants and other funding opportunities for those teaching theology or religion in graduate institutions and for administrators and project leaders who are seeking funding for institutional or collaborative projects. There are three types of funding opportunities described here: 1) grants for individual research and scholarship; 2) grant sources for collaborative research, institutional, and program support; and 3) funding associated with awards, travel grants, and honorary fellowships. The scope of coverage is broader than you might think. Of course, traditional religious studies are covered, but so are African studies, death and dying, economics, education, environment, folklore, gender studies, immigration, journalism, and peace and justice. You can search the database by either sponsor or subject. Most of the sponsoring organizations included in the directory have web sites and, in those cases, there is a link from the organization's name to its home page. In addition, for each funding opportunity, the following information is provided: award amount, deadline, description, eligibility, number awarded, and application process. Until 1998, the directory was also available in print and sold for $30.

Available from: Association of Theological Schools in the United States and Canada, 10 Summit Park Drive, Pittsburgh, PA 15275. *Telephone:* (412) 788-6505; *Fax:* (412) 788-6510; *E-mail:* ats@ats.edu
Web site: www.ats.edu

Grants for Individuals–Humanities–Visual Arts

Visual Arts

303

Artists' Communities: A Directory of Residencies in the United States That Offer Time and Space for Creativity

2nd ed. By the Alliance of Artists' Communities. New York: Allworth Press, 2000. 224p. ISBN 1-58115-044-X. $18.95. Paper.

Description: Compiled by the Alliance of Artists' Communities and updating the 1996 edition, this guide describes approximately 80 residence opportunities in the United States for visual and performing artists, composers, and writers. Some of these residencies charge and others offer financial support. The following information is provided for each: contact, art disciplines served, facilities, housing, meals, season and length of residency, number of artists in residence, deadlines and fees, stipends and expenses, duties, programs, history and mission, and well-known artists who have been in residence. A nice touch: a photograph of each community is provided.

Available from: Allworth Press, 10 East 23rd Street, Suite 510, New York, NY 10010. *Telephone:* (212) 777-8395; *Toll-free:* (800) 491-2808; *Fax:* (212) 777-8395; *E-mail:* pub@allworth.com

Web site: www.allworth.com

304

Artists & Writers Colonies: Retreats, Residencies, and Respites for the Creative Mind

2nd ed. By Robyn Middleton, et. al. Hillsboro, OR: Blue Heron Publishers, 2000. 352p. ISBN 0-936085-62-2. $19.95. Paper.

Description: Described here are approximately 200 residencies, retreats, and fellowships available to artists and writers. For more information about the publication, see entry 289 in the "Grants for Individuals—Humanities—Literature" section of this bibliography.

Available from: Blue Heron Publishers, 1234 S.W. Stark Street, Portland, OR 97205. *Telephone:* (503) 223-8098; *Fax:* (503) 223-9474; *E-mail:* info@blueheronpublishing.com

Web site: www.greatnorthwestbooks.com

305

NYFA Source

http://www.nyfa.org

Description: NYFA Source is the nation's most extensive free databank of grants, residencies, publications, and sources of information and assistance for visual and performing artists. For more information about the site, see entry 301 in the "Grants for Individuals—Humanities—Performing Arts" section of this bibliography.

Available from: New York Foundation for the Arts, 155 Avenue of the Americas, 14th Floor, New York, NY 10013-1507. *Telephone:* (212) 366-6900; *Fax:* (212) 366-1778; *E-mail:* nyfaweb@nyfa.org

Web site: www.nyfa.org

SCIENCES

General

306

GrantFinder: The Complete Guide to Postgraduate Funding Worldwide: Sciences

New York: Palgrave, 2000. 468p. ISBN 0-312-22895-3. $50. Hardcover.

Description: This guide to worldwide postgraduate funding in the sciences is one of a four-volume set extracted directly from the listings in the 2000 edition of the *Grants Register* (see entry 265). The other volumes in the set focus on the social sciences, arts/humanities, and medicine (see entries 0, 20960, and 315). Like the parent volume, this directory describes grants, prizes, and fellowships open to nationals of the United States, Canada, the United Kingdom, Ireland, Australia, New Zealand, South Africa, and the developing countries—but only those that relate to the sciences. There's nothing in here that you can't find in the *Grants Register,* which is more up to date as well.

Available from: Palgrave, 175 Fifth Avenue, New York, NY 10010. *Telephone:* (212) 982-3900; *Toll-free:* (800) 221-7945; *Fax:* (212) 777-6359

Web site: www.palgrave-usa.com

307

GrantsInfo.com: Social and Natural Sciences Report

http://www.arisnet.com/socnatu.html

Description: This inexpensive online searchable database information on hundreds of grant and fellowship opportunities in the natural and social sciences. For more information about the site, see entry 271 in the "Grants for Individuals—Social Sciences—General" section of this bibliography.

Grants for Individuals–Sciences–General

Available from: Academic Research Information System, Inc., 2940 16th Street, Suite 314, San Francisco, CA 94103. *Telephone:* (415) 558-8133; *Fax:* (415) 558-8135; *E-mail:* arisnet@dnai.com
Web site: www.arisnet.com

308

GrantsNet

http://www.grantsnet.org
Description: Because American scientists-in-training (postdoctorates, graduate students, undergraduates, and junior faculty members) are especially vulnerable in the area of competitive funding, the American Association for the Advancement of Science and the Howard Hughes Medical Institute created this searchable database of approximately 1,000 biomedical and scientific funding options from nonprofit organizations and federal agencies. For more information about the database, see entry 169 in the "Scholarships, Fellowships & Loans—Sciences—General" section of this bibliography.

Available from: American Association for the Advancement of Science, 1200 New York Avenue, N.W., Washington, DC 20005-3920. *Telephone:* (202) 326-6636; *Fax:* (202) 789-2008
Web site: www.grantsnet.org

309

National Science Foundation Guide to Programs: A Compilation of NSF Funding Opportunities

http://www.nsf.gov
Description: The National Science Foundation (NSF) was founded in 1950 to promote and advance scientific programs. Over the years, it has established a wide range of programs to support scientific, mathematical, and engineering research and education. Currently, the foundation makes more than 10,000 new awards each year. These programs are described in this annual guide, which used to be printed but, as of 2000, is now only available at NSF's web site as an HTML document or a .pdf file (latest edition: 2003). Entries supply information on program title, contact, address, eligibility requirements, application deadline, program purpose, application procedure, and type and amount of assistance available. Also covered are programs administered in cooperation with foreign countries. To update these listings, sign up for NSF's *E-Bulletin*, which is e-mailed daily and provides up-to-date information on deadlines and target dates for NSF programs. It replaces the *NSF Bulletin*, a print product, which ceased publication in September, 1998.

How to Find Out About Financial Aid and Funding

Available from: National Science Foundation, 4201 Wilson Boulevard, Arlington, VA 22230. *Telephone:* (703) 292-5111; *TDD:* (703) 292-5090; *E-mail:* pubs@nsf.gov
Web site: www.nsf.gov

310

ScienceWise

http://www.sciencewise.com
Description: Prior to being acquired by TheScientificWorld, Inc., Science-Wise was known as Federal Information Exchange & Research and Management Systems (or FIE-RAMS). ScienceWise developed two online searchable databases of funding opportunities: FEDIX and later the Minority Online Information System (MOLIS). Both of these services could be accessed from ScienceWise's web site (for more information about these services, see entries 203 and 240). ScienceWise also provided three other search services on its site: Research & Education Funding (where your could search for grant and contract opportunities from U.S. agencies, corporations, foundations, and the European Union); Science & Engineering Scholarships (a searchable database of science and engineering scholarships provided by the Scholarship Resource Network, a service described in entry 72), and Science & Engineering Jobs (a database of scientifically-relevant jobs provided by Scijobs.org). ScienceWise also provided a *fundingALERT* service, which was a daily customized content delivery and search service that identified approximately 200 new funding opportunities each month based on the keywords, organizations, and types of funding specified by each subscriber ($99/yr.). However, in mid-2002, ScienceWise suspended operations. Although the web site promised that "the combination of free and paid-for services" would resume as of December 2002, the site was still not operating in April of 2003 and e-mails sent to the posted contact were returned as undeliverable.
Available from: ScienceWise, 300 Professional Drive, Suite 200, Gaithersburg, MD 20879-3419. *Telephone:* (301) 975-0103; *Fax:* (301) 975-0109
Web site: www.sciencewise.com

Biological Sciences

311

Money for Graduate Students in the Biological & Health Sciences

By Gail Ann Schlachter and R. David Weber. El Dorado Hills, CA: Reference Service Press, 2001- . Biennial. (RSP Graduate Funding Set). ISBN 1-58841-075-7. $42.50 (2003-2005 ed.). Comb binding.

Grants for Individuals–Sciences–Earth Sciences

Description: Described here are more than 1,100 grants, fellowships, loans, and awards set aside just for students interested in working on a master's or doctoral degree in the biological or health sciences. For more information about the publication, see entry 174 in the "Scholarships, Fellowships & Loans—Sciences—Biological Sciences" section of this bibliography.

Available from: Reference Service Press, 5000 Windplay Drive, Suite 4, El Dorado Hills, CA 95762. *Telephone:* (916) 939-9620; *Fax:* (916) 939-9626; *E-mail:* findaid@aol.com
Web site: www.rspfunding.com

Earth Sciences

312

Money for Graduate Students in the Physical & Earth Sciences

By Gail Ann Schlachter and R. David Weber. El Dorado Hills, CA: Reference Service Press, 2001- . Biennial. (RSP Graduate Funding Set). ISBN 1-58841-077-3. $35 (2003-2005 ed.). Comb binding.

Description: Described here are 800 grants, fellowships, loans, and awards set aside just for students interested in working on a master's or doctoral degree in the earth or physical sciences. For more information about the publication, see entry 190 in the "Scholarships, Fellowships & Loans—Sciences—Physical Sciences" section of this bibliography.

Available from: Reference Service Press, 5000 Windplay Drive, Suite 4, El Dorado Hills, CA 95762. *Telephone:* (916) 939-9620; *Fax:* (916) 939-9626; *E-mail:* findaid@aol.com
Web site: www.rspfunding.com

Health and Medical Sciences

313

Directory of Biomedical and Health Care Grants

Westport, CT: Oryx, 1985- . Annual. ISSN 0883-5330. ISBN 1-57356-569-5. $84.50 (2003 ed.). Paper.

Description: Use this directory to locate descriptions of more than 3,000 funding sources open to individuals and organizations in the biomedical and health care areas (500 new to this edition). The programs described here are sponsored by corporations, foundations, professional organizations, and federal, state, and local governments. Most of the programs originate in the United

States and Canada, although some programs from other countries are included as well. In recent editions, a special effort has been made "to increase coverage of such areas as clinical and programmatic studies in gerontology and mental health; clinical studies of the cause, detection, and elimination of cancer; health care delivery and maintenance at the community level; and programs researching all areas relating to HIV and AIDS." Each program profile describes purpose, remuneration, eligibility, renewability, application deadlines, and sources of additional information. The entries are listed by program title and indexed by sponsoring organization, sponsoring organization by type (e.g., business and professional organizations, government agencies), specific subject terms, and (since the 1993 edition) program type. The programs listed in the directory are taken from Oryx's GrantSelect database (see entry 247), which is also the source for the *Directory of Research Grants* (entry 238); consequently, many of the programs included in the two publications are duplicates.

Available from: Oryx Press, 88 Post Road West, Westport, CT 06881. *Telephone:* (602) 265-2651; *Toll-free:* (800) 279-6799; *Fax:* (800) 279-4663; *E-mail:* info@oryxpress.com

Web site: www.oryxpress.com

314

Directory of International Grants and Fellowships in the Health Sciences

Bethesda, MD: Fogarty International Center, 2002. 108p. Free. Paper or online.

Description: Perhaps no activity is more international in scope than the pursuit of scientific knowledge for health. And with good reason, as the current pandemic of AIDS has vividly illustrated. Just as diseases cross national borders, so do the scientific activities that address them. To keep track of the funding available to support these activities, the Fogarty International Center for Advanced Study in the Health Sciences has prepared this directory. About 175 programs that fund doctoral or postdoctoral research in the health sciences in the United States or abroad are described here. The entries are arranged by type of funding (grants or fellowships) and sponsoring organization; they are indexed by medical focus and tenability. The following information is provided for each program: address and telephone number, e-mail and web site, fields of study, purpose, eligibility, financial provisions, duration, number awarded, and deadline dates. Since 1988, when the title was first introduced, this directory has become the National Institute of Health's most frequently requested publication. This directory is also available, in its entirety, at the Fogarty International Center's web site.

Available from: John E. Fogarty International Center for Advanced Study in the Health Sciences, National Institutes of Health, Building 31, Room B2C29, 31 Center Drive, MSC 2220, Bethesda, MD 20892-2220. *Telephone:* (301) 496-2075; *Fax:* (301) 594-1211; *E-mail:* ficinfo@nih.gov

Web site: www.nih.gov/fic

315

GrantFinder: The Complete Guide to Postgraduate Funding Worldwide: Medicine

New York: Palgrave, 2000. 394p. ISBN 0-312-22896-1. $50. Hardcover.

Description: This guide to worldwide postgraduate funding in medicine is one of a four-volume set extracted directly from the listings in the 2000 edition of the *Grants Register* (see entry 265). The other volumes in the set focus on arts and humanities, sciences, and social sciences (see entries 281, 306, and 269). Like the parent volume, this directory describes prizes, fellowships, and grants open to nationals of the United States, Canada, the United Kingdom, Ireland, Australia, New Zealand, South Africa, and the developing countries—but only those that relate to the medical sciences. There's nothing in here that you can't find in the *Grants Register*.

Available from: Palgrave, 175 Fifth Avenue, New York, NY 10010. *Telephone:* (212) 982-3900; *Toll-free:* (800) 221-7945; *Fax:* (212) 777-6359

Web site: www.palgrave-usa.com

316

GrantsInfo.com: Biomedical Sciences

http://www.arisnet.com/biomed.html

Description: For the past 20 years, ARIS (Academic Research Information System) has been providing information to individuals and organizations interested in federal and private grants, fellowships, scholarships, contracts, and awards in the biomedical sciences—previously in the printed *ARIS Funding Messenger: Biomedical Sciences Report* (ISSN 0747-9913) and now only on the Internet at GrantsInfo.com. The programs included in the online database cover biomedical research, health care and services, and the general biological sciences. Each entry provides address, telephone numbers, concise guidelines, and deadline dates. Although subscriptions for the now-defunct *Biomedical Sciences Report* used to run as high as $240 a year, the Internet version may be searched on an unlimited basis for the seemingly bargain price of $10. But beware, this "savings" comes at a price—much of the material in the database has not been updated since 2000.

Available from: Academic Research Information System, Inc., 2940 16th Street, Suite 314, San Francisco, CA 94103. *Telephone:* (415) 558-8133; *Fax:* (415) 558-8135; *E-mail:* arisnet@dnai.com

Web site: www.arisnet.com

317

Interorganizational Financial & Experiential Information Document: "If I'd" Only Known about That Scholarship

Prep. by the member organizations of the Interorganizational Council on Student Affairs. Washington, DC: Interorganizational Council on Student Affairs, 1999. Unpaged. Free. Paper or online.

Description: Aimed at undergraduate and graduate pharmacy students, this free listing provides (in tabular format) information on available grants, fellowships, loans, awards, experiential programs, and residencies. For more information about the listing, see entry 184 in the "Scholarships, Fellowships & Loans—Sciences—Health and Medical Sciences" section of this bibliography.

Available from: Interorganizational Council on Student Affairs, 2215 Constitution Avenue, N.W., Washington, DC 20037-2985. *Telephone:* (202) 429-7595; *Toll-free:* (800) 237-AphA, ext. 7595; *E-mail:* edt@mail.aphanet.org
Web site: www.aphanet.org/students/ifeid.html

318

Medical Research Funding Bulletin

New York: Science Support Center, 1972- . Bi-weekly. $75/yr. E-mail.

Description: Aimed at researchers in the scientific community, each issue identifies between 50 and 100 research grants and fellowships in medical sciences offered by federal and private organizations. The programs are listed chronologically by deadline (two months' lead time is usually given). Entries generally provide sponsoring organization contact information, along with program requirements and deadline date. Until mid-2001, the newsletter was distributed in both paper and e-mail versions; since then, it has been available only as an e-mail publication.

Available from: Science Support Center, P.O. Box 7507, FDR Center, New York, NY 10150-7507. *Telephone:* (212) 371-3398; *E-mail:* grants1@ATTglobal.net

319

Money for Graduate Students in the Biological & Health Sciences

By Gail Ann Schlachter and R. David Weber. El Dorado Hills, CA: Reference Service Press, 2001- . Biennial. (RSP Graduate Funding Set). ISBN 1-58841-075-7. $42.50 (2003-2005 ed.). Comb binding.

Description: Described here are more than 1,100 grants, fellowships, loans, and awards set aside just for students interested in working on a master's or doctoral degree in the health or biological sciences. For more information about

Grants for Individuals–Sciences–Physical Sciences

the publication, see entry 174 in the "Scholarships, Fellowships & Loans—Sciences—Biological Sciences" section of this bibliography.
Available from: Reference Service Press, 5000 Windplay Drive, Suite 4, El Dorado Hills, CA 95762. *Telephone:* (916) 939-9620; *Fax:* (916) 939-9626; *E-mail:* findaid@aol.com
Web site: www.rspfunding.com

320

RSP Funding for Nursing Students and Nurses

By Gail Ann Schlachter and R. David Weber. El Dorado Hills, CA: Reference Service Press, 1998- . Biennial. ISBN 1-58841-046-3, comb binding; 1-58841-081-1, eBook. $30 (2002-2004 ed.), comb binding or eBook.
Description: Described here are more than 600 grants, loans, fellowships, and scholarships set aside just for nursing students and nurses already in the field. For more information about the publication, see entry 188 in the "Scholarships, Fellowships & Loans—Sciences—Health and Medical Sciences" section of this bibliography.
Available from: Reference Service Press, 5000 Windplay Drive, Suite 4, El Dorado Hills, CA 95762. *Telephone:* (916) 939-9620; *Fax:* (916) 939-9626; *E-mail:* findaid@aol.com
Web site: www.rspfunding.com

Physical Sciences

321

Money for Graduate Students in the Physical & Earth Sciences

By Gail Ann Schlachter and R. David Weber. El Dorado Hills, CA: Reference Service Press, 2001- . Biennial. (RSP Graduate Funding Set). ISBN 1-58841-077-3. $35 (2003-2005 ed.). Comb binding.
Description: Described here are 800 grants, fellowships, loans, and awards set aside just for students interested in working on a master's or doctoral degree in the physical or earth sciences. For more information about the publication, see entry 190 in the "Scholarships, Fellowships & Loans—Sciences—Physical Sciences" section of this bibliography.
Available from: Reference Service Press, 5000 Windplay Drive, Suite 4, El Dorado Hills, CA 95762. *Telephone:* (916) 939-9620; *Fax:* (916) 939-9626; *E-mail:* findaid@aol.com
Web site: www.rspfunding.com

SPECIAL POPULATION GROUPS
Ethnic Groups

322

Financial Aid for African Americans

By Gail Ann Schlachter and R. David Weber. El Dorado Hills, CA: Reference Service Press, 1997- . Biennial. (Minority Funding Set). ISBN 1-58841-068-4. $40 (2003-2005 ed.). Hardcover.

Description: Described here are 1,500 grants, scholarships, fellowships, loans, awards, prizes, and internships—representing billions of dollars—open specifically to Black/African Americans. For more information about the publication, see entry 198 in the "Scholarships, Fellowships & Loans—Special Population Groups—Ethnic Groups" section of this bibliography.

Available from: Reference Service Press, 5000 Windplay Drive, Suite 4, El Dorado Hills, CA 95762. *Telephone:* (916) 939-9620; *Fax:* (916) 939-9626; *E-mail:* findaid@aol.com

Web site: www.rspfunding.com

323

Financial Aid for Asian Americans

By Gail Ann Schlachter and R. David Weber. El Dorado Hills, CA: Reference Service Press, 1997- . Biennial. (Minority Funding Set). ISBN 1-58841-069-2. $37.50 (2003-2005 ed.). Hardcover.

Description: More than 1,000 grants, awards, fellowships, scholarships, loans, and internships set aside for Asian Americans are described here. For more information about the publication, see entry 199 in the "Scholarships, Fellowships & Loans—Special Population Groups—Ethnic Groups" section of this bibliography.

Available from: Reference Service Press, 5000 Windplay Drive, Suite 4, El Dorado Hills, CA 95762. *Telephone:* (916) 939-9620; *Fax:* (916) 939-9626; *E-mail:* findaid@aol.com

Web site: www.rspfunding.com

324

Financial Aid for Hispanic Americans

By Gail Ann Schlachter and R. David Weber. El Dorado Hills, CA: Refer-

Grants for Individuals–Special Population Groups–Military , Etc.

ence Service Press, 1997- . Biennial. (Minority Funding Set). ISBN 1-58841-070-6. $40 (2003-2005 ed.). Hardcover.

Description: This directory identifies nearly 1,400 grants, fellowships, scholarships, loans, awards, and internships available to Hispanic Americans, including Mexican Americans, Puerto Ricans, Cuban Americans, and others of Latin American origin. For more information about the publication, see entry 200 in the "Scholarships, Fellowships & Loans—Special Population Groups—Ethnic Groups" section of this bibliography.

Available from: Reference Service Press, 5000 Windplay Drive, Suite 4, El Dorado Hills, CA 95762. *Telephone:* (916) 939-9620; *Fax:* (916) 939-9626; *E-mail:* findaid@aol.com
Web site: www.rspfunding.com

325

Financial Aid for Native Americans

By Gail Ann Schlachter and R. David Weber. El Dorado Hills, CA: Reference Service Press, 1997- . Biennial. (Minority Funding Set). ISBN 1-58841-071-4. $40 (2003-2005 ed.). Hardcover.

Description: Detailed information on nearly 1,500 grants, scholarships, fellowships, awards, loans, and internships open to American Indians, Native Alaskans, and Native Pacific Islanders (including Native Hawaiians and Samoans) is presented in this directory. For more information about the publication, see entry 201 in the "Scholarships, Fellowships & Loans—Special Population Groups—Ethnic Groups" section of this bibliography.

Available from: Reference Service Press, 5000 Windplay Drive, Suite 4, El Dorado Hills, CA 95762. *Telephone:* (916) 939-9620; *Fax:* (916) 939-9626; *E-mail:* findaid@aol.com
Web site: www.rspfunding.com

Military Personnel and Veterans

326

Code of Federal Regulations, Title 38: Pensions, Bonuses, and Veterans' Relief

Washington, DC: G.P.O. 2v. Annual. Vol. 1 (2002), $57; vol. 2, $58. Paper.

Description: The *Code of Federal Regulations* is a codification of the general and permanent rules published in the *Federal Register* (see entry 357) by the Executive departments and agencies of the federal government. The *Code* is divided into 50 titles; Title 38 contains the exact text of the laws related to veterans' benefits that come under the jurisdiction of the House Committee on Veterans' Affairs. Use this publication when you need the official wording of the authorizing legislation. For a more readable and considerably less expensive description of available veterans' benefits, see the annually revised *Federal Benefits for Veterans and Their Dependents* (entry 327). The complete text of *Title 38* is also available without charge on the Internet at GPO Access (see the URL below), where there are both browse and search features.

Available from: U.S. Government Printing Office, Superintendent of Documents, P.O. Box 371954, Pittsburgh, PA 15250-7954. *Telephone:* (202) 512-1800, press 1; *Toll-free:* (800) 669-8331; *Fax:* (202) 512-2250; *E-mail:* gpoaccess@gpo.gov

Web site: www.access.gpo.gov/su_docs

327

Federal Benefits for Veterans and Dependents

Prep. by the U.S. Department of Veterans Affairs. Washington, DC: G.P.O., 1969- . Annual. ISSN 0883-3370. ISBN 0-16-051085-6. $5 (2002 ed.), paper; free, online.

Description: One of the federal government's all-time best-selling publications, this booklet provides a comprehensive summary of federal government benefits (not all of which are monetary) to veterans and their dependents. It is updated annually and contains information on alcoholism treatment programs, aid for the blind, burial assistance, clothing allowances, compensation for service-connected disabilities, death payments, dental treatment, dependents' education, education and training loans, medical benefits, pensions for nonservice-connected disabilities, etc. The booklet concludes with a list of DVA facilities and an index. An online version of the latest edition can also be found at the DVA's web site: http://www.va.gov/opa/feature/index.htm. The online version is in both English and Spanish *(Beneficios Federales para los Veteranos y sus Dependientes)*. Over the years, the pamphlet has been issued under a number of titles, including *Handbook on Federal Benefits for Veterans* and *Federal Benefits for Veterans*. Brief information about some or all of the benefits covered in this annual can also be found in *Summary of Educational Benefits* and *A Summary of Department of Veterans Affairs Benefits*. These small pamphlets are available without charge from the Veterans Benefits Department, Department of Veterans Affairs, Washington, DC 20420.

Available from: U.S. Government Printing Office, Superintendent of Documents, P.O. Box 371954, Pittsburgh, PA 15250-7954. *Telephone:* (202) 512-1800, press 1; *Toll-free:* (800) 669-8331; *Fax:* (202) 512-2250; *E-mail:* gpoaccess@gpo.gov

Web site: www.access.gpo.gov/su_docs

Grants for Individuals–Special Population Groups–Military, Etc.

328

Financial Aid for Veterans, Military Personnel, and Their Dependents

By Gail Ann Schlachter and R. David Weber. El Dorado Hills, CA: Reference Service Press, 1988- . Biennial. ISSN 0896-7792. ISBN 1-58841-043-9. $40 (2002-2004 ed.). Hardcover.

Description: More than 1,100 grants/grants-in-aid, fellowships, scholarships, loans, and awards set aside for those with ties to the military are described in the latest edition (2002-2004) of this directory. For more information about the publication, see entry 216 in the "Scholarships, Fellowships & Loans—Special Population Groups—Military Personnel and Veterans" section of this bibliography.

Available from: Reference Service Press, 5000 Windplay Drive, Suite 4, El Dorado Hills, CA 95762. *Telephone:* (916) 939-9620; *Fax:* (916) 939-9626; *E-mail:* findaid@aol.com

Web site: www.rspfunding.com

329

Uniformed Services Almanac

Falls Church, VA: Uniformed Services Almanac, 1959- . Annual. $7.95 (2002 ed.) Paper.

Description: Issued annually, this handbook provides summary information not only on pay, retirement, travel and transportation, and military health care for active-duty military personnel, but on tax benefits, survivor benefits, educational benefits, and other monetary and nonmonetary benefits as well. Much of this information is available elsewhere (e.g., *Federal Benefits for Veterans and Their Dependents,* described in entry 327), but not in the tabular and summary forms presented here. Annually, the publisher also issues three other related guides, each for the same price: *National Guard Almanac, Reserve Forces Almanac,* and *Retired Military Almanac.*

Available from: Uniformed Services Almanac, Inc., P.O. Box 4144, Falls Church, VA 22044. *Telephone:* (703) 532-1631; *Toll-free:* (888) 872-9698; *Fax:* (703) 532-1635

Web site: www.militaryalmanac.com

330

Veterans' Benefits: A Guide to State Programs

By R.E. Armstrong and Terry P. Rizzauti. Westport, CT: Greenwood, 2001. 344p. ISBN 0-313-31905-7. $59.95. Paper.

How to Find Out About Financial Aid and Funding

Description: Written by two former members of the armed forces, this guide describes the benefits programs (some monetary, some not) offered to veterans by each of the 50 states. For more information about the guide, see entry 219 in "Scholarships, Fellowships & Loans—Special Population Groups—Military Personnel and Veterans" section of this bibliography.

Available from: Greenwood Publishing Group, Inc., 88 Post Road West, P.O. Box 5007, Westport, CT 06881-5007. *Telephone:* (203) 226-3571; *Toll-free:* (800) 225-5800; *Fax:* (203) 222-1502
Web site: www.greenwood.com

Persons with Disabilities

331

Financial Aid for the Disabled and Their Families

By Gail Ann Schlachter and R. David Weber. El Dorado Hills, CA: Reference Service Press, 1988- . Biennial. ISSN 0898-9222. ISBN 1-58841-042-0. $40 (2002-2004 ed.). Hardcover.

Description: This is the only comprehensive and up-to-date listing of grants-in-aid, awards, scholarships, fellowships, internships, and loans for individuals with disabilities and their families. For more information about the publication, see entry 222 in the "Scholarships, Fellowships & Loans—Special Population Groups—Persons with Disabilities" section of this bibliography.

Available from: Reference Service Press, 5000 Windplay Drive, Suite 4, El Dorado Hills, CA 95762. *Telephone:* (916) 939-9620; *Fax:* (916) 939-9626; *E-mail:* findaid@aol.com
Web site: www.rspfunding.com

332

How Do I Pay for It: A Guide to Funding Assistive Technology Equipment

Comp. by Mary Fitzpatrick and the Disability Law Project. Waterbury, Vermont Assistive Technology Project, 2000. 68p. Free. Paper.

Description: This resource guide is designed to give an overview of the many sources of funding available to Vermont residents to purchase assistive technology. Described here are dozens of funding sources from the federal government, Vermont state government, Vermont community programs, and out-of-state funders; two of these sections (federal government and out-of-state funders) would be of interest to residents in any state. Some of this information is also available on the Project's web site. A number of other states have pro-

Grants for Individuals–Special Population Groups–Religious Groups

duced similar guides to assistive technology funding; for example, *The Buck Starts Here...A Guide to Assistive Technology Funding in Kentucky,* (6th ed. 1998. 74p. Free. Spiral bound), which is available from the Kentucky Assistive Technology Service Network, 8412 Westport Road, Louisville, KY 40242.

Available from: Vermont Assistive Technology Project, Weeks Building, 103 South Main Street, Waterbury, VT 05671-2305. *Telephone:* (802) 241-2620; *Toll-free:* (800) 750-6355; *Fax:* (802) 241-2174

Web site: www.dad.state.vt.us/atp

333

Resources for People with Disabilities: A National Directory

2nd ed. Chicago: Ferguson Publishing, 2001. ISBN 0-89434-309-2, hardcover; 0-89434-256-8, CD-ROM. $89.95, 2-volume hardcover or CD-ROM single-user; $199, CD-ROM network.

Description: Persons with disabilities account for approximately 20 percent of the American population—making the disabled the largest "minority" group in the United States. This two-volume set contains more than 8,000 entries, grouped into several sections covering such topics as organizations and associations, publications, and assistive technology. One of the sections in the first volume provides information on funding sources available for technology, research, and education. Eligibility and deadline information is supplied. Not all of the programs covered are aimed directly at individuals with disabilities; a number are for researchers and organizations working to help the disabled. The publication is also available on a CD-ROM, which contains the same information as the book but also features hotlinks to web sites of interest and a Boolean search.

Available from: Ferguson Publishing Company, 200 West Jackson Boulevard, Chicago, IL 60606. *Toll-free:* (800) 306-9941; *Fax:* (800) 306-9942

Web site: www.fergpubco.com

Religious Groups

334

Faculty Grants Directory

http://www.ats.edu/faculty/fgdirtoc.htm

Description: The online Faculty Grants Directory is sponsored by the Association of Theological Schools and provides information, at no charge, on more than 750 grants and other funding opportunities for those teaching theology or religion in graduate institutions and for administrators and project leaders who are seeking funding for institutional or collaborative projects. For more informa-

tion about the online listing, see entry 302 in the "Grants for Individuals—Humanities—Religion" section of this bibliography.
Available from: Association of Theological Schools in the United States and Canada, 10 Summit Park Drive, Pittsburgh, PA 15275. *Telephone:* (412) 788-6505; *Fax:* (412) 788-6510; *E-mail:* ats@ats.edu
Web site: www.ats.edu

335

Princeton Theological Seminary Scholarship Guide

http://www.ptsem.edu/open/scholarships
Description: More than 100 grants, loans, and fellowships open to seminary students are described in this online directory. For more information about the site, see entry 229 in the "Scholarships, Fellowships & Loans—Special Population Groups—Religious Groups" section of this bibliography.
Available from: Princeton Theological Seminary, 64 Mercer Street, P.O. Box 821, Princeton, NJ 08542. *Telephone:* (609) 921-8300
Web site: www.ptsem.edu

Women

336

Directory of Financial Aids for Women

By Gail Ann Schlachter and R. David Weber. El Dorado Hills, CA: Reference Service Press, 1978- . Biennial. ISSN 0732-5215. ISBN 1-58841-067-6. $45 (2003-2005 ed.). Hardcover.
Description: This is the only extensive and regularly updated listing of grants, loans, fellowships, scholarships, awards/prizes, and internships available primarily or exclusively to women and women's organizations. For more information about the publication, see entry 232 in the "Scholarships, Fellowships & Loans—Special Population Groups—Women" section of this bibliography.
Available from: Reference Service Press, 5000 Windplay Drive, Suite 4, El Dorado Hills, CA 95762. *Telephone:* (916) 939-9620; *Fax:* (916) 939-9626; *E-mail:* findaid@aol.com
Web site: www.rspfunding.com

Grants for Organizations

Grants for organizations provide funds to support projects, programs, operating budgets, building and renovation, etc. Many are restricted by geographic location, purpose of the proposed program, or type of applicant. Described in this section of the guide are nearly 200 print, electronic, and Internet resources listing grants available to organizations on the international, national, and/or state levels. Of these directories, more than half (126) are general in their subject coverage: 8 have international scope, 48 have national scope, and 70 provide state coverage (only five states do not have at least one state-based listing of grants currently available). Of the remaining entries, 30 focus on grants in the social sciences, 10 cover the humanities, 17 deal with the sciences, and 9 are aimed at special population groups. If you are looking for a specific grants resource and you do not find it in this chapter, be sure to check the Title Index to see if it is covered elsewhere in the guide.

GENERAL
United States

337

America's New Foundations

Farmington Hills, MI: Taft Group, 1986-2000. Annual. ISBN 1-56995-373-2. $195 (2000 ed.). Hardcover.

Description: Described in the latest edition are nearly 3,000 private, corporate, and community foundations created since 1989 (about 600 of these are new to the 2000 edition). Profiles include contact information, gifts received, giving histories, typical recipients, officers and directors, application procedures, and the top 10 grants made by the foundation. With individual assets or annual giving of $100,000 or more, the funding organizations profiled here represent more than $15.1 billion in assets and $871 million in total giving. The 2000 edition is the latest available and no future editions are planned.

Available from: Taft Group, 27500 Drake Road, Farmington Hills, MI 48331-3535. *Toll-free:* (800) 877-TAFT; *Fax:* (800) 414-5043

Web site: www.galegroup.com/taft

338

Annual Register of Grant Support: A Directory of Funding Sources

Medford, NJ: Information Today, 1969- . Annual. ISSN 0066-4049. ISBN 1-57387-145-1. $229 (2003 ed.). Hardcover.

Description: Both organizational and individual grants in the United States and abroad are covered in this annual directory. For more information about the publication, see entry 235 in the "Grants for Individuals—General—United States" section of this bibliography.

Available from: Information Today, Inc., 143 Old Marlton Pike, Medford, NJ 08055-8750. *Telephone:* (609) 654-6266; *Fax:* (609) 654-4309; *E-mail:* custserv@infotoday.com

Web site: www.infotoday.com

339

Catalog of Federal Domestic Assistance

Prep. by the U.S. General Services Administration. Washington, DC: G.P.O., 1965- . Annual. ISSN 0097-7799. $63 (2002 ed.), looseleaf; $85, CD-ROM; online, free.

How to Find Out About Financial Aid and Funding

Description: This is the "what's what" of government grant programs. It is *the* definitive source of information on programs funded at the federal level. Nearly 1,500 domestic assistance programs and activities, administered by 60 different federal agencies and departments, are described in this annual publication: grants, loans, loan guarantees and shared revenue; provision of federal facilities; direct construction of goods and services; donation or provision of surplus property, technical assistance, and counseling; statistical and other information services; and service activities of regulatory agencies. These assistance programs are available to state and local governments, public and private organizations and institutions, and individuals. Excluded are automatic payment programs not requiring application; personal recruitment programs of individual federal departments other than the Civil Service Program; and inactive or unfunded programs. Each program entry contains information on purpose, availability, authorizing legislation, administering agency, and sources of additional information. The catalog contains three indexes: a functional index, a subject index, and an agency program index. It is issued once a year in a looseleaf format (usually published in June and distributed in August) and is updated 6 months after publication. Each annual edition contains more than 1,000 pages of information, making the listing cumbersome to use, even though there is extensive cross indexing. Users may find it easier to access the *Catalog* through the Federal Assistance Program Retrieval System (FAPRS), the official computerized guide to all federal grants found in the *Catalog*. With FAPRS ($53 subscription fee per year) and a modem, you can link up with the *Catalog's* database directly. Catalog contents and accompanying documents are also available on CD-ROM ($50 for a single copy and $85 for the complete June and December editions). The hard copy and CD-ROM versions contain grant-writing tutorials, and the CD-ROM comes with a database giving complete information on what programs received money in past awards. To order the electronic versions, write to: General Services Administration, Catalog Staff, The Reporter Building, 300 7th Street, S.W., Washington, DC 20407. To order the paper version, see the address below. Parts of the *Catalog* are also on the web site (http://www.cfda.gov) and can be searched, without charge, by keyword and program number.

Available from: U.S. Government Printing Office, Superintendent of Documents, P.O. Box 371954, Pittsburgh, PA 15250-7954. *Telephone:* (202) 512-1800, press 1; *Toll-free:* (800) 669-8331; *Fax:* (202) 512-2250; *E-mail:* gpoaccess@gpo.gov

Web site: www.access.gpo.gov/su_docs

340

CharityBrowser

Portland, OR: C&D Publishing. Quarterly. $100 per state (or $250 annually). CD-ROM.

Description: Produced by the same company that publishes numerous state *DataBooks* (see, for example, entry 389), this series of CD-ROMs provides data

Grants for Organizations–General–United States

on every active tax-exempt entity for each state in the United States ($100 per state, per quarter, or $250 per state annually). This includes nonprofit organizations, foundations, associations, and charitable trusts. The data come from IRS records. Each state-based CharityBrowser CD-ROM features two versions of the data: an Excel file and an ASCII tab-delimited text file for users wishing to import the data into other spreadsheet or database applications (e.g., Access, FileMaker Pro). The following information is provided for each entry, if available: organization name, address, city, state, zip, phone number, contact person, Employer Identification Number (EIN), tax year of the data, total assets, total revenues, year the organization became tax exempt (ruling year), National Taxonomy of Exempt Entities code, and NTEE code description. Each state-based CD-ROM also includes six ready-to-print reports in .pdf format; these reports break the data into two categories: foundations and all entities. For each of these categories, there are three reports: data by city name, data by entity name, and data by asset amount. Because the CD-ROMs are issued quarterly, the information on each is quite up to date.

Available from: C&D Publishing, 1017 Morrison Street S.W., Suite 500, Portland, OR 97205. *Telephone:* (503) 274-8780; *Toll-free:* (877) 924-7268

Web site: www.foundationdatabook.com

341

Chronicle Guide to Grants

http://philanthropy.com/grants

Description: Previously distributed on disk and CD-ROM, this service is now available only at the *Chronicle of Philanthropy's* web site and accessible only by subscription ($49 for one week, $95 for one month, $195 for six months; $295 for one year); current subscribers to the print version of the *Chronicle of Philanthropy* (see entry 342) or the *Chronicle of Higher Education* (entry 277) can search the past two issues at no charge or subscribe at a substantial discount. Using the online Chronicle Guide to Grants, subscribers can search the grant announcements published in either of the *Chronicles* since 1995 by 1) keywords; 2) grantmakers; and 3) recipient. More advanced searching is also possible. In addition, searches can be restricted to the current issue only. Program entries identify grant sponsor, grant recipient characteristics, application procedures, fiscal information, and date entry appeared in either *Chronicle* (but not the date when the grant was awarded).

Available from: Chronicle of Philanthropy, Attn: Subscription Department, 1255 23rd Street, N.W., Suite 700, Washington, DC 20037. *Telephone:* (202) 466-1200; *Toll-free:* (800) 728-2819; *E-mail:* subscriptions@philanthropy.com

Web site: philanthropy.com

342

Chronicle of Philanthropy

Washington, DC: Chronicle of Higher Education. Biweekly. ISSN 1040-676X. $69.50/yr. Paper.

Description: The *Chronicle of Philanthropy* is the newspaper of record for the nonprofit world. Published every other week (except at the end of December) by the *Chronicle of Higher Education* (see entry 277), the newspaper reports on various aspects of nonprofit and philanthropic activities. One of the regular departments, "Deadlines," lists a dozen or two government and private funding programs and gives contact and application deadline information. Another funding-related section, "New Grants," generally runs about 12 pages and covers more than $34 million in currently-available grants each issue. The information in the "Deadlines" section is also available on the *Chronicle's* web site and can be searched at no charge. The "New Grants" announcements printed in the newsletter since 1995 are also included in the Chronicle Guide to Grants, a database on the web that may be accessed only by subscription (see entry 341).

Available from: Chronicle of Philanthropy, Attn: Subscription Department, 1255 23rd Street, N.W., Suite 700, Washington, DC 20037. *Telephone:* (202) 466-1200; *Toll-free:* (800) 728-2819; *E-mail:* subscriptions@philanthropy.com

Web site: philanthropy.com

343

Community Foundation Locator

http://www.communityfoundationlocator.org/search/index.cfm

Description: Community foundations are tax-exempt public charities serving thousands of people who share a common concern: improving the quality of life in their area. To locate community foundations in your state, go to the Community Foundation Locator, a web site sponsored and maintained by the Council on Foundations. There you can click on the state map (the number of community foundations are indicated for each state) or search by name, region, state, or zip code. Basic contact information and links to the foundations' web sites are provided (although many of the links have not been kept up to date and do not work). This service is available without charge, but much of the rest of the Council's web site is open only to Council members.

Available from: Council on Foundations, 1828 L Street, N.W., Washington, DC 200036. *Telephone:* (202) 466-6512; *E-mail:* cflocator@cof.org

Web site: www.cof.org

Grants for Organizations–General–United States

344

Corporate Foundation Profiles

12th ed. New York: Foundation Center, 2002. 724p. ISBN 0-87954-972-6. $155. Hardcover.

Description: The 12th edition of *Corporate Foundation Profiles* provides grantseekers with current, indepth reports on 187 of the largest corporate grantmakers in the United States. Plus, there is an appendix listing core financial data on 1,300 additional corporate foundations that give at least $50,000 in grants every year. The directory is divided into three sections: 1) Foundation Portrait, which provides basic information on the listed foundations: contact information, purpose, giving limitations, and application guidelines; 2) Grants Analysis, which offers a detailed breakdown of the corporate foundation's grant program; and 3) Sample Grants, which lists up to 50 or more grants recently awarded by each foundation. Entries are indexed by names of donors, officers and trustees, subject areas funded, types of support preferred, geographic location, and international giving. No other published source provides a more thorough analysis of the 200 major corporate funders covered here, each of which gives at least $1.2 million annually.

Available from: Foundation Center, 79 Fifth Avenue, New York, NY 10003-3076. *Telephone:* (212) 807-3690; *Toll-free:* (800) 424-9836; *Fax:* (212) 807-3691

Web site: fdncenter.org

345

Corporate Giving Directory: Comprehensive Profiles of America's Major Corporate Foundations and Corporate Charitable Giving Programs

Farmington Hills, MI: Taft, 1977- . Annual. ISSN 1055-0623. ISBN 1-56995-458-5. $505 (2003 ed.). Hardcover.

Description: Taft is one of the oldest, largest, and best known of the information subscription services. This directory, first issued in 1977 and updated annually since then, profiles the 1,000 largest corporate foundations and corporate direct giving programs in the United States. Collectively, the companies described here donate $3.6 billion in cash and nonmonetary support each year—more than 50 percent of all corporate giving. The profiles are arranged by program name; each entry contains: full contact information; corporate revenue figures and Fortune 500 rankings; cash, nonmonetary, and corporate giving information; details about corporate matching gift and company-sponsored volunteer programs; analysis of the corporation's giving priorities and typical recipients; an expanded list of corporate operating locations; geographic giving preferences; application procedures and evaluative criteria; and biographical data on corporate and foundation officers and directors (profiles average one page in length). Multiple indexes are provided: state, field of interest, corporate operating location, contact persons, sponsoring company, and types of grants. New to this edition, an appendix identifies more than 1,000 abridged corporate foundation and corporate direct giving program entries that provide additional funding leads. There are a number of other sources that complement the listings included here: *Corporate 500, Foundation 1000, Foundation Directory,* and its companion, the *Foundation Grants Index* (each described elsewhere in this section of the guide). But, nearly one third of the profiles presented in the *Corporate Giving Directory* cover difficult-to-find corporate direct giving programs (these are not available from the IRS, corporate annual reports, or other directories). Further, the directory supplies more relevant biographical data than can be found in other grants resources. Although the directory was formerly available in both print and electronic formats, it is now issued only in print; however, you can use Taft's *Prospector's Choice* to access much of the same information on CD-ROM (see entry 383).

Available from: Taft Group, 27500 Drake Road, Farmington Hills, MI 48331-3535. *Toll-free:* (800) 877-TAFT; *Fax:* (800) 414-5043

Web site: www.galegroup.com/taft

346

Corporate Giving Yellow Pages: Guide to Corporate Giving Contacts

Farmington Hills, MI: Taft, 1983-2000. Annual. ISSN 1058-689X. ISBN 1-56995-332-5. $115 (2000 ed.). Paper.

Description: It is often more effective to address an initial inquiry to a specific contact person at a potential granting source than to submit an undirected letter. Until the year 2000, this directory could help in the process, providing information on 3,700 funding contact persons at major corporate giving programs and corporate foundations in the United States. More than half of the listed companies had direct giving programs (these are identified by "dg" after the name; foundation giving is indicated by "fdn"). Entries in the last edition (2000) are arranged by organization name and specify only contact name, company address and telephone numbers, and fax numbers. An asterisk identifies the corporations that are more fully described in the *Corporate Giving Directory* (see entry 345). The directory was last published in 2000 and no future editions are planned.

Available from: Taft Group, 27500 Drake Road, Farmington Hills, MI 48331-3535. *Toll-free:* (800) 877-TAFT; *Fax:* (800) 414-5043

Web site: www.galegroup.com/taft

Grants for Organizations–General–United States

347

COS Funding Opportunities

http://www.cos.com
Description: COS Funding Opportunities is a web-based subscription database that is updated daily and contains descriptions of more than 23,000 funding opportunities from around the world that support research, collaborative activities, travel, training, curriculum development, conferences, postdoctoral positions, equipment acquisition, and operating or capital expenses. For more information about the database, see entry 237 in the "Grants for Individuals—General—United States" section of this bibliography.
Available from: Community of Science, Inc., 1629 Thames Street, Suite 200, Baltimore, MD 21231. *Telephone:* (410) 563-2378; *Fax:* (410) 563-5389; *E-mail:* evd@cos.com
Web site: www.cos.com

348

Directory of Building and Equipment Grants: A Reference Directory Identifying Building, Renovation, and Equipment Grants Available to Nonprofit Organizations

7th ed. Ed. by Richard M. Eckstein. Loxahatchee, FL: Research Grant Guides, 2003. 184p. ISBN 0-945078-31-5. $69. Paper.
Description: Applicants seeking funding for building, equipment, or renovation often face greater challenges than other grantseekers, because many foundations exclude funding for those purposes. One of the ways to find available funding is to use this guide, which describes 950 foundations that award building and equipment grants. Entries are listed by state and specify contacts, areas of interest supported, geographic restrictions, grant ranges, and organizations funded. The profiles are indexed by subject, e.g., community development, elderly, environment, hospitals, libraries, recreation, and renovation.
Available from: Research Grant Guides, Inc., P.O. Box 1214, Loxahatchee, FL 33470-1214. *Telephone:* (561) 795-6129; *Fax:* (561) 795-7794

349

Directory of Corporate and Foundation Givers

Ed. by Katherine E. Jankowski. Farmington Hills, MI: Taft, 1999. 2v. ISBN 1-56995-253-1. $260. Paper.
Description: This guide is aimed at fundseekers who wish to reach the "next tier" of foundations and corporate givers: the smaller and more regional grantmakers. Covered in the 1999 edition are 1) 4,500 private foundations that have

at least $1.8 million in assets or distribute at least $250,000 in grants each year; and 2) nearly 4,000 corporate giving programs, including 1,500 corporate foundations and 2,400 corporate direct givers. Each entry provides address and telephone number, contact person, corporate or giving officers, financial summary of gifts, a brief summary of contribution categories, and a list of recent grants awarded. Some entries also detail application procedures, but these seem to be randomly supplied. Entries are indexed by location (headquarters and operations), grant type, nonmonetary support provided, recipient type, major products/industry, officers and directors, and recipients by state, followed by a master funder index. Much of the information provided here is also included in Taft's CD-ROM *Prospector's Choice* (see entry 383). The edition issued in 1999 is the latest available and no future editions are planned.

Available from: Taft Group, 27500 Drake Road, Farmington Hills, MI 48331-3535. *Toll-free:* (800) 877-TAFT; *Fax:* (800) 414-5043

Web site: www.galegroup.com/taft

350

Directory of International Corporate Giving in America and Abroad

10th ed. Ed. by Katherine E. Jankowski. Farmington Hills, MI: Taft, 1999. 826p. ISBN 1-56995-296-5. $215. Paper.

Description: In this age of global markets, many multinational corporations have set up international philanthropies. This comprehensive resource profiles more than 650 companies that give internationally—one of the few sources to provide this type of information. The directory is divided into two sections: Section One presents current information on the funding activities in the United States of 477 foreign-owned American companies; Section Two provides information on the international funding activities of nearly 200 U.S.-headquartered companies. This information can be accessed through 19 separate indexes. In all, more than $500 million in international corporate giving is identified in this directory. The last edition was issued in 1999 and no future editions are planned.

Available from: Taft Group, 27500 Drake Road, Farmington Hills, MI 48331-3535. *Toll-free:* (800) 877-TAFT; *Fax:* (800) 414-5043

Web site: www.galegroup.com/taft

351

Directory of Operating Grants

7th ed. Ed. by Richard M. Eckstein. Loxahatchee, FL: Research Grant Guides, 2003. 208p. ISBN 0-945078-29-3. $69. Paper.

Description: Operating grants are not restricted to a specified project or set of activities. They can be used to support general, on-going organizational expenses: salaries, rent, mortgage payments, utilities, office supplies, and other overhead expenses. The latest edition of *Directory of Operating Grants* identi-

Grants for Organizations–General–United States

fies 1,000 foundations that award that type of grant. Profiles are listed by state, are indexed by subject, and provide the following information: address, phone number, areas of interest supported, geographic restrictions, grant range, and organizations funded. Research Grants Guide publishes several other grants directories (each described elsewhere in the "Grants for Organizations" chapter of this bibliography); this is the publisher's best-selling title.

Available from: Research Grant Guides, Inc., P.O. Box 1214, Loxahatchee, FL 33470-1214. *Telephone:* (561) 795-6129; *Fax:* (561) 795-7794

352

Directory of Program Grants

2nd ed. Ed. by Richard M. Eckstein. Loxahatchee, FL: Research Grant Guides, 2002. 152p. ISBN 0-945078-28-5. $69. Paper.

Description: Included in the second edition of this directory is information on 775 foundations that provide funding for programs, including AIDS, animal welfare, culture, education, the elderly, the environment, health, higher education, hospitals, minorities, recreation, religion, social services, women and girls, and youth. Entries are listed by state and specify contacts, areas of interest supported, geographic restrictions, grant ranges, and organizations funded. The profiles are indexed by subject.

Available from: Research Grant Guides, Inc., P.O. Box 1214, Loxahatchee, FL 33470-1214. *Telephone:* (561) 795-6129; *Fax:* (561) 795-7794

353

Directory of Research Grants

Westport, CT: Oryx, 1975- . Annual. ISSN 0146-7336. ISBN 1-57356-570-9. $134.95 (2003 ed.). Paper.

Description: Research grants open to both organizations and individuals are described in this annual publication. For more information about the directory, see entry 238 in the "Grants for Individuals—General—United States" section of this bibliography.

Available from: Oryx Press, 88 Post Road West, Westport, CT 06881. *Telephone:* (602) 265-2651; *Toll-free:* (800) 279-6799; *Fax:* (800) 279-4663; *E-mail:* info@oryxpress.com
Web site: www.oryxpress.com

354

FC Search

New York: Foundation Center, 2002 (Version 6.0). ISBN 0-87954-540-2, CD-ROM stand-alone (single user); 0-87954-866-5, CD-ROM local area network (2-8 users). $1,195, CD-ROM stand-alone; $1,895, CD-ROM local area network.

Description: This is the most comprehensive fundraising CD-ROM. It describes more than 65,000 independent, community, and company-sponsored foundations as well as corporate giving programs and grantmaking public charities in the United States. In addition, it identifies close to 200,000 grants linked to the largest U.S. funders and lists approximately 290,000 trustees, officers, and donors. The data presented here can also be found, collectively, in the following seven Foundation Center print products: *The Foundation Directory* (see entry 359), *The Foundation Directory Part 2* (entry 361), *The Foundation Directory Supplement* (entry 362), *Guide to U.S. Foundation: Their Trustees, Officers and Donors* (entry 377), *National Directory of Corporate Giving* (entry 380), and *Foundation Grants Index* (entry 364). The CD-ROM's search engine enables users to select from among 21 different search criteria: grantmaker name, grantmaker state, grantmaker city, grantmaker type, geographic focus, establishment date, fields of interest, trustees and other officers, text search field, types of support, total assets, total giving, corporate name, corporate location, recipient name, recipient state, recipient city, subjects, grant amount, authorization year, and recipient type. Beginning with version 2.1, the CD-ROM also provides links to 2,500 grantmaker web sites, including the Foundation Center's web site (for users with access to the web and either Netscape's Navigator or Microsoft's Internet Explorer browser software), and 1,500 corporate web sites. For nonsubscribers, these links can also be found (and searched by subject or geographic keyword) in the "Grantmaker Info" section of the Foundation Center's web site. More than 60 percent of the entries have been updated since the last edition.

Available from: Foundation Center, 79 Fifth Avenue, New York, NY 10003-3076. *Telephone:* (212) 807-3690; *Toll-free:* (800) 424-9836; *Fax:* (212) 807-3691

Web site: fdncenter.org

355

Federal Assistance Monitor

Silver Spring, MD: CD Publications 1986- . Bi-weekly. ISSN 1050-3242. $349/yr. Paper or online.

Description: The *Federal Assistance Monitor* is published twice monthly and reviews federal funding announcements, private grants, and legislative actions affecting community programs, including education, economic development, housing, children and youth services, substance abuse, and health care. Each grant notice is categorized by subject matter. Indicated for foundations and organizations are areas of interest and projected grant awards, as well as funding priorities. *Federal Assistance Monitor* is one in a series of funding newsletters issued by CD Publications. The others (which cover both public and private grants) include: *Aid for Education* ($339/yr.), *Children and Youth Funding Report* ($349/yr.), *Community Health Funding Report* ($339/yr.), *Disability Funding News* ($339/yr.), *Family Services Funding Report* ($339/yr.), *State & Local Homeland Security Funding Report* ($347/yr.), and *Substance Abuse Funding News* ($339/yr.). Each of these newsletters also contains advice on grantseeking and proposal writing, along with tips from funding officials on what they look for in grant applications. Most of the newsletters are available either in print or as an online subscription at the same price.

Available from: CD Publications, 8204 Fenton Street, Silver Spring, MD 20910. *Telephone:* (301) 588-6380; *Toll-free:* (800) 666-6380; *Fax:* (301) 588-6385

Web site: www.cdpublications.com

356

Federal Grants & Contracts Weekly: Project Opportunities in Research, Training, and Services

Ed. by Pamela Moore. Frederick, MD: Aspen Publishers, 1974- . Weekly. ISSN 0194-2247. $489/yr. E-mail.

Description: Published 50 times a year by Aspen Publishers (formerly Capitol Publications), *Federal Grants & Contracts Weekly* serves as an "early warning" system, to alert readers to federal grant announcements, as well as to research, training, and technical services contracts. Previously issued as an eight-page weekly newsletter, the *Weekly* is now sent only by e-mail to subscribers. Each "issue" contains information on Requests for Proposals (RFPs), closing dates for grant programs, procurement-related regulatory news, contract awards, updates on federal budget action, and profiles on grant programs and federal agencies. Aspen Publishers also issues three other weekly "alerting" services: *Education Grants Alert* in a print version only, for elementary and secondary school grantseekers (50 issues; $486/yr.), *Foundation & Corporate Grants Alert* (12 issues; $383/yr.) in both print and e-mail versions, and *Health Grants & Contracts Weekly* (see entry 512).

Available from: Aspen Publishers, Inc., 7201 McKinney Circle, Frederick, MD 21704. *Toll-free:* (800) 638-8437; *Fax:* (301) 417-7550

Web site: www.aspenpublishers.com

How to Find Out About Financial Aid and Funding

357

Federal Register

Prep. by the U.S. Office of the Federal Register. Washington, DC: G.P.O., 1936- . Daily (Monday through Friday, except legal holidays). $674/yr., paper; $264/yr., microfiche.

Description: The *Federal Register* is issued every week day except holidays. It is the official source for the publication of public regulations and legal notices issued by more than 250 federal executive agencies and independent agencies. By law, all agency documents of public interest, documents required to be published by acts of Congress, federal agency documents of general applicability and legal effect, presidential proclamations, and Executive Orders are presented here. Thus, this is an excellent place to check for the latest information (including deadline date) on federally funded programs. But the information does not come cheap. A print subscription to the complete service costs $674 per year; a microfiche subscription costs $264. There is a separately published *Federal Register Subject Index* that is issued monthly; each issue is cumulative, with the December issue serving as the annual cumulative index ($30). The U.S. Government Printing Office maintains an online searchable database of the contents of the *Federal Register* back through 1995 (as well as the *U.S. Government Manual* and other important publications) which can be accessed without charge at the web site listed below. For a copy of the daily "Notices of Funding Availability" (announcements that invite applications to federal grant programs), go to this web site: http://ocd.usda.gov/nofa.htm (also referred to as "EZ/EC"). This page allows you to generate a customized listing of NOFAs by date, keyword, or agency.

Available from: U.S. Government Printing Office, Superintendent of Documents, P.O. Box 371954, Pittsburgh, PA 15250-7954. *Telephone:* (202) 512-1800, press 1; *Fax:* (202) 512-2250; *E-mail:* gpoaccess@gpo.gov

Web site: www.access.gpo.gov/su_docs

358

The Foundation Center's Guide to Grantseeking on the Web

2nd ed. Ed. by Kief Schladweiler. New York: Foundation Center, 2001. 764p. ISBN 0-87954-966-1, paper; 0-87954-967-X, CD-ROM. $29.95, paper or CD-ROM.

Description: This is the single best guide aimed at fundseekers interested in conducting funding research online. It is packed with details about more than 2,000 useful Internet sites that provide information on funding opportunities offered by private foundations, public charities, corporate grantmakers, federal and state agencies, and other related nonprofits. The sites referred to throughout the guide cover a wide range of subject areas; some are specialized, focusing on a specific topic, while others are portal sites with information and links that

Grants for Organizations–General–United States

span a number of topics. There's even a separate chapter focusing on web sites and strategies for researching individual donors. Supplementing the text are numerous screen shots chosen to "help you to visualize the sites and...prepare you for when you actually visit them." There are eight appendices and, collectively, they are very lengthy (more than 500 pages) and exceptionally helpful; detailed information is provided there on general search engines, individual foundations and other grantmakers on the web, resources available for further reading, and web-related terms. The guide is available either in print or on a CD-ROM—each at the bargain price of $29.95.

Available from: Foundation Center, 79 Fifth Avenue, New York, NY 10003-3076. *Telephone:* (212) 807-3690; *Toll-free:* (800) 424-9836; *Fax:* (212) 807-3691

Web site: fdncenter.org

359

The Foundation Directory

New York: Foundation Center, 1960- . Annual. ISSN 0071-8092. ISBN 0-87954-992-0, paper; 0-87954-060-5, CD-ROM single-user; 0-87954-061-3, CD-ROM local area network. $215 (2002 ed.), paper; $295, CD-ROM single-user; $595, CD-ROM local area network; various pricing, online subscription.

Description: Issued by the Foundation Center, the major nonprofit organization in the country focusing on the activities of private foundations, this directory sets the standard for listings of nongovernmental grantmaking foundations. It identifies nonprofit, nongovernmental organizations with assets in excess of $3 million or which make grants in excess of $200,000 in one year. Nearly 10,000 foundations are covered (1,000 more than in the previous edition). These represent only 10 percent of all grantmaking foundations but over 90 percent of all grant money distributed ($19 billion annually). Data on the foundations, arranged by state and then by name of agency, include: purpose, finances, person to contact, number of grants awarded, and average amount of the award. More than 46,000 descriptions of recently-awarded grants are also provided. Entries are indexed by type of support; field of interest; foundation name; geographic location; and donors, trustees, and administrators. For information on the next 10,000 largest foundations, see the *Foundation Directory Part 2* (described below). To update the information presented here, use the *Foundation Directory Supplement* (see entry 362). The directory is also available on a separate CD-ROM and as an Internet subscription (for more information on the online version, see Foundation Directory Online, entry 360).

Available from: Foundation Center, 79 Fifth Avenue, New York, NY 10003-3076. *Telephone:* (212) 807-3690; *Toll-free:* (800) 424-9836; *Fax:* (212) 807-3691

Web site: fdncenter.org

360

The Foundation Directory Online

http://www.fconline.fdncenter.org

Description: While the Basic version of the Foundation Directory Online corresponds to the print edition of the *Foundation Directory* (see entry 359), the other versions provide additional information. The Plus version covers the 10,000 largest foundations found in the Basic subscription but also offers access to the Foundation Center's database of 150,000+ grants awarded by the top 1,000 funders. The Premium version offers the same features found in the Plus subscription, plus information on an additional 10,000 mid-size funders. Finally, the Platinum version offers the most comprehensive coverage: 70,000+ foundations, corporate givers, and grantmaking public charities as well as 150,000+ grants. The prices directly correspond to the extent of coverage: Basic is $195/year or $19.95/month; Plus is $295/year or $29.95/month; Premium is $595/year or $59.95/month; and Platinum is $995/year or $149.95/month. In each version, fundseekers can select up to seven search fields to search for foundations. In the Plus, Premium, and Platinum versions, fundseekers can also use up to seven search fields to look for grants. The database is updated monthly and, like Foundation Finder (see entry 363), users can access the most recent 990-PF forms for each private foundation.

Available from: Foundation Center, 79 Fifth Avenue, New York, NY 10003-3076. *Telephone:* (212) 807-3690; *Toll-free:* (800) 424-9836; *Fax:* (212) 807-3691

Web site: fdncenter.org

361

The Foundation Directory Part 2

New York: Foundation Center, 1993- . Annual. ISBN 0-87954-993-9, paper; 0-87954-962-9, CD-ROM single-user; 0-87954-962-9, local area network. $185 (2002 ed.), paper; $495, CD-ROM single-user; $795, CD-ROM local area network; various pricing, online subscription.

Description: The listings in *Part 2* extend the scope of *The Foundation Directory* (see above), describing the next 10,000 largest foundations (those that are mid-sized) by total giving. *Part 2's* latest edition features more than 1,500 foundations that are covered for the first time and over 31,000 grant descriptions. To update the information presented here, use the *Foundation Directory Supplement* (see below). The information in the directory is also available on a CD-ROM along with part one of *The Foundation Directory* and as part of the Foundation Directory Online Plus on the web ($295 per year or $29.95 per month; see entry 360). Together, *The Foundation Directory* and *The Foundation Directory Part 2* constitute the most comprehensive source of information on the country's largest foundations.

Grants for Organizations–General–United States

Available from: Foundation Center, 79 Fifth Avenue, New York, NY 10003-3076. *Telephone:* (212) 807-3690; *Toll-free:* (800) 424-9836; *Fax:* (212) 807-3691
Web site: fdncenter.org

362

The Foundation Directory Supplement

New York: Foundation Center, 1982- . Annual. ISBN 1-931923-01-9. $125 (2002 ed.). Paper.

Description: This supplement (issued every year in September) provides updated information on the grantmaking foundations covered in *The Foundation Directory* and *The Foundation Directory Part 2* (both described above). In each supplement, approximately 2,000 entries are presented; these supply new fiscal data; changes in staff, trustees, officers, addresses, telephone numbers, deadlines, application procedures, and funding priorities; and information on major foundations that terminated during the previous year. Subject, foundation, and personnel indexes complete the work. The information in the *Supplement* is also included in *FC Search,* the Foundation Center's CD-ROM product (see entry 354).

Available from: Foundation Center, 79 Fifth Avenue, New York, NY 10003-3076. *Telephone:* (212) 807-3690; *Toll-free:* (800) 424-9836; *Fax:* (212) 807-3691
Web site: fdncenter.org

363

Foundation Finder

htttp://fdncenter.org/finder.html

Description: This free look-up tool provided on the Foundation Center's web site offers basic information on approximately 70,000 active grantmaking foundations in the United States: full legal name, address, telephone number, contact person, and, when available, supplemental address, additional phone numbers, fax numbers, e-mail addresses, URL addresses, type of foundation (e.g., community, company sponsored, independent), fiscal data, assets, total giving, IRS employer identification number, and, with the help of GrantSmart (see entry 374), a .pdf file of the most recent IRS Form 990-PF filings. Also available are links to the 1,700 grantmakers that have web sites; use the Grantmaker and Sector Search to access this service. The data are updated monthly. Foundations can be searched by name, city, and state. Excluded from the Foundation Finder site are direct corporate giving programs and public charities.

Available from: Foundation Center, 79 Fifth Avenue, New York, NY 10003-3076. *Telephone:* (212) 807-3690; *Toll-free:* (800) 424-9836; *Fax:* (212) 807-3691

Web site: fdncenter.org

364

The Foundation Grants Index on CD-ROM

New York: Foundation Center, 1971- . Annual. ISSN 0090-1601. ISBN 1-931923-21-3. $165 (2003 ed., Version 3.0), CD-ROM.

Description: Originally issued as a print product, the *Foundation Grants Index* is now available only on CD-ROM. The *Index* provides detailed subject access to 125,000 grants made in excess of $10,000 during the year of record by 1,000 leading foundations. This represents combined giving of $7.9 billion and about 57 percent of all foundation giving. Information is taken from foundation annual reports, surveys, and IRS Form 990s. Grant descriptions can be accessed in 12 different ways: recipient name, recipient state, recipient city, recipient type, grantmaker name, grantmaker state, geographic focus, subject, types of support, grant amount, year authorized, and full text. Entries include the amount and date of the grant, name and location of the recipients, a description of the grant, and any known limitations in the foundation's giving pattern. While not comprehensive, the *Index* is useful in representing recent grants made by large national foundations, thus providing insight into their current interest. You can use the *Index* to find foundations active in your field, check for foundations that made grants in your geographic area, review the recent grants of 1,000 large foundations, and identify which nonprofits have been successful in obtaining grants. The information in the *Foundation Grants Index* is also sorted by subject and made available in the Foundation Center's *Grant Guides* (see entry 369). This information is also included in *FC Search* (see entry 354).

Available from: Foundation Center, 79 Fifth Avenue, New York, NY 10003-3076. *Telephone:* (212) 807-3690; *Toll-free:* (800) 424-9836; *Fax:* (212) 807-3691

Web site: fdncenter.org

365

Foundation Reporter: Comprehensive Profiles and Analyses of America's Major Private Foundations

Farmington Hills, MI: Taft, 1977- . Annual. ISSN 1055-4998. ISBN 1-56995-448-8. $490 (2003 ed.). Hardcover.

Description: This is one of the best, most detailed, and most expensive of the grants directories. Included annually in this definitive resource are nearly 1,000 indepth profiles and analyses of America's leading private foundations, which collectively contribute more than $6 billion each year. All foundations listed have at least $10 million in assets or a minimum of $500,000 in annual giving. Lengthy entries provide information on the history of the foundation, officers, directors, types of foundations, areas of interest, fiscal activities, types of grants awarded, grants distribution, sample grants, application requirements, and contact persons. A "new initiatives" section alerts fundseekers to any new programs instituted by a foundation. Thirteen indexes are supplied, including state, type of grant, field of interest, and officers/directors by name, place of birth, and alma mater. Also included, since the 2002 edition, is an appendix containing more than 1,000 abridged private foundation entries that provide additional funding leads. Although this title used to be issued, also, on diskette and magnetic tape, it is now only available in print. The companion newsletter that used to update the directory, *Foundation Giving Watch,* ($149), has also ceased publication. In the past, the directory was known as *Taft Foundation Reporter: Comprehensive Profiles and Analysis of America's Private Foundations.*

Available from: Taft Group, 27500 Drake Road, Farmington Hills, MI 48331-3535. *Toll-free:* (800) 877-TAFT; *Fax:* (800) 414-5043

Web site: www.galegroup.com/taft

366

The Foundation 1000

New York: Foundation Center, 1977- . Annual. ISSN 1067-7828. ISBN 0-931923-12-4. $295 (2002-2003 ed.). Paper.

Description: Of all the Foundation Center's general directories, *The Foundation 1000* provides the most detailed treatment but covers the smallest number of foundations. In all, only 1,000 grantmaking organizations are included, with entries averaging three to six pages each. These are the wealthiest foundations, accounting for 60 percent of the total annual giving of all U.S. foundations (close to 250,000 grants worth $10 billion annually). Each profile provides information on the foundation's areas of giving, types of grants, and types of recipients; the profiles also list up to 50 or more recent grants, often the best indicators of funding interests. All varieties of foundations are represented, including over 200 company-sponsored foundations and more than 25 community foundations. Entries are indexed by foundation name, subject field, type of support, geographic locations, and officers/donors/trustees. A separate index tracks foundations that award international grants. This work was previously published under the title *Source Book Profiles.* In 1992, the publication changed both its frequency (to annual) and its title to *The Foundation 1000.* Use this directory to identify the 1,000 largest grantgivers, their giving priorities, who receives their grants, how much they receive, and how you can apply.

Available from: Foundation Center, 79 Fifth Avenue, New York, NY 10003-3076. *Telephone:* (212) 807-3690; *Toll-free:* (800) 424-9836; *Fax:* (212) 807-3691

Web site: fdncenter.org

How to Find Out About Financial Aid and Funding

367

Fundsnet

http://www.fundsnetservices.com

Description: Fundsnet has been online since 1996. It is a information-rich site, covering grants for organizations, grants for individuals, and financial aid for students, along with some other miscellaneous categories: grantwriting resources, fundraising books, and the Fundsnet message board. Be sure to check the site list, or you could miss out on a number of site offerings. Each entry on the site is linked to further information from the sponsoring organization on the web, and most of these links are annotated. Although information/links on funding programs are grouped into categories (e.g., women grants and resources, government grants and information, disability grants, international funders), users can only browse through the listings; there is no search feature. In some channels (for example, Foundations Online, Community Foundations) this is easier, because the entries are arranged alphabetically or geographically. But most of the channels consist of profiles either randomly or chronologically (by deadline date) listed. Thus, using the site is not only time consuming, but hit-or-miss as well.

Available from: Fundsnet Online Services, 419 Immaculada Street, San Juan, PR 00915. *E-mail:* info@fundsnetservices.com

Web site: www.fundsnetservices.com

368

Government Assistance Almanac

By J. Robert Dumouchel. Detroit: Omnigraphics, 1985- . Annual. ISSN 0883-8690. ISBN 0-7808-0580-1. $225 (2002-2003 ed.). Hardcover.

Description: This is another publication based on the *Catalog of Federal Domestic Assistance* (see entry 339). Dumouchel's work summarizes rather than reproduces all the information in the *Catalog's* 2,500 pages and nearly 1,500 entries. Brief information is provided: program purpose, type of assistance (e.g., grants, loans, services), activity level (number of claims or awards), monetary award, eligibility, and contact information (including address, telephone, fax, e-mail, and web site). In addition, the *Almanac* adds its own index and provides a system of finding federal office contacts, but it does cost considerably more than the *Catalog*. If you are interested in the essentials rather than the details of current federal programs, this volume could prove less cumbersome to use than the *Catalog's* looseleaf system. However, readers who have checked or plan to check the *Catalog of Federal Domestic Assistance,* either in print on online, can skip this source.

Available from: Omnigraphics, Inc., 615 Griswold Street, Detroit, MI 48226. *Telephone:* (313) 961-1340; *Toll-free:* (800) 234-1340; *Fax:* (800) 875-1340; *E-mail:* info@omnigraphics.com

Grants for Organizations–General–United States

Web site: www.omnigraphics.com

369

The Grant Guides

New York: Foundation Center, 1983- . Annual. $75 each (2002/2003 ed.). Paper.

Description: Originally entitled *COMSEARCH Printouts,* this is a series of 35 computer-produced subject guides to foundation funding. Each one deals with a different topic: arts, culture, and the humanities; children and youth; elementary and secondary education; environmental protection and animal welfare; film, media, and communications; foreign and international programs; higher education; libraries and information services; mental health, addictions, and crisis services; minorities; physically and mentally disabled; religion, religious welfare and religious education; scholarships, student aid, and loans; social services; and women and girls. The reports provide the same data that can be found in the *Foundation Grants Index* (see entry 364), but the listing is arranged according to specific subjects. Each subject-based guide identifies foundation grants of $10,000 or more and indexes the entries by subject, geographic preferences, and recipients. The number of pages in each report varies greatly, from 111 pages in the *Libraries & Information Services Grant Guide* to 554 pages in the *Children & Youth Grant Guide,* but the price for each is the same.

Available from: Foundation Center, 79 Fifth Avenue, New York, NY 10003-3076. *Telephone:* (212) 807-3690; *Toll-free:* (800) 424-9836; *Fax:* (212) 807-3691

Web site: fdncenter.org

370

Grants on Disc

Farmington Hills, MI: Taft. Annual, with quarterly updates. ISBN 1-56995-349-X. $695 (1999 ed.). CD-ROM.

Description: This Windows-based CD-ROM offers information on close to 300,000 grants awarded during the past year by more than 5,200 independent U.S. foundations, corporate foundations, and corporate direct givers. Details are provided on grant recipients, including name and locations, dollar amount of recent grants, purpose of the grant, subject focus, recipient type, and contact; all of this can be viewed simultaneously in different windows. Both keyword and Boolean searches can be conducted, so it is possible to target a search by funder, recipient, or grant characteristics. Since the focus of this product is on the grants awarded and the recipients of those grants, fundseekers can use the product to identify funders awarding money to organizations and programs like their own, to locate funders in specific geographic area, to determine a funder's priorities and trends, and to uncover the amounts generally awarded by a particular funder. In the 1999 edition, an archival disk for 1992-1993 is also included. This is the latest edition, and no future updates are planned.

Available from: Taft Group, 27500 Drake Road, Farmington Hills, MI 48331-3535. *Toll-free:* (800) 877-TAFT; *Fax:* (800) 414-5043

Web site: www.galegroup.com/taft

371

GrantScape

Frederick, MD: Aspen Publishers. Annual. ISBN 0-8342-2003-2. $715 (Version 4.0, 2001). CD-ROM.

Description: *GrantScape* identifies funding from corporate foundations, the federal government, and foundations. Collectively, more than 14,000 grantmakers are covered. Each funder profile includes: funder contact information, employer identification number, geographic restrictions, eligibility restrictions, giving priorities, grant types, financial information, application information and guidelines, and organization directors, officers, and trustees. Up to 50 recent grant descriptions are included in many of the entries. In addition, hypertext links to web sites for a number of the sponsors are supplied. This information is also available (to subscribers only) at the publisher's web site. Although GrantScape is issued as an electronic product, it has not been updated since 2001. Information in *GrantScape* is used to produce a number of other directories issued by the publisher, including *Grants for At-Risk Youth* (see entry 490), *Grants for K-12 Schools* (entry 476), and *Grants for Technology* (entry 517).

Available from: Aspen Publishers, Inc., 7201 McKinney Circle, Frederick, MD 21704. *Toll-free:* (800) 638-8437; *Fax:* (301) 417-7550

Web site: www.aspenpublishers.com

372

The Grantseeker's Handbook of Essential Internet Sites

By Mollie Mudd. Frederick, MD: Aspen Publishers, 2000. ISBN 0-8342-1800-3, paper; 0-8342-1868-2, CD-ROM. $99. Paper or CD-ROM.

Description: Less comprehensive than the Foundation's Center's *Guide to Grantseeking on the Web* (see entry 358), this guide—available in print or electronically—identifies and describes 500 of the web sites determined by the editor to be of particular importance to nonprofit fundraisers and other executives. Entries are grouped into the following categories: corporations, foundations and associations, government, and research. This information can also be accessed through two indexes: sites by alphabetical order and corporate and foundation sites by major category of giving. A chapter on resource sites for nonprofit executives completes the book.

Available from: Aspen Publishers, Inc., 7201 McKinney Circle, Frederick, MD 21704. *Toll-free:* (800) 638-8437; *Fax:* (301) 417-7550

Grants for Organizations–General–United States

Web site: www.aspenpublishers.com

373

GrantSelect

http://www.grantselect.com
Description: Updated daily and used to generate Oryx Press's print funding directories, GrantSelect identifies more than 10,000 grants (for organizations and individuals) sponsored by organizations and agencies in the United States and other countries. For more information about the database, see entry 247 in the "Grants for Individuals—General—United States" section of this bibliography.
Available from: Oryx Press, 88 Post Road West, Westport, CT 06881. *Telephone:* (602) 265-2651; *Toll-free:* (800) 279-6799; *Fax:* (800) 279-4663; *E-mail:* info@oryxpress.com
Web site: www.oryxpress.com

374

GrantSmart

http://www.grantsmart.com
Description: GrantSmart is an informational and interactive resource center for and about the nonprofit community. The site is operated on a nonprofit basis by Canyon Research, with funding and support from the J.C. Downing Foundation. Featured here is a searchable database of tax-related information on each of over 60,000 private foundations that file Form 990-PF with the IRS. The database includes images of the most recently-filed forms and information from key fields within each tax return. Searching is by name, location, assets, EIN, or web sites by keyword. In addition, foundation tax returns from the GrantSmart database are accessible through links included in the Foundation Center's *Foundation Finder* (see entry 363) and *Foundation Directory Online* (entry 360). Note: if you can't find a particular organization at the GrantSmart site, it may be because they filed a Form 990 instead of a Form 990-PF; only private foundations file IRS Form 990-PF (general churches, hospitals, schools, or other publicly-supported organizations file IRS Form 990).
Available from: Canyon Research, PMB 422, 10755 Scripps Poway Parkway, Suite F, San Diego, CA 92131-3924. *E-mail:* info@grantsmart.org
Web site: www.grantsmart.org

375

GrantStation

http://www.grantstation.com
Description: Produced by Cynthia M. Adams, author of the *Alaska Funding and Resource Guide* (see entry 385), GrantStation.com is an online searchable database designed to connect nonprofits with the more than $35 billion in grants given annually in the United States. Although the service is intended to provide customized searches by state, not all states are available (currently, local search upgrades are offered only for Alaska, California, Colorado, Hawaii, Idaho, Montana, New Mexico, Ohio, Oregon, Washington, and Wyoming). Two levels of subscriptions are offered: GrantStation Basic ($399/yr.), which provides access to 2,000 active national grantmakers (ones that make grants in all 50 states); and GrantStation Pro ($599/yr.), which provides information on 4,000 local, regional, and national funders. The listings represent the full gamut of nonprofits, including private foundations, corporate foundations, corporate contribution programs, religious funders, association grant programs, and selected federal and state programs. The following information is provided for each: contacts, funding priorities, geographic scope, application deadlines and procedures, links to funders' e-mail and web site, notes that provide "insider" information on selected funders, and access to IRS Form 990-PF.
Available from: GrantStation.com, Inc., 3677 College Road, Suite 11B, Fairbanks, AK 99709. *Telephone:* (907) 457-6601; *Toll-free:* (877) 784-7268; *Fax:* (907) 458-7277; *E-mail:* info@grantstation.com
Web site: www.grantstation.com

376

Guide to Federal Funding for Governments & Nonprofits

Washington, DC: Government Information Services, 1977- . Annual. $339 (2002 ed.). 2v. Looseleaf.
Description: More than 750 federal programs offering $80 billion in grants and other financial aid to state and local governments and nonprofit organizations are described in detail in this directory. These include funding programs for housing, community development, roads and highways, law enforcement, pollution clean-up, energy conservation, homeless shelters, job training, volunteers, food and nutrition assistance, day care, drug abuse prevention, public health, and social services. Entries are grouped by function. Detailed information is provided for each of the programs: eligibility, uses of the funds, matching requirements, application procedures, selection criteria and priorities, budget levels, and federal contact. A unique feature is the publisher's five star "Funding Opportunity Index," which shows at a glance how competitive a program is (i.e., what an eligible applicant's chances are of winning a grant); ratings are based on a program's grantmaking history, current funding level, award policies, and

Grants for Organizations–General–United States

discussions with government officials. In addition to the *Guide,* subscribers receive quarterly updates, twice-monthly federal grant deadline calendars, and search access to the deadline calendars on the publisher's web site. Government Information Services (an affiliate of Thompson Publishing Group since 1997) also issues a number of other government grant sources, including the weekly *Local/State Funding Report* ($298/yr.).

Available from: Government Information Services, 1725 K Street, N.W., 7th Floor, Washington, DC 20006. *Telephone:* (202) 872-4000; *Toll-free:* (800) 876-0226; *Fax:* (800) 926-2012

Web site: www.grantsandfunding.com

377

Guide to U.S. Foundations: Their Trustees, Officers, & Donors

New York: Foundation Center, 1975- . Annual. ISSN 1071-202X. ISBN 0-87954-994-7. $295 (2002 ed.). Paper.

Description: This is the only publication that lists all foundations giving more than $1 per year. It is the best single source for information on small foundations. The current edition contains brief descriptions of 58,000 independent, corporate, and community foundations in the United States (more than any other published source); 3,000 of these are new to the 2002 edition. A two-volume set, the first volume arranges foundations by state and provides information for each on name, address, principal officers, market value of assets, grants paid, gifts received, fiscal period, and annual reports; the second volume, which features foundations listed by state (and, within each state, from highest to lowest grant amounts), serves as an index to the entries in the first volume. The introduction to the set provides various statistical analyses, including numerical distribution, dollar totals, and percentages of foundation assets. Detailed charts illustrate the geographic concentration of foundation wealth as well as the patterns of economic distribution. You can use this resource to find the address of any active U.S. foundation, locate all foundations in a particular city or zip code area, profile foundation assets or giving levels by states or region, identify all foundations issuing annual reports, and determine the number and size of small foundations by community. The first edition of this directory was published in 1972 under the title *Foundation Center Data Book.* Since 1981, the directory has been released on an annual basis, first as *National Data Bank* and now as *Guide to U.S. Foundations.* The information in the guide is also available in *FC Search,* the Foundation Center's CD-ROM product (see entry 354).

Available from: Foundation Center, 79 Fifth Avenue, New York, NY 10003-3076. *Telephone:* (212) 807-3690; *Toll-free:* (800) 424-9836; *Fax:* (212) 807-3691

Web site: fdncenter.org

How to Find Out About Financial Aid and Funding

378 🕸 ¢

GuideStar

http://www.guidestar.org
Description: GuideStar's free online searchable database contains information on more than 850,000 organizations in the United States that are classified by the IRS as nonprofits (i.e., public charities, private nonoperating foundations, and private operating foundations). Grantseekers can search the database by federal identification number, keywords, location (city, state, and/or zip code), nonprofit type, and/or income range ($0 to unlimited). The following information is given for each organization: address, contact name, telephone number, brief description, program/activities, funding base, geographic reach, EIN, assets, income, tax year, ruling year, number of board members, number of employees, number of volunteers, and audited statements available to the public. Financial data are taken from the IRS Business Master File and/or Form 990 (a public report that all 501(c)(3) public charities with revenues exceeding $25,000 must file with the IRS). A special section provides links to more than 300 disaster-relief and assistance organizations, from the Cantor Fitzgerald Relief Fund to the Adirondack Rescue Dog Association. GuideStar, along with the Idealist (see entry 635) provides a replacement for the now defunct Nonprofit Locator. Another way to obtain an IRS 990-PF return for a specific nonprofit is by contacting the Internal Revenue Service directly (toll-free: (800) 829-3676); ask for form 4506, or download the form from the IRS web site: www.irs.ustreas.gov. The cost for a copy of each return is free for the first 100 pages and $.20 per page after that. There is no charge to inspect a return at an IRS office. Keep in mind: corporate giving programs that are not organized as separate foundations do not file IRS Form 990-PF returns; information about those funders are not available either in GuideStar or with form 4506 (you'll need to search through the parent business for that).
Available from: Philanthropic Research, Inc., Attn: GuideStar Customer Service, 427 Scotland Street, Williamsburg, VA 23185. *Telephone:* (757) 229-4631
Web site: www.guidestar.org

379 🕸

IRIS (Illinois Researcher Information Service)

Urbana: Illinois Researcher Information Service (IRIS). Updated daily. Annual Internet subscription fees range from $400 (for institutions with fewer than 3,000 students and faculty) to $2,000 (more than 15,000 students and faculty or more than $50 million annual research volume).
Description: Some of the 8,000 funding opportunities in this subscription database are open to academic institutions (the rest are aimed at individual graduate students, researchers, scholars, and faculty). For more information about

Grants for Organizations–General–United States

the service, see entry 249 in the "Grants for Individuals—General—United States" section of this bibliography.

Available from: Illinois Researcher Information Service (IRIS), University of Illinois at Urbana-Champaign, 128 Observatory, 901 South Mathews Avenue, Urbana, IL 61801. *Telephone:* (217) 333-0284; *Fax:* (217) 333-7011; *E-mail:* a-trehub@uiuc.edu
Web site: www.library.uiuc.edu/iris

380

National Directory of Corporate Giving

8th ed. New York: Foundation Center, 2002. 1,165p. ISBN 0-931923-05-1. $195. Paper.

Description: First published in 1989, this directory now serves as one of the most comprehensive sources of information on the corporate philanthropic sector. In the eighth edition, detailed profiles are presented for 3,300 corporate foundations and direct giving programs; these companies annually award more than $7 billion. The following information is provided: application procedures, names of key personnel, types of support generally awarded, giving limitations, financial data, and purpose and activities statements. In addition, many entries include descriptions of recently-awarded grants. Organized by corporate name, the entries are indexed by subject area, geographic location, type of business practiced, type of grant generally awarded, foundation name, and the names of the officers, donors, and trustees. An international giving index tracks funders by country, continent, and region. The information presented here is also available in *FC Search,* the Foundation Center's CD-ROM product (see entry 354). For more indepth information on the 250 largest corporate foundations described here (those that grant at least $1.2 million annually), see *Corporate Foundation Profiles* (entry 344), also published by the Foundation Center.

Available from: Foundation Center, 79 Fifth Avenue, New York, NY 10003-3076. *Telephone:* (212) 807-3690; *Toll-free:* (800) 424-9836; *Fax:* (212) 807-3691
Web site: fdncenter.org

381

National Directory of Corporate Public Affairs

21st ed. Ed. by Valerie S. Sheridan, Natacha Leonard, Diane R. Murphy, and Katherine Adjemian. Washington, DC: Columbia Books, 2003. 1,158p. ISSN 0749-9736. ISBN 0-9715487-2-2. $159. Paper.

Description: Using data from questionnaires, augmented by information taken from other sources, this directory focuses on companies and individuals involved in public affairs programs. In the latest edition (21st ed., 2003), the listing is divided into two sections. The first is an alphabetical catalog of 1,700 organizations of varied sizes with public affairs programs. The following information is provided: address of corporate headquarters, address of foundation or corporate giving program, political action committees and the candidates they support, corporate philanthropic programs and their beneficiaries, corporate publications, and names of the company's public affairs and related activities personnel. The second section, "The People," consists of an alphabetical list of 15,000 corporate officers engaged in the informational, political, or philanthropic aspects of public affairs in the United States. The entries in both sections are indexed by industry and by geographic location. New to this edition: 250 companies included for the first time, thousands of new e-mail addresses, names of company chairs and chief executive officers, and a "Major Changes at a Glance" section that quickly identifies the past year's major company mergers and name changes (and contains a list of the new companies added). Because of its currency, this directory is a good source to use to identify appropriate contact people, to determine who has public affairs responsibility in a given company, or to discover where to get more information on a public affairs program. However, since public affairs is such a broad field, some of this information can be found elsewhere (e.g., *Corporate Foundation Profiles,* described in entry 344).

Available from: Columbia Books, Inc., 1825 Connecticut Avenue, N.W., Suite 625, Washington, DC 20009. *Telephone:* (202) 464-1662; *Toll-free:* (888) 265-0600; *Fax:* (202) 464-1775; *E-mail:* info@columbiabooks.com

Web site: www.columbiabooks.com

382

Operating Grants for Nonprofit Organizations

Westport, CT: Oryx, 2002. 312p. ISBN 1-57356-565-2. $36.50. Paper.

Description: Similar to Eckstein's *Directory of Operating Grants* (see entry 351) but at half the price, this directory identifies more than 1,000 grants available to support the general operating expenses of nonprofit and other organizations in such fields as the arts and humanities, community development, health care, social services, and education. Entries are grouped by state and include the following information: contact name and title, phone and fax numbers, e-mail and web sites, requirements and restrictions, sample awards, and sponsor's area of interest. Additional access is provided by subject, sponsor, and geographic indexes. Like the other Oryx publications in this bibliography, the entries in *Operating Grants for Nonprofit Organizations* are taken directly from GrantSelect, the publisher's comprehensive funding database (see entry 247).

Available from: Oryx Press, 88 Post Road West, Westport, CT 06881. *Telephone:* (602) 265-2651; *Toll-free:* (800) 279-6799; *Fax:* (800) 279-4663; *E-mail:* info@oryxpress.com

Web site: www.oryxpress.com

Grants for Organizations–General–United States

383

Prospector's Choice

Farmington Hills, MI: Taft. Annual. ISBN 1-56995-452-6. $849 (2003 ed.). CD-ROM.

Description: Now available in a Windows format, this CD-ROM provides detailed profiles of nearly 10,000 foundations and corporate giving programs. The following is provided in each entry: contact information, financial summary, contributions summary, giving officers, application information, grant analysis, and a list of up to 50 recent grants and their recipients. This information can be searched by seven functions: funders by name, officers by name, officers by alma mater, funders by location, recipients by location, grants by type, and recipients by type. In addition, there is a Quick Search function for keyword searching. What makes this source different than the Foundation Center's *FC Search* (see entry 354) is the extensive biographical information provided on the people who make the funding decisions—the officers, treasurers, and presidents—even down to their alma mater and club affiliations. Much of the information included here is also available in Taft's *Directory of Corporate and Foundation Givers* (see entry 349).

Available from: Taft Group, 27500 Drake Road, Farmington Hills, MI 48331-3535. *Toll-free:* (800) 877-TAFT; *Fax:* (800) 414-5043

Web site: www.galegroup.com/taft

384

Sources of Operating Grants

4th ed. Ed. by Mollie Mudd. Frederick, MD: Aspen Publishers, 2002. 384p. ISBN 0-8342-1896-8. $119. Paper.

Description: Prepared by Aspen Publishers (formerly Capitol Publications), the fourth edition of this directory identifies funding for regular personnel, administrative, and other nonprogram-related operating expenses. In all, there are profiles of more than 550 private sector funders. Each profile contains the following: address, telephone number, e-mail address, primary contact name, eligibility requirements, application process, geographic restrictions, giving properties, financial data, samples of recent grants awarded, and names of directors, officers, and trustees (when available). Also included in the directory are an appendix listing resources offering additional help to funders and an alphabetical index to funders. Like other directories published by Aspen, this one consists of data taken directly from GrantScape, the publisher's electronic funding database (see entry 371). Of the three directories listing operating grants (for the other two, see entries 351 and 382), this one costs the most and provides the least number of entries.

Available from: Aspen Publishers, Inc., 7201 McKinney Circle, Frederick, MD 21704. *Toll-free:* (800) 638-8437; *Fax:* (301) 695-7931

Web site: www.aspenpublishers.com

Alaska

385

Alaska Funding and Resource Guide: The Directory of Foundations, Corporate Giving and Technical Assistance Programs for Alaskan-based Organizations

Ed. by Cynthia M. Adams. Fairbanks, AK: Funding Exchange, 2003. 149p. $74, spiral bound; $54, CD-ROM.

Description: Formerly issued as the *Alaska Funding Guide,* the 2003 edition highlights foundations and corporate giving programs that are either located in Alaska or that fund projects in the state. More than 125 different grantmakers are covered (generally, one entry to a page). Entries identify contact, type of grantmaking organization, application deadlines, areas of interest, grant range, etc. No information, however, is provided on specific grants or past recipients. The directory is also available on CD-ROM ($54). In addition, the same information, and more, can be found in the Exchange's affiliate online business, GrantStation.com (see entry 375).

Available from: Alaska Funding Exchange, Inc., P.O. Box 92456, Anchorage, AK 99509. *Telephone:* (907) 569-4233; *Fax:* (907) 569-4253; *E-mail:* info@funding-exchange.org

Web site: www.funding-exchange.org

386

Philanthropy Northwest Member Directory

6th ed. Seattle: Pacific Northwest Grantmakers Forum, 2002. 234p. $91, paper; $126, online.

Description: This directory (also available as an online subscription) provides descriptive information on the grantgiving activities of the members of Philanthropy Northwest: community foundations, corporate foundations, corporate giving programs, private foundations, public foundations, and trusts in Alaska, Washington, Oregon, Montana, and Idaho. For more information about the publication and its online version, see entry 449 in the "Grants for Organizations—General—Washington" section of this bibliography.

Available from: Philanthropy Northwest, 2815 Second Avenue, Suite 290, Seattle, WA 98121. *Telephone:* (206) 770-9423; *E-mail:* info@PhilanthropyNW.org

Web site: www.pngf.org

Arizona

387

Arizona Guide to Grants & Giving

8th ed. Glendale, AZ: JUST GRANTS! Arizona, 2003. $60, paper; $95, online.

Description: More than 1,000 corporations and foundations with a history of making grants in Arizona are described in the latest edition (2003) of this directory. The following information is provided: address and telephone numbers, contacts, priorities, and application guidelines. Much of this information is supplied by the grantmakers in response to a questionnaire. A web version is also available on a subscription basis ($95/yr.), which permits searches in nine areas of grantmaker interest (art, civic, education, environment, health, international, religion, science, and social services) as well as several "target group" categories: child, youth, family, elderly, minority, women, men, low income, working poor, urban, and rural. Keyword searches can also be done to identify grant activity by county or community, specialized topics (e.g., literacy, dance, museums), or specific grantees. Note: the database includes only sample grants, rather than the entire inventory of each funder's grant offerings, so search results are indicative rather than comprehensive.

Available from: JUST GRANTS! Arizona, P.O. Box 5456, Glendale, AZ 85312-5456. *Telephone:* (623) 412-8650; *Fax:* (623) 412-8776; *E-mail:* mboess@azgrants.com

Web site: www.azgrants.com

Arkansas

388

Arkansas Funding Directory

Little Rock: Nonprofit Resources, 1998- . Biennial. $70 (2001-2002 ed.). Paper.

Description: Described in the latest edition of this directory (2001-2002) are 1) private foundations and other grantmakers located in Arkansas as well as 2) funders outside the state that have an interest in making grants in the state. Also provided is information on grants from state agencies.

Available from: Nonprofit Resources, 3805 West 12th Street, Suite 104, Little Rock, AR 72204. *Telephone:* (501) 379-1558; *Fax:* (501) 374-6548

Web site: www.nonprofitarkansas.org

California

389

California Foundation DataBook

1st ed. By Ford T. Pearson. Portland: C&D Publishing, 2000. 768p. $150, book; $250, book and CD-ROM set.

Description: One in a series of state-based directories (the others focus on Iowa, Louisiana, Nebraska, Oklahoma, Oregon, and Washington; see entries 405, 408, 424, 435, 437, and 450), the first edition was issued in 2000 and describes 220 (mostly large) California-based foundations; specifically excluded are foundations located outside of California, even if they make substantial grants within the state. The following information, most of which is taken from 990-PF forms, is provided for each grantmaker: contact information, financial data, giving restrictions, and geographic focus. While the coverage of grantmakers is selective, the information provided on their grantmaking activity is comprehensive: all grants made by a listed foundation during the most recent fiscal year are identified. This is a real plus for the serious fundseeker; most other directories only list representative grants and do not provide as complete a picture as Pearson does of a funder's giving patterns. Information is available both in book form and on CD-ROM.

Available from: C&D Publishing, 1017 Morrison Street S.W., Suite 500, Portland, OR 97205. *Telephone:* (503) 274-8780; *Toll-free:* (877) 924-7268
Web site: www.foundationdatabook.com

390

Guide to California Foundations

San Francisco: Northern California Grantmakers, 1976-1999. Biennial. ISBN 0-9618375-2-7. $27.50 (11th ed.), paper; $60, CD-ROM.

Description: Published from 1976-1999, this directory has provided descriptive information on private charitable foundations based in California that make at least $40,000 in grants each year. Some corporations and a few smaller foundations are also included. In the last (11th) edition, nearly 1,400 foundations are covered—a 25 percent increase from the previous edition. Combined, these foundations control $46.7 billion in assets and award more than $2 billion in grants annually. For each entry, information is given on purpose and fields of granting interest; total amount, number, and range of grants; geographic limits and other restrictions; contact person, officers, and directors; application deadlines and procedures; and five sample grants reflecting giving patterns. The information is based primarily on returns filed with the IRS or records in the California Attorney General's Office and, to a much lesser extent, on data supplied by foundations completing questionnaires. Arranged by foundation name, the directory is indexed by primary interest, geographic area, and name of foundation. Also included are sections on applying for grants, foundation vocabulary, foundations new to this edition, foundations deleted from this edition, and name changes. The directory has been a joint venture of Northern California Grantmakers and the Southern California Association for Philanthropy. The final edition was issued in 1999, both in print and bundled with a CD-ROM ($60). In 2004, an online database of California foundations will be available on subscription, and a CD-ROM version may be offered as well.

Available from: Northern California Grantmakers, 116 New Montgomery Street, Suite 720, San Francisco, CA 94105-3416. *Telephone:* (415) 777-5761; *Fax:* (415) 777-1714; *E-mail:* ncg@ncg.org

Web site: www.ncg.org

Colorado

391

Colorado Grants Guide

7th ed. Ed. by Jane Marsh. Denver: Community Resource Center, 2003. 394p. $135, spiral bound; $70-$200, online.

Description: Presented here is detailed information on approximately 400 Colorado foundations, trusts, corporations, state government agencies, and religious institutions. The listing is not intended to be comprehensive. Foundations and trusts are included only if they are Denver-based and annually grant more than $50,000, are located primarily in rural areas and grant more than $10,000 annually, or are of particular interest to groups in a specific field or geographic area. Corporations are included only if they make grants in excess of $75,000 annually to Colorado nonprofit organizations. State departments with major grant programs are covered, as are major religious denominational programs that make grants. Organizational profiles are grouped by type (foundations and trusts, corporations, etc.) and listed alphabetically; for most, the following information is provided: contact information, purpose, trustees, areas of interest, types of grants (scholarships and professorships are excluded), restrictions, financial data, application process, proposal deadline, examples of recent grants, and other relevant information. Indexes provide access by specific area of interest, geographic location or type of grant, and application deadlines. Although this is the 2003-2004 edition, most of the data included date back to 2000. Since 2001, the information presented here is also available online ($200 for a one-year subscription, $120 for a 6-month subscription, or $70 for a 3-month subscription).

Available from: Community Resource Center, 655 Broadway, Suite 300, Denver, CO 80203-3426. *Telephone:* (303) 623-1540; *Toll-free:* (800) 516-6284; *Fax:* (303) 623-1567; *E-mail:* info@crcamerica.org

Web site: www.crcamerica.org

Connecticut

392

Guide to Connecticut Grantmakers

1st ed. Hartford, CT: Connecticut Council for Philanthropy, 1999. 350p. $75. Paper with updated CD-ROM.

Description: The Connecticut Council for Philanthropy (formerly the Coordinating Council for Foundations) is a nonprofit membership association of 90 family, independent, and community foundations, corporate foundations, giving programs, and federated funds in the Connecticut area. In 1999, it published the *Guide to Connecticut Grantmakers*, which was previously issued by D.A.T.A. as the *Connecticut Foundation Directory* (7th ed. 1994. 406p. ISBN 1-882445-10-4. $35). The *Guide* provides the most complete listing of Connecticut funders available; it supplies information on more than 1,500 foundations, corporate giving programs, federal funds, and charitable trusts registered in the state or that have targeted giving programs in the state. Entries indicate types of programs funded, assets, largest and smallest grants made, types of support, etc. Additional access is provided through a number of indexes: areas of interest, types of support for organizations, types of support for individuals; target populations, geographic locations, officers and staff, and grantmakers (alphabetically by name). The 1999 edition of the book is sold with a searchable CD-ROM formatted for Windows; the CD-ROM is intended to be updated annually, but the latest available is 2001. The price for the book/CD-ROM combination ranges from $75, for a stand-alone license to $250 for a network in a for-profit institution; the 2001 updated CD-ROM is available for $30. Rather than update the book version in the future, the Council plans to make the information available only on their web site or in electronic form.

Available from: Connecticut Council for Philanthropy, 221 Main Street, Hartford, CT 06106. *Telephone:* (860) 525-5585; *Fax:* (860) 525-0436; *E-mail:* ccp@CTphilanthropy.org
Web site: www.CTphilanthropy.org

District of Columbia

393

Guide to Greater Washington D.C. Grantmakers on CD-ROM

New York: Foundation Center, 1994- . Biennial. ISBN 0-87954-996-3, CD-ROM single user; 1-931923-06-X, CD-ROM local area network. $75 (2002 ed.), CD-ROM single-user; $125, CD-ROM local area network.

Grants for Organizations–General–Florida

Description: Aimed at grantseekers in the D.C. area (including portions of Maryland and Virginia), this directory provides information on more than 1,500 foundations, corporations, and public charities that make grants there, as well as 300 funders in 30 different states that have an interest in D.C.-area nonprofits. All profiles supply the following information: address, financial data, giving limitations, and names of key officials. For the larger foundations (those that give at least $50,000 in grants each year), the directory provides even more information, including application procedures and giving interest statements. The volume also features more than 1,800 descriptions of recently-awarded grants, which are often the best indication of giving priorities. This directory is produced as a collaborative project of the Washington Regional Association of Grantmakers and the Foundation Center. Originally issued as a print directory, its format changed to CD-ROM with the 2000 edition. This is one of five geographically-based funding directories available from the Foundation Center (the others cover Michigan, Missouri, New York, and Ohio and are described in entries 416, 421, 431, and 434).

Available from: Foundation Center, 79 Fifth Avenue, New York, NY 10003-3076. *Telephone:* (212) 807-3690; *Toll-free:* (800) 424-9836; *Fax:* (212) 807-3691

Web site: fdncenter.org

394

Maryland/DC Foundation Directory Online

http://www.grantsdirect.com

Description: This subscription-based online directory, which is updated monthly, provides information on more than 1,450 grantmakers in Washington, D.C., Maryland, and northern Virginia. For more information about the online guide, see entry 413 in the "Grants for Organizations—General—Maryland" section of this bibliography.

Available from: Jankowski Associates, Inc., 216 West Patrick Street, Frederick, MD 21701. *Telephone:* (301) 696-0797; *Fax:* (301) 696-0798; *E-mail:* info@grantsdirect.com

Web site: www.grantsdirect.com

Florida

395

The Complete Guide to Florida Foundations

Miami: Florida Funding Publications, 1985- . Annual. ISSN 1070-7840. ISBN 1-879543-22-2 (2003 ed.). $90. Paper.

Description: This is the most comprehensive but not the most detailed of the directories that list Florida foundations. Nearly 3,500 organizations (private and corporate) that award $798 million annually in grants are identified here, including almost 500 new to the 2003 edition. But, many of these are small, are unstaffed, or only give to preselected grantees. Further, the directory-type information provided for each funder is very brief and, sometimes, quite dated. Entries are arranged alphabetically by foundation and indexed by county and city, corporate and community foundations, area of interest, geographic areas of support, assets, and giving. To update some of this listing, use *Florida Funding—The Monthly Newsletter for Florida Grantseekers* ($142/yr.) or the *Florida Information Network Database* (also known as F.I.N.D. $445, CD-ROM), both produced by Florida Funding Publications.

Available from: Florida Funding Publications, Inc., 8925 S.W. 148 Street, Suite 110, Miami, FL 33176. *Telephone:* (305) 251-2203; *Fax:* (305) 251-2773; *E-mail:* info@floridafunding.com

Web site: www.floridafunding.com

396

Florida State Grant Programs

Ed. by John L. Adams and Frances S. Passannante. Miami: Florida Funding Publications, 2002. ISSN 1070-7832. ISBN 1-879543-18-4. 290p. $80. Paper.

Description: The purpose of this guide is "to assist users in identifying the grant programs most applicable to their program needs and to provide general information concerning Florida assistance programs." It serves as a companion to Florida Funding Publications' *Complete Guide to Florida Foundations* (see entry 395). The directory provides detailed profiles of more than 200 state and federal grant programs (representing billions of dollars in funding) that are administered by the State of Florida. The program profiles are divided by level (federal and state), grouped by sponsoring agency (e.g., Department of Commerce), and indexed by deadline and subject area. For each program, the following information is provided: program title, program description, type of assistance, matching requirements, other requirements, eligibility, funds available, source of funds, deadline, and point of contact. New and deleted programs are listed in a separate section. To update this listing, use *Florida Funding—The Monthly Newsletter for Florida Grantseekers* ($142/yr.) or the *Florida Information Network Database* (also known as F.I.N.D. $445, CD-ROM), both produced by Florida Funding Publications. In the past, this source was published under the title *A Guide to Florida State Programs*.

Available from: Florida Funding Publications, Inc., 8925 S.W. 148 Street, Suite 110, Miami, FL 33176. *Telephone:* (305) 251-2203; *Fax:* (305) 251-2773; *E-mail:* info@floridafunding.com

Web site: www.floridafunding.com

Georgia

397

Georgia Foundation Directory

Atlanta: Sinclair, Townes and Co., 2002. 2v. Updated quarterly. $350. Paper.

Description: More than 900 foundations located in Georgia are listed in this directory. The entries are arranged alphabetically by grantmaker name and indexed geographically by region and city. The following information is provided for each foundation: address and telephone number, contact, purpose, assets, range of grants awarded, restrictions and limitations, application information, board members, sample grants, and sources of information. Fundseekers who do not wish to purchase the entire directory can take advantage of the publisher's research service: the same information can be provided for any of the grantmakers in the directory for $15 each.

Available from: Sinclair, Townes and Co., 230 Peachtree Street, N.W., Suite 1601, Atlanta, GA 30303. *Telephone:* (404) 688-4047; *Fax:* (404) 688-6543; *E-mail:* info@sinclairtownes.com
Web site: www.sinclairtownes.com

Hawaii

398

Directory of Charitable Trusts and Foundations: A Guide for Hawai'i's Nonprofit Organizations

Comp. by Alberta Freidus-Flagg. Honolulu: Helping Hands Hawai'i, 1999. 227p. $30. Spiral bound.

Description: The 1999-2000 edition of this directory provides information on local trusts and foundations that give grants to organizations and individuals in Hawaii. The listing is divided into three sections: Hawaii foundations, foundations for persons in Hawaii who are in need, and mainland foundations that include Hawaii within their geographic area of funding. Close to 200 foundations are covered. For each entry, the following information is included: name of trust and foundation, address, date established in Hawaii, purpose, type of support, limitations, latest financial data, sample grants, deadlines for applications, application procedures, and officers/trustees. A "Fields of Interest" index facilities access to the entries. In the past, the directory was published under the title *Directory of Charitable Trusts and Foundations for Hawaii's Non-Profit Organizations.* Although a new edition was scheduled for 2001/2002, it has not yet been released.

Available from: Helping Hands Hawai'i, 2100 North Nimitz Highway, Honolulu, HI 96819. *Telephone:* (808) 536-7234; *Fax:* (808) 536-7235
Web site: www.helpinghandshawaii.org

Idaho

399

Directory of Idaho Foundations

10th ed. Ed. by Elaine C. Leppert. Caldwell, ID: Caldwell Public Library, 2001. ISSN 1058-0689. Unpaged. $15. Comb binding

Description: The *Directory of Idaho Foundations* is published by the Caldwell Public Library as a service to nonprofit organizations, foundations, and others interested in philanthropy in Idaho. It was first issued in 1978 as an eight-page pamphlet. The latest (2001) edition covers more than 200 foundations and corporations "either headquartered in Idaho or with a history of giving in Idaho." The entries are grouped by type (foundations, scholarship-granting foundations, foundations with designated grantees, inactive, and national foundations/corporate funders in Idaho) and listed alphabetically by foundation name. The information in each entry (e.g., assets, grants, major areas of interest) was taken primarily from 990-PF returns filed with the IRS. Appendices list foundations by deadline date and geographic orientation. Entries are indexed by application deadlines, headquarters' location, and name of grantmaker. There is a brief bibliography of additional sources.

Available from: Caldwell Public Library, 1010 Dearborn Street, Caldwell, ID 83605-4195. *Telephone:* (208) 459-3242; *Fax:* (208) 459-7344; *E-mail:* caldwellpl@yahoo.com

400

Philanthropy Northwest Member Directory

6th ed. Seattle: Pacific Northwest Grantmakers Forum, 2002. 234p. $91, paper; $126, online.

Description: This directory (also available as an online subscription) provides descriptive information on the grantgiving activities of the members of Philanthropy Northwest: community foundations, corporate foundations, corporate giving programs, private foundations, public foundations, and trusts in Idaho, Washington, Oregon, Montana, and Alaska. For more information about the listing and its online version, see entry 449 in the "Grants for Organizations—General—Washington" section of this bibliography.

Grants for Organizations–General–Illinois

Available from: Philanthropy Northwest, 2815 Second Avenue, Suite 290, Seattle, WA 98121. *Telephone:* (206) 770-9423; *E-mail:* info@philanthropynw.org
Web site: www.philanthropynw.org

Illinois

401

Catalog of State Assistance to Local Governments

8th ed. Springfield: Illinois Commission on Intergovernmental Cooperation, 2001. 273p. Free. Paper or online.

Description: The relationship between Illinois state government and the more than 5,800 units of local government and special districts in the state involves the transfer of nearly $6 billion a year. Issued biennially by the Illinois Commission on Intergovernmental Cooperation, this directory is intended to serve as a comprehensive source of information on this state and local assistance (not all of which is monetary). Described here are nearly 400 "state programs providing financial and technical assistance to counties, municipalities, townships and special districts (excluding school districts)." The entries are grouped by sponsoring agency and indexed by funding interest. The following information is provided for each program: objective, eligibility, funding, official source of further information, and contact (address and telephone number). Additional access to funding interests is provided by an 11-page index. The report is also available in .pdf format online, at the "Living In Illinois" web site (www.100.state.il.us/living/grants.cfm); links to information on other state and federal funding opportunities can also be found there.

Available from: Illinois Commission on Intergovernmental Cooperation, 707 Stratton Building, Springfield, IL 62706. *Telephone:* (217) 782-6924; *Fax:* (202) 273-4749

402

The Directory of Illinois Foundations

7th ed. Chicago: Donors Forum, 2002. 411p. $83.50, members; $103.50, nonmembers. Paper.

Description: Identified in the seventh edition of this directory (2002-2004) are foundations (private, independent, family, company-sponsored) and corporate programs in Illinois. Detailed descriptions are provided for 29 corporate giving programs and 465 Illinois foundations with assets of at least $100,000 and/or grantgiving of at least $50,000 annually. Information supplied for these foundations includes: contact persons, geographic limits, application procedures,

How to Find Out About Financial Aid and Funding

deadlines, total grants, grant range, officers, and directors. Brief information for an additional 1,700 smaller foundations in Illinois is presented in the appendix. Together, these foundations and giving programs (25 percent more than listed in the previous edition) represent an asset base of more than $14 billion and grantgiving of more than $570 million per year. A series of tables (e.g., 100 largest Illinois foundations by total assets) and a set of eight indexes (program interests, types of support, foundation name, etc.) complete the work. This is one of the best organized and most complete of the state funding guides. In the past, the directory was issued under the title *Illinois Foundation Profile.* Until the 2000-2002 edition, the directory was also available in a CD-ROM version; beginning with 2002, however, the CD-ROM version has been replaced by a fully-searchable online subscription service: Illinois Funding Source (see entry 403).

Available from: Donors Forum of Chicago, 208 South LaSalle Street, Suite 740, Chicago, IL 60604-1006. *Telephone:* (312) 578-0090; *Fax:* (312) 578-0103; *E-mail:* info@donorsforum.org

Web site: www.donorsforum.org

403

Illinois Funding Source

http://www.donorsforum.org.

Description: This is more than an online version of the *Directory of Illinois Foundations* (see entry 402). It combines two powerful tools: FoundationSource, a searchable directory of more than 2,500 Illinois foundations, and GrantSource, a research database that indexes more than $2.5 billion in grant dollars awarded by local funders. The information in both sections is updated monthly. Three subscription options are offered: 1) the complete Illinois Funding Source (including FoundationSource and GrantSource), which runs from $200 for a single user who belongs to the Donors Forum to $500 for 6+ users who are nonmembers; 2) FoundationSource, which can be searched by name, type, budget, interests, or types of grants and costs from $160 to $400; and 3) GrantSource, which offers a database of 70,000 grants that can be searched by foundation, support type, beneficiary, or recipient and costs from $80 to $200 per year.

Available from: Donors Forum of Chicago, 208 South LaSalle Street, Suite 740, Chicago, IL 60604-1006. *Telephone:* (312) 578-0090; *Fax:* (312) 578-0103; *E-mail:* info@donorsforum.org

Web site: www.donorsforum.org

Indiana

404

Directory of Indiana & Kentucky Grantmakers

Ed. by Susan R. Wilson. Indianapolis: Indiana Grantmakers Alliance, 2001. 1,300p. $80, members, paper; $100, nonmembers, paper; $100, members, CD-ROM; $125, nonmembers, CD-ROM.

Description: The 2001-2002 print edition of this directory combines two previously separate publications: *Directory of Indiana Grantmakers* and *Directory of Kentucky Grantmakers*. Included here are profiles of more than 2,000 private foundations, corporate foundations, and community foundations headquartered in Indiana and Kentucky, along with foundations headquartered elsewhere but which have been known to give grants to those states. Entries include typical directory information: contact (including fax, e-mail, and web site), range of grants, eligibility, geographic and program preferences, limitations, and application process. Although many of the listed foundations do award scholarships to residents of the two states, these agencies are hard to spot; they are not identified in a separate section, and it is often necessary to read an entire program entry to determine if scholarships are offered. The appendices list foundations by type, program interest, headquarters location, geographic preferences, fixed assets, amount of grants paid, and contact person, but the brief table of contents and the way the sections are typeset make it difficult to use these sections efficiently. This information is also available on a CD-ROM, entitled *Directory of Indiana & Kentucky Grantmakers Searchable Database*. The next edition of both versions is scheduled for late 2003.

Available from: Indiana Grantmakers Alliance, Inc., 32 East Washington Street, Suite 1100, Indianapolis, IN 46204-3583. *Telephone:* (317) 630-5200; *Fax:* (317) 630-5210

Web site: www.ingrantmakers.org

Iowa

405

Iowa Foundation DataBook

2nd ed. By Ford T. Pearson. Portland: C&D Publishing, 2002. 550p. $100, book; $250, book and CD-ROM set.

Description: Like the other titles in the Foundation DataBook series (see entries 389, 408, 424, 435, 437, and 450), this directory focuses on a single state and provides data on the grantmaking foundations there. In all, 1,116 Iowa

How to Find Out About Financial Aid and Funding

foundations are covered, Together, the combined assets of these foundations total more than $2.2 billion. The following information, most of which is taken from 990-PF forms, is provided for each grantmaker: contact information, financial data, giving restrictions, and geographic focus. A special feature: all grants made by a listed foundation during the most recent fiscal year are identified (including the amount of the grant, the purpose of the grant, and the grant recipient). This is a real plus for the serious fundseeker; most other directories only list representative grants and do not provide as complete a picture as Pearson does of a funder's giving patterns. Indexes include a Grants Deadline Calendar, foundations listed by grantee categories, foundations listed by fund balance, foundations listed by amount of grants paid, and foundations listed by name. Information is available both in book form and on CD-ROM. The first edition of the directory was issued in 2000.

Available from: C&D Publishing, 1017 Morrison Street S.W., Suite 500, Portland, OR 97205. *Telephone:* (503) 274-8780; *Toll-free:* (877) 924-7268
Web site: www.foundationdatabook.com

Kansas

406

The Directory of Kansas Foundations

Topeka: Kansas Non Profit Association, 2002. 279p. $65, members; $75, nonmembers. Spiral bound.

Description: Currently, more than 725 foundations with combined assets exceeding $1.1 billion are operating in Kansas (nearly 150 more than listed in the previous edition). These foundations give away more than $64 million each year. Up-to-date descriptions of these foundations and other Kansas funding sources are provided in the latest edition of *The Directory of Kansas Foundations,* which was previously published by the Topeka and Shawnee County Public Library. Profiles are arranged alphabetically by foundation and supply the following information: address, telephone number, funding priorities, limitations, financial data (assets, high and low grants, total number and amount of grants), board members, sample grants, and contact person. Entries are indexed by city, name of the foundation, and funding priority.

Available from: Kansas Non Profit Association, P.O. Box 47054, Topeka, KS 66647-0054. *Telephone:* (785) 266-6886; *Toll-free:* (800) 582-1428; *Fax:* (785) 266-2113; *E-mail:* knpa@inlandnet.com
Web site: www.ksnonprofitassoc.net

Kentucky

407

Directory of Indiana & Kentucky Grantmakers

Ed. by Susan R. Wilson. Indianapolis: Indiana Grantmakers Alliance, 2001. 1,300p. $80, members, paper; $100, nonmembers, paper; $100, members, CD-ROM; $125, nonmembers, CD-ROM.

Description: This directory profiles more than 2,000 active grantmaking foundations, trusts, and scholarship programs in Kentucky and Indiana, including a number that are located elsewhere but have a history of funding in the state. For more information about the listing, see entry 404 in the "Grants for Organizations—General—Indiana" section of this bibliography.

Available from: Indiana Grantmakers Alliance, Inc., 32 East Washington Street, Suite 1100, Indianapolis, IN 46204-3583. *Telephone:* (317) 630-5200; *Fax:* (317) 630-5210

Web site: www.ingrantmakers.org

Louisiana

408

Louisiana Foundation DataBook

1st ed. Ed. by Ford T. Pearson. Portland: C&D Publishing, 2002. 374p. $100, book; $250, book and CD-ROM set.

Description: This is the newest title in a series of *Foundation DataBooks* published by C&D Publishing (for the others, see entries 389, 405, 424, 435, 437, and 450). It identifies all 896 foundations in Louisiana, with comprehensive profiles provided for the largest 220 foundations (whose assets represent 98 percent of all Louisiana foundation assets). The following information, most of which is taken from 990-PF forms, is provided for each grantmaker: contact information, financial data, giving restrictions, and geographic focus. A special feature: all grants made by a listed foundation during the most recent fiscal year are identified (including the amount of the grant, the purpose of the grant, and the grant recipient). This is a real plus for the serious fundseeker; most other directories only list representative grants. Information is available both in book form and on CD-ROM.

Available from: C&D Publishing, 1017 Morrison Street S.W., Suite 500, Portland, OR 97205. *Telephone:* (503) 274-8780; *Toll-free:* (877) 924-7268

Web site: www.foundationdatabook.com

409

Louisiana Funding Guide

1st ed. Baton Rouge: Louisiana Association of Nonprofit Organizations, 2001. 257p. ISBN 0-9701878-1-5. $45, members; $75, nonmembers. Paper.

Description: The first edition of this directory describes 525 foundations that make grants in Louisiana. It also includes a section on "philanthropy in Louisiana" and a "grantseekers toolkit."

Available from: Louisiana Association of Nonprofit Organizations, P.O. Box 3808, Baton Rouge, LA 70821. *Telephone:* (225) 343-5266; *Fax:* (225) 343-5363; *E-mail:* contactus@lano.org

Web site: www.lano.org

Maine

410

Directory of Maine Grantmakers

Ed. by Priscilla Miller and Frances L. Rice. Portland: University of Southern Maine, 1973- . Irreg. $20 (2001 ed.). Paper or online.

Description: Based on 990-PF returns filed with the IRS, this edition, issued in 2001, is divided into three sections: Maine grantmakers, Maine foundations awarding scholarships, and out-of-state grantmakers giving in Maine. For each record, the following information is provided (taken from 990-PF forms): address, contact person, telephone number, assets, number of grants, total of grants awarded, representative grants, limitations, and any appropriate notes. Currently, this title is available both in print and on the university's web site. In the past, this title was issued as *A Directory of Foundations in the State of Maine.*

Available from: Maine Philanthropy Center, University of Southern Maine Library, P.O. Box 9301, Portland, ME 04104-9301. *Telephone:* (207) 780-5039; *Fax:* (207) 780-4649; *E-mail:* Jread@megrants.org

Web site: www.megrants.org

Grants for Organizations–General–Maryland

Maryland

411

Index to Private Foundation Reports

Baltimore: Maryland Office of the Attorney General, 1979- . Irreg. $95 (2000 ed.). Paper.

Description: Compiled by the Maryland Office of the Attorney General, the latest edition (2000) provides brief information on more than 500 foundations in the state: name, address, employer identification number, foundation manager, application process, total assets in book and market value, contributions paid during the fiscal year, and contributions approved for future payment. The source is arranged alphabetically by foundation name (there are no indexes) and the entries consist of data taken from 2000 returns received by the state Attorney General's Office. Unfortunately, it takes approximately two years before the data are published, so the 2000 edition, based on the 2000 returns, was published in 2002. A supplemental index, consisting of those foundations that submitted their 990-PF forms to the office after December of each year, is compiled and sent free of charge in mid-April of the next year to those who had purchased the *Index*. In the past, this title was issued as *Annual Index Foundation Reports*. Currently, some of the information in the *Index* is also included in the Maryland Department of Planning's free Maryland Grants Searchable Database (see entry 255), but not information on eligibility or application procedures, so it will be necessary for you to contact directly any foundation identified in the search process.

Available from: Maryland Attorney General Office, Attn: Denise Manuli, 200 St. Paul Place, Baltimore, MD 21202-2021. *Telephone:* (410) 576-6491; *Toll-free:* (888) 743-0023; *Fax:* (410) 576-6404; *E-mail:* dmanuli@oag.state.md.us

Web site: www.oag.state.md.us

412

Maryland Funders

Ed. by Ann von Lossberg. Ellicott City, MD: Hieu Press, 2001. 268p. $95. Paper.

Description: The 2001-2002 edition of this directory provides information on grantmakers located in or interested in making grants in Maryland. Covered here are foundations, corporations, nonprofit organizations, and public agencies. The book is divided into sections: funders that accept unsolicited proposals or issue RFPs; funders that award less than $20,000 per year; funders that do not accept unsolicited proposals; and individual donors. Basic information for each is provided.

Available from: Hieu Press, 9676 Gwynn Park Drive, Ellicott City, MD 21042. *Telephone:* (410) 465-3493; *Fax:* (410) 465-7679; *E-mail:* mdfunders2@starpower.net

413

Maryland/DC Foundation Directory Online

http://www.grantsdirect.com

Description: This subscription-based online directory, which is updated monthly, provides information on more than 1,450 grantmakers in Maryland, northern Virginia, and the Washington, D.C. area. The following information is given for each foundation: contact, financial, officers and director, number of grants, amount of grants, priorities, geographic giving, and application information. The information profiles can be searched free-text or using the following search fields: foundation name, corporate sponsor, grantmaker city, grantmaker state, recipient name, purpose, recipient city, recipient state/country, organization type, grant amount, and grant year. Visitors to the web site can "test drive" an abridged database, to evaluate the service before subscribing (annual subscriptions cost $499).

Available from: Jankowski Associates, Inc., 216 West Patrick Street, Frederick, MD 21701. *Telephone:* (301) 696-0797; *Fax:* (301) 696-0798; *E-mail:* info@grantsdirect.com

Web site: www.grantsdirect.com

414

The Red Book: Catalog of State Assistance Programs

http://www.mdp.state.md.us/clhouse/redbook/redbook.html

Description: Over $2.25 billion in grants, loans, scholarships, technical assistance, and other services available from the state and federal government to public sector agencies and the general public in Maryland is identified in this source. For more information about the listing, see entry 255 in the "Grants for Individuals—General—Maryland" section of this bibliography.

Available from: Maryland Department of Planning, 301 West Preston Street, Room 1101, Baltimore, MD 21201-2365. *Telephone:* (410) 767-4500; *Toll-free:* (877) 767-6272; *Fax:* (410) 767-4480; *E-mail:* dczerwinski@mdp.state.md.us

Web site: www.op.state.md.us

Massachusetts

415

Massachusetts Grantmakers Directory

Boston: Associated Grantmakers of Massachusetts, 1999. 339p. ISSN 0898-7025. $50. Paper with online updates.

Description: Nearly 500 grantmaking foundations in Massachusetts are covered in this directory. The entries describing the foundations' activities are arranged alphabetically by foundation name and indexed by program areas, city, and foundations granting support to individuals. For each of the foundations included in the main section, the following information is provided: trustees, contact person, emphasis, areas of interest, geographic focus, types of support offered, application procedures, total grants, range, and assets. The data presented were taken from the returns filed with the IRS and from questionnaires answered by the foundations. The latest edition (1999-2000) of the directory is now out of print; a new edition is scheduled for 2003. In between, members can access updated information on AGM's web site; nonmembers can search the database at selected locations in Massachusetts (these are listed on the web site). Also note: links to many of the foundations listed in the directory are provided, at no charge, on the web site. In the past, *Massachusetts Grantmakers* was published as the *Massachusetts Foundation Directory* and, for information about funding for individuals, the *Massachusetts Foundation Directory Supplement: Sources of Private Support for Individuals.*

Available from: Associated Grantmakers of Massachusetts, 55 Court Street, Suite 520, Boston, MA 02108. *Telephone:* (617) 426-2606; *Fax:* (617) 426-2849; *E-mail:* agm@agmconnect.org
Web site: www.agmconnect.org

Michigan

416

Michigan Foundation Directory

Prep. by the Council of Michigan Foundations and the Foundation Center. Lansing: Michigan League for Human Services, 1976- . Biennial. ISSN 0362-1561. ISBN 1-891445-01-4. $80 (2002 ed.). Paper or CD-ROM.

Description: First published in 1976, this excellent directory is more comprehensive than many of the other state listings; more than 2,300 foundation profiles are provided, including 300 new to the latest (13th) edition. These profiles are arranged alphabetically by name and indexed by donors, officers, and

How to Find Out About Financial Aid and Funding

trustees; types of support; subject; grantmaker name; and geographic location of principal office. In addition to typical directory information, entries also specify time of the year requests are preferred, type of initial contact preferred, types of requests the foundation will consider, whether an application or special format is required, and a list of selected grants (up to 10) for foundations with annual giving of at least $50,000. Since 1999 (11th edition), this publication has been available not only in print, but in CD-ROM ($80) and in a bundled CD-ROM and book package as well ($95). The title is jointly published by the Council of Michigan Foundations and the Foundation Center in New York; both organizations sell the book and CD-ROM. Most of the information included here can also be found in various Foundation Center publications, including the *Foundation Directory* (see entry 359), *Guide to U.S. Foundations* (entry 377), and *National Directory of Corporate Giving* (entry 380).

Available from: Council of Michigan Foundations, One South Harbor Avenue, Suite 3, P.O. Box 599, Grand Haven, MI 49417. *Telephone:* (616) 842-7080; *Fax:* (616) 842-1760

Web site: www.cmif.org

Minnesota

417

Guide to Minnesota Grantmakers

Minneapolis: Minnesota Council on Foundations, 1977- . Biennial. $45 (2001-2002 ed.), paper; $100, CD-ROM stand-alone; $150, CD-ROM network; online, $160-$960/yr.

Description: This directory, which was issued in the past under the title *Guide to Minnesota Foundations and Corporate Giving Programs,* is designed to help individuals and organizations seeking grants in Minnesota, as well as to aid grantmakers and the general public. Covered in the latest edition (2001-2002) are more than 1,000 private, corporate, and community foundations in Minnesota (nearly 150 more than in the previous edition). Information about them is taken primarily from IRS returns. The 52 corporate sources listed account for 40 percent of the grants awarded annually. About one third of the entries in the directory have detailed profiles; specified in each of those entries are: statement of purpose, interests, funding limits, financial data, application procedures, geographic orientation, sample grants, and officers. Also included are a section on proposal writing; a description of foundations' review processes; lists of inactive foundations; foundations with designated recipients; foundations making grants only outside of Minnesota; and indexes of foundations, types of organizations, types of organizations funded, and grantmakers by size. The stand-alone and networked versions of the CD-ROM edition both feature 1) automatic searching for grantmakers based on geography, areas of interest, types of support, intended beneficiaries, grantmaker name, grantmaker city, and more; and 2) automatic sorting of search results by grants paid, total assets, grant range, and city or zip code. The results can be printed or downloaded in text format. The CD-ROM versions are available only for the PC (there are no Mac editions). The information in the book and CD-ROM versions can also be searched online, using Minnesota Grantmakers Online. The basic online subscription, which provides access to the database of 1,000 Minnesota foundations and corporate grantmakers, ranges in price from $160 to $795/yr. The "deluxe" subscription, which also provides access to a database of more than 50,000 grants awarded by these foundations, costs between $240 and $960/yr. Note: free access to Minnesota Grantmakers Online is available at the five Foundation Center Cooperating Collection locations in Minnesota.

Available from: Minnesota Council on Foundations, 15 South Fifth Street, Suite 600, Minneapolis, MN 55402-1570. *Telephone:* (612) 338-1989; *Fax:* (612) 337-5089; *E-mail:* info@mcf.org
Web site: www.mcf.org

418

Minnesota Foundation Directory

Minnetonka, MN: Foundation Data Center, 2003. 800p. $300. Looseleaf with online updates.

Description: Issued annually for the past 30 years, this directory covers all 1,600+ foundations registered in Minnesota and on file with the Internal Revenue Service. Detailed information is provided on the largest 50 percent of these (type, assets, giving, areas of interest, geographic range, officers and trustees, donors, and complete details of each gift); brief information is presented on 400 of the rest, and the remainder are simply listed. Index access is provided for banks and trust companies acting as corporate trustees, areas of interest, and donors, trustees, and administrators. Each annual renewal (called the *Minnesota Foundation Directory Update Service*) costs $240 and provides looseleaf replacement pages for the original directory. Subscribers are also given access to the web site, where information is available on all 1,600 Minnesota foundations. They can check for updates or search for foundations and sort their results by the following: grantmaker name, city, market value at year end, total recipients for the latest fiscal year available, total gifts for the latest fiscal year available, and report year. In the future, an Internet-only subscription may be offered.

Available from: Foundation Data Center, Inc., 401 Kenmar Circle, Minnetonka, MN 55305-1019. *Telephone:* (952) 542-8582; *Toll-free:* 800-716-0055; *Fax:* (952) 542-8582; *E-mail:* fdc@capriotti.com
Web site: www.capriotti.com/fdc

419

Minnesota Grants Directory

St. Paul: Minnesota Council of Nonprofits, 2003. 82p. $40. Paper.

Description: According to a recent Minnesota Council on Foundations' report, 870 foundations and corporate giving programs in Minnesota grant an estimated $630 million to nonprofits annually. About 83 percent of the total giving is carried out by only 15 percent of these Minnesota grantmakers. The latest edition (2003) of the *Minnesota Grants Directory* is designed to provide an overview of the state's most active foundations and corporate giving programs. Less inclusive than the other Minnesota grant directories, this source provides information on only 73 Minnesota foundation, corporate, and religious giving programs. Entries (one to a page) are arranged by organization name and provide typical directory information: contact person, deadlines, availability of funds, giving priorities, geographic focuses, types of grants, staff, trustees, and sample lists of grants. The graphs and charts that accompany most entries give the presentation visual punch.

Available from: Minnesota Council of Nonprofits, 2314 University Avenue West, Suite 20, St. Paul, MN 55114-1802. *Telephone:* (651) 642-1904; *Toll-free:* (800) 289-1904; *Fax:* (651) 642-1517; *E-mail:* info@mncn.org
Web site: www.mncn.org

Missouri

420

The Directory of Missouri Foundations

Ed. by Anne Borman. St. Louis: Directory of Missouri Foundations, 1985- . Biennial. ISSN 0884-7223. $62 (2001-2002 ed.). Paper.

Description: More than 400 private, corporate, and community foundations registered in Missouri are briefly described in the 170-page Millennium edition (2001-2002) of this directory. The information presented is taken from 990-PF income tax returns and questionnaires completed by foundation officials. Foundation profiles are grouped into three sections: foundations making contributions to organizations, foundations providing assistance to individuals (scholarships, loans, and emergency funding), and designated foundations (those that do not accept separate applications). Entries specify names of executive officers, mailing address, telephone number, total assets, limitations, geographic restrictions, largest and smallest grants made recently, major interests, and application procedures/deadlines. Additional sections list inactive, terminated, and relocated foundations. Two indexes provide access by city location and by foundation name. Formerly, this directory was published by Swift Associates.

Grants for Organizations–General–Montana

Available from: Directory of Missouri Foundations, 8122 Edinburgh Drive, St. Louis, MO 63105. *Telephone:* (314) 725-6834; *Fax:* (314) 725-0211; *E-mail:* foundations@primary.net

421

Directory of Missouri Grantmakers

4th ed. New York: Foundation Center, 2001. 159p. ISBN 0-87954-956-4. $75. Paper.

Description: This is one of five geographically-based funding directories available from the Foundation Center (the others cover the District of Columbia, Michigan, New York, and Ohio and are described in entries 393, 416, 431, and 434). Intended to be comprehensive, this directory describes the grantmaking activities of approximately 1,300 foundations, corporate giving programs, and direct charities in Missouri. Organization profiles indicate amounts, fields of interest, purpose, and selected grants. Entries can be accessed using the following indexes: subject, types of support, and names of key personnel. Produced as a collaborative project of the Foundation Center and the regional association of grantmakers serving metropolitan St. Louis, most of the information included here can also be found in various Foundation Center publications, including the *Foundation Directory* (see entry 359), *Guide to U.S. Foundations* (entry 377), and *National Directory of Corporate Giving* (entry 380).

Available from: Foundation Center, 79 Fifth Avenue, New York, NY 10003-3076. *Telephone:* (212) 807-3690; *Toll-free:* (800) 424-9836; *Fax:* (212) 807-3691

Web site: fdncenter.org

Montana

422

Montana Foundation Directory

14th ed. Ed. by Joan Bares. Billings: Montana State University at Billings, 2002. 155p. $25. Spiral bound.

Description: Covered in this directory are more than 200 foundations in Montana. The profiles presented are based on information extracted from 990-PF returns; this includes foundation name, address, telephone number, contact person, and areas of funding interest. The entries are arranged by foundation. The directory also covers foundations located outside of Montana but involved in funding within the state. The latest edition also provides information on application submission, purpose, restrictions, and amount and number awarded. Foundations offering scholarships (rather than grants to organizations) can be identified in the index. Prior to the fifth edition, this directory also included similar information for the state of Wyoming and was issued under the title *Montana and Wyoming Foundations Directory*. Laramie County Community College in Cheyenne, Wyoming now publishes a separate directory that covers only Wyoming foundations (see entry 454).

Available from: Montana State University at Billings, Grants Development Office, 1500 University Drive, Billings, Montana 59101-298. *Telephone:* (406) 657-1654; *Fax:* (406) 657-2264; *E-mail:* jbares@msubillings.edu

Web site: www.msubillings.edu/library/grants/index.html

423

Philanthropy Northwest Member Directory

6th ed. Seattle: Pacific Northwest Grantmakers Forum, 2002. 234p. $91, paper; $126, online.

Description: This directory (also available as an online subscription) provides descriptive information on the grantgiving activities of the members of Philanthropy Northwest: community foundations, corporate foundations, corporate giving programs, private foundations, public foundations, and trusts in Montana, Washington, Oregon, Idaho, and Alaska. For more information about the listing and its online version, see entry 449 in the "Grants for Organizations—General—Washington" section of this bibliography.

Available from: Philanthropy Northwest, 2815 Second Avenue, Suite 290, Seattle, WA 98121. *Telephone:* (206) 770-9423; *E-mail:* info@philanthropynw.org

Web site: www.philanthropynw.org

Nebraska

424

Nebraska Foundation DataBook

1st ed. By Ford T. Pearson. Portland: C&D Publishing, 2002. 358p. $100, book; $250, book and CD-ROM set.

Description: More than 700 foundations located in Nebraska are covered in the first edition of this directory. Comprehensive profiles are provided for the largest 222 foundations (whose assets represent 97 percent of all Nebraska foundation assets), including a listing of the grants they awarded during the most recent year on record; brief entries are included for 500 additional grantmakers in the state. The combined assets of all the foundations profiled exceed $1 billion. Specifically excluded from the listing are foundations located outside Nebraska, even if they make grants within the state. The following information,

Grants for Organizations–General–Nevada

most of which is taken from 990-PF forms, is provided for each grantmaker: contact information, financial data, giving restrictions, and geographic focus. Information is available both in book form and on CD-ROM. The *Nebraska Foundation Databook* is one in a series of state-based directories issued by C&D Publishing; the others focus on California, Iowa, Louisiana, Oklahoma, Oregon, and Washington (see entries 389, 405, 408, 435, 437, and 450).

Available from: C&D Publishing, 1017 Morrison Street S.W., Suite 500, Portland, OR 97205. *Telephone:* (503) 274-8780; *Toll-free:* (877) 924-7268
Web site: www.foundationdatabook.com

425

Nebraska Foundation Directory

Omaha: Junior League of Omaha, 1979- . Irreg. $25 (2000 ed.). Paper.

Description: Approximately 200 Nebraska foundations are listed alphabetically by foundation name in the latest edition of this directory (which, recently, has been updated on a three-year cycle). This is every foundation in the state for which a 990-PF form filed with the IRS was available. Identified for each foundation are address, purpose, restrictions, assets, grants paid (high and low), officers, and contact. There are no indexes. The price ($25) is rather high for the amount of information provided in this 30-page pamphlet.

Available from: Junior League of Omaha, 608 North, 108th Court, Omaha, NE 68154. *Telephone:* (402) 493-8818; *Fax:* (402) 493-5823
Web site: www.juniorleagueomaha.org

Nevada

426

Nevada Funding Directory

Las Vegas, NV: Las Vegas-Clark County Library District, 1984-2000. Irreg. $15 (2000 ed.). Paper.

Description: Information is presented here on approximately 300 foundations either located in Nevada or having a history of giving in the state. Entries are arranged alphabetically by foundation name and are indexed by fields of interest and geographic location. The following information is provided for each foundation: funding interests, amounts awarded, contact persons, and typical grants, The data presented were taken from 990-PF forms filed with the Internal Revenue Service and from interviews with foundation officials. In addition to the descriptions of active foundations in Nevada, the directory also includes lists of inactive or defunct foundations and national foundations that in the past have funded projects in Nevada. Through 1994, this directory was issued as the

How to Find Out About Financial Aid and Funding

Nevada Foundation Directory. The current edition (4th) was edited by Ellen B. Reed and published in 2000; no future editions are planned.
Available from: Las Vegas-Clark County Library District, Special Collections, Grants, 1401 East Flamingo Road, Las Vegas, NV 89119. *Telephone:* (702) 733-3642; *Fax:* (202) 733-1173
Web site: www.lvccld.org

New Hampshire

427

New Hampshire Directory of Foundations

2nd ed. Ed. by Christine Graham. Shaftsbury, VT: CPG Enterprises, 2002. 60p. $48. Spiral bound.
Description: Produced by CPG Enterprises, which also publishes the *Vermont Directory of Foundations* (see entry 446), the second edition of this directory lists all active foundations incorporated in New Hampshire plus several outside the state that have "giving or guidelines that include New Hampshire organizations and projects." The following information is provided for each entry: contact, assets, typical grant ranges, application procedures, areas of giving, restrictions, and recent New Hampshire grantees. Also included are an introduction on grant research and a bibliography of sources for further research (both print and Internet resources).
Available from: CPG Enterprises, P.O. Box 199, Shaftsbury, VT 05262. *Telephone:* (802) 862-0327; *E-mail:* cpgraham@cpgfundraising.com
Web site: www.cpgfundraising.com

New Jersey

428

The Mitchell Guide: A Directory of New Jersey Foundations

10th ed. Ed. by Janet A. Mitchell. Pennington, NJ: Mitchell Guide, 2001. 312p. ISSN 0743-9601. $75. Paper.
Description: Published earlier as the *New Jersey Mitchell Guide: Foundations, Corporations, and Their Managers,* the 2001 edition identifies more than 550 foundations in New Jersey that have assets of at least $150,000 or make total annual grants of at least $15,000; these include 300 foundations that accept unsolicited applications, 260 foundations that pre-select their grantees, 11 "emerging" foundations, and 62 foundations dropped from the current edition.

Arranged alphabetically by foundation name, the entries present information taken from IRS returns (mostly 1999), along with data supplied by the foundations themselves. The following information is provided: application procedures, proposal requirements, geographic limits and, when known, fields of interest. Entries are indexed by foundation trustees, county, and field of interest. In between editions, free updates and corrections are sent to purchasers via e-mail.

Available from: Mitchell Guide, P.O. Box 626, Pennington, NJ 08534-0626. *Telephone:* (609) 730-8247; *Fax:* (609) 730-8247; *E-mail:* grantsnj@aol.com

429

New Jersey Grants Guide

2nd ed. Ed. by Shanan Y. Miller and Mandy M. Rigg. Denver: Grant Guides Plus, 2000. 984p. ISBN 0-9658306-3-2. $100, Center for Non-Profit Corporations members; $150, nonmembers. Paper.

Description: Prepared by Grant Guides Plus in cooperation with the Center for Non-Profit Corporations, the second edition of this guide (2000-2002) provides profiles on 400 foundations, 150 state agency funders, and 30 religious funders within the state of New Jersey. The following information is given for each: areas of interest, assets, amount of New Jersey giving, examples of recent grants, application procedures, application deadlines, contact names, funding levels, types of support, and officers and trustees. The entries are indexed in a number of ways, including by name, trustees, areas of interest, geographic location, and types of support. All subscribers to the guide receive updates containing revised contact information, funding priority changes, and new funding sources every six months at no additional charge. The publisher, Grant Guides Plus, is no longer in business; the 2000-2002 edition of the guide is now only available from the Center for Non-Profit Corporations. The three other state-based funding directories previously published by the now-defunct Grant Guides Plus are no longer in print: *New York State Grants Guide* (1998. ISBN 0-9658306-6-7); *Ohio Grants Guide* (1997. ISBN 0-9658306-0-8); and *Pennsylvania Grants Guide* (1998. ISBN 0-9658306-5-9).

Available from: Center for Non-Profit Corporations, 1501 Livingston Avenue, North Brunswick, NJ 08902. *Telephone:* (732) 227-0800; *Fax:* (732) 227-0087; *E-mail:* center@njnonprofits.org

Web site: www.njnonprofits.org

How to Find Out About Financial Aid and Funding

New Mexico

430

The New Mexico Funding Directory

5th ed. Ed. by Denise A. Wallen and Amy Elder. Albuquerque: University of New Mexico, 1999. 175p. $40, paper; free, online.

Description: The fifth edition of the *New Mexico Funding Directory* identifies more than 300 funding programs located in or interested in funding in the state. Included are state government grant programs, corporate direct giving programs, private organizations, community and corporate foundations, and awards offered by the University of New Mexico. This information is also available on the University of New Mexico's Office of Research Services' web site. Although some of the databases on this site are restricted to the University of New Mexico community using either a UNM machine or UNM or New Mexico Technet dial ups, the funding directory is in the "public domain" section and can be searched by keyword by anyone visiting the site; no fees are charged. A new print edition was planned for 2002 but has not yet been released; however, a searchable version of the planned edition is currently available on the web site.

Available from: University of New Mexico, Attn: Office of Research Services, Scholes Hall 102, Albuquerque, NM 87131-6003. *Telephone:* (505) 277-2256; *Fax:* (505) 277-5567; *E-mail:* research@unm.edu

Web site: www.unm.edu/~ors

New York

431

New York State Foundations

7th ed. New York: Foundation Center, 2001. 1,095p. ISBN 0-87954-955-6. $180. Paper.

Description: This is the most comprehensive listing of foundations located in New York state. More than 5,900 foundations are profiled, along with 1,200 out-of-state grantmakers with an interest in funding in the state. These grantmakers award more than $3 billion each year—one fifth of all foundation grant giving in the United States. The profiles are organized by county and indexed by city. All entries provide basic information: application address, financial data, giving limitations, and key officials. Additional information is presented for the large foundations (those that give at least $50,000 annually): application procedures, purpose, and activities statements. Many entries also include descriptions of recently-awarded grants; in all, over 12,000 sample grants are listed. Produced by the Foundation Center, most of the information included here can also be found in various Foundation Center publications, including the *Foundation Directory* (see entry 359), *Guide to U.S. Foundations* (entry 377), and *National Directory of Corporate Giving* (entry 380). This is one of five geographically-based funding directories available from the Foundation Center; the others cover the District of Columbia, Michigan, Missouri, and Ohio and are described in entries 393, 416, 421, and 434.

Available from: Foundation Center, 79 Fifth Avenue, New York, NY 10003-3076. *Telephone:* (212) 807-3690; *Toll-free:* (800) 424-9836; *Fax:* (212) 807-3691

Web site: fdncenter.org

North Carolina

432

North Carolina Giving

4th ed. Raleigh, NC: Capital Development Services, 1999. 1,092p. ISBN 0-9624910-7-1. $120, paper; $110, online.

Description: North Carolina's first foundation—The Winston-Salem Foundation—was established in 1919. Today, North Carolina is home to 1,100 foundations with assets totaling nearly $8 billion and annual giving approaching $400 million. These foundations are described in detail in the fourth edition of *North Carolina Giving* (previous editions were issued in 1990, 1993, and 1996). Information on corporate giving in North Carolina is not covered here but was included in the last edition (1995) of the publisher's *North Carolina Corporate Giving*. In the 1999 edition of *North Carolina Giving,* foundation profiles are grouped by size ($1 million or more in assets or $100,000 or more in grants; $200,000 to $1 million in assets or $25,000 to $100,000 in grants; less than $200,000 in assets or $25,000 in grants) and indexed by subject, county, state (listing foundations located in North Carolina that have funded programs in the District of Columbia or Maryland), individual, and foundation name. Each profile provides the following information: address, telephone number, contact, board of directors, financial data, purpose and activities, restrictions, grant analysis, grants awarded by subject categories, application guidelines, and sample grants. The information in this directory is now also available as an online product, North Carolina Giving Online, which permits subscribers to access the data electronically; as a result, online subscribers are able to see the latest information posted on these foundations. The price for the online product is $110; if purchased with the print directory, the bundled price is $220. Although Capital Development has provided the same type of coverage in the past for Georgia (*Georgia Giving*) and Virginia *(Virginia Giving* and *Virginia Corporate Giving),* these publications have not been updated in several years and there are no plans to print them again in the future.

Available from: Capital Development Services, Inc., 111 Hampton Woods Lane, Raleigh, NC 27607. *Telephone:* (919) 854-9775; *Toll-free:* (800) 729-4553; *Fax:* (919) 854-9740; *E-mail:* info@capdev.com

Web site: www.capdev.com

Ohio

433

Charitable Foundations Directory of Ohio

Columbus, OH: Office of the Attorney General, 1973- . Biennial. $7.50 (13th ed.). Paper.

Description: Prepared by the Ohio State Attorney General's Office, this directory is intended to benefit individuals and organizations seeking grants and other types of assistance from charitable foundations in Ohio. The 13th edition includes all organizations reporting to the Attorney General's Office under Ohio Revised Code 109.31 and the Federal Tax Reform Act of 1969, regardless of the extent of assets or distribution. Because of this loose definition of "foundation," there are a surprising number of entries (2,600), some of which are trusts wholly devoted to named recipients and a number with zero assets and grants. The source is arranged alphabetically by foundation and indexed by counties and purpose. Each entry specifies, in addition to the usual data, the name of the individual handling grants, restrictions, trust number, and purpose. The latest edition (1999-2000) was published in 2001; the next biennial edition will be released in mid-2003 and cover 2001-2002.

Available from: Ohio Attorney General's Office, Attn: Charitable Law Section, 101 East Town Street, 4th Floor, Columbus, OH 43215-5148. *Telephone:* (614) 466-3180; *Fax:* (614) 466-9788

Web site: www.ag.state.oh.us

434

Guide to Ohio Grantmakers

1st ed. New York: Foundation Center, 2001. 596p. ISBN 0-87954-975-0. $125. Paper.

Description: This is one of five geographically-based funding directories available from the Foundation Center (the others cover the District of Columbia, Michigan, Missouri, and New York and are described in entries 393, 416, 421, and 431). Like the others, the first edition of this directory is intended to be comprehensive; covered here are more than 3,000 foundations in Ohio, plus 300

Grants for Organizations–General–Oklahoma

funders outside the state that make grants in Ohio. Organization profiles indicate amounts, fields of interest, purpose, and selected grants. Entries can be accessed using the following indexes: subject, types of support, and names of key personnel. Produced as a collaborative project of the Foundation Center and the Ohio Association of Nonprofit Organizations, most of the information included here can also be found in various Foundation Center publications, including the *Foundation Directory* (see entry 359), *Guide to U.S. Foundations* (entry 377), and *National Directory of Corporate Giving* (entry 380).

Available from: Foundation Center, 79 Fifth Avenue, New York, NY 10003-3076. *Telephone:* (212) 807-3690; *Toll-free:* (800) 424-9836; *Fax:* (212) 807-3691

Web site: fdncenter.org

Oklahoma

435

Oklahoma Foundation DataBook

1st ed. Ed. by Ford T. Pearson. Portland: C&D Publishing, 2002. 420p. $100, book; $250, book and CD-ROM set.

Description: Covered here are all grantmaking foundations in Oklahoma (close to 1,100). And, while comprehensive information is provided for only a quarter of those, the combined assets of that segment (213 foundations) represent more than 99 percent of all Oklahoma foundation assets. The following information, most of which is taken from 990-PF forms, is provided for each grantmaker: contact information, financial data, giving restrictions, and geographic focus. A special feature: all grants made by a listed foundation during the most recent fiscal year are identified (including the amount of the grant, the purpose of the grant, and the grant recipient). This is a real plus for the serious fundseeker; most other directories only list representative grants. Information is available both in book form and on CD-ROM. *Oklahoma Foundation DataBook* is one in a series of state-based foundation directories; the others focus on California, Iowa, Louisiana, Nebraska, Oregon, and Washington (see entries 389, 405, 408, 424, 437, and 450).

Available from: C&D Publishing, 1017 Morrison Street S.W., Suite 500, Portland, OR 97205. *Telephone:* (503) 274-8780

Web site: www.foundationdatabook.com

Oregon

436

Guide to Oregon Foundations

Portland, OR: Guide Line, 1977- . Annual. $46 (2003 ed.). Spiral bound.

Description: Oregon is not particularly foundation rich, especially when compared to states like New York and California; Oregon foundations make up only one percent of the national total. Further, the majority of foundations in Oregon are small operations, awarding less than $5,000 in grants each year. Most of these foundations (400 in the 2003 edition) are described here. The data are taken primarily from 990-PF, 990-AR, and CT-12 forms filed with the Oregon Register of Charitable Trusts. Entries are listed alphabetically and include information on contact, establishment, purpose, restrictions, type of foundation, geographic location, and finances (total assets, total number of grants, range of grants, etc.). Additional access to these entries is provided by geographic focus and field of interest (arts, disabled, elderly, education, general, health, nature, minority, religion, sexual minority, women, or youth). The guide has been a collaboration between the United Way Columbia-Willamette and Guide Line since it began in 1977.

Available from: Guide Line, Inc., 621 S.W. Alder Street, Suite 660, Portland, OR 97205. *Telephone:* (503) 226-3099; *Fax:* (503) 226-3099

437

Oregon Foundation DataBook

7th ed. Ed. by Craig McPherson. Portland: C&D Publishing, 2002. 624p. $100, book; $250, book and CD-ROM set.

Description: Similar to the other *Foundation DataBooks* published by C&D Publishing (see entries 389, 405, 408, 424, 435, and 450), the 2002 edition of this directory provides detailed descriptions of nearly 350 foundations based in Oregon; foundations located outside of Oregon are not included, even if they have a history of grantmaking in the state. The following information, most of which is taken from 990-PF forms, is provided for each grantmaker: contact information, financial data, giving restrictions, and geographic focus. A special feature: all grants made by a listed foundation during the most recent fiscal year are identified (including the amount of the grant, the purpose of the grant, and the grant recipient). This is a real plus for the serious fundseeker; most other directories only list representative grants. Information is available both in book form and on CD-ROM.

Available from: C&D Publishing, 1017 Morrison Street S.W., Suite 500, Portland, OR 97205. *Telephone:* (503) 274-8780; *Toll-free:* (877) 924-7268
Web site: www.foundationdatabook.com

Grants for Organizations–General–Pennsylvania

438

Philanthropy Northwest Member Directory

6th ed. Seattle: Pacific Northwest Grantmakers Forum, 2002. 234p. $91, paper; $126, online.

Description: This directory (also available as an online subscription) provides descriptive information on the grantgiving activities of the members of Philanthropy Northwest: community foundations, corporate foundations, corporate giving programs, private foundations, public foundations, and trusts in Oregon, Washington, Idaho, Montana, and Alaska. For more information about the listing and its online version, see entry 449 in the "Grants for Organizations—General—Washington" section of this bibliography.

Available from: Philanthropy Northwest, 2815 Second Avenue, Suite 290, Seattle, WA 98121. *Telephone:* (206) 770-9423; *E-mail:* info@philanthropynw.org
Web site: www.philanthropynw.org

Pennsylvania

439

Directory of Pennsylvania Foundations

7th ed. Comp. by S. Damon Kletzien. Springfield, PA: Triadvocates Press, 2001. 580p. ISBN 0-9616806-4-4. $85, paper; $235, nonprofits, CD-ROM; $385, for-profits, CD-ROM.

Description: The main section of this directory describes 1,600 Pennsylvania foundations (330 new to this edition) with assets of more than $150,000 or grantmaking of more than $7,500; it is arranged alphabetically within five geographic regions. In total, the assets of these foundations exceed $21 billion and their annual giving tops $1 billion; this represents a 45 percent increase over aggregate assets reported in the previous edition. Each profile indicates: representative grants or an analysis of the grantmaking process, funding areas, application guidelines, financial data, availability of published reports, telephone numbers, and names of trustees, directors, and principal officers. Smaller foundations (an additional 2,100) are also listed, but not profiled. The information presented is taken either from earlier 990-PF returns filed with the IRS or from questionnaires returned by the foundations. There are five indexes: officers, directors, and trustees; funding interests; foundation name; county; and deadline date. A CD-ROM version of the directory is also available at $235 for nonprofit organizations and $385 for consultants and other for-profit businesses. This price also includes a print copy of the directory.

Available from: Triadvocates Press, P.O. Box 336, Springfield, PA 19064-0336. *Telephone:* (610) 544-6927; *Fax:* (610) 328-2805; *E-mail:* DirPaFdns@aol.com
Web site: www.upenn.edu/research/PAfoundations.htm

Rhode Island

440

Rhode Island Grantsbook: A Resource for Grant Seekers in Rhode Island

4th ed. Providence, RI: Nonprofit Resources of Southern New England, 2002. Unpaged. $45, members; $75, all others. Paper.

Description: Previously published as *Grantsbook: A Resource Guide to Fundraising in Rhode Island,* this biennially-issued directory provides the following information for approximately 200 foundations in Rhode Island: contact, assets, number of grants awarded annually, high and low grants, type of support, purpose and activity, restrictions, fields of interest, application process, and deadline. The publisher, Nonprofit Resources of Southern New England, was formerly known as the Support Center of Rhode Island. This title is sometimes cited as *RI Grantsbook.*

Available from: Nonprofit Resources of Southern New England, 160 Broad Street, Providence, RI 02903. *Telephone:* (401) 861-1920; *Fax:* (401) 861-8198
Web site: www.nonprofitresourcessne.org

South Carolina

441

South Carolina Foundation Directory

7th ed. Columbia: South Carolina State Library, 2000. 506p. $15. Spiral bound.

Description: As state foundation directories go, this one is a bargain. More than 500 pages of information for only $15! Described in some detail are 399 active South Carolina private and community foundations and grantmaking public charities. Together, these foundations make more than 6,000 grants each year, totaling more than $56 million dollars. Most information is taken from annual reports and from 990-PF forms. The entries are arranged alphabetically by foundation and indexed by name, city, and areas of interest. The following information is provided for each of the foundations: officers, areas of interest, geographical restrictions, assets, total grants awarded, number awarded, and range of grants. Listed in separate sections are inactive foundations new to the seventh edition, inactive foundations listed in the sixth edition, terminated foundations, and South Carolina foundation facts.

Available from: South Carolina State Library, Attn: Karen McMullen, 1500 Senate Street, P.O. Box 11469, Columbia, SC 29211. *Telephone:* (803) 734-8026; *Fax:* (803) 734-8676; *E-mail:* reference@leo.scsl.state.sc.us

Web site: www.myscgov.com

South Dakota

442

South Dakota Grant Directory

http://www.sdstatelibrary.com/grants/index.cfm

Description: This directory, "designed specifically for use by South Dakotans and their organizations," was last issued in print in 1995 (4th ed. 172p. $7, paperback). The 2000 edition, when completed, will be available only on the Internet; however, as of the beginning of 2003, the database is still "under construction." That means that both "the number of foundations and grants described here and the tables/additional resource links are incomplete." Additional records will be added to the database on an ongoing basis. Currently, there are 411 South Dakota grantmakers covered online (i.e., foundations, trusts, and major corporate giving programs headquartered in South Dakota; foundations and corporations located outside the state that have shown interest in funding within the state; South Dakota state government programs; South Dakota foundations awarding scholarships; and nongranting foundations in the state). This listing can be searched at no charge by foundation or grant name and/or fields of interest. No information is provided on federal programs, except those administered competitively at the state level. Information is taken from questionnaires completed by the foundations during 1999, their most recent annual report, and the 990-PF forms filed with the Internal Revenue Service. When completed, the database will contain the most inclusive listing of grantmakers in or focused on the state.

Available from: South Dakota State Library, Attn: Public Services Department, The MacKay Building, 800 Governors Drive, Pierre, SD 57501-2294. *Telephone:* (605) 773-3131; *Toll-free:* (800) 423-6665 (within SD); *Fax:* (605) 773-4950

Web site: www.sdstatelibrary.com/grants/index.cfm

Tennessee

443

A Grantseeker's Guide to Tennessee Funders

4th ed. Nashville: Center for Nonprofit Management, 2002. $160. CD-ROM.

Description: This searchable directory on CD-ROM offers the most current and comprehensive coverage of Tennessee foundations and corporate giving programs. In-depth profiles for 319 foundations and 210 corporate giving programs are provided; the following information is supplied: application procedures, deadlines, board members and contacts, and examples of past grants (if available). Those who purchase the guide also receive access to online updates. This is the first edition of the guide to be issued solely as a CD-ROM product.

Available from: Center for Non-Profit Management, 44 Vantage Way, Suite 230, Nashville, TN 37228. *Telephone:* (615) 259-0100; *Fax:* (615) 259-0400

Web site: www.cnm.org

Texas

444

Directory of Texas Foundations

San Antonio: Nonprofit Resource Center of Texas, 1990- . Annual. ISSN 1087-9692. $175 (2003 ed.). Paper or online.

Description: Published until 1990 under the title *Hooper Directory of Texas Foundations,* this annual provides information on approximately 2,400 private and community foundations in Texas (300 are new to this edition). In total, these foundations annually grant more than a billion dollars to nonprofits in the state. Information in the directory can be accessed by areas of interest, city, foundation name, trustees and officers, types of support, deadline dates, and foundation solicitation requirements. Also available is an Internet subscription, Directory of Texas Foundations Online, which costs from $175/yr. for a single user to $275/yr. for multiple users. The online version includes information on 3,264 foundations registered in Texas and complete profiles on 2,200 foundations; it can be searched by areas of interest, total assets, foundation name, total grants, location, types of support, trustees and officers, and zip codes.

Available from: Nonprofit Resource Center of Texas, P.O. Box 27215, San Antonio, TX 78227-0215. *Telephone:* (210) 227-4333; *Fax:* (210) 227-0310; *E-mail:* fic@fic.org

Web site: www.nprc.org

Utah

445

Philanthropic Foundations of Utah Directory

Ed. by Roger Henry Plothow. Provo, UT: Henry Dean Publishing, 2002. 278p. $59. Paper or CD-ROM.

Description: Available in either a print or CD-ROM edition, this biennially-issued directory covers 425 philanthropic foundations, awarding nearly $100 million annually, that are located in the state of Utah; of these, 105 are new to this edition. The entries are listed alphabetically. Basic directory type information is provided: addresses and telephone numbers, names of officers and managers, purposes and interests, fiscal data and lists of grants, etc. The directory is published every two years; an addendum, with updating information, is included in alternate years.

Available from: Henry Dean Publishing, Inc., 1254 North 1220 West, Provo, UT 84604. *Telephone:* (801) 375-1068
Web site: www.idahomall.com/grantwriting/direct.html

Vermont

446

Vermont Directory of Foundations

11th ed. Ed. by Christine Graham. Shaftsbury, VT: CPG Enterprises, 2002. 60p. $45. Spiral bound.

Description: This directory is organized into two sections: foundations incorporated in the state of Vermont and foundations incorporated out of state that have demonstrated an interest in funding Vermont nonprofits. The criterion for inclusion is "foundations that have given more than $2,500, or have been in business for several years, giving a fluctuating amount which has at least once reached $2,500." There are approximately 80 to 100 foundations described in each section. The following information is provided: contact, assets, areas of interest, sample grants, application procedures, requirements, and deadlines. The introduction covers "how to apply for a grant." CPG Enterprises also publishes a bi-monthly newsletter, *Nonprofit Vermont Newsletter* ($24/yr.), which can be used sometimes to update the listings here.

Available from: CPG Enterprises, P.O. Box 199, Shaftsbury, VT 05262. *Telephone:* (802) 862-0327; *E-mail:* cpgraham@cpgfundraising.com
Web site: www.cpgfundraising.com

Virginia

447

Directory of Virginia Foundations

Richmond, VA: Grants Connection. Updated weekly. ISBN 0-9709031-4-6, looseleaf; 0-9709031-5-4, CD-ROM. $150, looseleaf; $195, disk; $225, CD-ROM; $350, online.

Description: The *Directory of Virginia Foundations* provides information on 1,000 private, corporate, and community foundations incorporated in the Commonwealth of Virginia. The directory is available in four different formats: CD-ROM, diskette, looseleaf binder, and online subscription. The latest information is available not only online, but in the other formats as well, since the CD-ROM, diskette, and looseleaf versions are produced only when an order is received. The database used to generate the four versions is updated weekly and is available to all subscribers on the Grants Connection's web site.

Available from: Grants Connection, Inc., 8522 Ben Nevis Drive, Richmond, VA 23235-3408. *Telephone:* (804) 301-5038; *Toll-free:* (800) 532-7934; *Fax:* (804) 320-4222; *Telephone:* brownie3@cox.net

Web site: www.grantsconnection.com

Washington

448

Charitable Trust Directory

Olympia, WA: Office of the Secretary of State, 2001. 387p. $20. Paper.

Description: More than 900 Washington foundations are covered in this biennially-issued directory. The information presented is based on registration and reporting forms gathered by the Secretary of State's Office under the Washington Charitable Trust Act. The main section of the work is arranged alphabetically by organization. Standard directory-type information is presented for each institution. General information about charitable trusts (e.g., address, purpose of the organization, contact person) is also available at no charge by calling the Secretary of State's Charities Hotline at (800) 332-GIVE (within WA) or (360) 753-0863 (outside the state). Similar information can also be accessed, without charge, at the Charitable Organizations and Commercial Fundraisers Registration Search section of the office's web site; the listings there are updated daily and can be accessed by organization name, location, UBI and EIN numbers, and purpose.

Grants for Organizations–General–Washington

Available from: Washington Secretary of State, Attn: Charities Program, 801 Capitol Way South, P.O. Box 40234, Olympia, WA 98504-0234. *Telephone:* (360) 753-0863; *Toll-free:* (800) 332-GIVE (within WA); *Fax:* (360) 664-4250; *TDD:* (888) 658-1485; *E-mail:* charities@secstate.wa.gov
Web site: www.secstate.wa.gov/charities

449

Philanthropy Northwest Member Directory

6th ed. Seattle: Pacific Northwest Grantmakers Forum, 2002. 234p. $91, paper; $126, online.

Description: Philanthropy Northwest (formerly Pacific Northwest Grantmakers Forum) is composed of organizations that fund in the Northwestern states of Alaska, Idaho, Montana, Oregon, and Washington. There are a total of 135 members, including community foundations, corporate foundations, corporate giving programs, private foundations, public foundations, and trusts. Their annual giving ranges from $5,000 to more than $19 million. The following information is presented for each of the members in the 2002-2003 membership directory: contact person, funding areas, geographic limitations, typical grant size, number of grants made per year, total yearly giving, application procedures, and available publications. Grantseekers can access the information by type of support (e.g., capital building funds, start-up funding, multiple-year funding) and funding areas (e.g., visual arts, literacy/ESL, programs for women and girls). The directory is also available as an online subscription ($126/yr.). Previously, the directory was issued as the *Pacific Northwest Grantmakers Forum Member Directory.*

Available from: Philanthropy Northwest, 2815 Second Avenue, Suite 290, Seattle, WA 98121. *Telephone:* (206) 770-9423; *E-mail:* info@philanthropynw.org
Web site: www.philanthropynw.org

450

Washington Foundation DataBook

2nd ed. Ed. by Craig McPherson. Portland: C&D Publishing, 2002. 660p. $100, book; $250, book and CD-ROM set.

Description: Released by C&D Publishing, which also publishes similar *Foundation DataBooks* for several other states (see entries 389, 405, 408, 424, 435, and 437), the second edition of this directory provides information on more than 350 Washington-based foundations; foundations located outside of Washington are not included, even if they have a history of grantmaking in the state. The following information, most of which is taken from 990-PF forms, is provided for each grantmaker: contact information, financial data, giving restrictions, and geographic focus. A special feature: all grants made by a listed foundation during the most recent fiscal year are identified (including the amount of the grant, the purpose of the grant, and the grant recipient). This is a real plus for the serious fundseeker; most other directories only list representative grants. Information is available both in book form and on CD-ROM. The first edition of the directory was issued in 2000.

Available from: C&D Publishing, 1017 Morrison Street S.W., Suite 500, Portland, OR 97205. *Telephone:* (503) 274-8780; *Toll-free:* (877) 924-7268
Web site: www.foundationdatabook.com

451

Washington Foundation Directory: How to Get Your Slice of the Pie

3rd ed. Ed. by Mardell Moore and Charna Klein. Seattle: Consultant Services Northwest, 2000. 439p. ISBN 0-6141493-1-2. $38. Paper.

Description: Descriptions of more than 600 foundations located in or interested in funding projects in Washington state are profiled in this directory. The information presented was taken from IRS 990-PF forms. Each entry provides the following, when available: contact information, assets or total monetary value of the foundation, subject interest area(s), types of support offered, and types of recipients(s) funded. The entries are arranged alphabetically by foundation name and indexed by subject, support types, recipients types, and geographic coverage. First published in 1991, the directory has been updated twice since then, in 1994 and 2000.

Available from: Consultant Services Northwest, Inc., 6521 36th Avenue, N.E., Seattle, WA 98115. *Telephone:* (206) 524-1950; *E-mail:* csklein14@juno.com

Wisconsin

452

Foundations in Wisconsin: A Directory

Ed. by Mary C. Frenn. Milwaukee, WI: Marquette University Memorial Library Funding Center, 1975- . Annual. ISSN 0360-8042. $63 (2002 ed.), spiral bound; $190, online.

Description: First issued in 1975, the latest edition (2002) describes 1,151 currently-active Wisconsin foundations (representing nearly $3 billion in assets and $300 million in grantmaking). The listing is intended to be inclusive. Since there are no size qualifications for inclusion, assets vary from more than $10 million to zero. Each foundation profile includes: foundation names, address and telephone number, contact person, fiscal year reporting, total asset value (at market value), total grants paid, grant range and median, areas of interest, officers

Grants for Organizations–General–Wyoming

and directors, and sample grant list. Arranged alphabetically by foundation name, the entries contain information based on returns filed with the IRS. Additional access is provided through the county, foundation managers, and funding interest indexes. The information presented here is also available as an online subscription; this replaces the CD-ROM version issued previously. *Foundations in Wisconsin* is the only directory that covers every active grantmaking foundation in the state. It is produced by the staff of the Funding Information Center located in Marquette University's Memorial Library.

Available from: Marquette University Memorial Library, Attn: Dean's Office, P.O. Box 3141, Milwaukee, WI 53201-3141. *Telephone:* (414) 288-1515; *Fax:* (414) 288-7813; *E-mail:* Mary.Frenn@marquette.edu
Web site: www.marquette.edu/library/fic

Wyoming

453

Catalog of Wyoming State Grants

http://cowgirl.state.wy.us/grantscat
Description: This web site offers a starting point for potential grant applicants in Wyoming and provides basic information on representative grants. The programs included are available to a range of applicants, generally unsolicited, and competitive in some sense. Programs with doubtful futures are excluded from the database, as are entitlement programs. The listing can be searched by program title, by agency, or by subject focus. A paper copy of the catalog is available upon request. Given the limited nature of this listing, grantseekers in Wyoming should check other, more inclusive sources, particularly the latest edition of the *Wyoming Foundations Directory* (see entry 454).

Available from: Wyoming State Library, 2301 Capitol Avenue, Cheyenne, WY 82002-0060. *Telephone:* (307) 777-6333; *Fax:* (307) 777-6289
Web site: will.state.wy.us

454

Wyoming Foundations Directory: A Guide to Private Foundations

8th ed. Ed. by M. Ann Miller. Cheyenne, WY: Laramie County Community College, 2002. Unpaged. $8. Paper.
Description: The purpose of this pamphlet is "to provide a comprehensive up-to-date reference on the composition and funding policies of philanthropic foundations in the State of Wyoming." These foundations provide funding for research grants, scholarships, loans, and the special needs of citizens in Wyoming. Approximately 230 foundations are covered. Foundations that specifically

identify themselves as "charitable testamentary trusts," with governing documents that stipulate particular grantees as their sole beneficiaries, have been omitted. Information is provided on purpose, contact person, application process, deadline, assets, and grantmaking. Entries are divided into two sections (multipurpose foundations and educational scholarships/loans) and indexed by foundation name.

Available from: Laramie County Community College, Instructional Resources Center, 1400 East College Drive, Cheyenne, WY 82007-3299. *Telephone:* (307) 778-1206; *Fax:* (307) 778-1309; *E-mail:* ktaylor@lccc.cc.wy.us

Web site: www.lccc.cc.wy.us/library/foundation/foundation.asp

International

455

Annual Register of Grant Support: A Directory of Funding Sources

Medford, NJ: Information Today, 1969- . Annual. ISSN 0066-4049. ISBN 1-57387-145-1. $229 (2003 ed.). Hardcover.

Description: Both organizational and individual grants abroad and in the United States are covered in this annual directory. For more information about the publication, see entry 235 in the "Grants for Individuals—General—United States" section of this bibliography.

Available from: Information Today, Inc., 143 Old Marlton Pike, Medford, NJ 08055-8750. *Telephone:* (609) 654-6266; *Fax:* (609) 654-4309; *E-mail:* custserv@infotoday.com

Web site: www.infotoday.com

456

COS Funding Opportunities

http://www.cos.com

Description: COS Funding Opportunities is a web-based subscription database that is updated daily and contains descriptions of more than 23,000 funding opportunities from around the world that support research, collaborative activities, travel, training, curriculum development, conferences, postdoctoral positions, equipment acquisition, and operating or capital expenses. For more information about the database, see entry 237 in the "Grants for Individuals—General—United States" section of this bibliography.

Available from: Community of Science, Inc., 1629 Thames Street, Suite 200, Baltimore, MD 21231. *Telephone:* (410) 563-2378; *Fax:* (410) 563-5389; *E-mail:* evd@cos.com

Web site: www.cos.com

Grants for Organizations–General–International

457

Directory of International Corporate Giving in America and Abroad

10th ed. Ed. by Katherine E. Jankowski. Farmington Hills, MI: Taft, 1999. 826p. ISBN 1-56995-296-5. $215. Paper.

Description: Grantseekers with global aspirations can find more than $500 million in international corporate giving covered in the last edition of this directory. For more information about the publication, see entry 350 in the "Grants for Organizations—General—United States" section of this bibliography.

Available from: Taft Group, 27500 Drake Road, Farmington Hills, MI 48331-3535. *Toll-free:* (800) 877-TAFT; *Fax:* (800) 414-5043

Web site: www.galegroup.com/taft

458

Directory of Research Grants

Westport, CT: Oryx, 1975- . Annual. ISSN 0146-7336. ISBN 1-57356-570-9. $134.95 (2003 ed.). Paper.

Description: Although the emphasis is on U.S. and Canadian programs, some grants, scholarships, fellowships, and loans sponsored by other countries are also included in this directory. For more information about the publication, see entry 238 in the "Grants for Individuals—General—United States" section of this bibliography.

Available from: Oryx Press, 88 Post Road West, Westport, CT 06881. *Telephone:* (602) 265-2651; *Toll-free:* (800) 279-6799; *Fax:* (800) 279-4663; *E-mail:* info@oryxpress.com

Web site: www.oryxpress.com

459

GrantSelect

http://www.grantselect.com

Description: Updated daily and used to generate Oryx Press's print funding directories, GrantSelect identifies more than 10,000 grants for organizations and individuals sponsored by organizations and agencies in the United States and Canada (some of which can be used abroad). For more information about the database, see entry 247 in the "Grants for Individuals—General—United States" section of this bibliography.

Available from: Oryx Press, 88 Post Road West, Westport, CT 06881. *Telephone:* (602) 265-2651; *Toll-free:* (800) 279-6799; *Fax:* (800) 279-4663; *E-mail:* info@oryxpress.com

Web site: www.oryxpress.com

460

Guide to Funding for International and Foreign Programs

6th ed. New York: Foundation Center, 2002. 358p. ISBN 0-87954-995-5. $125. Paper.

Description: This directory identifies 1,300 American foundations, corporate direct givers, and public charities that have supported a wide range of projects with an international focus, both in this country and abroad. These include international relief, conferences, disaster assistance, human rights, civil liberties, community development, education, and many other related subjects. Organizational profiles specify foundation name, address and telephone number, contact person, asset amount, gifts received, amount and number of grants awarded, grantmaker's statement of purpose and activities, types of support generally awarded, geographic limitations, and application deadline. In addition, the directory provides 9,000 descriptions of recently-awarded grants. Entries are indexed by subject field, geographic area, and type of grant.

Available from: Foundation Center, 79 Fifth Avenue, New York, NY 10003-3076. *Telephone:* (212) 807-3690; *Toll-free:* (800) 424-9836; *Fax:* (212) 807-3691

Web site: fdncenter.org

461

International Foundation Directory

11th ed. London: Europa (dist. by Gale), 2002. 825p. ISSN 1366-8048. ISBN 1-85743-127-8. $350. Hardcover.

Description: This is not a listing of foundations around the world. Rather, this publication identifies foundations, trusts, and other similar nonprofit organizations that operate on an international basis, offer fellowships or similar awards to applicants from outside their own countries, or operate within their own national territory on a scale large enough to establish international importance. While these foundations are located in more than 100 countries, not all geographic locations are equally represented; the emphasis is on international foundations in North America and Europe. The 2,200 profiles are arranged alphabetically by country and then by foundation name within the country. The amount of information on each foundation varies, but the listings generally include: history of the organization, activities and interests, publications issued (if any), financial status, officers and trustees, and addresses, telephone numbers, fax numbers, and e-mail addresses. Additional access to the entries is provided through the name and broad subject categories indexes.

Available from: The Gale Group, P.O. Box 9187, Farmington Hills, MI 48333-9187. *Telephone:* (248) 699-GALE; *Toll-free:* (800) 877-GALE; *Fax:* (800) 414-5043; *E-mail:* galeord@gale.com

Web site: www.galegroup.com

462

World Guide to Foundations

2nd ed. Ed. by Michael Zils. Munchen: K.G. Saur Verlag (dist. by Gale), 2001. 2v. ISBN 3-598-11315-3. $313. Hardcover.

Description: Foundations around the world offer a broad spectrum of support for causes and issues, ranging from free speech to human rights and environmental protections. This directory describes more than 41,000 of these foundations, located in 115 countries, from Albania to Zimbabwe. Entries are divided into two volumes: Volume 1 covers 20,743 foundations in Europe and Volume 2 covers 20,500 grantmakers in Africa, Asia, America, and Oceania. Within these volumes, the foundation profiles are grouped by country and indexed by foundation name and subject focus. The following information is provided for each: foundation's name, abbreviation, and year of origin; address, phone and fax numbers, and e-mail addresses; key personnel, including chairpersons, managing directors, and donors; financial resources and annual income and expenses; type of foundation and its aims; and publications. Previously, the guide was published by Bowker; it is now published by K.G. Saur Verlag and distributed in the United States by Gale.

Available from: The Gale Group, P.O. Box 9187, Farmington Hills, MI 48333-9187. *Telephone:* (248) 699-GALE; *Toll-free:* (800) 877-GALE; *Fax:* (800) 414-5043; *E-mail:* galeord@gale.com

Web site: www.galegroup.com

SOCIAL SCIENCES
General

463

Grantmakers Directory: A Resource for Social Change Funders & Grantseekers

6th ed. Comp. by Nicole Trombley. Brooklyn: National Network of Grantmakers, 1994- . Irreg. ISBN 1-891460-02-1. $50 (2000-2001 ed.). Spiral bound.

Description: The National Network of Grantmakers (NNG) is an organization of progressive funders who work for systematic change, both in the United States and abroad, to create social, political, economic, and environmental justice. This is a membership directory and is intended to serve "as a reference tool and working document for NNG members, their grantmaking programs, and grantseekers." However, nonmembers as well as members can purchase the directory. The sixth edition features 200 grantmaking institutions and related organizations. Profiles describing each of the member organizations are

How to Find Out About Financial Aid and Funding

arranged alphabetically and include information on current mission, contact address and telephone numbers, primary areas of interest, priority grants and grant limitations, application process, and financial data. Entries are indexed by organization name, grantmaking interests, target population, and geographic area. Previously, this publication was issued as the *National Network of Grantmakers Membership Directory*.

Available from: National Network of Grantmakers, 150 Court Street, Second Floor, Brooklyn, NY 11201. *Telephone:* (718) 923-1400, ext. 242; *Fax:* (718) 923-2869; *E-mail:* nng@nng.org

Web site: www.nng.org

464

GrantsInfo.com: Social and Natural Sciences Report

http://www.arisnet.com/socnatu.html

Description: This inexpensive online searchable database provides information on hundreds of grant and fellowship opportunities for organizations and individuals in the social and natural sciences. For more information about the site, see entry 271 in the "Grants for Individuals—Social Sciences—General" section of this bibliography.

Available from: Academic Research Information System, Inc., 2940 16th Street, Suite 314, San Francisco, CA 94103. *Telephone:* (415) 558-8133; *Fax:* (415) 558-8135; *E-mail:* arisnet@dnai.com

Web site: www.arisnet.com

465

Progressive Publications Foundation Database

http://www.progressivepubs.com/foundations

Description: This free online database, offered by ProgressivePubs.com (formerly Progressive Resources Publications), provides information on hundreds of progressive grantmaking foundations. The entries can be searched by topic or browsed by name, but you have to register to search the database. The following information is provided for each of the progressive foundations included in the database: contact, program officers, giving priorities, average grant size, and deadlines. Users are encouraged to post comments (positive or critical) about specific foundations.

Available from: ProgressivePubs.com, Inc., P.O. Box 11335, Washington, DC 20008. *E-mail:* webmaster@progressivepubs.com

Web site: www.progressivepubs.com

Grants for Organizations–Social Sciences–Business & Economics

Business and Economics

466 🕸 ¢

CBD*Net*

http://cbdnet.access.gpo.gov
Description: Until January, 2002, CBD*Net* provided the electronic version of *Commerce Business Daily,* which listed all proposed procurements of $25,000 or more by civil and military agencies, including potential research interest; all contract awards of $25,000 or more for the benefit of potential subcontractors; non-U.S. government procurement; surplus U.S. government property sales; non-U.S. government standards that may affect U.S. exports; special notices; and occasional announcements of business-related events, such as procurement conferences and symposia. On January 4, 2002, the Department of Commerce ceased publishing *Commerce Business Daily (CBD)* and began posting all appropriate listings on the Federal Business Opportunities (FedBizOpps) web site (see entry 467). The postings printed in *CBD* prior to January 4, 2002 are being maintained in an archival database on the CBD*Net* website. For listings since then, you will need to check the Federal Business Opportunities site.
Available from: U.S. Department of Commerce, 14th Street between Constitution Avenue and E Street, N.W., Washington, DC 20230. *Telephone:* (202) 512-1800
Web site: www.doc.gov

467 🕸 ¢

Federal Business Opportunities

http://www.fedbizopps.gov
Description: Prior to 2002, all government procurement invitations, contract awards, subcontracting leads, notices of sales of surplus property, foreign business opportunities, and research and development sources were printed in *Commerce Business Daily* and reproduced on its online version, CBD*Net.* Since the beginning of 2002, however, in accordance with recent changes in the Federal Acquisition Regulation (FAR), these two resources have been replaced by a single point of universal electronic public access on the Internet for government-wide Federal procurement opportunities: Federal Business Opportunities (also referred to as FedBizOpps). The scope and purpose of the site remains unchanged; posted here are all proposed procurements of $25,000 or more by civil and military agencies, including potential research interest; all contract awards of $25,000 or more for benefit of potential subcontractors; non-U.S. government procurement; surplus U.S. government property sales; non-U.S. government standards that may affect U.S. exports; special notices; and occasional announcements of business-related events, such as procurement conferences and

symposia. Entries briefly describe the service or item involved, the address and contact for the particular action, and the deadline established. Archives of previous *Commerce Daily Business* issues are being maintained on the former CBD*Net* web site: http://cbnet.access.gpo.gov; for more information on these archival listings, see entry 466. Although Federal Business Opportunities is only available online, some commercial vendors are selling subscriptions to printed versions of the listings. For a current list of these vendors, go to: http://oamweb.osec.doc.gov/cbdnet.htm.

Available from: U.S. Department of Commerce, 14th Street between Constitution Avenue and E Street, N.W., Washington, DC 20230. *Telephone:* (202) 512-1387

Web site: www.doc.gov

468

Funding Sources for Community and Economic Development: A Guide to Current Sources for Local Programs and Projects

Westport, CT: Oryx, 2003. 752p. ISSN 1080-6318. ISBN 1-57356-568-7. $64.95. Paper.

Description: For the purposes of this compilation, "community development" is defined as projects that enrich or improve the lives of community residents. The listing is aimed at citizen groups, government agencies, nonprofit groups, and community foundations that are interested in learning about funding available at the local level for special school programs, health care, business development, civic affairs, and arts and humanities projects. Identified in the 2003 edition are 3,000 funding sources. Entries indicate grant purpose, restrictions, requirements, funding amount, application/renewal date, and sponsor information. In addition to sponsoring organization/program title, geographic, and program type indexes, there is an extensive subject index. Like other Oryx funding directories, the information provided here was taken from the publisher's GrantSelect database (see entry 247).

Available from: Oryx Press, 88 Post Road West, Westport, CT 06881. *Telephone:* (602) 265-2651; *Toll-free:* (800) 279-6799; *Fax:* (800) 279-4663; *E-mail:* info@oryxpress.com

Web site: www.oryxpress.com

469

The PRI Directory: Charitable Loans and Other Program-Related Investments by Foundations

New York: Foundation Center, 2001. 155p. ISBN 0-87954-915-7. $75. Paper.

Description: Program-Related Investing (PRI) is an alternative financing approach developed by certain foundations for supplying capital to the nonprofit sector. PRIs have been used to support community revitalization, low-income housing, microenterprise development, historic preservation, human services, and other related activities. This directory, issued for the first time in 2001 by the Foundation Center, lists leading PRI providers; entries indicate the funder's name and state; recipient's name, city, and state; and a description of the project funded. These entries are indexed by foundation/recipient location, subject/type of support, and recipient name, as well as officers, donors, and trustees.

Available from: Foundation Center, 79 Fifth Avenue, New York, NY 10003-3076. *Telephone:* (212) 807-3690; *Toll-free:* (800) 424-9836; *Fax:* (212) 807-3691

Web site: fdncenter.org

Education

470

Chronicle of Higher Education

Washington, DC: Chronicle of Higher Education, 1966- . Weekly. ISSN 0009-5982. $82.50. Paper.

Description: Included in each weekly print issue (and on the web site) are foundation and grant news items and deadline dates. The programs covered here represent all fields of study and are of interest principally to academic teaching faculty, researchers, and administrators. For more information about the *Chronicle,* see entry 277 in the "Grants for Individuals—Social Sciences—Education" section of this bibliography.

Available from: Chronicle of Higher Education, Attn: Circulation Department, 1255 23rd Street, N.W., Suite 700, Washington, DC 20037. *Telephone:* (202) 466-1000; *Toll-free:* (800) 728-2803; *E-mail:* circulation@chronicle.com

Web site: chronicle.com

471

Distance Learning Funding $ourcebook: A Guide to Foundation, Corporate and Government Support for Telecommunications and the New Media

4th ed. By Arlene Krebs. Dubuque, IA: Kendall/Hunt, 1999. 448p. ISBN 0-7872-4980-7. $48. Paper.

Description: The purpose of this guide is to provide the "latest research on funding sources for telecommunications and interactive technology" for distance education. The funding opportunities identified are open to public and private schools, institutions of higher education, community organizations, health care and social service agencies, arts and cultural organizations, museums, libraries, and other organizations seeking funding for telecommunications and technology. Indepth analyses are provided for each funding agency (these include corporate and federal); the following information is supplied: recently-awarded telecommunications and technology grants, contact names, address, telephone and fax numbers, application guidelines, and e-mail and Internet resources. In addition, key trends in philanthropic giving among foundations, corporations, federal agencies, the telephone companies, and the cable systems operators are described in the introductions to each of the chapter.

Available from: Kendall/Hunt Publishing Company, 4050 Westmark Drive, P.O. Box 1840, Dubuque, IA 52004-1840. *Telephone:* (563) 589-1000; *Toll-free:* (800) 228-0810; *Fax:* (800) 772-9165

Web site: www.kendallhunt.com

472

FedMoney.org

http://www.fedmoney.org
Description: This is a little confusing. While FedMoney.org describes itself as "the most comprehensive free full-text online resource covering all U.S. federal government student financial aid programs," the site is not really aimed at students. Rather, it consists of detailed descriptions of 130 different government programs that grant money to academic institutions and other appropriate agencies involved in education which, in turn, use the funds to offer loans, scholarships, fellowships, and traineeships to students, faculty, professionals, and others. The listings can be browsed but are not searchable. The site is offered as a free service to the public by IDI Magic Tech Corp., creators of *Federal Money Retriever* (an online or CD-ROM guide to U.S. government grants and loans that costs between $39.95 and $179).

Available from: IDI Magic Tech Corp., P.O. Box 97655, Las Vegas, NV 89193. *Toll-free:* (800) 804-5270; *Fax:* (800) 390-1315

Web site: www.fedmoney.org

473

Funding Sources for K-12 Education

Westport, CT: Oryx, 2002. 976p. ISBN 1-57356-566-0. $49.95. Paper.
Description: Another Oryx directory that's drawn from the publisher's GrantSelect database (see entry 247), but priced considerably less, this annual describes 1,600 funding opportunities for K-12 schools and related educational organizations (museums, libraries, adult basic education programs) in the United States and Canada; funding for students interested in working on an education-

related degree is also, but randomly and incompletely, covered. Entries indicate purpose, restrictions, requirements, funding amount, application process, deadline, and sponsor. A number of indexes provide access to this information: geographic location, sponsor/program title, program type, and subject. In addition, the volume offers web site addresses for sponsoring organizations and a 17-page guide to proposal planning and writing. Previously, this title was issued as *Funding Sources for K-12 Schools and Adult Basic Education.*

Available from: Oryx Press, 88 Post Road West, Westport, CT 06881. *Telephone:* (602) 265-2651; *Toll-free:* (800) 279-6799; *Fax:* (800) 279-4663; *E-mail:* info@oryxpress.com

Web site: www.oryxpress.com

474

The Grant Advisor

Charlottesville, VA: The Grant Advisor, 1983- . Monthly, except July. ISSN 0740-5383. $198/yr., paper; $398, online.

Description: Since 1983, *The Grant Advisor* has been issued as a newsletter that contains information on fellowship and grant opportunities for U.S. institutions of higher education and their faculty offered by federal agencies (except the National Institutes of Health), private foundations, corporations, and professional organizations. Published monthly except in July, each issue contains 20 to 25 program reviews that specify eligibility requirements, special criteria, funding amounts, and contact (including phone and fax numbers, e-mail and web addresses). The remainder of the newsletter consists of a "Deadline Memo:" more than 300 listings of grant and fellowship programs with deadlines closing during the coming four months; these listings are organized into eight academic divisions: fine arts, humanities, sciences, social sciences, education, international, health, and unrestricted/other. A subscription to the newsletter, alone, is $198. However, the newsletter is also available online as part of a *Grant Advisor Plus* subscription ($398/yr.); this subscription provides an online version of the newsletter, along with deadline memo hyperlinks (to all organizations listed in the "Deadline Memo" section that have web sites), a searchable database, links to 200 funding sources (federal/related sources and foundation/independent sources), and a series of articles providing useful advice and tips for the grantsperson in higher education.

Available from: The Grant Advisor, 1946 Lonicera Way, Charlottesville, VA 22911. *Telephone:* (434) 975-9098; *Fax:* (815) 361-2971; *E-mail:* info@grantadvisor.com

Web site: www.grantadvisor.com

475

Grants and Funding for Higher Education

Boston: Quinlan Publishing. Monthly. $129. Paper.

Description: Like the other current awareness services published by Quinlan, this monthly identifies available grants, foundations, programs, and business partnerships. In this case, the focus is on grants and funding of interest to institutions of higher learning. Also included is a list of important deadlines from the *Federal Register* (see entry 357), online resource listings, and a regional grants update. Subscribers also receive the GRANTSHOTLINE weekly e-mail updates.

Available from: Quinlan Publishing Group, 23 Drydock Avenue, Boston, MA 02210-2387. *Telephone:* (617) 542-0048; *Toll-free:* (800) 229-2084; *Fax:* (617) 345-9646; *E-mail:* info@quinlan.com

Web site: www.grantshotline.com

476

Grants for K-12 Schools

Ed. by Mollie Mudd. Frederick, MD: Aspen Publishers, 2001. 371p. ISBN 0-8342-1893-3. $145. Hardcover.

Description: More and more schools are getting into the grantseeking game. To go after those grants, schools have to develop efficient, organized systems for seeking out funding sources, writing grant proposals, and working with funding officers. This guide is designed to help in the process; it replaces the fourth edition of Aspen's *Grants for Schools*. The first part of the source deals with preparing a proposal; the rest of the book describes 75 federal and 500 private sources of grants for schools. The following information is provided in each entry: address, telephone number, range and types of grants available, geographic preferences, eligibility requirements, application guidelines, deadlines, and examples of recent grants awarded. A useful bibliography plus some other instructive materials (e.g., Internet sites for grantseekers and sample forms) complete the work. While this is not the most comprehensive or detailed of the education grant directories, it is certainly one of the more attractive. Another, more focused education-related title issued by Aspen Publishers (formerly Capitol Publications) may also be of interest to fundseekers in this area: *Grants for Special Education and Rehabilitation* (entry 478).

Available from: Aspen Publishers, Inc., 7201 McKinney Circle, Frederick, MD 21704. *Toll-free:* (800) 638-8437; *Fax:* (301) 417-7550

Web site: www.aspenpublishers.com

Grants for Organizations–Social Sciences–Education

477

Grants for School Districts

Boston: Quinlan Publishing. Bi-weekly or monthly. $149, biweekly; $109, monthly. Paper.

Description: Issued as either a bi-weekly or monthly subscription, this current awareness service provides information on available grants, foundations, school programs, and business partnerships of interest to school districts. Also included is a list of important deadlines from the *Federal Register* (see entry 357), online resource listings, and a regional grants update. Quinlan also publishes a number of other newsletters dealing with grants in the education field, including *Public Schools Grants and Funding Opportunities* ($129, bi-weekly; $99, monthly); *Funding Private Schools* ($129, monthly); *Grants for K-12 Hotline* ($149, bi-weekly), and *School Administrator's Title I Hotline* ($139, monthly). Subscribers to any of these publications also receive the GRANTSHOTLINE weekly e-mail updates.

Available from: Quinlan Publishing Group, 23 Drydock Avenue, Boston, MA 02210-2387. *Telephone:* (617) 542-0048; *Toll-free:* (800) 229-2084; *Fax:* (617) 345-9646; *E-mail:* info@quinlan.com

Web site: www.grantshotline.com

478

Grants for Special Education and Rehabilitation: How to Find and Win Funds for Research, Training and Services

4th ed. Frederick, MD: Aspen Publishers, 2000. 215p. ISBN 0-8342-1785-6. $119. Paper.

Description: Described here are 350 federal, private, and corporate funding opportunities in the field of special education. Each of these entries provides the following information: contact, geographic restrictions, funding interests, examples of recent grants awarded, guidelines, deadlines, and names of directors, officers, and trustees (when available). Also included in the fourth edition are a number of items from other publications produced by Aspen Publishers (formerly Capitol Publications), including an annotated bibliography, sample forms, and a checklist for deciding to apply. For more comprehensive coverage of relevant federal programs, see the *Catalog of Federal Domestic Assistance* (entry 339 in the "Grants for Organizations—General—United States" section); for private programs, see the *Directory of Research Grants* (entry 238).

Available from: Aspen Publishers, Inc., 7201 McKinney Circle, Frederick, MD 21704. *Toll-free:* (800) 638-8437; *Fax:* (301) 695-7931

Web site: www.aspenpublishers.com

479

A Guide to Federal Funding for Education

Arlington, VA: Education Funding Research Council, 1981- . Annual. ISSN 0275-8393. $297 (2002 ed.), 2-volume looseleaf or online subscription.

Description: This source describes more than $65 million in federal funding available for elementary, secondary, and higher education. Introductory narratives for each of the 23 topic areas (e.g., desegregation, bilingual education, vocational education) provide information on the evolution of grant programs, new developments, and potential funding opportunities for the year covered. Within each of the topic sections, entries are arranged by program title and supply information on purpose, eligibility requirements, type of assistance offered, application procedures, legislative authority, and information contacts. A unique feature (since the 21st edition) is the *Guide's* five star "Funding Opportunity Index," a feature not available in other similar directories; this index shows what an eligible applicant's chances are of winning a grant (ratings are based on the program's grantmaking history, current level of funding, award policies, and discussions with government officials). Indexing is by program title and subject. An annual subscription to the *Guide* includes the periodic *New Program Updates,* plus the twice-monthly *Federal Grant Deadline Calendar.* Furthermore, subscribers have unlimited access to the Grant Deadline Monitor database on the Internet, where the most recently announced federal grants are listed. The information in the guide is also available on a subscription basis on the publisher's web site ($297 for the online version only; $396 for the print and online bundle). Although focusing on education, the guide does not comprehensively cover the field. Just over 800 federal programs are described each year in the *Guide,* while well over half of the programs listed in the *Catalog of Federal Domestic Assistance* (see entry 339) can be labeled educational. And the *Catalog* costs considerably less (although the *Guide to Federal Funding for Education* is much easier to read). *Guide to Federal Funding for Education* is published by Education Funding Research Council, an affiliate of Thompson Publishing Group since 1997, which also issues the weekly newsletter *Education Funding News* ($298/yr.).

Available from: Education Funding Research Council, 1725 K Street, N.W., 7th Floor, Washington, DC 20006. *Telephone:* (202) 872-4000; *Toll-free:* (800) 876-0226; *Fax:* (800) 926-2012

Web site: www.grantsandfunding.com

480

National Guide to Funding for Elementary and Secondary Education

5th ed. Washington, DC: Foundation Center, 1999. 725p. ISBN 0-87954-880-0. $140. Paper.

Grants for Organizations–Social Sciences–Education

Description: Another title in the Foundation Center's "National Guide to Funding" series, this one identifies more than 3,300 philanthropic foundations and corporations that are either interested in supporting K-12 education or have recently given at least $10,000 to schools. Funding interests include nationwide research initiatives, bilingual programs, cooperative/community education, drop-out prevention, educational testing, gifted programs, remedial reading, math initiatives, and vocational/trade schools. Like the other volumes in this series, entries are arranged geographically by state and then alphabetically by foundation name. Entries provide full information: address, financial data, giving priorities, application procedures, contact names, and key officials. Many entries also identify recently-awarded grants (8,800 listed in the latest edition). The information in this volume is indexed by subject, geographic areas preferred, types of grants generally awarded, foundation name, and names of key personnel. Completing the volume are a user's guide, glossary, bibliography, list of other Foundation Center publications and services, and list of Foundation Center cooperating reference collections. Last published in 1999, the information provided here is now becoming dated.

Available from: Foundation Center, 79 Fifth Avenue, New York, NY 10003-3076. *Telephone:* (212) 807-3690; *Toll-free:* (800) 424-9836; *Fax:* (212) 807-3691

Web site: fdncenter.org

481

National Guide to Funding in Higher Education

6th ed. Washington, DC: Foundation Center, 2000. 1,275p. ISBN 0-87954-905-X. $175. Paper.

Description: This directory identifies more than 7,200 foundations, corporate direct giving programs, and public charities that have an interest in funding higher education projects and institutions. The grantmakers listed here award millions of dollars each year to colleges, universities, professional and technical schools, scholarship funds, and a range of other related programs and projects. Entries are arranged alphabetically by state and indexed by key officials, geographic preference, type of support, subject, and foundation name. Each foundation profile provides information on address and contact, source of funding, financial status (including market value and total expenditures for the year), funding interests and purposes, limitations on giving, names of key officials, and application process. Many entries also include a list of recently-awarded grants (18,000 in the sixth edition).

Available from: Foundation Center, 79 Fifth Avenue, New York, NY 10003-3076. *Telephone:* (212) 807-3690; *Toll-free:* (800) 424-9836; *Fax:* (212) 807-3691

Web site: fdncenter.org

482

Nyquist Report on Funding for Community, Junior, and Technical Colleges

New Paltz, NY: Nyquist Associates. Monthly. $159/yr. Paper.

Description: A one-year subscription includes 12 monthly funding memoranda on current "General Funding Opportunities and Resources for Two-Year Colleges," 12 monthly funding memoranda on current "Federal Funding Opportunities and Resources for Two-Year Colleges," and 18 special reports produced during the subscription period on such topics as "Funding for Nursing Education," "Funding for Faculty Renewal and Development," and "Federal Sources for Community-Oriented Programs." Of the three components, the last (special reports) will be the most helpful to the grantseeker. Described in each of the reports (which range from 4 to 21 pages) are organizations making grants to two-year colleges in that area.

Available from: Nyquist Associates, 140 Huguenot Street, New Paltz, NY 12561-1018. *Telephone:* (845) 255-3003; *Toll-free:* (800) 550-0110; *Fax:* (845) 256-9609; *E-mail:* nyq@hvi.net

Web site: www.nyquistassoc.com

483

School Technology Funding Directory

3rd ed. Bethesda: eSchool News, 2002. 298p. ISBN 0-9703007-3-5. $169. Paper.

Description: Covered here are more than 500 grants and other sources of school technology funding from federal, state, and local government agencies, corporate foundations, private endowments, charitable organizations, and community foundations. For more information about the directory, see entry 519 in the "Grants for Organizations—Sciences—Technology" section of this bibliography.

Available from: eSchool News, 7920 Norfolk Avenue, Suite 900, Bethesda, MD 20814. *Toll-free:* (800) 394-0115; *Fax:* (301) 913-0119; *E-mail:* cpugh@eschoolnews.com

Web site: www.eschoolnews.com

Librarianship

484

The Big Book of Library Grant Money: Profiles of Private and Corporate Foundations and Direct Corporate Givers Receptive to Library Grant Proposals

Prep. by the Taft Group. Chicago: American Library Association, 2002. 1,486p. ISSN 1086-0568. ISBN 0-8389-3520-6. $225, members; $250, nonmembers. Paper.

Description: With diminished budgets and increasing demand for innovative service, librarians must now be more creative than ever in locating available funding. The latest edition of this directory (2002-2003), developed by the Taft Group by tapping their database of top private-sector givers, identifies more than $11 billion in funding available to libraries. The organizations listed here have either funded library programs in the past or expressed a willingness to consider proposals from libraries in the future. Funders of "information" projects were not included unless they indicated specific library interest. A total of 2,200 funders are covered in this edition—more than four times the number of library-interested funders identified in any other source. Organization profiles, which are arranged by state, include the following information: contact, financial summary, contribution summary, corporate and program officers, application procedures, "other things to know," grant analyses, and summaries of up to five recent grants. Biographical data on more than 34,000 foundation officers, directors, trustees, and corporate officers is also included. Information for these profiles is taken from foundation annual reports, recent tax forms, questionnaire responses, press releases, telephone interviews, standard business publications, and publication surveys. An introductory chapter providing practical tips from the American Library Association's development office and an index of recent library projects funded by the givers complete the work. As valuable as the *Big Book* is, the price may put this out of the reach of the very libraries that need grants the most.

Available from: American Library Association, Attn: ALA Editions, Order Fulfillment, 155 North Wacker Drive, Chicago, IL 60606-1719. *Telephone:* (312) 836-9958; *Toll-free:* (800) 545-2433, press 7; *Fax:* (312) 440-9374
Web site: www.alastore.ala.org

485

The Bowker Annual Library and Book Trade Almanac

Medford, NJ: Information Today, 1955- . Annual. ISSN 0068-0540. ISBN 1-57387-165-6. $199 (2003 ed.). Hardcover.

How to Find Out About Financial Aid and Funding

Description: Generally, each edition contains a list of library fellowships and up-to-date information on library legislation, funding, and grantmaking agencies. For more information about the publication, see entry 559 in the "Awards and Prizes—Social Sciences—Librarianship" section of this bibliography.
Available from: Information Today, Inc., 143 Old Marlton Pike, Medford, NJ 08055-8750. *Telephone:* (609) 654-6266; *Fax:* (609) 654-4309; *E-mail:* custserv@infotoday.com
Web site: www.infotoday.com

486

Grants for Libraries Hotline

Boston: Quinlan Publishing. Monthly. $129. Paper.
Description: Like the other current awareness services published by Quinlan, this monthly identifies available grants, foundations, alternative funding programs, and business partnerships. In this case, the focus is on grants and funding of interest to libraries. Also included is a "Consultants Corner" column, a technology column, and lists of volunteer resources. Quinlan also publishes a number of other grants newsletters in related fields, including *Grants for Cities and Towns* ($149) and *Public and Safety Funding Hotline* ($149), which was formerly issued as *Funding Law Enforcement Hotline.* Subscribers to any of these publications also receive the GRANTSHOTLINE weekly e-mail updates.
Available from: Quinlan Publishing Group, 23 Drydock Avenue, Boston, MA 02210-2387. *Telephone:* (617) 542-0048; *Toll-free:* (800) 229-2084; *Fax:* (617) 345-9646; *E-mail:* info@quinlan.com
Web site: www.grantshotline.com

487

National Guide to Funding for Libraries and Information Services

6th ed. Washington, DC: Foundation Center, 2001. 209p. ISBN 0-87954-953-X. $115. Paper.
Description: Another in the Foundation Center's "National Guide to Funding" series, this title focuses on grantmaking foundations and direct corporate giving programs (a total of about 900) that have shown "substantial interest" in awarding grants (totaling $100 million each year) to libraries and information services, including nonprofit information clearinghouses, databases, and public service centers. Entries are arranged alphabetically by state and, within state, by foundation names. Over 1,600 recently-awarded grants are also described. In addition, there are six indexes, a glossary of terms used by grantmakers and grantseekers, and a bibliography of publications on funding for libraries and information services. A new edition is scheduled for release in mid-2003. For similar but more comprehensive coverage (nearly four times as many entries), see the American Library Association's *Big Book of Library Grant Money*

Grants for Organizations–Social Sciences–Sociology & Social Services

(entry 484). Grantseekers in this area will also be interested in one of the Foundation Center's *Grant Guides* (see entry 369): *Grants for Libraries and Information Services,* which complements the *National Guide* by describing foundation grants ($10,000 or more), organizing them by state, and indexing them by subject and geographic coverage (2002/2003, $75).

Available from: Foundation Center, 79 Fifth Avenue, New York, NY 10003-3076. *Telephone:* (212) 807-3690; *Toll-free:* (800) 424-9836; *Fax:* (212) 807-3691

Web site: fdncenter.org

Sociology and Social Services

488

Fund Raiser's Guide to Human Service Funding

Ed. by Mollie B. Mudd. Farmington Hills, MI: Taft Group, 1999. 1,450p. ISBN 1-56995-338-4. $145. Paper.

Description: Use this guide to identify which private and corporate foundations were funding child welfare, homeless shelters, spouse abuse shelters, and volunteer service programs in 1999. Described here are nearly 1,900 grantmakers donating more than $4.5 billion annually in those areas. Many of the corporate direct givers are not covered in any other source. Entries offer information on contacts, giving policies (including what activities and organizations are not supported), financial history, and up to 50 recent grants. Both monetary and nonmonetary support is listed. The indexes make it possible to locate grantmakers by headquarters state, denominational preference, geographical preference, grant type, recipient type, officers and directors, and grant recipients by location. The edition issued in 1999 is the latest available and no future editions are planned.

Available from: Taft Group, 27500 Drake Road, Farmington Hills, MI 48331-3535. *Toll-free:* (800) 877-TAFT; *Fax:* (800) 414-5043

Web site: www.galegroup.com/taft

489

Funding Sources for Children and Youth Programs

2nd ed. Westport, CT: Oryx, 2003. 342p. ISBN 1-57356-588-1. $37.95. Paper.

Description: Another Oryx directory that's drawn from the publisher's GrantSelect database (see entry 247), but priced considerably less than the others, the second edition of this directory identifies more than 1,500 grant resources for children and youth programs. Entries indicate purpose, restrictions,

How to Find Out About Financial Aid and Funding

requirements, funding amount, application process, deadline, and sponsor. A number of indexes provide access to this information: geographic location, sponsor/program title, program type, and subject. Although not as current, the listing in the Foundation Center's *National Guide to Funding for Children, Youth and Families* is four times more comprehensive (see entry 491).

Available from: Oryx Press, 88 Post Road West, Westport, CT 06881. *Telephone:* (602) 265-2651; *Toll-free:* (800) 279-6799; *Fax:* (800) 279-4663; *E-mail:* info@oryxpress.com
Web site: www.oryxpress.com

490

Grants for At-Risk Youth

Frederick, MD: Aspen Publishers, 2003. 400p. ISBN 0-8342-2148-9. $155. Paper.

Description: Programs serving at-risk youth (students who are in danger of dropping out of school) are chronically underfunded and overpopulated. To help agencies interested in winning funds for this type of project, this directory identifies more than 200 private, corporate, and federal sources that make grants in that area. Each funder profile includes contact information, the scope and areas of grants available, total giving amounts, eligibility requirements, application procedure, deadlines, and examples of recent grants. Appendices list Internet sites for grantseekers and grantseeking resources. Indexes provide access by name to private and federal funders and by headquarters to private funders. Additionally, the application forms of some of the funders listed in the directory are available on a disk included with this volume. Previously published by Capitol Publications, which is now Aspen Publishers, the directory consists of data taken directly from GrantScape, the publisher's electronic funding database (see entry 371).

Available from: Aspen Publishers, Inc., 7201 McKinney Circle, Frederick, MD 21704. *Toll-free:* (800) 638-8437; *Fax:* (301) 417-7550
Web site: www.aspenpublishers.com

491

National Guide to Funding for Children, Youth and Families

5th ed. New York: Foundation Center, 1999. 1,664p. ISBN 0-87954-877-0. $150. Paper.

Description: Covered here are 5,100 foundations and corporate giving programs interested in funding in the areas of child development and welfare, family planning, family services, delinquency prevention, youth centers, and other related programs. Nearly $1 billion in grants is awarded in these areas each year. Foundation profiles are arranged by state and then alphabetically by name. Entries specify address and contact name, financial data, giving priorities and

Grants for Organizations–Humanities–General

limitations, application guidelines, names of key officials, and recently-awarded grants (a total of 19,000 in this edition). This information is indexed by names of donors, officers, and trustees; subject fields; geographic areas; and preferred types of support. Last published in 1999, the information provided here is now dated.

Available from: Foundation Center, 79 Fifth Avenue, New York, NY 10003-3076. *Telephone:* (212) 807-3690; *Toll-free:* (800) 424-9836; *Fax:* (212) 807-3691

Web site: fdncenter.org

492

National Guide to Funding in Aging

6th ed. New York: Foundation Center, 2000. 294p. ISBN 0-87954-904-1. $115. Paper.

Description: This directory is aimed at agencies serving the 25 million Americans who are over the age of 65. Information is provided here on 1,200 foundations, corporations, and charitable organizations that annually award millions of grant dollars to senior citizen programs, hospitals, community centers, nursing homes, continuing education facilities, and organizations concerned with legal rights, housing, employment, health, veterans affairs, cultural affairs, nutrition, and other issues related to an aging population. Each profile supplies contact information, financial data, giving priorities, application procedures, and key officials. More than 500 foundation entries also include descriptions of several recent grants (the best indication of grantmaker funding interests).

Available from: Foundation Center, 79 Fifth Avenue, New York, NY 10003-3076. *Telephone:* (212) 807-3690; *Toll-free:* (800) 424-9836; *Fax:* (212) 807-3691

Web site: fdncenter.org

HUMANITIES
General

493

Arts & Culture Funding Report

Arlington, VA: Capitol City Publishers, 1989- . Monthly. ISSN 1047-3297. $198/yr. Paper.

Description: Capitol City Publishers issues this and several other funding reports, including: *Criminal Justice Funding Report* (ISSN 1092-5163, 26 issues, $278/yr.), *The Welfare Reporter* (ISSN 1097-8356, 12 issues, $279/yr.), and *Justice Technology Monitor* (ISSN 1521-9569, 12 issues, $278/yr.). Each of these reports contains a "Grant Alert" section, which highlights upcoming grant application deadlines for federal and private sector aid (including foundations and corporations).

Available from: Capitol City Publishers, 1408 North Fillmore Street, Suite 3, Arlington, VA 22201-3819. *Telephone:* (703) 525-3080; *Toll-free:* (888) 854-3080; *Fax:* (703) 525-3044; *E-mail:* inquiry@capitolcitypublishers.com

Web site: capitolcitypublishers.com

494

Directory of Grants in the Humanities

Westport, CT: Oryx, 1986- . Annual. ISSN 0877-0551. ISBN 1-57356-567-9. $84.95 (2002-2003 ed.). Paper.

Description: This annual directory identifies grants (for organizations and individuals), awards, and fellowships in literature, languages, history, anthropology, philosophy, ethics, religion, the fine arts, and performing arts (including painting, dance, photography, sculpture, music, drama, crafts, folklore, and mime). For more information about the publication, see entry 280 in the "Grants for Individuals—Humanities—General" section of this bibliography.

Available from: Oryx Press, 88 Post Road West, Westport, CT 06881. *Telephone:* (602) 265-2651; *Toll-free:* (800) 279-6799; *Fax:* (800) 279-4663; *E-mail:* info@oryxpress.com

Web site: www.oryxpress.com

495

GrantsInfo.com: Creative Arts and Humanities

http://www.arisnet.com/arts.html

Description: This inexpensive online searchable database provides information on regional, national, and international grants, fellowships, and awards for individuals and organizations in the humanities, performing arts, and visual arts. For more information about the site, see entry 282 in the "Grants for Individuals—Humanities—General" section of this bibliography.

Available from: Academic Research Information System, Inc., 2940 16th Street, Suite 314, San Francisco, CA 94103. *Telephone:* (415) 558-8133; *Fax:* (415) 558-8135; *E-mail:* arisnet@dnai.com

Web site: www.arisnet.com

Grants for Organizations–Humanities–Applied Arts

496

National Guide to Funding in Arts and Culture

7th ed. Washington, DC: Foundation Center, 2002. 1,138p. ISBN 0-87954-998-X. $155. Paper.

Description: This edition provides information on more than 7,500 foundations and corporate giving programs with a history of making grants in the areas of arts and culture. Foundation profiles, which are arranged by state location of the grantmaker, provide descriptive information on more than $800 million in support available for projects in the visual arts, music, theater, dance, literature and writing, film and video, public radio and television, historic preservation, museums, botanical gardens, festivals and conferences, and arts education. Each entry supplies data on the grantmaker's address and contact person, financial status, program policies, application information, and officers and directors. Also included are 16,500 brief descriptions of recently-awarded grants and six indexes (including subject interests, geographic interests, and type of grant).

Available from: Foundation Center, 79 Fifth Avenue, New York, NY 10003-3076. *Telephone:* (212) 807-3690; *Toll-free:* (800) 424-9836; *Fax:* (212) 807-3691

Web site: fdncenter.org

Applied Arts

497

Directory of Grants for Crafts: How to Write a Winning Proposal

By James Dillehay. Torreon, NM: Warm Snow, 2000. 216p. ISBN 0-9629923-4-8. $19.95. Paper.

Description: This publication identifies, in 140 pages of appendices, hundreds of foundations, government agencies, public arts programs, residency programs, arts agencies, and other related sources that offer grants to craft organizations. For more information about the publication, see entry 285 in the "Grants for Individuals—Humanities—Visual Arts" section of this bibliography.

Available from: Warm Snow Publishers, P.O. Box 75, Torreon, NM 87061. *Telephone:* (505) 384-1195; *Toll-free:* (800) 235-6570; *E-mail:* info@craftmarketer.com

Web site: www.craftmarketer.com/warm_snow_publishers.htm

Religion

498

Catholic Funding Guide: A Directory of Resources for Catholic Activity

2nd ed. Ed. by Kerry A. Robinson. Washington, DC: FADICA, 2001. 504p. ISBN 1-891646-02-8. $60. Paper.

Description: While FADICA is an association of private grantmaking foundations, its main function is to offer continuing education on trends impacting Catholic philanthropy. It does not provide grant assistance or direction for individual grantseekers. However, FADICA does publish a book for those seeking to locate sources of funding for Catholic projects: *Catholic Funding Guide*. Use this directory to find information on funding offered by more than 800 private and corporate foundations, church-based funding agencies, fraternal organizations, and religious orders (300 more entries than in the previous edition). Each of these grantmakers has a history of providing funding to the Catholic sector, including Catholic schools, colleges, social service agencies, missionary programs, hospitals, parish projects and retirement facilities.

Available from: FADICA, Inc., 1350 Connecticut Avenue, N.W., Suite 303, Washington, DC 20036-1701. *Telephone:* (202) 223-3550; *Fax:* (202) 296-9295; *E-mail:* info@fadica.org

Web site: www.fadica.org

499

Faculty Grants Directory

http://www.ats.edu/faculty/fgdirtoc.htm

Description: Described here are 750 grants available for institutional programs as well as individual research and scholarship in the areas of theology or religion. For more information about the site, see entry 302 in the "Grants for Individuals—Humanities—Religion" section of this bibliography.

Available from: Association of Theological Schools in the United States and Canada, 10 Summit Park Drive, Pittsburgh, PA 15275. *Telephone:* (412) 788-6505; *Fax:* (412) 788-6510; *E-mail:* ats@ats.edu

Web site: www.ats.edu

Grants for Organizations–Humanities–Religion

500

Fund Raiser's Guide to Religious Philanthropy

Farmington Hills, MI: Taft Group, 2000. 1,149p. ISBN 1-56995-374-0. $175. Paper.

Description: This directory provides approximately 1,000 detailed profiles and funding histories of philanthropic grantmakers responsible for giving a total of $751 million each year to religious causes; 89 percent of these each donated more than $100,000 to religious organizations and all of them contributed at least $50,000. The latest edition of the directory features 88 new profiles of grantmakers that provided more than $46 million to religious organizations and interests and more than 2,000 new biographical listings of foundation officers, directors, and trustees. Entries include a list of up to 20 recent religious grants and 20 historical grants, along with information on foundation donors, denominational and geographic preferences, funding priorities, and more. An appendix identifies more than 2,000 foundations and corporations that contributed at least $10,000 to religious organizations in their most recent reporting period. The indexes make it possible to access the directory listings by headquarters, denominational preference, geographical preference, grant type, recipient type, officers and directors, and grant recipients by location. The 2000 edition is the latest available and no future editions are planned.

Available from: Taft Group, 27500 Drake Road, Farmington Hills, MI 48331-3535. *Toll-free:* (800) 877-TAFT; *Fax:* (800) 414-5043

Web site: www.galegroup.com/taft

501

National Guide to Funding in Religion

6th ed. Washington, DC: Foundation Center, 2001. 1,690p. ISBN 0-87954-952-1. $155. Paper.

Description: Published every two years, this directory describes 8,400 foundations and corporate direct giving programs that have a history of making grants to churches, synagogues, mosques, missionary societies, religious schools, youth groups, and other religious-affiliated projects, including building preservation and humanitarian aid. Entries are arranged by state and then alphabetically by foundation name; they are indexed by geographic location, type of support, subject, and names of key officials. Full information is given on the listed grantmakers: address and contact names, financial data, giving interests, application guidelines, and names of key officials. Many entries list sample grants (a total of 10,000 in the 2001 edition). The work also includes an excellent introduction to support in religion and a glossary of related terms. A new edition is scheduled for release in mid-2003.

Available from: Foundation Center, 79 Fifth Avenue, New York, NY 10003-3076. *Telephone:* (212) 807-3690; *Toll-free:* (800) 424-9836; *Fax:* (212) 807-3691
Web site: fdncenter.org

502

Religious Funding Resource Guide

16th ed. Ed. by Mary Eileen Paul and Andrea Flores. Washington, DC: ResourceWomen, 2000. 515p. ISBN 1-883542-10-3. $85, individuals; $95, libraries and universities. Paper.

Description: Philanthropic giving by organized religion in the United States exceeds that of all of the nation's secular foundations and corporations combined. This guide (formerly issued as the *Church Funding Resource Guide*) has been published since 1983 "to enable organizations working for change which are not denominationally or religiously based to identify sources of support for their important work." Nonprofit, service, and social justice agencies will find this compilation particularly helpful. Although the 2000 edition is more than an inch thick, it covers only 39 programs (from Episcopal, Jewish, Lutheran, Presbyterian, Catholic, Unitarian, Methodist, and United Church of Christ funders). Specifically excluded are African American church bodies and ethnic churches, such as the Greek Orthodox Church. What makes up the bulk of the publication are complete application packets for each of these programs. This is a handy, if one of the few programs included here matches your funding needs. If not, you'll need a more inclusive listing of sponsors that give to religious groups. For that, see the Foundation Center's *National Guide to Funding in Religion* (entry 501 in this section of the bibliography).

Available from: ResourceWomen, 4527 South Dakota Avenue, N.E., Washington, DC 20017. *Telephone:* (202) 832-8071; *TTY:* (202) 832-8073; *Fax:* (202) 832-8078; *E-mail:* rswmn@aol.com

SCIENCES
General

503

GrantsInfo.com: Social and Natural Sciences Report

http://www.arisnet.com/socnatu.html

Description: This inexpensive online searchable database provides information on hundreds of grant and fellowship opportunities for organizations and individuals in the natural and social sciences. For more information about the

Grants for Organizations–Sciences–Agricultural Sciences

site, see entry 271 in the "Grants for Individuals—Social Sciences—General" section of this bibliography.

Available from: Academic Research Information System, Inc., 2940 16th Street, Suite 314, San Francisco, CA 94103. *Telephone:* (415) 558-8133; *Fax:* (415) 558-8135; *E-mail:* arisnet@dnai.com

Web site: www.arisnet.com

504 ¢

National Science Foundation Guide to Programs: A Compilation of NSF Funding Opportunities

http://www.nsf.gov

Description: Described in this free annual guide (available at NSF's web site) are grants for organizations or individuals and fellowships sponsored by the National Science Foundation or administered in cooperation with foreign countries. For more information about the listing, see entry 309 in the "Grants for Individuals—Sciences—General" section of this bibliography.

Available from: National Science Foundation, 4201 Wilson Boulevard, Arlington, VA 22230. *Telephone:* (703) 292-5111; *TDD:* (703) 292-5090; *E-mail:* pubs@nsf.gov

Web site: www.nsf.gov

Agricultural Sciences

505 ¢

Federal Funding Sources for Rural Areas

Comp. by M. Louise Reynnells and Melinda L. Surratt. Beltsville, MD: Rural Information Center. Annual. (Rural Information Center Publications Series, No. 75). Free (2002 ed.). Paper or online.

Description: This directory is prepared annually by the Rural Information Center (RIC), which is a joint project of the U.S.D.A. Cooperative State Research, Education & Extension Service and the National Agricultural Library (NAL). The federal funding programs available to rural areas described in this free document were selected from the *Catalog of Federal Domestic Assistance*, using FAPRS (Federal Assistance Programs Retrieval System); both of these sources are described in entry 339. The information included here is also available in full text (in html or .pdf) and keyword searchable versions on the Internet at RIC's web site. This is just one of several funding publications made available in print and online by the National Agricultural Library; among the other titles offered are *Rural Health Services Funding: A Resource Guide; Federal*

How to Find Out About Financial Aid and Funding

Support for Rural Health: A Compendium of Federal Programs That Support the Provision of Health Care in Rural Areas; and *Capital Assistance Funding: A Rural Health Resource Guide.*

Available from: National Agricultural Library, Attn: Rural Information Center, 10301 Baltimore Avenue, Room 304, Beltsville, MD 20705-2351; *Toll-free:* (800) 633-7701; *Fax:* (301) 504-5181; *E-mail:* ric@nal.usda.gov

Web site: www.nal.usda.gov/ric

Biological Sciences

506

National Guide to Funding for the Environment and Animal Welfare

6th ed. Washington, DC: Foundation Center, 2002. 527p. ISBN 1-931923-02-7. $115. Paper.

Description: The sixth edition provides full information on more than 2,900 foundations and corporate direct giving programs that award millions of dollars each year to nonprofit institutions and projects involved with animal welfare and environmental programs. For more information about the publication, see entry 508 in the "Grants for Organizations—Sciences—Environmental Sciences" section of this bibliography.

Available from: Foundation Center, 79 Fifth Avenue, New York, NY 10003-3076. *Telephone:* (212) 807-3690; *Toll-free:* (800) 424-9836; *Fax:* (212) 807-3691

Web site: fdncenter.org

Environmental Sciences

507

Environmental Grantmaking Foundations

Cary, NC: Resources for Global Sustainability, 1992- . Annual. ISBN 0-9631943-6-4. $105 (2001 ed.), paper; $115, CD-ROM.

Description: Resources for Global Sustainability has a large database containing detailed information on environmental grants awarded by independent, community, operating, and company-sponsored foundations in the United States and Canada. Using the database, the institute produces this directory of environmental grantmaking foundations. Profiled in the most recent edition are 900 of the most significant foundations that fund environmental projects. These foundations give more than $600 million a year for environmental purposes. Profiles are arranged alphabetically by grantmaker name. Each entry contains information on: contact, history and philosophy, officers and directors, grantgiving, environmental issues funded, sample grants, application process, emphasis, and limitations. Indexing is by grantmaker location, recipient location, activity region, funding emphasis, funding limitations, environmental issues, and officers, trustees, directors, and contacts. Since the 1997 edition, the information has been available on CD-ROM as well as in print form. Through the fourth edition, the directory was published by Environmental Data Research Institute. Although this is intended to be an annual, no edition was published in 2002; a 2003 edition is planned.

Available from: Resources for Global Sustainability, Inc., P.O. Box 3665, Cary, NC 27519-3665. *Toll-free:* (800) 724-1857; *Fax:* (919) 363-9841; *E-mail:* rgs@environmentalgrants.com

Web site: www.environmentalgrants.com

508

National Guide to Funding for the Environment and Animal Welfare

6th ed. Washington, DC: Foundation Center, 2002. 527p. ISBN 1-931923-02-7. $115. Paper.

Description: The sixth edition provides full information on more than 2,900 foundations and corporate direct giving programs that award millions of dollars each year to nonprofit institutions and projects involved with environmental and animal welfare programs, including animals, botanical gardens, conservation, ecology, energy, forests, global warming, recycling, pollution control, waste management, water pollution, and water resources. Entries are arranged geographically and then alphabetically by foundation name; they provide the following information: address and telephone number, contact person, asset amounts, gifts received, amount and number of grants awarded, grantmaker's statement of purpose and activities, types of support generally awarded, geographical limitations, application deadlines, and—for many entries—brief descriptions of sample grants (7,200 in the 2002 edition). There are several indexes provided: names of key officials, preferred types of support, geographic region, subject interest, and grantmaker name. A bibliography lists additional sources of information on grantseeking in the field.

Available from: Foundation Center, 79 Fifth Avenue, New York, NY 10003-3076. *Telephone:* (212) 807-3690; *Toll-free:* (800) 424-9836; *Fax:* (212) 807-3691

Web site: fdncenter.org

Health and Medical Sciences

509

Directory of Biomedical and Health Care Grants

Westport, CT: Oryx, 1985- . Annual. ISSN 0883-5330. ISBN 1-57356-569-5. $84.50 (2003 ed.). Paper.

Description: The current edition of this directory identifies 3,000 grants (to organizations and individuals), awards, and fellowships in the biomedical and health care areas. For more information about the publication, see entry 313 in the "Grants for Individuals—Sciences—Health and Medical Sciences" section of this bibliography.

Available from: Oryx Press, 88 Post Road West, Westport, CT 06881. *Telephone:* (602) 265-2651; *Toll-free:* (800) 279-6799; *Fax:* (800) 279-4663; *E-mail:* info@oryxpress.com

Web site: www.oryxpress.com

510

GrantsInfo.com: Biomedical Sciences

http://www.arisnet.com/biomed.html

Description: This inexpensive online searchable database provides information on hundreds of grants and fellowships for organizations and individuals in the biomedical sciences. For more information about the site, see entry 316 in the "Grants for Individuals—Sciences—Health and Medical Sciences" section of this bibliography.

Available from: Academic Research Information System, Inc., 2940 16th Street, Suite 314, San Francisco, CA 94103. *Telephone:* (415) 558-8133; *Fax:* (415) 558-8135; *E-mail:* arisnet@dnai.com

Web site: www.arisnet.com

511

Health Funds Grants Resources Yearbook

9th ed. Allenwood, NJ: Health Resources, 2001. 545p. ISBN 1-882364-58-9. $165. Paper.

Description: Although this is more of a yearbook than a grants directory, the latest edition does provide information on the health grants priorities of the major foundations, corporations, community foundations, and federal government agencies. Program entries contain financial data, descriptions of previous grant recipients, and details of future funding trends. Entries are grouped into

Grants for Organizations–Sciences–Health & Medical Sciences

chapters: AIDS research and health services, cancer, elderly health services, adolescent health care, etc. The rest of the yearbook consists of suggested development strategies, tips for grantseeking, and a guide to grantseeking on the Internet. To update the information presented here, use the monthly *Health Grants Funding Alert,* which identifies current opportunities in health care offered by federal, corporate, and foundation grantmakers ($237/yr.). Health Resources also publishes another handbook that might be of interest to health grantseekers: *Grant Funding for Elderly Health Services* (4th ed., 2002, $95); while not a directory, the guide does provide details on grants from such major funding sources as the Robert Wood Johnson Foundation, the Hartford Foundation, the Commonwealth Fund, and the W.K. Kellogg Foundation.

Available from: Health Resources Publishing, P.O. Box 456, Allenwood, NJ 08720. *Telephone:* (732) 292-1100; *Toll-free:* (800) 516-4343; *Fax:* (732) 292-111; *E-mail:* info@healthresourcesonline.com

Web site: www.healthresourcesonline.com

512

Health Grants & Contracts Weekly: Project Opportunities in Research, Training, and Services

Ed. by Pamela Moore. Frederick, MD: Aspen Publishers, 1974- . Weekly. ISSN 0194-2452. $459/yr. Paper or e-mail.

Description: Published 50 times a year by Aspen Publishers (formerly Capitol Publications), *Health Grants & Contracts Weekly* serves as an "early warning" system, to alert readers to federal grant announcements, as well as to research, training, and technical service contracts in health and related social service areas (including medical sciences, biological sciences, behavioral sciences, and social sciences). Every health-related area is covered, including AIDS, maternal and child health, substance abuse, disease and injury prevention, basic biology, disabilities, Alzheimer's disease and related disorders, family violence, social sciences, biotechnology, environmental health, health education, health services for the homeless, nutrition research and education, biomedical research and equipment, and health training. Each eight-page issue is published on Monday and contains information on Requests for Proposals (RFPs), closing dates for grant programs, procurement-related regulatory news, contract awards, updates on federal budget action, and profiles on grant programs and federal agencies. RFP entries include the following information: title of project, brief description, length of project, date proposal due, RFP number, date appearing in FedBizOpps, and contact name and address. Subscribers may order either a print or an e-mail version of the weekly.

Available from: Aspen Publishers, Inc., 7201 McKinney Circle, Frederick, MD 21704. *Toll-free:* (800) 638-8437; *Fax:* (301) 417-7550

Web site: www.aspenpublishers.com

513

National Guide to Funding in AIDS

2nd ed. New York: Foundation Center, 2001. 170p. ISBN 0-87954-950-5. $115. Paper.

Description: Current information is provided on more than 550 foundations, corporate giving programs, and public charities that have stated or demonstrated a commitment to AIDS-related services and research. Most entries list recently-awarded grants, to illustrate the kind of AIDS-related projects the grantmaker has funded. The directory is arranged alphabetically by state and then by foundation or organization name. In addition, there is an introductory section that provides a brief overview of AIDS-HIV funding, an essay describing steps to follow when trying to obtain funding, a glossary of terms, a bibliography of funding for AIDS-HIV, and multiple indexes: donors, officers, and trustees; geographic location; types of support; subject; and grantmaking organizations. Previously, this directory was known as *AIDS Funding*. A new edition is scheduled for release in mid-2003.

Available from: Foundation Center, 79 Fifth Avenue, New York, NY 10003-3076. *Telephone:* (212) 807-3690; *Toll-free:* (800) 424-9836; *Fax:* (212) 807-3691

Web site: fdncenter.org

514

National Guide to Funding in Health

7th ed. Washington, DC: Foundation Center, 2001. 2,447p. ISBN 0-87954-951-3. $155. Paper.

Description: The seventh edition of this guide provides information on more than 10,000 foundations, corporate giving programs, and grantmaking public charities that have an interest in funding health-related programs and institutions. The foundation profiles, which are organized by state, supply the following: address and contact name, financial data, giving interests and restrictions, application process, and names of key officials. Many entries also include brief descriptions of recently-awarded grants (a total of 16,000 are identified in this edition). The information included here is indexed by donors, officers, and trustees; subjects; geographic area; and preferred types of support. A new edition is scheduled for release in mid-2003.

Available from: Foundation Center, 79 Fifth Avenue, New York, NY 10003-3076. *Telephone:* (212) 807-3690; *Toll-free:* (800) 424-9836; *Fax:* (212) 807-3691

Web site: fdncenter.org

Technology

515 📖

Directory of Computer and High Technology Grants: A Reference Directory Identifying Computer, Software, and High-Tech Grants Available to Nonprofit Organizations

4th ed. Ed. by Richard M. Eckstein. Loxahatchee, FL: Research Grant Guides, 1999. 116p. ISBN 0-945078-23-4. $69. Paper.

Description: Nonprofit organizations looking for funding to purchase computers, software, and other technology will be interested in this guide. Information on 750 foundations making grants in these areas is provided in the latest (fourth) edition—this is 250 more than in the previous edition. Entries are listed by state and specify contacts, areas of interest supported, geographic restrictions, grant ranges, and organizations funded. The profiles are indexed by subject, including computer grants, office equipment, and software. Issued every three years (approximately), the next edition should be released before the end of 2003.

Available from: Research Grant Guides, Inc., P.O. Box 1214, Loxahatchee, FL 33470-1214. *Telephone:* (561) 795-6129; *Fax:* (561) 795-7794

516 📖

Distance Learning Funding $ourcebook: A Guide to Foundation, Corporate and Government Support for Telecommunications and the New Media

4th ed. By Arlene Krebs. Dubuque, IA: Kendall/Hunt, 1999. 448p. ISBN 0-7872-4980-7. $48. Paper.

Description: The purpose of this guide is to provide current information on funding for telecommunications and interactive technology for distance education. For more information about the publication, see entry 471 in the "Grants for Organizations—Social Sciences—Education" section of this bibliography.

Available from: Kendall/Hunt Publishing Company, 4050 Westmark Drive, P.O. Box 1840, Dubuque, IA 52004-1840. *Telephone:* (563) 589-1000; *Toll-free:* (800) 228-0810; *Fax:* (800) 772-9165

Web site: www.kendallhunt.com

517

Grants for Technology

Frederick, MD: Aspen Publishers, 2000. 328p. ISBN 0-8342-1894-1. $145. Paper.

Description: Prepared by Aspen Publishers (formerly Capitol Publications), this directory focuses on funding available for technology hardware, software, and technical assistance programs; it replaces the third edition of Aspen's *Grants for School Technology*. Nearly 400 private and corporate funders are profiled. Each entry includes name, address, telephone number, types of grants available, eligibility and use requirements, applications guidelines, deadlines, and examples of recently-funded grants. Appendices cover Internet sites for grantseekers and grantseeking resources. Sample forms are also provided. Like other directories published by Aspen, this one consists of data taken directly from GrantScape, the publisher's electronic funding database (see entry 371).

Available from: Aspen Publishers, Inc., 7201 McKinney Circle, Frederick, MD 21704. *Toll-free:* (800) 638-8437; *Fax:* (301) 417-7550

Web site: www.aspenpublishers.com

518

National Guide to Funding for Information Technology

2nd ed. Washington, DC: Foundation Center, 1999. 336p. ISBN 0-87954-879-7. $115. Paper.

Description: Covered here are 700 foundations and corporate direct giving programs that have a history of awarding money to projects involving computer science, engineering, technology, telecommunications, media, communications, and other areas directly related to information technology. Each entry provides: address, financial data, giving priorities, application procedures, contact names, and key officials. The volume also includes more than 2,400 descriptions of recently-awarded grants. Indexes access the information by specific program areas and geographic areas preferred by the grantmakers. Published last in 1999, much of the information included is now dated.

Available from: Foundation Center, 79 Fifth Avenue, New York, NY 10003-3076. *Telephone:* (212) 807-3690; *Toll-free:* (800) 424-9836; *Fax:* (212) 807-3691

Web site: fdncenter.org

Grants for Organizations–Special Population Groups–Ethnic Groups

519 📖 🕸 ¢

School Technology Funding Directory

3rd ed. Bethesda: eSchool News, 2002. 298p. ISBN 0-9703007-3-5. $169. Paper.

Description: Federal mandates to "wire" schools have educators looking for funds to connect to the Internet and to prepare for the digital age. They will find help here, in the latest edition of *School Technology Funding Directory*, where more than 500 grants and other sources of funding for K-12 technology from federal, state, and local government agencies, corporate foundations, private endowments, charitable organizations, and community foundations are described. Each entry contains the following information: funding priorities, limitations, deadlines, and financial data. Also included in the directory are: advice from grantseekers on how to research funding prospects; common myths about writing proposals; links to key Internet resources; and other information related to searching for technology grants. You can update these listings at no charge in the "Upcoming Grant Deadlines" section of eSchool News's web site. eSchool News also publishes another title that might be of interest to school technology grantseekers: *School Technology OneBook* ($199), which provides contact information for more than 15,000 funders, vendors, service providers, and information resources in the school technology field.

Available from: eSchool News, 7920 Norfolk Avenue, Suite 900, Bethesda, MD 20814. *Toll-free:* (800) 394-0115; *Fax:* (301) 913-0119; *E-mail:* cpugh@eschoolnews.com

Web site: www.eschoolnews.com

SPECIAL POPULATION GROUPS
Ethnic Groups

520 📖

Grants: Corporate Grantmaking for Racial and Ethnic Communities

Prep. by National Committee for Responsive Philanthropy. Kingston, RI: Moyer Bell, 2000. 733p. ISBN 1-55921-280-2. $89.95. Paper.

Description: African Americans, Hispanics and Latinos, Native Americans, and Asian Pacific Americans are the fastest growing population segments in the United States, according to the U.S. Census Bureau. By 2050, it is projected that people of color will constitute at least half of the U.S. population. This directory provides a listing of 124 American corporations that make over 10,000 grants each year (totaling more than $1.3 billion) to organizations serving these

How to Find Out About Financial Aid and Funding

groups. The book, prepared by the National Committee for Responsive Philanthropy, traces the giving patterns of these grantmakers by company and location. Although issued in 2000, the directory is based on information collected in 1995. In addition, the page headings are confusing and there is a lack of indexing. Use with care.

Available from: Moyer Bell, Ltd., 549 Old North Road, Kingston, RI 02881. *Telephone:* (401) 783-5480; *Toll-free:* (888) 789-1945; *Fax:* (401) 284-0959; *E-mail:* info_acorn@yahoo.com

Web site: www.moyerbellbooks.com

521

National Directory of Corporate Philanthropy for Native Americans

Ed. by Phyllis A. Meiners. Kansas City, MO: CRC Publishing, 2001. 160p. ISBN 0-9633694-7-4. $98.95. Paper.

Description: The focus here is on corporate giving programs and corporate foundations that have made multiple grants to Native American tribes and organizations between 1992 and 2000. Profiles specify contact person, number of corporate employees, philanthropic budget, sample grants, application deadlines, geographic and subject interests, and application procedures. Indexes provide access to grantmakers by subject and geographic priorities. Both national and regional/multi-state funders are included. Even so, only 39 sources of corporate philanthropy for Native Americans are covered; at $98.95, you're paying quite a hefty price tag for a limited amount of data—most of which can be found in any standard grants directory. A complementary publication issued earlier by CRC Publishing, *National Directory of Foundation Grants for Native Americans,* covers foundations that "specifically target American Indian agencies, who have presented more than one grant to Indian groups in recent years, or who have granted large dollar amounts for native studies or activities;" however, that listing, which also costs nearly $100, has not been updated since 1998.

Available from: CRC Publishing Company, P.O. Box 22583, Kansas City, MO 64113-2583. *Telephone:* (816) 361-2059; *Toll-free:* (800) 268-2059; *Fax:* (816) 361-2115; *E-mail:* books@crcpub.com

Web site: www.crcpub.com

522

National Directory of Seed Money Grants for American Indian Projects

Ed. by Phyllis A. Meiners. Kansas City, MO: CRC Publishing, 2001. 280p. ISBN 0-9633694-9-0. $109.95. Paper.

Description: Published first in 1997 and then updated in 2001, this sourcebook identifies just 56 private sector seed money grants for start-up and innova-

Grants for Organizations–Special Population Groups–Gays, Lesbians, Etc.

tive programs managed by Native Americans. Small, "alternative" foundation grantmakers who focus on projects of self determination and social change are featured. Profiles provide information on contact person, typical grants, deadlines, geographic preferences, special interests, and application procedures. In addition, a section is devoted to American Indian foundations (grants from American Indians to American Indians). Subject and geographic indexes complete the source.

Available from: CRC Publishing Company, P.O. Box 22583, Kansas City, MO 64113-2583. *Telephone:* (816) 361-2059; *Toll-free:* (800) 268-2059; *Fax:* (816) 361-2115; *E-mail:* books@crcpub.com

Web site: www.crcpub.com

Gays, Lesbians, Etc.

523

Funders of Lesbian, Gay, Bisexual and Transgender Programs: A Directory for Grantseekers

New York: Funders for Lesbian and Gay Issues, 2002. $15, paper; free, online.

Description: This is the only national directory that identifies funders who support lesbian, gay, bisexual, and transgender programs. The latest edition lists nearly 300 foundations and corporate giving programs (including foundations that support international organizations). The following information is provided for each funder: funding priorities, grant types, limitations, area, how to apply, and average grant. In addition, a limited number of scholarship funds and fellowships available for lesbian and gay students, as well as for those pursuing gay and lesbian studies, are described in a separate section. Paper copies of the directory are available for purchase ($15 each) or the database can be accessed, without charge, on the Funders for Lesbian and Gay Issues' web site.

Available from: Funders for Lesbian and Gay Issues, 116 East 16th Street, 7th Floor, New York, NY 10003. *Telephone:* (212) 475-2930; *Fax:* (212) 982-3321; *E-mail:* info@lgbtfunders.org

Web site: www.lgbtfunders.org

How to Find Out About Financial Aid and Funding

Persons with Disabilities

524

Directory of Grants for Organizations Serving People with Disabilities: A Reference Directory Identifying Grants Available to Nonprofit Organizations

Ed. by Richard M. Eckstein. Loxahatchee, FL: Research Grant Guides, 1978- . Biennial. ISSN 0733-4752. ISBN 0-945078-25-0. $69 (11th ed.). Paper.

Description: Published biennially since 1978, first under the title *Handicapped Funding Directory* and now as the *Directory of Grants for Organizations Serving People with Disabilities,* this guide identifies more than 700 foundations, corporations, associations, and agencies that have funded programs and services in the following areas: mentally retarded, speech impaired, emotionally disturbed, health impaired, hard of hearing, deaf, visually handicapped, orthopedically impaired, and learning disabled. However, only very brief information is provided for the agencies (address, telephone number, areas of interest, geographic restrictions, grant range, and, sometimes, a list of organizations funded). A number of the listed organizations do not have ongoing funding programs for the disabled but only a record of having issued at least one grant at least one time during the past in at least one of the areas listed above. Additional access to the entries is provided by two indexes to foundations (alphabetical and by subject or category of disability) and an index to federal programs (about 50). A list of organizations that publish information for people with disabilities completes the work. This listing is aimed at nonprofits. Funding programs for individuals with disabilities are not covered here; for that information, see *Financial Aid for the Disabled and Their Families* (described in entry 222).

Available from: Research Grant Guides, Inc., P.O. Box 1214, Loxahatchee, FL 33470-1214. *Telephone:* (561) 795-6129; *Fax:* (561) 795-7794

525

Resources for People with Disabilities: A National Directory

2nd ed. Chicago: Ferguson Publishing, 2001. ISBN 0-89434-309-2, hardcover; 0-89434-256-8, CD-ROM. $89.95, 2-volume hardcover or CD-ROM single-user; $199, CD-ROM network.

Description: Not all of the programs covered here are aimed directly at individuals with disabilities; a number are for organizations and researchers working to help the disabled. For more information about the publication, see entry 333 in the "Grants for Individuals—Special Population Groups—Persons with Disabilities" section of this bibliography.

Available from: Ferguson Publishing Company, 200 West Jackson Boulevard, Chicago, IL 60606. *Toll-free:* (800) 306-9941; *Fax:* (800) 306-9942

Web site: www.fergpubco.com

Religious Groups

526

Catholic Funding Guide: A Directory of Resources for Catholic Activity

2nd ed. Ed. by Kerry A. Robinson. Washington, DC: FADICA, 2001. 504p. ISBN 1-891646-02-8. $60. Paper.

Description: Each of the grantmakers listed in this book has a history of providing funding to the Catholic sector, including Catholic schools, colleges, social service agencies, missionary programs, hospitals, parish projects and retirement facilities. For more information about this title, see entry 498 in the "Grants for Organizations—Humanities—Religion" section of this bibliography.

Available from: FADICA, Inc., 1350 Connecticut Avenue, N.W., Suite 303, Washington, DC 20036-1701. *Telephone:* (202) 223-3550; *Fax:* (202) 296-9295; *E-mail:* info@fadica.org
Web site: www.fadica.org

Women

527

Directory of Financial Aids for Women

By Gail Ann Schlachter and R. David Weber. El Dorado Hills, CA: Reference Service Press, 1978- . Biennial. ISSN 0732-5215. ISBN 1-58841-067-6. $45 (2003-2005 ed.). Hardcover.

Description: This is the only extensive and regularly updated listing of grants, loans, fellowships, scholarships, awards/prizes, and internships available primarily or exclusively to women's organizations and women. For more information about the publication, see entry 232 in the "Scholarships, Fellowships & Loans—Special Population Groups—Women" section of this bibliography.

Available from: Reference Service Press, 5000 Windplay Drive, Suite 4, El Dorado Hills, CA 95762. *Telephone:* (916) 939-9620; *Fax:* (916) 939-9626; *E-mail:* findaid@aol.com
Web site: www.rspfunding.com

528

National Guide to Funding for Women and Girls

5th ed. Washington, DC: Foundation Center, 1999. 414p. ISBN 0-87954-881-9. $115. Paper.

Description: The title of this publication could be misunderstood. This is not a guide to funding *for* women and girls but to nonprofit organizations that serve women and girls. Described here are more than 1,200 foundations and corporate direct giving programs with a specific interest in funding projects related to women and girls, including child care, health care, civil rights, homeless and abuse shelters, education, legal defense, employment programs, rape prevention, and family planning. In addition to summarizing more than 5,400 sample grants, the directory also provides information on the grantmakers address and contact, financial features, giving priorities, application guidelines, and key officials. But use with care; last published in 1999, much of the information provided here is now dated. To update these listings, use the Foundation Center's *Grant Guide* that focuses on women and girls (see entry 369).

Available from: Foundation Center, 79 Fifth Avenue, New York, NY 10003-3076. *Telephone:* (212) 807-3690; *Toll-free:* (800) 424-9836; *Fax:* (212) 807-3691

Web site: fdncenter.org

Awards & Prizes

Awards—including prizes, competitions, and honoraria—are granted on local, state, regional, national, and international levels to recognize, reward, or support notable achievement. Included in this chapter are 77 print, electronic, and Internet resources listing awards and prizes. Of these, 27 are general in nature (covering either international or American awards); 4 deal with the social sciences; the vast majority focus on the humanities (31 entries), particularly fine and applied arts, journalism, and literature; 7 cover the sciences; and 8 are aimed at special population groups. If you are looking for a specific awards resource and you do not find it in this chapter, be sure to check the Title Index to see if it is covered elsewhere in the guide.

GENERAL

United States

529

Annual Register of Grant Support: A Directory of Funding Sources

---

Medford, NJ: Information Today, 1969- . Annual. ISSN 0066-4049. ISBN 1-57387-145-1. $229 (2003 ed.). Hardcover.

Description: Despite its title, this annual covers awards and prizes as well as grant opportunities. For more information about the publication, see entry 235 in the "Grants for Individuals—General—United States" section of this bibliography.

Available from: Information Today, Inc., 143 Old Marlton Pike, Medford, NJ 08055-8750. *Telephone:* (609) 654-6266; *Fax:* (609) 654-4309; *E-mail:* custserv@infotoday.com

Web site: www.infotoday.com

530

Awards, Honors and Prizes: An International Directory of Awards and Their Donors

---

21st ed. Ed. by Donna Batten. Farmington Hills, MI: Gale, 2002. 2v. ISSN 0196-6316. ISBN 0-7876-6223-2, volume 1; 0-7876-6224-0, volume 2. $275, volume 1; $305, volume 2. Hardcover.

Description: This is the single most comprehensive source of information on awards offered in the United States, Canada, and 100 other countries. The publication is divided into two volumes. Volume 1, *United States and Canada,* contains up-to-date information on approximately 17,000 awards, honors, and prizes given in the two countries in the areas of advertising and public relations, art, business, government, finance, science, engineering, literature, technology, sports, religion, public affairs, law, publishing, international affairs, transportation, architecture, journalism, music, photography, theater, and the performing arts. Excluded from the listing are scholarships, fellowships, study awards to students, prizes received as a result of entering contests where something is achieved only for the purpose of the contest, and local and regional awards. The volume is divided into four sections: 1) the main listing for each award, where the following information is provided: name, address, e-mail and URLs, title of award, purpose, eligibility, form of award, frequency, date established, and who established the award; 2) a list of subjects and "see also" references (each award is indexed by subject and/or areas of interest); 3) an alphabetical index to the specific names of each award; and 4) an organization index. Volume 2 adds international coverage by describing 4,000 organizations and 8,000 awards given in countries other than the United States or Canada. Recent editions include e-mail addresses and web site URLs in the contact information.

Available from: The Gale Group, P.O. Box 9187, Farmington Hills, MI 48333-9187. *Telephone:* (248) 699-GALE; *Toll-free:* (800) 877-GALE; *Fax:* (800) 414-5043; *E-mail:* galeord@gale.com

Web site: www.galegroup.com

531

Chronicle Financial Aid Guide: Scholarships and Loans for High School Students, College Undergraduates, Graduates, and Adult Learners

Moravia, NY: Chronicle Guidance Publications, 1978- . Annual. ISSN 1063-7915. ISBN 1-55631-310-1. $24.98 (2002-2003 ed.). Paper.

Description: In addition to scholarship programs, a number of awards and loans for high school and undergraduate students are described in this annual directory. For more information about the publication, see entry 8 in the "Scholarships, Fellowships & Loans—General—United States" section of this bibliography.

Available from: Chronicle Guidance Publications, 66 Aurora Street, Moravia, NY 13118-3576. *Telephone:* (315) 497-0330; *Toll-free:* (800) 899-0454; *Fax:* (315) 497-3359; *E-mail:* customerservice@chronicleguidance.com

Web site: www.chronicleguidance.com

532

College Student's Guide to Merit and Other No-Need Funding

By Gail Ann Schlachter and R. David Weber. El Dorado Hills, CA: Reference Service Press, 1996- . Biennial. ISSN 1099-9086. ISBN 1-58841-041-2. $32 (2002-2004 ed.). Hardcover.

Description: Both awards and scholarships are described in this guide, which identifies more than 1,200 funding opportunities for students in or returning to college that never consider income in the selection process. For more information about the publication, see entry 16 in the "Scholarships, Fellowships & Loans—General—United States" section of this bibliography.

Available from: Reference Service Press, 5000 Windplay Drive, Suite 4, El Dorado Hills, CA 95762. *Telephone:* (916) 939-9620; *Fax:* (916) 939-9626; *E-mail:* findaid@aol.com

Web site: www.rspfunding.com

Awards & Prizes–General–United States

533

Collegeboard.com Scholarship Search

http://www.collegeboard.com
Description: Available without charge on the College Board's web site, this database describes 2,300 awards, loans, scholarships, and other types of financial aid sponsored by national, state, and private sources. For more information about the service, see entry 17 in the "Scholarships, Fellowships & Loans—General—United States" section of this bibliography.
Available from: College Board Publications, Box 886, New York, NY 19191-0886. *Telephone:* (212) 713-8000; *Toll-free:* (800) 323-7155; *Fax:* (212) 713-8143; *E-mail:* expan@collegeboard.org
Web site: www.collegeboard.org

534

Directory of Research Grants

Westport, CT: Oryx, 1975- . Annual. ISSN 0146-7336. ISBN 1-57356-570-9. $134.95 (2003 ed.). Paper.
Description: Awards, internships, scholarships, fellowships, and loans are described in this annual directory, in addition to research grants. For more information about the publication, see entry 238 in the "Grants for Individuals—General—United States" section of this bibliography.
Available from: Oryx Press, 88 Post Road West, Westport, CT 06881. *Telephone:* (602) 265-2651; *Toll-free:* (800) 279-6799; *Fax:* (800) 279-4663; *E-mail:* info@oryxpress.com
Web site: www.oryxpress.com

535

ExPAN

New York: College Board. Annual. $595/yr., Widows and Macintosh versions.
Description: The FundFinder section of ExPAN provides information on thousands of awards, loans, scholarships, fellowships, and other financial aid opportunities offered by national, state, and private sources. For more information about the product, see entry 26 in the "Scholarships, Fellowships & Loans—General—United States" section of this bibliography.
Available from: College Board Publications, Box 886, New York, NY 19191-0886. *Telephone:* (212) 713-8000; *Toll-free:* (800) 323-7155; *Fax:* (212) 713-8143; *E-mail:* expan@collegeboard.org
Web site: www.collegeboard.org

536

FASTaid

http://www.fastaid.com
Description: Thousands of financial aid opportunities (including awards) that are open to students from high school through postdoctorate are briefly described here. For more information about the service, see entry 27 in the "Scholarships, Fellowships & Loans—General—United States" section of this bibliography.
Available from: National Scholarship Research Service, 5577 Skyland Boulevard, Suite 6A, Santa Rosa, CA 95403. *Toll-free:* (800) 432-3782; *E-mail:* editor@www.fastaid.com
Web site: www.fastaid.com

537

Getting Money for Graduate School: More than 1,000 Scholarships, Grants, Prizes, Forgivable Loans, and Fellowships

1st ed. Lawrenceville, NJ: Peterson's Guides, 2002. 404p. ISBN 0-7689-1294-6. $16.95. Paper.
Description: Described here are 1,100 prizes, grants, forgivable loans, and fellowships, not all of which are open to graduate students (despite the title). For more information about the publication, see entry 39 in the "Scholarships, Fellowships & Loans—General—United States" section of this bibliography.
Available from: Peterson's Guides, Princeton Pike Corporate Center, 2000 Lenox Drive, P.O. Box 67005, Lawrenceville, NJ 08648. *Telephone:* (609) 896-1800; *Toll-free:* (800) 338-3282; *Fax:* (609) 896-4544; *E-mail:* sales@petersons.com
Web site: www.petersons.com

538

The Grants Register: The Complete Guide to Postgraduate Funding Worldwide

Ed. by Sara Hackwood. New York: Palgrave, 1969- . Annual. ISSN 0072-5471. ISBN 0-333-96474-8. $185 (2003 ed.). Hardcover.
Description: This annual directory describes awards, fellowships, and grants open to nationals of the United States, Canada, the United Kingdom, Ireland, Australia, New Zealand, South Africa, and the developing countries. For more information about the publication, see entry 265 in the "Grants for Individuals—General—International" section of this bibliography.

Awards & Prizes–General–United States

Available from: Palgrave, 175 Fifth Avenue, New York, NY 10010. *Telephone:* (212) 982-3900; *Toll-free:* (800) 221-7945; *Fax:* (212) 777-6359
Web site: www.palgrave-usa.com

539

GrantSelect

http://www.grantselect.com
Description: Updated annually and used to generate Oryx Press's print funding directories, GrantSelect identifies more than 10,000 awards and other funding opportunities sponsored by organizations and agencies in the United States and other countries. For more information about the database, see entry 247 in the "Grants for Individuals—General—United States" section of this bibliography.
Available from: Oryx Press, 88 Post Road West, Westport, CT 06881. *Telephone:* (602) 265-2651; *Toll-free:* (800) 279-6799; *Fax:* (800) 279-4663; *E-mail:* info@oryxpress.com
Web site: www.oryxpress.com

540

GrantsInfo.com: Student Funding Sources

http://www.arisnet.com/newstu.html
Description: This site provides both undergraduate and graduate students with information on awards, grants, scholarships, fellowships, and internships in the arts and sciences, including creative arts, humanities, social sciences, natural sciences, and biomedical sciences. For more information about the site, see entry 44 in the "Scholarships, Fellowships & Loans—General—United States" section of this bibliography.
Available from: Academic Research Information System, Inc., 2940 16th Street, Suite 314, San Francisco, CA 94103. *Telephone:* (415) 558-8133; *Fax:* (415) 558-8135; *E-mail:* arisnet@dnai.com
Web site: www.arisnet.com

541

High School Senior's Guide to Merit and Other No-Need Funding

By Gail Ann Schlachter and R. David Weber. El Dorado Hills, CA: Reference Service Press, 1996- . Biennial. ISBN 1-58841-044-7. $29.95 (2002-2004 ed.). Hardcover.

How to Find Out About Financial Aid and Funding

Description: More than 1,100 awards, scholarships, and other funding opportunities set aside for college-bound high school seniors are described here. For more information about the publication, see entry 45 in the "Scholarships, Fellowships & Loans—General—United States" section of this bibliography.

Available from: Reference Service Press, 5000 Windplay Drive, Suite 4, El Dorado Hills, CA 95762. *Telephone:* (916) 939-9620; *Fax:* (916) 939-9626; *E-mail:* findaid@aol.com

Web site: www.rspfunding.com

542

Kaplan Scholarships

Ed. by Gail A. Schlachter, R. David Weber, and the Staff of Reference Service Press. New York: Kaplan/Simon & Schuster, 2003. 638p. ISSN 1090-9052. ISBN 0-7432-3044-2. $27. Paper.

Description: The latest edition of this directory (2003) identifies nearly 3,200 awards and scholarships that can be used to support study in any discipline in junior and community colleges, vocational and technical institutes, four-year colleges, and universities in the United States. For more information about the publication, see entry 48 in the "Scholarships, Fellowships & Loans—General—United States" section of this bibliography.

Available from: Simon & Schuster, Attn: Order Department, 100 Front Street, Riverside, NJ 08075. *Toll-free:* (800) 223-2336; *Fax:* (800) 445-6991

Web site: www.simonsays.com

543

NASSP National Advisory List of Contests and Activities

http://www.nhs.us/scaa

Description: Issued annually as a pamphlet from 1940 to 1998 (which last sold for $8 in 1998), this advisory list of regional and national contests and activities suitable for inclusion in a school program or curriculum is now available only on the National Honor Society's web site. The contests and activities listed here are "designed solely to benefit secondary school youth in educational, civic, social and ethical development." They are open to all secondary students, regardless of race, creed, sex, or national origin. Excluded from the compilation are unsupervised essay and poster contests, scholarship programs, and national contests that require team or group competition at a common site. Some music festivals and music-travel programs are included. The contests and activities are listed alphabetically or can be searched by keyword. The following information is provided for each entry: sponsors' address, program title, description, grade level, deadlines, and program dates.

Awards & Prizes–General–United States

Available from: National Association of Secondary School Principals, Attn: National Honor Society, 1904 Association Drive, Reston, VA 22091-1537. *Telephone:* (703) 860-0200; *Toll-free:* (800) 253-7746; *Fax:* (703) 476-5432
Web site: www.principals.org

544

Peterson's Complete Guide to Financial Aid

1st ed. Lawrenceville, NJ: Peterson's Guides, 2002. 1,500p. ISBN 0-7689-1115-X. $49.95. Hardcover.

Description: Since it incorporates information from *Peterson's Scholarships, Grants & Prizes* (see entry 34650), awards (as well as others types of financial aid) are covered here. For more information about the publication, see entry 54 in the "Scholarships, Fellowships & Loans—General—United States" section of this bibliography.

Available from: Peterson's Guides, Princeton Pike Corporate Center, 2000 Lenox Drive, P.O. Box 67005, Lawrenceville, NJ 08648. *Telephone:* (609) 896-1800; *Toll-free:* (800) 338-3282; *Fax:* (609) 896-4544; *E-mail:* sales@petersons.com
Web site: www.petersons.com

545

Peterson's Scholarship Search

http://www.petersons.com

Description: This free search service, sponsored by a well-known publisher, identifies awards and scholarships available to support college study. For more information about the service, see entry 56 in the "Scholarships, Fellowships & Loans—General—United States" section of this bibliography.

Available from: Peterson's Guides, Princeton Pike Corporate Center, 2000 Lenox Drive, P.O. Box 67005, Lawrenceville, NJ 08648. *Telephone:* (609) 896-1800; *Toll-free:* (800) 338-3282; *Fax:* (609) 896-4544; *E-mail:* sales@petersons.com
Web site: www.petersons.com

546

Peterson's Scholarships, Grants & Prizes: Sources of Financial Aid That Anyone Can Apply For

Lawrenceville, NJ: Peterson's Guides, 1996- . Annual. ISSN 1089-9898. ISBN 0-7689-0905-8. $29.95 (2003 ed.). Paper with CD-ROM.

Description: This annual directory describes in some detail approximately 2,000 awards and scholarships available to support college studies that are offered by civic, corporate, state, and other sources. For more information about the publication, see entry 57 in the "Scholarships, Fellowships & Loans—General—United States" section of this bibliography.

Available from: Peterson's Guides, Princeton Pike Corporate Center, 2000 Lenox Drive, P.O. Box 67005, Lawrenceville, NJ 08648. *Telephone:* (609) 896-1800; *Toll-free:* (800) 338-3282; *Fax:* (609) 896-4544; *E-mail:* sales@petersons.com

Web site: www.petersons.com

547

RSP Funding for Graduate Students

El Dorado Hills, CA: Reference Service Press (dist. by Ovid), 1996- . Annual, with semi-annual update. $695 and up. CD-ROM, disk, or online.

Description: *RSP Funding for Graduate Students* contains up-to-date information on more than 4,000 awards, fellowships, loans, loan forgiveness programs, loan repayment programs, and grants open to students entering, continuing, or returning to graduate school. For more information about the product, see entry 59 in the "Scholarships, Fellowships & Loans—General—United States" section of this bibliography.

Available from: Ovid Technologies, 100 River Ridge Drive, Norwood, MA 02062. *Telephone:* (781) 769-2599; *Toll-free:* (800) 343-0064; *Fax:* (781) 769-8763

Web site: www.ovid.com

548

RSP Funding for Postdoctorates and Professionals

El Dorado Hills, CA: Reference Service Press (dist. by Ovid), 1996- . Annual, with semi-annual update. $695 and up. CD-ROM, disk, or online.

Description: *RSP Funding for Postdoctorates and Professionals* contains current information on more than 5,000 awards and other funding programs available to professionals and postdoctorates for recognition, research, study, training, creative activities, conference attendance, travel, etc. For more information about the product, see entry 251 in the "Grants for Individuals—General—United States" section of this bibliography.

Available from: Ovid Technologies, 100 River Ridge Drive, Norwood, MA 02062. *Telephone:* (781) 769-2599; *Toll-free:* (800) 343-0064; *Fax:* (781) 769-8763

Web site: www.ovid.com

Awards & Prizes–General–International

549

RSP Funding for Undergraduates

El Dorado Hills, CA: Reference Service Press (dist. by Ovid), 1996- . Annual, with semi-annual update. $695 and up. CD-ROM, disk, or online.

Description: *RSP Funding for Undergraduates* contains current information on more than 5,000 portable (not single-school based) awards and other financial aid programs open specifically to students entering, currently enrolled in, or returning to college. For more information about the product, see entry 60 in the "Scholarships, Fellowships & Loans—General—United States" section of this bibliography.

Available from: Ovid Technologies, 100 River Ridge Drive, Norwood, MA 02062. *Telephone:* (781) 769-2599; *Toll-free:* (800) 343-0064; *Fax:* (781) 769-8763

Web site: www.ovid.com

550

The Scholarship Book: The Complete Guide to Private-Sector Scholarships, Fellowships, Grants, and Loans for the Undergraduate

9th ed. By Daniel J. Cassidy. Englewood Cliffs, NJ: Prentice-Hall, 2002. 592p. ISSN 1528-9079. ISBN 0-7352-0276-1. $30. Paper with CD-ROM.

Description: This directory lists approximately 1,500 awards, loans, scholarships, and internships available to undergraduate students. For more information about the publication, see entry 64 in the "Scholarships, Fellowships & Loans—General—United States" section of this bibliography.

Available from: Prentice Hall, P.O. Box 11075, Des Moines, IA 50336-1075. *Toll-free:* (800) 947-7700; *Fax:* (515) 264-6719

Web site: www.phdirect.com

International

551

Annual Register of Grant Support: A Directory of Funding Sources

Medford, NJ: Information Today, 1969- . Annual. ISSN 0066-4049. ISBN 1-57387-145-1. $229 (2003 ed.). Hardcover.

Description: Although it focuses on North American programs, the *Annual Register* also describes a number of awards available to support activities abroad. For more information about the publication, see entry 235 in the "Grants for Individuals—General—United States" section of this bibliography.

Available from: Information Today, Inc., 143 Old Marlton Pike, Medford, NJ 08055-8750. *Telephone:* (609) 654-6266; *Fax:* (609) 654-4309; *E-mail:* custserv@infotoday.com

Web site: www.infotoday.com

552

Awards, Honors, and Prizes: An International Directory of Awards and Their Donors

21st ed. Ed. by Donna Batten. Farmington Hills, MI: Gale, 2002. 2v. ISSN 0196-6316. ISBN 0-7876-6223-2, volume 1; 0-7876-6224-0, volume 2. $275, volume 1; $305, volume 2. Hardcover.

Description: Volume two of this widely-used reference work provides comprehensive coverage of awards and prizes given in countries other than the United States or Canada. For more information about the publication, see entry 530 in the "Awards and Prizes—General—United States" section of this bibliography.

Available from: The Gale Group, P.O. Box 9187, Farmington Hills, MI 48333-9187. *Telephone:* (248) 699-GALE; *Toll-free:* (800) 877-GALE; *Fax:* (800) 414-5043; *E-mail:* galeord@gale.com

Web site: www.galegroup.com

553

Directory of Research Grants

Westport, CT: Oryx, 1975- . Annual. ISSN 0146-7336. ISBN 1-57356-570-9. $134.95 (2003 ed.). Paper.

Description: Although the emphasis is on U.S. and Canadian programs, some awards, scholarships, fellowships, and research grants sponsored by other countries are also included in this directory. For more information about the publication, see entry 238 in the "Grants for Individuals—General—United States" section of this bibliography.

Available from: Oryx Press, 88 Post Road West, Westport, CT 06881. *Telephone:* (602) 265-2651; *Toll-free:* (800) 279-6799; *Fax:* (800) 279-4663; *E-mail:* info@oryxpress.com

Web site: www.oryxpress.com

Awards & Prizes–Social Sciences–General

554

The Grants Register: The Complete Guide to Postgraduate Funding Worldwide

Ed. by Sara Hackwood. New York: Palgrave, 1969- . Annual. ISSN 0072-5471. ISBN 0-333-96474-8. $185 (2003 ed.). Hardcover.

Description: This annual directory describes awards, fellowships, and grants open to nationals of the United States, Canada, the United Kingdom, Ireland, Australia, New Zealand, South Africa, and the developing countries. For more information about the publication, see entry 265 in the "Grants for Individuals—General—International" section of this bibliography.

Available from: Palgrave, 175 Fifth Avenue, New York, NY 10010. *Telephone:* (212) 982-3900; *Toll-free:* (800) 221-7945; *Fax:* (212) 777-6359

Web site: www.palgrave-usa.com

555

GrantSelect

http://www.grantselect.com

Description: Updated daily and used to generate Oryx Press's print funding directories, GrantSelect identifies more than 10,000 awards and other funding opportunities sponsored by organizations and agencies in the United States and Canada (some of which can be used abroad). For more information about the database, see entry 247 in the "Grants for Individuals—General—United States" section of this bibliography.

Available from: Oryx Press, 88 Post Road West, Westport, CT 06881. *Telephone:* (602) 265-2651; *Toll-free:* (800) 279-6799; *Fax:* (800) 279-4663; *E-mail:* info@oryxpress.com

Web site: www.oryxpress.com

SOCIAL SCIENCES
General

556

GrantFinder: The Complete Guide to Postgraduate Funding Worldwide: Social Sciences

New York: Palgrave, 2000. 516p. ISBN 0-312-22894-5. $50. Hardcover.

How to Find Out About Financial Aid and Funding

Description: This guide describes awards, fellowships, and grants in the social sciences that are open to nationals of the United States, Canada, the United Kingdom, Ireland, Australia, New Zealand, South Africa, and the developing countries. For more information about the publication, see entry 269 in the "Grants for Individuals—Social Sciences—General" section of this bibliography.

Available from: Palgrave, 175 Fifth Avenue, New York, NY 10010. *Telephone:* (212) 982-3900; *Toll-free:* (800) 221-7945; *Fax:* (212) 777-6359

Web site: www.palgrave-usa.com

557

Money for Graduate Students in the Social & Behavioral Sciences

By Gail Ann Schlachter and R. David Weber. El Dorado Hills, CA: Reference Service Press, 1996- . Biennial. (RSP Graduate Funding Set). ISBN 1-58841-078-1. $42.50 (2003-2005 ed.). Comb binding.

Description: *Money for Graduate Students in the Social & Behavioral Sciences* identifies nearly 1,100 awards, loans, fellowships, and grants—representing millions of dollars—available to support study or research on the master's or doctoral level in those fields. For more information about the publication, see entry 127 in the "Scholarships, Fellowships & Loans—Social Sciences—General" section of this bibliography.

Available from: Reference Service Press, 5000 Windplay Drive, Suite 4, El Dorado Hills, CA 95762. *Telephone:* (916) 939-9620; *Fax:* (916) 939-9626; *E-mail:* findaid@aol.com

Web site: www.rspfunding.com

Law

558

University of Richmond School of Law Legal Essay Contest Catalogue

http://www.law.richmond.edu/essaycontests

Description: Prepared by the University of Richmond's School of Law, this is an excellent and up-to-date listing of approximately 100 law essay contests which can be accessed online (at no charge) by deadline, prize amount, and area of law—ranging from "Accounting and Law" to "World Affairs/World Order Under Law." Most entries are briefly annotated; the following information is provided: contact, links to the sponsor's web site, prize amount, essay topic, length requirements, and deadline. A number of other law schools also provide

Awards & Prizes–Social Sciences–Librarianship

lists of writing competitions but, while current, they tend to be less comprehensive; two of the best of these are: George Washington University Law School's Technology Law Moot Court and Writing Competitions (www.law.gwu.edu) and Saint Louis University School of Law's Writing Competitions (law.slu.edu).

Available from: University of Richmond, School of Law, Richmond, VA 23173. *Telephone:* (804) 289-8208; *Fax:* (804) 289-8992; *E-mail:* amajor@richmond.edu

Web site: www.law.richmond.edu

Librarianship

559

The Bowker Annual Library and Book Trade Almanac

Medford, NJ: Information Today, 1955- . Annual. ISSN 0068-0540. ISBN 1-57387-165-6. $199 (2003 ed.). Hardcover.

Description: This annual focuses on library and book trade developments. The specific aspects covered vary somewhat from year to year. Generally, each edition contains a section on book statistics, prices, and prizes as well as a list of library fellowships and up-to-date information on library legislation, funding, and grantmaking agencies. Previously published by Bowker (hence its name), the guide is now issued by Information Today.

Available from: Information Today, Inc., 143 Old Marlton Pike, Medford, NJ 08055-8750. *Telephone:* (609) 654-6266; *Fax:* (609) 654-4309; *E-mail:* custserv@infotoday.com

Web site: www.infotoday.com

HUMANITIES
General

560

Art Deadlines List

Ed. by Richard Gardner. Cambridge, MA: Art Deadlines List. Monthly. $36, paper; $18, e-mailed.

Description: Every month (either through the mail or e-mail), subscribers receive an international list of 600 to 900 competitions, contests (primarily), call for entries/papers, grants, scholarships, fellowships, residencies, internships, and other opportunities for artists, art educators, and art students of any age. Related areas are also covered, but to a lesser extent: poetry, writing, sculpture, multimedia, journalism, cartooning, photography, video, film, music, and dance. Some of the listed events take place only on the Internet. The information provided for each competition is often very brief and, reducing the reference value of the listing, the formal name of the competition is rarely given. The listing is also partially available in a free version, either on the web or as an e-mail sent to you monthly; but, many of the entries in the free version are events, contests, or job openings that the sponsors have paid to be included in the list.

Available from: Art Deadlines List, Box 381067, Harvard Square Station, Cambridge, MA 02238-1067. *Telephone:* (617) 576-1214; *Fax:* (617) 926-9519; *E-mail:* contact@artdeadlineslist.com

Web site: www.artdeadlineslist.com

561

Directory of Grants in the Humanities

Westport, CT: Oryx, 1986- . Annual. ISSN 0877-0551. ISBN 1-57356-567-9. $84.95 (2002-2003 ed.). Paper.

Description: This annual directory identifies awards, fellowships, and grants in literature, languages, history, anthropology, philosophy, ethics, religion, the fine arts, and performing arts (including painting, dance, photography, sculpture, music, drama, crafts, folklore, and mime). For more information about the publication, see entry 280 in the "Grants for Individuals—Humanities—General" section of this bibliography.

Available from: Oryx Press, 88 Post Road West, Westport, CT 06881. *Telephone:* (602) 265-2651; *Toll-free:* (800) 279-6799; *Fax:* (800) 279-4663; *E-mail:* info@oryxpress.com

Web site: www.oryxpress.com

562

GrantFinder: The Complete Guide to Postgraduate Funding Worldwide: Arts and Humanities

New York: Palgrave, 2000. 476p. ISBN 0-312-22893-7. $50. Hardcover.

Description: This guide describes awards, fellowships, and grants in the arts and humanities that are open to nationals of the United States, Canada, the United Kingdom, Ireland, Australia, New Zealand, South Africa, and the developing countries. For more information about the publication, see entry 281 in the "Grants for Individuals—Humanities—General" section of this bibliography.

Available from: Palgrave, 175 Fifth Avenue, New York, NY 10010. *Telephone:* (212) 982-3900; *Toll-free:* (800) 221-7945; *Fax:* (212) 777-6359

Web site: www.palgrave-usa.com

Awards & Prizes–Humanities–Applied Arts

563

GrantsInfo.com: Creative Arts and Humanities

http://www.arisnet.com/arts.html
Description: This inexpensive online searchable database provides information about regional, national, and international awards, fellowships, and grants in the humanities, performing arts, and visual arts. For more information about the site, see entry 282 in the "Grants for Individuals—Humanities—General" section of this bibliography.
Available from: Academic Research Information System, Inc., 2940 16th Street, Suite 314, San Francisco, CA 94103. *Telephone:* (415) 558-8133; *Fax:* (415) 558-8135; *E-mail:* arisnet@dnai.com
Web site: www.arisnet.com

564

Money for Graduate Students in the Arts & Humanities

By Gail Ann Schlachter and R. David Weber. El Dorado Hills, CA: Reference Service Press, 1996- . Biennial. (RSP Graduate Funding Set). ISBN 1-58841-076-5. $40 (2003-2005 ed.). Comb binding.
Description: This biennially-issued directory identifies 1,000 awards, grants, and fellowships available to support graduate work in the arts and humanities. For more information about the publication, see entry 143 in the "Scholarships, Fellowships & Loans—Humanities—General" section of this bibliography.
Available from: Reference Service Press, 5000 Windplay Drive, Suite 4, El Dorado Hills, CA 95762. *Telephone:* (916) 939-9620; *Fax:* (916) 939-9626; *E-mail:* findaid@aol.com
Web site: www.rspfunding.com

Applied Arts

565

Artweek

San Jose, CA: Artweek, 1970- . Monthly (10 issues/yr.). ISSN 0004-4121. $32/yr., individuals; $36/yr., institutions. Paper.
Description: Despite its name, this is now a monthly, not a weekly. The "Competitions" section of *Artweek* identifies approximately 50 art contests and festivals each month. International, national, and regional competitions are covered. Entries for each competition specify event name, address, telephone num-

ber, contact persons, deadline, location, dates, eligibility, media accepted, entry fees, awards offered, and whether or not juried. These lists are arranged by geographic restrictions, subdivided by deadline date.

Available from: Artweek, P.O. Box 26340, San Jose, CA 95159-6340. *Telephone:* (408) 288-7555; *Toll-free:* (800) 733-2916; *Fax:* (408) 288-7494; *E-mail:* info@artweek.com

Web site: www.artweek.com

566

Photographer's Market: Places to Sell Your Photographs

Ed. by Donna Poehner. Cincinnati, OH: Writer's Digest, 1978- . Annual. ISSN 0147-247X. ISBN 1-58297-121-8. $24.99 (2003 ed.). Paper.

Description: Included in each annual guide to the photography market is a short section (generally 50 to 100 entries) briefly describing contests "that are excellent for aspiring photographers who want to measure their talent and progress." The listings are arranged alphabetically by program title and contain the basic information needed to be able to contact the sponsoring organization and to determine the styles or media eligible for submission. Both national and international photography contests are represented.

Available from: Writer's Digest Books, 1507 Dana Avenue, Cincinnati, OH 45207. *Telephone:* (513) 531-2222; *Toll-free:* (800) 289-0963; *Fax:* (888) 590-4082

Web site: www.writersdigest.com

Communications and Mass Media

567

AV Market Place

Medford, NJ: Information Today, 1969- . Annual. ISSN 1044-0445. ISBN 1-57387-156-7. $195 (2003 ed.). Paper.

Description: The latest edition of this one-stop guide to the AV industry identifies more than 7,500 audio/video producers, distributors, and services, plus associations, film commissions, unions, and other organizations active in or serving the audio/video fields in the United States or Canada. The volume is divided into 10 sections. One of the sections, "Awards & Festivals," lists (in a dozen or so pages) events open to professional, student, educational, and industrial media products. The entries are arranged by program name and specify address, telephone number, media, award, date presented, deadline, and entry fee (if any). In the past, this publication was issued under the titles *Audio Video Market Place* and *Audiovisual Market Place*.

Awards & Prizes–Humanities–Communications & Mass Media

Available from: Information Today, Inc., 143 Old Marlton Pike, Medford, NJ 08055-8750. *Telephone:* (609) 654-6266; *Fax:* (609) 654-4309; *E-mail:* custserv@infotoday.com
Web site: www.infotoday.com

568

Editor & Publisher Journalism Awards and Fellowships Directory

New York: Editor & Publisher Company. Annual. ISSN 0013-094X. $15 (2002 ed.). Paper.

Description: Published each year as a special pull-out section in the last issue of *Editor & Publisher* (the "only independent weekly journal of newspapering"), this directory describes over 500 awards, scholarships, and fellowships available in the field of journalism. It can also be ordered separately, for $15. The focus is on programs for reporters, columnists, editors, cartoonists, and photographers. The entries are arranged alphabetically within four main sections: national and international awards; regional contests for media, honorary awards and citations; and fellowships, grants and scholarships. The following information is provided for each program: sponsoring organization, address (including e-mail addresses and web sites), requirements, and deadlines. Many entries also list the previous year's winners. A subject index completes the source.

Available from: Editor & Publisher, 770 Broadway, New York, NY 10003-9595. *Telephone:* (646) 654-5270; *Toll-free:* (800) 722-6658; *Fax:* (646) 654-5370; *E-mail:* edpub@mediainfo.com
Web site: www.mediainfo.com

569

Journalism Awards and Fellowships

http://ajr.org

Description: Described on the American Journalism Review's web site are nearly 100 awards, fellowships, and scholarships available to students and practicing journalists interested in careers in broadcast, radio, online, and print journalism. The entries are listed alphabetically by program type, are concisely described (generally a paragraph), and are linked—when appropriate—to the sponsors' web sites. The entire list is searchable by keyword. Many of the competitions are annual events; if the deadline has passed, this is noted and readers are "encouraged to prepare for next year." This information is also published in the October issue of *American Journalism Review* and can be purchased for $3.95 from the address listed below.

Available from: American Journalism Review, Attn: Awards Issue, University of Maryland, 1117 Journalism Building, College Park, MD 20742-7111. *Telephone:* (301) 405-8803; *Toll-free:* (800) 827-0771; *Fax:* (301) 405-8223
Web site: ajr.org

History

570

Grants, Fellowships, and Prizes of Interest to Historians

Ed. by Pillarisetti Sudhir, with Kim Foote and Jesse Erdheim. Washington, DC: American Historical Association, 1978-2000. Annual. ISSN 0275-830X. $10, members; $12, nonmembers (2000-2001 ed.). Paper.

Description: Last issued in 2000, this directory identifies and describes more than 450 awards, prizes, fellowships, and travel grants of interest to graduate students, postdoctoral researchers, and scholars in history. For more information about the listing and its online replacement, see entry 287 in the "Grants for Individuals—Humanities—History" section of this bibliography.

Available from: American Historical Association, 400 A Street, S.E., Washington, DC 20003-3889. *Telephone:* (202) 544-2422; *Fax:* (202) 544-8307; *E-mail:* pubsales@theaha.org

Web site: www.theaha.org

Literature

571

Children's Books: Awards & Prizes

http://www.cbcbooks.org/html/awards.html

Description: The Children's Book Council (CBC) has been publishing *Children's Books: Awards and Prizes* since 1969. The last edition of this standard work was issued in 1996 (ISBN 0-93363-303-3. $75). There are no plans to continue issuing the source in print form. Instead, beginning sometime in 2003, CBC will make available a revised and updated searchable online edition on its web site.

Available from: Children's Book Council, Inc., 12 West 37th Street, Second Floor, New York, NY 10018-7480. *Telephone:* (212) 966-1990; *Toll-free:* (800) 999-2160; *Fax:* (212) 966-2073; *E-mail:* staff@cbcbooks.org

Web site: www.cbcbooks.org

Awards & Prizes–Humanities–Literature

572

Children's Writer's & Illustrator's Market

Ed. by Alice Pope. Cincinnati, OH: Writer's Digest, 2002. ISSN 0897-9790. ISBN 1-58297-148-X. $24.99. Paper.

Description: Like the other Writer's Digest's "Market" books (for example, see *Writer's Market,* entry 582), one section of this guide lists contests and awards for children's writers and illustrators. More than 150 are covered each year. Brief descriptions are provided, specifying frequency, year established, purpose, submission requirements, monetary awards, and deadline dates. Contests listed in previous editions but not included in the current edition of *Children's Writer's & Illustrator's Market* can be identified in the General Index in the back of the book.

Available from: Writer's Digest Books, 1507 Dana Avenue, Cincinnati, OH 45207. *Telephone:* (513) 531-2222; *Toll-free:* (800) 289-0963; *Fax:* (888) 590-4082

Web site: www.writersdigest.com

573

The Complete Guide to Literary Contests

Comp. by William F. Fabio, James M. Plagianos, and Jerome Madramootoo. Amherst, NY: Prometheus Books, 1999- . Annual. ISSN 1532-0367. ISBN 1-57392-850-X. $30 (2001 ed.). Paper.

Description: Compiled by the national contest experts at Literary Fountain, this listing identifies awards for fiction, nonfiction, poetry, and plays in the United States and (beginning with the 2001 edition) in Canada. Prizes for both published and unpublished authors are covered—ranging from such major contests as the Pulitzer Prize to smaller-scale competitions, e.g., Pro Dogs National Charity and the Key West Theatre Festival. The following information is provided for each award: contact information, guidelines, rules, judging, entry forms, application procedures, and deadlines. Entries are arranged by sponsoring organization; there is no index. Despite its title, this guide is by no means "complete." Its program descriptions are fuller than *Literary Market Place* (see entry 577) or *Writer's Market* (entry 582), but the number of listings can't compare to *Grants and Awards Available to American Writers* (described in entry 575 in this section of the bibliography). Despite the fact that the directory was announced as an annual, no editions have been published since 2001.

Available from: Prometheus Books, 59 John Glenn Drive, Amherst, NY 14228-2197. *Telephone:* (716) 691-0133; *Toll-free:* (800) 421-0351; *Fax:* (716) 691-0137; *E-mail:* marketing@prometheusbooks.com

Web site: www.prometheusbooks.com

574

Dramatists Sourcebook: Complete Opportunities for Playwrights, Translators, Composers, Lyricists, and Librettists

Ed. by Kathy Sova, Samantha R. Healy, and Jennifer Sokolov. New York: Theatre Communications Group, 1982- . Annual. ISSN 0733-1606. ISBN 1-55936-217-0. $21.95 (2002-2003 ed.). Paper.

Description: While one half of this directory focuses on "script opportunities" (theaters willing to review unpublished plays), there are four separate sections that provide funding information: prizes (the most useful and complete), fellowships and grants, colonies and residencies, and emergency funds. The entries in these sections are arranged by sponsoring organization and subdivided by specific programs. The information presented includes eligibility, financial arrangements, purpose, application process, and deadlines. The *Sourcebook* also contains a short bibliography of useful publications, a handy submission calendar for the programs described, a special interests index, a sponsoring organization index, and several helpful essays in the prologue. Use the Theatre Communications Group's monthly magazine, *American Theatre,* to update the listings in the sourcebook; the "opportunities" column there announces new grants and contests as well as revised deadlines.

Available from: Theatre Communications Group, 355 Lexington Avenue, New York, NY 10017-6603. *Telephone:* (212) 697-5230; *Fax:* (212) 983-4847; *E-mail:* tcg@tcg.org
Web site: www.tcg.org

575

Grants and Awards Available to American Writers

New York: P.E.N. American Center, 1969- . Biennial. ISSN 0092-5268. ISBN 0-934638-20-9. $15 (2002-2003 ed.), individuals; $18, libraries and institutions. Paper.

Description: First published in 1969 as a pamphlet, this directory is now updated as a book every two years by P.E.N. American Center, an association of literary writers. Described in the directory are grants and awards, in excess of $500, available to American writers for use in the United States and abroad. According to the editors, this is the only reference work "which combines both domestic and foreign grants for American writers." The more than 1,000 entries listed here (104 new to this edition) are arranged alphabetically by organization and indexed by award title, type of literature, and sponsoring organization. There is no subject index. Each listing specifies purpose of the award, amount available, eligibility, and application procedures; also included are the sponsors' fax numbers, e-mail addresses, and web site locations. The programs covered are open to playwrights, poets, journalists, fiction writers, researchers, and scholars. In the past, competitions open solely to Canadian writers have also been included (in a separate section), but beginning with this edition, those programs have been excluded. To find information on programs open only to Canadian writers, check the booklet *Awards, Competitions, and Prizes* published by the Writers Union of Canada (24 Ryerson Avenue, Toronto, Ontario M5T 2P3). Since many of the awards described in *Grants and Awards Available to American Writers* require prior publication or are open only to nominees, this listing will prove most useful to writers with experience and reputation. To update the listing, use the *P.E.N. American Center Newsletter.*

Available from: P.E.N. American Center, 568 Broadway, Suite 401, New York, NY 10012-3225. *Telephone:* (212) 334-1660; *Fax:* (212) 334-2181; *E-mail:* pen@pen.org

Web site: www.pen.org

576

International Literary Market Place: The Directory of the International Book Publishing Industry

Medford, NJ: Information Today, 1965- . Annual. ISSN 0074-6827. ISBN 1-57387-144-3. $229 (2003 ed.), paper; $389, online.

Description: The current edition of this guide identifies more than 18,000 publishers, booksellers, and book-related organizations in 180 countries outside of the United States and Canada. Entries in each annual volume are arranged by country and subdivided by 15 subject headings (e.g., book trade organizations, remainder dealers, book clubs, major libraries, literary periodicals). One of these subsections in the directory covers international literary awards and prizes. There is also an Internet version ($389/yr.) that includes information from both this source and its companion publication, *Literary Market Place* (see entry 577). Subscribers can search the online database by company, personal name, keyword, places, subject categories, and more. Some of this information can also be accessed at the web site at no charge (but you will need to register).

Available from: Information Today, Inc., 143 Old Marlton Pike, Medford, NJ 08055-8750. *Telephone:* (609) 654-6266; *Fax:* (609) 654-4309; *E-mail:* custserv@infotoday.com

Web site: www.literarymarketplace.com

577

Literary Market Place: The Directory of the American Book Publishing Industry

Medford, NJ: Information Today, 1972- . Annual. ISSN 0000-1155. ISBN 1-57387-148-6. $299 (2003 ed.), paper; $389, online.

Description: Originally designed as a register of personnel in American publishing and allied fields, over the years the print directory has been expanded to include 16,000 entries in a dozen major sections (e.g., book trade events, book manufacturing, agents and agencies). One of the main sections focuses on "Literary Awards, Contests & Grants." Covered here are major awards given to books, authors, publishers, libraries, or librarians by various organizations; prizes that may be applied for by writing to the sponsor; and scholarships, fellowships, and grants-in-aid of interest to the American writer. There is also an Internet version ($389/yr.) that includes information from both this source and its companion publication, *International Literary Market Place* (see entry 576). You can search the database by company, personal name, keyword, places, subject categories, and more. Some of this information can also be accessed at the product's web site for no charge (but you will need to register).

Available from: Information Today, Inc., 143 Old Marlton Pike, Medford, NJ 08055-8750. *Telephone:* (609) 654-6266; *Fax:* (609) 654-4309; *E-mail:* custserv@infotoday.com

Web site: www.literarymarketplace.com

578

Novel & Short Story Writer's Market: Places to Sell Your Fiction

Ed. by Anne Bowling, with Nancy Breen. Cincinnati: Writer's Digest, 1994- . Annual. ISSN 0897-9812. ISBN 1-58297-147-1. $24.99 (2003 ed.). Paper.

Description: Like the other titles issued in the "Writer's Digest" family of publications, *Novel & Short Story Writer's Market* identifies thousands of markets and other opportunities for fiction writers. Each entry indicates the kinds of fiction that are needed, how much they pay, how to contact them, and how to submit. In addition, a separate chapter identifies more than 250 contests and awards for the short or long fiction writer. For each competition, the following information is provided: contact information, description of the competition, monetary awards, submission requirements, and deadline date. In the past, this title was issued as *Fiction Writer's Market*.

Available from: Writer's Digest Books, 1507 Dana Avenue, Cincinnati, OH 45207. *Telephone:* (513) 531-2222; *Toll-free:* (800) 289-0963; *Fax:* (888) 590-4082

Web site: www.writersdigest.com

579

Poet's Market

Ed. by Nancy Breen. Cincinnati: Writer's Digest, 1985- . Annual. ISSN 0883-5470. ISBN 1-58297-124-2. $24.99 (2003 ed.). Paper.

Description: Included here are detailed market analyses of more than 1,800 poetry publishers in the United States and Canada. In addition, the annual also contains a separate chapter listing 200 poetry and other literary contests and

Awards & Prizes–Humanities–Literature

awards. Each entry provides contact information, description of the competition, submission requirements, amount of the awards, and deadline. At the end of the chapter, there is a list of more than 200 "additional contests and awards" that are included elsewhere in the book. But, to find the descriptions of these additional contests, the reader must first identify the contest sponsor of interest in the list, go to the General Index in the back of the book, find on which page the contest is described, and turn there for information about the contest. Not very user friendly.

Available from: Writer's Digest Books, 1507 Dana Avenue, Cincinnati, OH 45207. *Telephone:* (513) 531-2222; *Toll-free:* (800) 289-0963; *Fax:* (888) 590-4082

Web site: www.writersdigest.com

580

Poets & Writers Magazine

New York: Poets & Writers Magazine, 1972- . Bimonthly. ISSN 0891-6136. $19.95/yr. Paper.

Description: Published six times a year, this is an excellent source of information on awards, fellowships, and grants for poets and other writers. For more information about the magazine and its online bimonthly issues, see entry 295 in the "Grants for Individuals—Humanities—Literature" section of this bibliography.

Available from: Poets & Writers Inc., 72 Spring Street, Suite 301, New York, NY 10012. *Telephone:* (212) 226-3586; *Fax:* (212) 226-3963

Web site: www.pw.org

581

The Writer's Handbook

Ed. by Elfrieda Abbe. Boston: The Writer, 1936- . Annual. ISSN 0084-2710. ISBN 0-87116-196-6. $29.95 (2003 ed.). Paper.

Description: In addition to identifying 3,300 markets for the sale of literary manuscripts, this annual presents a number of special lists, including a briefly annotated list of 150 awards and prizes open to American writers. Most of the competitions listed here are for unpublished manuscripts and usually offer publication in addition to cash prizes. To update this list, check the monthly "Prize Offerings" column in *The Writer* magazine ($28/yr.).

Available from: Kalmbach Publishing Company, 21027 Crossroads Circle, P.O. Box 1612, Waukesha, WI 53187-1612. *Toll-free:* (800) 533-6644

Web site: www.writermag.com

582

Writer's Market: Places to Sell What You Write

Ed. by Kirsten C. Holm. Cincinnati, OH: Writer's Digest, 1922- . Annual. ISSN 0084-2729. ISBN 1-58297-120-X, paper; 1-58297-125-0, CD-ROM. $29.99 (2003 ed.), paper; $49.99, CD-ROM; $2.99/month, online.

Description: Described in the latest edition are 8,000 places for authors to sell their books, articles, poetry, and features. Listings include the names and addresses of editors, how much they pay, their needs, and how to contact them. There are more than 900 new listings provided each year. In addition, annual volumes present interviews with magazine and book editors, tips on how to analyze the markets, a postal chart, and answers to frequently asked questions about copyright. A separate section lists by genre the most important literary contests and awards. Nearly 500 awards for writers of nonfiction, fiction, plays, poetry, screenplays, newspaper articles, and children's books are briefly described here. In addition to the print edition, there is an online subscription available at http://www.writersmarket.com ($2.99/month or $29.99/yr.) and an "electronic" version, entitled *Writer's Market Online,* that consists of a CD-ROM (Windows or Mac platform) and online access bundled with the print edition.

Available from: Writer's Digest Books, 1507 Dana Avenue, Cincinnati, OH 45207. *Telephone:* (513) 531-2222; *Toll-free:* (800) 289-0963; *Fax:* (888) 590-4082

Web site: www.writersdigest.com

583

The Young Writer's Guide to Getting Published

1st ed. Ed. by Kathy Henderson. Cincinnati, OH: Writer's Digest, 2002. ISBN 1-58297-057-2. $18.99. Paper.

Description: Stephen King published his first story at age 13. For other young hopefuls with writings they hope to publish, this book could be the key they need to get their words into print. The first edition of Henderson's guide (which replaces her *Market Guide for Young Writers*) is full of suggestions for formatting, query and cover letters, e-publishing, developing writing and marketing skills; it also includes information from now-famous people who were first published as young writers. One of the nine chapters in the guide focuses on contests (including information on contests to avoid); more than 100 markets and contests that accept submissions from young writers are described, including literary genre, contest rules, prizes, and remarks and suggestions from the editor. No other literary directory identifies, in any depth, contests aimed at young writers.

Available from: Writer's Digest Books, 1507 Dana Avenue, Cincinnati, OH 45207. *Telephone:* (513) 531-2222; *Toll-free:* (800) 289-0963; *Fax:* (888) 590-4082

Awards & Prizes–Humanities–Music

Web site: www.writersdigest.com

Music

584

Career Guide for Singers

6th ed. Washington, DC: Opera America, 2003. 294p. ISBN 0-885131-03-8. $40, members; $70, nonmembers. Paper.

Description: The sixth edition of Opera America's *Career Guide for Singers* identifies 1,000 opportunities for aspiring opera singers. The book is organized into five sections, one of which—describing 100 opera-related competitions and grants—relates directly to financial aid. The programs in that section are grouped alphabetically by program name within two divisions: 1) United States and Canada, and 2) Foreign (including Europe, Central and South America, and Australia). Each entry contains a brief description, specifying address, telephone number, e-mail address and web page, contact name, age limitations, residency requirements, prerequisites, application procedures, deadlines, application fee, competition dates and location, repertoire requirements, accompanist information, top prize awarded, total number and value of prizes awarded, and other details. These entries are indexed by sponsoring organization, geographic location, and deadline date. This publication represents a merger of two previously-issued publications: *A Singer's Guide to the Professional Opera Companies* and the Central Opera Service's *Career Guide for Young American Singers*. A bimonthly newsletter, *Career Guide Update*, provides current information on the auditions and deadlines listed in the last edition of the *Career Guide*.

Available from: Opera America, 1156 15th Street, Suite 810, Washington, DC 20005-1704. *Telephone:* (202) 293-4466; *Fax:* (202) 393-0735; *E-mail:* frontdesk@operaam.org

Web site: www.operaam.org

585

Dramatists Sourcebook: Complete Opportunities for Playwrights, Translators, Composers, Lyricists, and Librettists

Ed. by Kathy Sova, Samantha R. Healy, and Jennifer Sokolov. New York: Theatre Communications Group, 1982- . Annual. ISSN 0733-1606. ISBN 1-55936-217-0. $21.95 (2002-2003 ed.). Paper.

Description: There are a number of sections in this sourcebook that describe various financial aid programs for composers, lyricists, and librettists, including awards, fellowships, grants, colonies and residencies, and emergency funds. For

more information about the publication, see entry 574 in the "Awards and Prizes—Humanities—Literature" section of this bibliography.
Available from: Theatre Communications Group, 355 Lexington Avenue, New York, NY 10017-6603. *Telephone:* (212) 697-5230; *Fax:* (212) 983-4847; *E-mail:* tcg@tcg.org
Web site: www.tcg.org

586

Musical America: International Directory of the Performing Arts

East Windsor, NJ: Commonwealth Business Media, 1899- . Annual. ISBN 1-891131-26-5. $115 (2003 ed.). Paper or online.

Description: *Musical America* started in 1898 as a weekly newspaper covering drama, music, and the arts and became an annual in 1960. One of the sections in the latest edition of the 800-page directory, "Contests, Foundations, and Awards," provides brief information on awards, grants, and competitions in music and the performing arts. Similar information can also be found on the web site, which launched in 1999 and is divided into three sections: industry news, directory articles, and listings. In the industry news section, online subscribers can link directly to grantmakers and contest sponsors. The subscription price for the annual is $115. For the online version, users can subscribe annually ($115) or monthly ($11.95). Or, nonsubscribers can find (at no charge) information about contests, foundations, and awards in the listing section (click on the Listing Search).

Available from: Commonwealth Business Media, Inc., 400 Windsor Corporate Park, 50 Millstone Road, Suite 200, East Windsor, NJ 08520-1415. *Telephone:* (609) 371-7700; *Toll-free:* (800) 221-5488, ext. 7783; *Fax:* (609) 371-7879; *E-mail:* info@musicalamerica.com
Web site: www.musicalamerica.com

587

Opportunities in New Music

10th ed. New York: American Music Center, 2002. 49p. $15, members; $30, nonmembers. Spiral bound.

Description: This is a listing of ongoing American and foreign competitions, grants, awards, commissioning programs, workshops, calls for scores, and residencies. These programs are open to individuals or ensembles, in both the fields of jazz and contemporary concert music. Entries are grouped into four sections: opportunities without entry fees, opportunities requiring entry fees, artist colonies without application fees, and artist colonies requiring application fees. Entries are indexed by title and subject. The following information is provided for each: contact and telephone number, eligibility, application procedures, amount awarded, number awarded, and deadline date. In the past, this publica-

Awards & Prizes–Humanities–Performing Arts

tion was issued under the title *Organizations for Composers*. American Music Center members (only) can update the information in the 2002 edition by checking the listings in *Opportunity Update,* which is mailed without charge to members monthly.
Available from: American Music Center, 30 West 26th Street, Suite 1001, New York, NY 10010-2011. *Telephone:* (212) 366-5260; *Fax:* (212) 366-5265; *E-mail:* center@amc.net
Web site: www.amc.net

588

Songwriter's Market

Ed. by Ian C. Bessler. Cincinnati, OH: Writer's Digest, 1979- . Annual. ISSN 0161-5971. ISBN 0-89879-980-5. $24.99 (2003 ed.). Paper.

Description: *Songwriter's Market* was first introduced in 1978 as a guide for songwriters seeking markets for their songs. The bulk of the 2003 annual consists of 2,000 markets seeking songs or songwriters' services. Listings feature the name and address of the person to contact, special requirements, and payment arrangements. In addition, there is a separate section on opportunities and services available to songwriters. One of the subsections included here covers relevant contests and awards. The contests listed (generally 50 or more each year) encompass all types of music and all levels of competition. Entries indicate purpose, requirements, and awards offered for each of the contests.

Available from: Writer's Digest Books, 1507 Dana Avenue, Cincinnati, OH 45207. *Telephone:* (513) 531-2222; *Toll-free:* (800) 289-0963; *Fax:* (888) 590-4082

Web site: www.writersdigest.com

Performing Arts

589

Musical America: International Directory of the Performing Arts

East Windsor, NJ: Commonwealth Business Media, 1899- . Annual. ISBN 1-891131-26-5. $115 (2003 ed.). Paper or online.

Description: One of the sections in both the print and online versions of the directory identifies contests and awards in music and the performing arts. For more information about the listing, see entry 586 in the "Awards and Prizes—Humanities—Music" section of this bibliography.

Available from: Commonwealth Business Media, Inc., 400 Windsor Corporate Park, 50 Millstone Road, Suite 200, East Windsor, NJ 08520-1415. *Tele-*

phone: (609) 371-7700; *Toll-free:* (800) 221-5488, ext. 7783; *Fax:* (609) 371-7879; *E-mail:* info@musicalamerica.com
Web site: www.musicalamerica.com

Visual Arts

590

Artweek

San Jose, CA: Artweek, 1970- . Monthly (10 issues/yr.). ISSN 0004-4121. $32/yr., individuals; $36/yr., institutions. Paper.

Description: The "Competitions" section of *Artweek* identifies approximately 50 international, national, and regional art contests and festivals each month. For more information about the publication, see entry 565 in the "Awards and Prizes—Humanities—Applied Arts" section of this bibliography.

Available from: Artweek, P.O. Box 26340, San Jose, CA 95159-6340. *Telephone:* (408) 288-7555; *Toll-free:* (800) 733-2916; *Fax:* (408) 288-7494; *E-mail:* info@artweek.com
Web site: www.artweek.com

SCIENCES

General

591

GrantFinder: The Complete Guide to Postgraduate Funding Worldwide: Sciences

New York: Palgrave, 2000. 468p. ISBN 0-312-22895-3. $50. Hardcover.

Description: This guide describes awards, fellowships, and grants in the sciences that are open to nationals of the United States, Canada, the United Kingdom, Ireland, Australia, New Zealand, South Africa, and the developing countries. For more information about the publication, see entry 306 in the "Grants for Individuals—Sciences—General" section of this bibliography.

Available from: Palgrave, 175 Fifth Avenue, New York, NY 10010. *Telephone:* (212) 982-3900; *Toll-free:* (800) 221-7945; *Fax:* (212) 777-6359
Web site: www.palgrave-usa.com

Biological Sciences

592

Money for Graduate Students in the Biological & Health Sciences

By Gail Ann Schlachter and R. David Weber. El Dorado Hills, CA: Reference Service Press, 2001- . Biennial. (RSP Graduate Funding Set). ISBN 1-58841-075-7. $42.50 (2003-2005 ed.). Comb binding.

Description: Described here are more than 1,100 awards, grants, fellowships, and loans set aside just for students interested in working on a master's or doctoral degree in the biological or health sciences. For more information about the publication, see entry 174 in the "Scholarships, Fellowships & Loans—Sciences—Biological Sciences" section of this bibliography.

Available from: Reference Service Press, 5000 Windplay Drive, Suite 4, El Dorado Hills, CA 95762. *Telephone:* (916) 939-9620; *Fax:* (916) 939-9626; *E-mail:* findaid@aol.com

Web site: www.rspfunding.com

Earth Sciences

593

Money for Graduate Students in the Physical & Earth Sciences

By Gail Ann Schlachter and R. David Weber. El Dorado Hills, CA: Reference Service Press, 2001- . Biennial. (RSP Graduate Funding Set). ISBN 1-58841-077-3. $35 (2003-2005 ed.). Comb binding.

Description: Described here are 800 awards, grants, fellowships, and loans set aside just for students interested in working on a master's or doctoral degree in the earth or physical sciences. For more information about the publication, see entry 190 in the "Scholarships, Fellowships & Loans—Sciences—Physical Sciences" section of this bibliography.

Available from: Reference Service Press, 5000 Windplay Drive, Suite 4, El Dorado Hills, CA 95762. *Telephone:* (916) 939-9620; *Fax:* (916) 939-9626; *E-mail:* findaid@aol.com

Web site: www.rspfunding.com

Health and Medical Sciences

594

Directory of Biomedical and Health Care Grants

Westport, CT: Oryx, 1985- . Annual. ISSN 0883-5330. ISBN 1-57356-569-5. $84.50 (2003 ed.). Paper.

Description: The current edition of this directory identifies 3,000 awards, fellowships, and grants in the biomedical and health care areas. For more information about the publication, see entry 313 in the "Grants for Individuals—Sciences—Health and Medical Sciences" section of this bibliography.

Available from: Oryx Press, 88 Post Road West, Westport, CT 06881. *Telephone:* (602) 265-2651; *Toll-free:* (800) 279-6799; *Fax:* (800) 279-4663; *E-mail:* info@oryxpress.com

Web site: www.oryxpress.com

595

Grantfinder: The Complete Guide to Postgraduate Funding Worldwide: Medicine

New York: Palgrave, 2000. 394p. ISBN 0-312-22896-1. $50. Hardcover.

Description: This guide describes prizes, fellowships, and grants in the medical sciences that are open to nationals of the United States, Canada, the United Kingdom, Ireland, Australia, New Zealand, South Africa, and the developing countries. For more information about the publication, see entry 315 in the "Grants for Individuals—Sciences—Health and Medical Sciences" section of this bibliography.

Available from: Palgrave, 175 Fifth Avenue, New York, NY 10010. *Telephone:* (212) 982-3900; *Toll-free:* (800) 221-7945; *Fax:* (212) 777-6359

Web site: www.palgrave-usa.com

596

Money for Graduate Students in the Biological & Health Sciences

By Gail Ann Schlachter and R. David Weber. El Dorado Hills, CA: Reference Service Press, 2001- . Biennial. (RSP Graduate Funding Set). ISBN 1-58841-075-7. $42.50 (2003-2005 ed.). Comb binding.

Description: Described here are more than 1,100 awards, grants, fellowships, and loans set aside just for students interested in working on a master's or doctoral degree in the health or biological sciences. For more information about

Awards & Prizes–Sciences–Physical Sciences

the publication, see entry 174 in the "Scholarships, Fellowships & Loans—Sciences—Biological Sciences" section of this bibliography.
Available from: Reference Service Press, 5000 Windplay Drive, Suite 4, El Dorado Hills, CA 95762. *Telephone:* (916) 939-9620; *Fax:* (916) 939-9626; *E-mail:* findaid@aol.com
Web site: www.rspfunding.com

Physical Sciences

597

Money for Graduate Students in the Physical & Earth Sciences

By Gail Ann Schlachter and R. David Weber. El Dorado Hills, CA: Reference Service Press, 2001- . Biennial. (RSP Graduate Funding Set). ISBN 1-58841-077-3. $35 (2003-2005 ed.). Comb binding.
Description: Described here are 800 awards, grants, fellowships, and loans set aside just for students interested in working on a master's or doctoral degree in the physical or earth sciences. For more information about the publication, see entry 190 in the "Scholarships, Fellowships & Loans—Sciences—Physical Sciences" section of this bibliography.
Available from: Reference Service Press, 5000 Windplay Drive, Suite 4, El Dorado Hills, CA 95762. *Telephone:* (916) 939-9620; *Fax:* (916) 939-9626; *E-mail:* findaid@aol.com
Web site: www.rspfunding.com

SPECIAL POPULATION GROUPS
Ethnic Groups

598

Financial Aid for African Americans

By Gail Ann Schlachter and R. David Weber. El Dorado Hills, CA: Reference Service Press, 1997- . Biennial. (Minority Funding Set). ISBN 1-58841-068-4. $40 (2003-2005 ed.). Hardcover.
Description: Described here are 1,500 awards, scholarships, fellowships, grants, loans, and internships—representing billions of dollars—available specifically to Black/African Americans. For more information about the publication, see entry 198 in the "Scholarships, Fellowships & Loans—Special Population Groups—Ethnic Groups" section of this bibliography.

How to Find Out About Financial Aid and Funding

Available from: Reference Service Press, 5000 Windplay Drive, Suite 4, El Dorado Hills, CA 95762. *Telephone:* (916) 939-9620; *Fax:* (916) 939-9626; *E-mail:* findaid@aol.com
Web site: www.rspfunding.com

599

Financial Aid for Asian Americans

By Gail Ann Schlachter and R. David Weber. El Dorado Hills, CA: Reference Service Press, 1997- . Biennial. (Minority Funding Set). ISBN 1-58841-069-2. $37.50 (2003-2005 ed.). Hardcover.

Description: More than 1,000 awards, fellowships, scholarships, loans, grants, and internships set aside for Asian Americans are described here. For more information about the publication, see entry 199 in the "Scholarships, Fellowships & Loans—Special Population Groups—Ethnic Groups" section of this bibliography.

Available from: Reference Service Press, 5000 Windplay Drive, Suite 4, El Dorado Hills, CA 95762. *Telephone:* (916) 939-9620; *Fax:* (916) 939-9626; *E-mail:* findaid@aol.com
Web site: www.rspfunding.com

600

Financial Aid for Hispanic Americans

By Gail Ann Schlachter and R. David Weber. El Dorado Hills, CA: Reference Service Press, 1997- . Biennial. (Minority Funding Set). ISBN 1-58841-070-6. $40 (2003-2005 ed.). Hardcover.

Description: This directory identifies nearly 1,400 awards, fellowships, scholarships, loans, grants, and internships available to Hispanic Americans, including Mexican Americans, Puerto Ricans, Cuban Americans, and others of Latin American origin. For more information about the publication, see entry 200 in the "Scholarships, Fellowships & Loans—Special Population Groups—Ethnic Groups" section of this bibliography.

Available from: Reference Service Press, 5000 Windplay Drive, Suite 4, El Dorado Hills, CA 95762. *Telephone:* (916) 939-9620; *Fax:* (916) 939-9626; *E-mail:* findaid@aol.com
Web site: www.rspfunding.com

Awards & Prizes–Special Population Groups–Military, Etc.

601

Financial Aid for Native Americans

By Gail Ann Schlachter and R. David Weber. El Dorado Hills, CA: Reference Service Press, 1997- . Biennial. (Minority Funding Set). ISBN 1-58841-071-4. $40 (2003-2005 ed.). Hardcover.

Description: Detailed information on nearly 1,500 awards, grants, scholarships, fellowships, loans, and internships open to American Indians, Native Alaskans, and Native Pacific Islanders (including Native Hawaiians and Samoans) is presented in this directory. For more information about the publication, see entry 201 in the "Scholarships, Fellowships & Loans—Special Population Groups—Ethnic Groups" section of this bibliography.

Available from: Reference Service Press, 5000 Windplay Drive, Suite 4, El Dorado Hills, CA 95762. *Telephone:* (916) 939-9620; *Fax:* (916) 939-9626; *E-mail:* findaid@aol.com

Web site: www.rspfunding.com

Military Personnel and Veterans

602

Financial Aid for Veterans, Military Personnel, and Their Dependents

By Gail Ann Schlachter and R. David Weber. El Dorado Hills, CA: Reference Service Press, 1988- . Biennial. ISSN 0896-7792. ISBN 1-58841-043-9. $40 (2002-2004 ed.). Hardcover.

Description: More than 1,100 awards, fellowships, scholarships, loans, and grants-in-aid set aside for those with ties to the military are described in the latest edition (2002-2004) of this directory. For more information about the publication, see entry 216 in the "Scholarships, Fellowships & Loans—Special Population Groups—Military Personnel and Veterans" section of this bibliography.

Available from: Reference Service Press, 5000 Windplay Drive, Suite 4, El Dorado Hills, CA 95762. *Telephone:* (916) 939-9620; *Fax:* (916) 939-9626; *E-mail:* findaid@aol.com

Web site: www.rspfunding.com

Persons with Disabilities

603

Financial Aid for the Disabled and Their Families

By Gail Ann Schlachter and R. David Weber. El Dorado Hills, CA: Reference Service Press, 1988- . Biennial. ISSN 0898-9222. ISBN 1-58841-042-0. $40 (2002-2004 ed.). Hardcover.

Description: This is the only comprehensive and up-to-date listing of awards, grants-in-aid, scholarships, fellowships, internships, and loans for individuals with disabilities and their families. For more information about the publication, see entry 222 in the "Scholarships, Fellowships & Loans—Special Population Groups—Persons with Disabilities" section of this bibliography.

Available from: Reference Service Press, 5000 Windplay Drive, Suite 4, El Dorado Hills, CA 95762. *Telephone:* (916) 939-9620; *Fax:* (916) 939-9626; *E-mail:* findaid@aol.com

Web site: www.rspfunding.com

Religious Groups

604

Financial Support for Jewish College Students

http://www.thebagel.org/financial_aid/matcher.php

Description: This searchable database identifies more than 100 awards, loans, scholarships, fellowships, and internships available to Jewish students for study, research, or other activities in the United States or abroad (particularly in Israel). For more information about the publication, see entry 227 in the "Scholarships, Fellowships & Loans—Special Population Groups—Religious Groups" section of this bibliography.

Available from: Los Angeles Hillel Council, 6505 Wilshire Boulevard, Suite 450, Los Angeles, CA 90048. *Telephone:* (323) 761-8555; *Fax:* (323) 761-8566; *E-mail:* mail@lahillel.org

Web site: www.lahillel.org

Awards & Prizes–Special Population Groups–Women

Women

605

Directory of Financial Aids for Women

By Gail Ann Schlachter and R. David Weber. El Dorado Hills, CA: Reference Service Press, 1978- . Biennial. ISSN 0732-5215. ISBN 1-58841-067-6. $45 (2003-2005 ed.). Hardcover.

Description: This is the only extensive and regularly updated listing of awards/prizes, loans, grants, fellowships, scholarships, and internships available primarily or exclusively to women and women's organizations. For more information about the publication, see entry 232 in the "Scholarships, Fellowships & Loans—Special Population Groups—Women" section of this bibliography.

Available from: Reference Service Press, 5000 Windplay Drive, Suite 4, El Dorado Hills, CA 95762. *Telephone:* (916) 939-9620; *Fax:* (916) 939-9626; *E-mail:* findaid@aol.com

Web site: www.rspfunding.com

Internships

Internships provide work experience opportunities and often monetary support for students (high school through postdoctoral), professionals, and other workers who are interested in short-term placements. Some internships can be held while pursuing other activities (e.g., school, job), but most of the programs listed in commercially available directories require a concentrated commitment for a limited time period (one month, a summer, an intersession, a semester, or a year). Many students find internships to be an excellent source of financial assistance. Included in this chapter are 76 print, electronic, and Internet resources listing work experience programs. Of these, 36 are general in coverage, 5 focus on the social sciences, 14 cover the humanities, 9 deal with the sciences, and 12 are aimed at special population groups. If you are looking for a specific internship resource and you do not find it in this chapter, be sure to check the Title Index to see if it is covered elsewhere in the guide.

GENERAL

United States

606

The Back Door Guide to Short-Term Job Adventures: Internships, Extraordinary Experiences, Seasonal Jobs, Volunteering, Work Abroad

3rd ed. By Michael Landes. Berkeley, CA: Ten Speed Press, 2003. 328p. ISBN 1-58008-449-4. $21.95. Paper.

Description: Written by the former associate director for internships and cooperative education at California State University, Chico, this directory describes approximately 1,000 internships, seasonal jobs, volunteer assignments, work abroad opportunities, and what the author labels "extraordinary experiences" in the United States and other countries. The entries range from working at a dance festival in Massachusetts to teaching English to students in Africa. Entries provide information on application requirements, work assignments, location, duration, compensation, etc. Some "adventures" offer compensation and/or room and board; others do not. Programs geared specifically to college students or recent graduates are marked. The source—which is written in a breezy style—is peppered with "motivational" messages from the author. Some of the listings included here are also available on the Internet, at backdoorjobs.com (although the site is more promotional than informational).

Available from: Ten Speed Press, P.O. Box 7123, Berkeley, CA 94707. *Telephone:* (510) 559-1632; *Toll-free:* (800) 841-BOOK; *Fax:* (510) 559-1629; *E-mail:* order@tenspeed.com
Web site: www.tenspeed.com

607

Best 109 Internships

By Mark Oldman and Samer Hamadeh. New York: Princeton Review (dist. by Random House), 1994- . Annual. ISSN 1073-5801. ISBN 0-375-76319-8. $21 (9th ed.). Paper.

Description: There's nothing new about supervised practical experience. References to apprenticeships can be found as early as 2100 B.C. in the Code of Hammurabi. Internships continue to be a popular practice. According to the National Society for Experiential Education, one third of all college students complete an internship before graduation. In their junior year in college, the authors of this guide were searching for internships themselves. They found the existing internship directories lacking. After they graduated, they conducted surveys, interviews, and onsite visits to identify the "best" internships available.

How to Find Out About Financial Aid and Funding

Based on the authors' *Internship Bible* (see entry 619), the latest edition (2003) is intended to be selective rather than comprehensive; it describes in detail the "top" 109 paid and unpaid internships in America. The number of interns selected by each of these "top" programs varies greatly, from under 10 to as many as 1,000. Each entry provides information on selectivity, compensation (from nothing to $1,200 or more per week), quality of life, locations, field, duration, prerequisites, deadlines, job description, selection, application procedure, overview, and contact. The internship profiles are arranged alphabetically by employer. An appendix groups internships by a number of interesting categories: highest compensation, most selective, etc. Formerly, the guide was published as *America's Top 100 Internships, America's Top Internships,* and the *Best 106 Internships.*
Available from: Random House, 400 Hahn Road, Westminster, MD 21157. *Telephone:* (212) 751-2600; *Toll-free:* (800) 733-3000
Web site: www.randomhouse.com/princetonreview

608

The College Board Scholarship Handbook

New York: College Board, 1998- . Annual. ISBN 0-87447-684-4. $25.95 (2003 ed.). Paper with CD-ROM.
Description: Covered here are more than 2,300 funding opportunities, including private, federal, and state scholarships, grants, internships, and loans. For more information about the publication, see entry 11 in the "Scholarships, Fellowships & Loans—General—United States" section of this bibliography.
Available from: College Board Publications, Box 886, New York, NY 19191-0886. *Telephone:* (212) 713-8000; *Fax:* (212) 713-8143; *Toll-free:* (800) 323-7155
Web site: www.collegeboard.com

609

Collegeboard.com Scholarship Search

http://www.collegeboard.com
Description: Available without charge on the College Board's web site, this database describes 2,300 internships, awards, loans, scholarships, and other types of financial aid sponsored by national, state, and private sources. For more information about the service, see entry 17 in the "Scholarships, Fellowships & Loans—General—United States" section of this bibliography.
Available from: College Board Publications, Box 886, New York, NY 19191-0886. *Telephone:* (212) 713-8000; *Toll-free:* (800) 323-7155; *Fax:* (212) 713-8143; *E-mail:* expan@collegeboard.org
Web site: www.collegeboard.org

Internships–General–United States

610

Connections: A Directory of Volunteer Opportunities

http://www.pallotticenter.org
Description: Prior to 2002, this free annual directory was issued only in print. Beginning with the 2002 edition, the listing is available both in a print version (latest edition: *Connections 2003*) and on the Center's web site. There are three ways to search the online listing: 1) click on the name of the Catholic-based volunteer agency that interests you, 2) search among the programs to identify those that accept medical personnel, or 3) answer a few personal questions (e.g., length of service, geographic areas of interest) and receive a list of opportunities that match your answers. Although you wouldn't know it from its title, many of the opportunities described in *Connections* provide stipends, housing allowances, transportation, and other monetary benefits to individuals interested in working with volunteer service organizations in the United States or abroad. Program entries specify purpose, geographic areas of service, term of service, personnel needed, ages, eligibility requirements, benefits given to the participant, and application deadline.

Available from: St. Vincent Pallotti Center for Apostolic Development, 415 Michigan Avenue, N.E., Washington, DC 20017-1518. *Telephone:* (202) 529-3330; *Fax:* (202) 529-0911; *E-mail:* pallotti01@aol.com

Web site: www.pallotticenter.org

611

Directory of Research Grants

Westport, CT: Oryx, 1975- . Annual. ISSN 0146-7336. ISBN 1-57356-570-9. $134.95 (2003 ed.). Paper.

Description: Internships, awards, scholarships, fellowships, and loans are described in this annual directory, in addition to research grants. For more information about the publication, see entry 238 in the "Grants for Individuals—General—United States" section of this bibliography.

Available from: Oryx Press, 88 Post Road West, Westport, CT 06881. *Telephone:* (602) 265-2651; *Toll-free:* (800) 279-6799; *Fax:* (800) 279-4663; *E-mail:* info@oryxpress.com

Web site: www.oryxpress.com

612

FASTaid

http://www.fastaid.com

How to Find Out About Financial Aid and Funding

Description: Thousands of financial aid opportunities (including internships) that are open to students from high school through postdoctorate are briefly described here. For more information about the service, see entry 27 in the "Scholarships, Fellowships & Loans—General—United States" section of this bibliography.

Available from: National Scholarship Research Service, 5577 Skyland Boulevard, Suite 6A, Santa Rosa, CA 95403. *Toll-free:* (800) 432-3782; *Fax:* (707) 546-6785; *E-mail:* editor@www.fastaid.com

Web site: www.fastaid.com

613

The Financial Aid Book

3rd ed. Prep. by Student Financial Services. Seattle: Perpetual Press, 1999. 601p. ISBN 1-881199-01-0. $24.95. Paper.

Description: While scholarships make up the bulk of the 3,300 entries in this directory, 600 internships, fellowships, and research funding programs are also briefly described. For more information about the publication, see entry 31 in the "Scholarships, Fellowships & Loans—General—United States" section of this bibliography.

Available from: Perpetual Press, P.O. Box 3956, Seattle, WA 98124. *Toll-free:* (800) 807-3030; *Fax:* (707) 221-1418; *E-mail:* sales@perpetualpress.com

Web site: www.FinancialAidFinder.com

614

Gaining the Co-op Edge: A Student Guide to Cooperative Education

Boston: National Commission for Cooperative Education, 1972. Irreg. Unpaged. Free. Paper.

Description: This free publication, available from the National Commission for Cooperative Education, identifies more than 300 community colleges, colleges, and universities that offer cooperative education. These programs provide students with the opportunity of alternating periods of off-campus career-related work with on-campus academic study. Very brief information on the co-op programs offered at each school is provided, along with links to the college's web site. The latest edition of the guide (2000) is also available on the Commission's web site; a 2002-3 edition has been announced there but is not yet available. Two other web sites that will help students interested in cooperative education are offered by the Cooperative Education & Internship Association (http://www.ceiainc.org) and the Cooperative Education Network (http://www.co-op.uc.edu/home), both of which provide links to co-op programs. Previously, similar pamphlets were issued by the Commission under the titles *Co-op Education Undergraduate Program Directory, Undergraduate Programs of Cooperative Education,* and *Co-op College Roster.*

Internships–General–United States

Available from: National Commission for Cooperative Education, 360 Huntington Avenue, 384CP, Boston, MA 02115-5096. *Telephone:* (617) 373-3770; *Fax:* (617) 373-3463; *E-mail:* ncce@lynx.neu.edu
Web site: www.co-op.edu

615

Get Outside!

Washington, DC: American Hiking Society, 2002. 41p. $12.95. Paper.
Description: If you like working outdoors and are looking for an unusual internship opportunity, this listing will interest you. Published annually by the American Hiking Society, this directory identifies volunteer work assignments and internships (many of which are paid) on public lands. These range from trail maintenance, cave inventory, and recreational planning to campground hosts and curatorial assistance. Until 2002, the directory was published under the title *Helping Out in the Outdoors: Your Source for Outdoor Volunteer Opportunities*. Entries in *Get Outside* are arranged alphabetically by states or regions and indexed by type of activity. Each entry provides the following information: location, work assignment, benefits, and contact address This information, which is compiled in cooperation with the Bureau of Land Management, is also available to be searched by state online (at no charge), in the society's Hiker's Info Center (http://www.americanhiking.org/infocenter/index.html).

Available from: American Hiking Association, 1422 Fenwick Lane, Silver Spring, MD 20910. *Telephone:* (301) 565-6704; *Toll-free:* (800) 972-8608; *Fax:* (301) 565-6714; *E-mail:* info@americanhiking.org
Web site: www.americanhiking.org

616

GrantSelect

http://www.grantselect.com
Description: Updated daily and used to generate Oryx Press's print funding directories, GrantSelect identifies more than 10,000 internships and other opportunities sponsored by organizations and agencies in the United States and other countries. For more information about the database, see entry 247 in the "Grants for Individuals—General—United States" section of this bibliography.

Available from: Oryx Press, 88 Post Road West, Westport, CT 06881. *Telephone:* (602) 265-2651; *Toll-free:* (800) 279-6799; *Fax:* (800) 279-4663; *E-mail:* info@oryxpress.com
Web site: www.oryxpress.com

617

GrantsInfo.com: Student Funding Sources

http://www.arisnet.com/newstu.html
Description: This site provides both undergraduate and graduate students with information on internships, traineeships, awards, grants, scholarships, and fellowships in the arts and sciences, including creative arts, humanities, social sciences, natural sciences, and biomedical sciences. For more information about the site, see entry 44 in the "Scholarships, Fellowships & Loans—General—United States" section of this bibliography.
Available from: Academic Research Information System, Inc., 2940 16th Street, Suite 314, San Francisco, CA 94103. *Telephone:* (415) 558-8133; *Fax:* (415) 558-8135; *E-mail:* arisnet@dnai.com
Web site: www.arisnet.com

618

idealist.org

http://www.idealist.org
Description: This site offers information on volunteer opportunities (nearly 6,500 volunteer projects) and internships (opportunities at nearly 2,000 organizations) in the U.S. and abroad. For more information about the listing, see entry 635 in the "Internships—General—International" section of this bibliography.
Available from: Action Without Borders, Inc., 79 Fifth Avenue, 17th Floor, New York, NY 10003. *Telephone:* (212) 843-3973; *Fax:* (212) 564-3377; *E-mail:* info@idealist.org
Web site: www.idealist.org

619

The Internship Bible

By Mark Oldman and Samer Hamadeh. New York: Princeton Review (dist. by Random House), 2003. 656p. ISBN 0-375-76307-4. $25. Paper.
Description: Written by Mark Oldman and Samer Hamadeh, who have trademarked themselves as the "Internship Informants," this annual listing of internships is intended to be inclusive (for an abridged list of the "best" internships included here, see the authors' *Best 109 Internships,* described in entry 607). More than 1,000 organizations offering internships in 100 different fields are identified, including Intel Corporation, the Metropolitan Museum of Art, and the TV program Nightline. The following information is provided for each: how selective the internship is, the compensation (both paid and unpaid programs are covered) and perks, application process, and deadline. A fun touch: inter-

Internships–General–United States

views with such famous former interns as Jodie Foster, Tipper Gore, and professional golfer Tom Lehman are included. This is one of the two most comprehensive sources of information on internships available in the United States (the other is *Peterson's Internships,* entry 623). Similar information can also be found on Princeton Review's web site; click on "Careers" and then on "Find an Internship." There you'll be able to search for internships, at no charge, by location, career, field, who's eligible to apply, and more. Each entry provides links to the sponsor as well as the same kind of information presented in the *Internship Bible.*

Available from: Random House, 400 Hahn Road, Westminster, MD 21157. *Telephone:* (212) 751-2600; *Toll-free:* (800) 733-3000

Web site: www.randomhouse.com/princetonreview

620

InternshipPrograms.com

http://www.internshipprograms.com

Description: By far, this is the most extensive listing of internship opportunities available in cyberspace today. More than 2,000 internship opportunities (offering more than 200,000 positions) are described in considerable detail in this database, which is updated daily or so. The database can be browsed within categories (e.g., law, journalism) by company or by region. Each entry begins with a section that identifies the employer's web site, application address, phone and fax numbers, and deadline date(s). This is followed by a lengthy description of internship opportunities at that location, which is written by the employing agency. Generally, these descriptions contain more information than can be found in printed internships directories, like *Peterson's Internships* (see entry 623); this includes URLs for electronic resumes and campus recruiting schedules, deadline dates, eligibility requirements, programs features, compensation package, majors recruited, geographic locations, and type of work assignments. Many of the entries connect directly to the employer's web site, where interested students can complete internship applications online. Only opportunities in the United States are covered.

Available from: WetFeet, 609 Mission Street, Suite 400, San Francisco, CA 94105. *Telephone:* (415) 284-7900; *Toll-free:* (800) 926-4JOB; *Fax:* (415) 284-7910

Web site: www.wetfeet.com

621

Internships-USA.com

http://www.internships-usa.com

Description: Internships-USA offers an Internet subscription to a database with information on more than 3,000 organizations offering internships to col-

333

lege and professional students. The online service costs $200 per year and provides unlimited access to the database plus the user's choice of any four of the 13 internship books published by Career Education Institutes: *Internships in International Affairs* (internships in the United States and abroad with international policy organizations, government agencies, international trade organizations, nongovernmental organizations, and relief organizations); *History Internship Book* (internship opportunities with historical sites, museums, historic research organizations, state archives, historical preservations groups, or living history programs); *Human Rights Internship Book* (internships with 150 organizations working for democracy and justice throughout the world); *Resort Internship and Seasonal Employment Guide* (information on positions at 250 resorts nationwide); *Sports Internship Directory* (250 internship programs with sports teams, arenas, leagues, college athletic departments, sports media, sports agents, sports lawyers, and sports marketing companies); *Women's Rights Internship Book* (internships with organizations working for women's rights nationwide, including advocacy groups, domestic violence prevention programs, human rights commissions, and reproductive health organizations); *Internships with America's Advertising Agencies* (internships with the advertising industry, including marketing, public relations, communications, and graphics); *Internships with America's Top Companies* (internships at 100 of the Fortune 500 corporations); *Congressional Internship Book* (internships with members of Congress, Congressional committees, and state or district offices serving constituents); *Big Green Internship Book* (internships at 300 conservation groups, wildlife preserves, environmental advocacy organizations, environmental education centers, and nature centers nationwide); *Media Internship Guide* (internships at 180 organizations in the media, including journalism, broadcasting, English, graphic arts, web design, and marketing); *Complete Guide to Seasonal State Park Employment* (identifies 20,000 positions in the nation's state parks); and *Washington Internships in Law and Policy* (internships at 250 organizations interested in policy, the environment, government reform, criminal justice, international issues, and human rights). Both paid and volunteer internships are covered in the books, each of which sells for $36.95.

Available from: Career Education Institutes, P.O. Box 11171, Winston-Salem, NC 27116. *Telephone:* (336) 768-2999; *Fax:* (336) 774-0675; *E-mail:* CEIbill@worldnet.att.net

Web site: www.internships-usa.com

622

National Internships Guide

College Park, MD: National Internships, 2003. ISBN 0-9726288-0-0. $99.95. Looseleaf.

Description: The *National Internships Guide* is a looseleaf compilation of all the internship pamphlets published by National Internships (each of which sells separately for $7.95); these include the *Student's Guide to International Internships,* more than a dozen regional internship listings (Alaska, Atlanta,

Internships–General–United States

Boston, Chicago, Denver, Florida, New Jersey, New York, North Carolina, Northern California, Ohio, Philadelphia, Seattle, Southern California, Texas, and Washington, D.C.), and several subject-focused listings, covering environmental internships, information technology internships, and legal internships. Each of these guides identifies internships offered by corporate, governmental, nonprofit, and educational entities. Both paid and unpaid opportunities are described (including ones that qualify for college credit). For most listings, the following information is given: sponsoring organization's URL, brief overview of the organization, a description of the internships opportunities, a summary of required qualifications, and data on how to apply (including e-mail address, physical address, phone and fax numbers).

Available from: National Internships Online/American Campus Company, 8322 Potomac Avenue, College Park, MD 20740. *Telephone:* (301) 474-2834; *Toll-free:* (877) 816-7511; *Fax:* (301) 982-5334; *E-mail:* poster1@aol.com

Web site: www.internships.com

623

Peterson's Internships: The Largest Source of Internships Available

Lawrenceville, NJ: Peterson's Guides, 1981- . Annual. ISSN 0272-5460. ISBN 0-7689-0904-X. $26.95 (2003 ed.). Paper.

Description: A professional internship can provide a real edge for students in today's competitive job market. Plus, internships can supply cash for college (in stipends, subsequent scholarships, or both). One of the best ways to find out about internship opportunities is with a copy of the latest edition of this directory, which identifies more than 2,000 organizations offering more than 50,000 paid and unpaid on-the-job training opportunities in such fields as architecture, business, communications, and sciences. True to its subtitle, this is the "largest source of internships available." Program entries describe length and duration of the position, rates of pay, desired qualifications, duties, training involved, availability of college credit, and application contacts, procedures, and deadlines. The focus is on work opportunities in the United States (only a few foreign countries are included). The book is arranged by categories of job sponsors as they relate to college disciplines; to narrow down your search, use the General or the Geographic-Cross Index. Completing the volume are helpful articles on selecting, applying for, and interviewing for an internship position. In the past, this title was known as *Internships: 30,000 On-the-Job Training Opportunities for Today's Job Market* and *Peterson's Internships: More than 50,000 Opportunities to Get an Edge in Today's Competitive Job Market.*

Available from: Peterson's Guides, Princeton Pike Corporate Center, 2000 Lenox Drive, P.O. Box 67005, Lawrenceville, NJ 08648. *Telephone:* (609) 896-1800; *Toll-free:* (800) 338-3282; *Fax:* (609) 896-4544; *E-mail:* sales@petersons.com

Web site: www.petersons.com

624 🕸 ¢

Rising Star Internships

http://www.rsinternships.com
Description: Students can browse for internships posted by employers and sponsors on this highly visible free site. Listings are grouped into approximately 100 subject categories (e.g., accounting, biology, editing, film, law, zoology). Each posting contains the following information: organization profile, position description, internship period, location, sectors (i.e., subject fields), salary and stipend, tuition assistance offered, college credits, application deadline, application process, and contact information (including direct links to the internship sponsor's site, when available). There are a number of other similar posting sites on the web; some examples: InternJobs.com (www.internjobs.com) and the related sites of SummerJobs.com, OverseasJobs.com, and ResortJobs.com; MonsterTRAK (campus.monster.com); and such specialized sites as EntertainmentCareers.net (www.entertainmentcareers.net).

Available from: Rising Star Internships, 1904 Hidden Point Road, Annapolis, MD 21401. *Telephone:* (410) 974-4783; *E-mail:* info@rsinternships.com
Web site: www.rsinternships.com

625 📖🖱

The Scholarship Book: The Complete Guide to Private-Sector Scholarships, Fellowships, Grants, and Loans for the Undergraduate

9th ed. By Daniel J. Cassidy. Englewood Cliffs, NJ: Prentice-Hall, 2002. 592p. ISSN 1528-9079. ISBN 0-7352-0276-1. $30. Paper with CD-ROM.

Description: This directory lists approximately 1,500 internships, loans, scholarships, and awards available to undergraduate students. For more information about the publication, see entry 64 in the "Scholarships, Fellowships & Loans—General—United States" section of this bibliography.

Available from: Prentice Hall, P.O. Box 11075, Des Moines, IA 50336-1075. *Toll-free:* (800) 947-7700; *Fax:* (515) 264-6719
Web site: www.phdirect.com

626 📖🕸 ¢

Summer Jobs for Students: Where the Jobs Are and How to Get Them

Lawrenceville, NJ: Peterson's Guides, 1952- . Annual. ISSN 1064-6701. ISBN 1-7689-0725-X. $18.95 (2002 ed.). Paper.

Description: Summer employment opportunities often function as internships. For over 40 years, this directory has been providing college students, high

Internships–General–United States

school students, and teachers with detailed information on 55,000 summer jobs at 800 resorts, camps, parks, businesses, and government offices in the United States. Arrangement is geographical and then by type of employer (camp, restaurants, etc.). Each listing specifies who to contact, application address, payment rates, qualifications needed, and number of openings available. Much of this information can also be accessed without charge on Peterson's web site; click on "Summer Opportunities" and then "Search for Summer Programs," which has a searchable database of more than 1,000 summer jobs and internships. For similar coverage of summer opportunities in foreign countries, see two other annual directories also published by Peterson's Guides: *Overseas Summer Jobs* and *Summer Jobs Britain,* both of which are described in the "Internships—General—International" section of this bibliography. In the past, *Summer Jobs for Students* was published under slightly different titles: first *Summer Employment Directory of the United States* and then *Summer Jobs.*

Available from: Peterson's Guides, Princeton Pike Corporate Center, 2000 Lenox Drive, P.O. Box 67005, Lawrenceville, NJ 08648. *Telephone:* (609) 896-1800; *Toll-free:* (800) 338-3282; *Fax:* (609) 896-4544; *E-mail:* sales@petersons.com

Web site: www.petersons.com

627

Summer Opportunities for Kids and Teenagers

Lawrenceville, NJ: Peterson's Guides, 1983- . Annual. ISSN 0894-9417. ISBN 0-7689-0844-2. $29.95. (2003 ed.). Paper.

Description: This book is dedicated to the idea that "there is a perfect summer program—and a wonderful summer vacation—awaiting every young person." Described in the latest edition of this annually-issued directory are more than 2,500 summer programs for children between the ages of 7 and 18 that are offered across the United States, Canada, the Caribbean, Europe, the Mediterranean, and the Far East by private schools, colleges, camps, religious organizations, travel groups, and special programs for the gifted, mentally retarded, and physically disabled. Nearly 600 of the camps and programs described offer employment opportunities for high school and college students in a variety of internship-like capacities. Much of this information can also be accessed without charge on Peterson's web site; click on "Summer Opportunities" and then "Search for Summer Programs" to access the information by sponsor, geographic location, or keyword.

Available from: Peterson's Guides, Princeton Pike Corporate Center, 2000 Lenox Drive, P.O. Box 67005, Lawrenceville, NJ 08648. *Telephone:* (609) 896-1800; *Toll-free:* (800) 338-3282; *Fax:* (609) 896-4544; *E-mail:* sales@petersons.com

Web site: www.petersons.com

628

Yale Daily News Guide to Internships

By Kalpana Srinivasan and the staff of the Yale Daily News. New York: Kaplan/Simon & Schuster, 2000. 425p. ISBN 0-684-86283-2. $25. Paper.

Description: According to Bob Filipczak in *Training* magazine (April, 1998): in 1985, "only one out of 36 college graduates had participated in some kind of internship; in 1995, one out of three grads had done some kind of internship." A number of internship directories have been published recently to respond to this developing interest. Some provide fairly comprehensive listings of available internship opportunities (e.g., *Peterson's Internships,* described in entry 623). However, the *Yale Daily News Guide* is not one of them. While there are nearly 600 pages in the 2000 edition of this directory, only around 500 unique internships offered by 225 companies and organizations are covered. A great deal of space in the directory is wasted by the format used; no matter how long or short the internship descriptions are, only two entries are provided on a page. The entries are grouped by type of internship (e.g., print journalism, business, entertainment, public service) and indexed by the companies offering internships and by the geographic location of these companies. These indexes have limited value, however, since they only identify the chapter which contains the internship profile (rather than the specific page or an entry number); to use the indexes, readers will have to go from the chapter reference to the Table of Contents (to find where the chapter starts), and then scan through the chapter to find the specific program in the alphabetically-arranged group of internship entries. Given the limited scope of the directory, it's just not worth the effort.

Available from: Simon & Schuster, Attn: Order Department, 100 Front Street, Riverside, NJ 08375. *Toll-free:* (800) 223-2336; *Fax:* (800) 445-6991

Web site: www.simonsays.com

New Jersey

629

New Jersey Internships

4th ed. Ed. by Michael Graham. Austin: Research Communications, 2001. 112p. ISBN 1-8832-1633-8. $24.95. Paper.

Description: This slight publication, last issued in 2001, lists various types of internships available in New Jersey. Entries are grouped by category (administrative, communications, education, legal, science, etc.) and contain the following information: address, phone and fax, eligibility requirements, duration, application procedure, and contact name and title. The indexes are perhaps the most interesting; you can search for paid and unpaid internships, internships that offer college credit, graduate level internships, and more. Previous edition were published in 1997, 1999, and 2000.

Available from: Research Communications, Inc., 3724 Jefferson Street, Suite 201, Austin, TX 78731. *Telephone:* (512) 458-2021; *Toll-free:* (800) 331-5076; *Fax:* (512) 458-2059; *E-mail:* researchcomm@austin.rr.com

Web site: researchcomm.com

International

630

Alternatives to the Peace Corps: A Directory of Third World & U.S. Volunteer Opportunities

9th ed. Ed. by Joan Powell. Oakland, CA: Food First, 2001. 128p. ISBN 0-935028-83-8. $9.95. Paper.

Description: Since 1961, more than 130,000 Americans have worked abroad through the Peace Corps' voluntary service program. But, there are many other ways to gain international experience in addition to the Peace Corps. This guide provides information on selected voluntary service organizations, technical services programs, work brigades, and study tours that offer alternative service options. These programs place volunteers in positions that complement the work of local people, grassroots organizations, and nongovernmental organizations. While many of these programs use only volunteers (and some even require participants to pay), a number listed here offer stipends, travel allowances, or other forms of financial assistance. Organizational profiles are grouped into three categories (international voluntary service organizations, U.S. voluntary service organizations, and alternative travel and study programs overseas) and indexed by organization name. Each listing provides the organization's name, address, telephone and fax numbers, web site, e-mail address, and an informative description of the program. A brief bibliography of other guides to overseas activities completes this pamphlet.

Available from: Food First Books, Institute for Food and Development Policy, 398 60th Street, Oakland, CA 94618-1212. *Telephone:* (510) 654-4400; *Toll-free:* (800) 243-0138; *Fax:* (510) 654-4551

Web site: www.foodfirst.org

How to Find Out About Financial Aid and Funding

631

The Back Door Guide to Short-Term Job Adventures: Internships, Extraordinary Experiences, Seasonal Jobs, Volunteering, Work Abroad

3rd ed. By Michael Landes. Berkeley, CA: Ten Speed Press, 2003. 328p. ISBN 1-58008-449-4. $21.95. Paper.

Description: This directory describes approximately 900 internships, seasonal jobs, volunteer assignments, work abroad opportunities, and "extraordinary experiences" that range from teaching English as a second language to students in Africa to working at a dance festival in Massachusetts. For more information about the publication, see entry 606 in the "Internships—General—United States" section of this bibliography.

Available from: Ten Speed Press, P.O. Box 7123, Berkeley, CA 94707. *Telephone:* (510) 559-1632; *Toll-free:* (800) 841-BOOK; *Fax:* (510) 559-1629; *E-mail:* order@tenspeed.com

Web site: www.tenspeed.com

632

Connections: A Directory of Volunteer Opportunities

http://www.pallotticenter.org

Description: This is a listing of volunteer and paid opportunities with volunteer service organizations in the United States and abroad. For more information about the listing, see entry 610 in the "Internships—General—United States" section of this bibliography.

Available from: St. Vincent Pallotti Center for Apostolic Development, 415 Michigan Avenue, N.E., Washington, DC 20017-1518. *Telephone:* (202) 529-3330; *Fax:* (202) 529-0911; *E-mail:* pallotti01@aol.com

Web site: www.pallotticenter.org

633

Directory of Research Grants

Westport, CT: Oryx, 1975- . Annual. ISSN 0146-7336. ISBN 1-57356-570-9. $134.95 (2003 ed.). Paper.

Description: Although the emphasis is on U.S. and Canadian research grants (and other types of financial aid), some internships sponsored by other countries are also included in this directory. For more information about the publication, see entry 238 in the "Grants for Individuals—General—United States" section of this bibliography.

Internships–General–International

Available from: Oryx Press, 88 Post Road West, Westport, CT 06881. *Telephone:* (602) 265-2651; *Toll-free:* (800) 279-6799; *Fax:* (800) 279-4663; *E-mail:* info@oryxpress.com
Web site: www.oryxpress.com

634

GrantSelect

http://www.grantselect.com
Description: Updated annually and used to generate Oryx Press's print funding directories, GrantSelect identifies more than 10,000 internships and other opportunities sponsored by organizations and agencies in the United States and Canada (some of which can be used abroad). For more information about the database, see entry 247 in the "Grants for Individuals—General—United States" section of this bibliography.
Available from: Oryx Press, 88 Post Road West, Westport, CT 06881. *Telephone:* (602) 265-2651; *Toll-free:* (800) 279-6799; *Fax:* (800) 279-4663; *E-mail:* info@oryxpress.com
Web site: www.oryxpress.com

635

Idealist.org

http://www.idealist.org
Description: First called the Contact Center Network, Action Without Borders was founded in 1995 to build a network of neighborhood Contact Centers that would provide a one-stop shop for volunteer opportunities and nonprofit services in communities around the world. A web site was started in 1996, to create a "virtual Contact Center" that would promote the mission and activities of nonprofits worldwide. Since then, idealistic.org has grown dramatically, and today offers information provided by 26,000 organizations in 153 countries. This information is grouped into categories, two of which are related to interning: "volunteer opportunities," which describes nearly 6,500 volunteer projects; and "internships," which describes opportunities at nearly 2,000 organizations. Each of these listings can be browsed by continent or searched by location, area of focus, or project description. Users can also sign up to receive personal e-mail updates of new projects that match their interests.
Available from: Action Without Borders, Inc., 79 Fifth Avenue, 17th Floor, New York, NY 10003. *Telephone:* (212) 843-3973; *Fax:* (212) 564-3377; *E-mail:* info@idealist.org
Web site: www.idealist.org

636

Internships-USA.com

http://www.internships-usa.com
Description: Internships-USA provides 1) an online database with information on more than 3,000 organizations in the United States and abroad offering internships to college and professional students as well as 2) 13 separate internship directories. For more information about these products, see entry 621 in the "Internships—General—United States" section of this bibliography.

Available from: Career Education Institutes, P.O. Box 11171, Winston-Salem, NC 27116. *Telephone:* (336) 768-2999; *Fax:* (336) 774-0675; *E-mail:* CEIbill@worldnet.att.net

Web site: www.internships-usa.com

637

National Internships Guide

College Park, MD: National Internships, 2003. ISBN 0-9726288-0-0. $99.95. Looseleaf.

Description: One of the nearly two dozen pamphlets published collectively as the *National Internships Guide* is the *Student's Guide to International Internships* (3rd ed., $7.95), which identifies hundreds of international internships and placement programs in the private, nonprofit, and government sectors. For more information about the national compilation, see entry 622 in the "Internships—General—United States" section of this bibliography.

Available from: National Internships Online/American Campus Company, 8322 Potomac Avenue, College Park, MD 20740. *Telephone:* (301) 474-2834; *Toll-free:* (877) 816-7511; *Fax:* (301) 982-5334; *E-mail:* poster1@aol.com

Web site: www.internships.com

638

Online Study Abroad Directory

http://www.istc.umn.edu
Description: Internship opportunities are identified in two of the databases offered on this site: the Volunteer Database, which describes approximately 150 volunteer opportunities in developing countries and eastern Europe, and the Work & Intern Database, which describes internships intended for American undergraduate students interested in going abroad. For more information on this Internet site, see entry 119 in the "Scholarships, Fellowships & Loans—General—International" section of this bibliography.

Internships–General–International

Available from: University of Minnesota, Attn: International Study and Travel Center, 94 Blegen Hall, 269 19th Avenue South, Minneapolis, MN 55455. *Telephone:* (612) 626-ISTC; *Toll-free:* (800) 770-ISTC; *Fax:* (612) 626-0979; *E-mail:* istc@umn.edu
Web site: www.istc.umn.edu

639

Summer Jobs Abroad

Ed. by Andrew James and David Woodworth. Lawrenceville, NJ: Peterson's Guides, 1980- . Annual. ISSN 0308-7123. ISBN 1-85458-272-0. $17.95 (2003 ed.). Paper.

Description: Revised annually, this directory (which was formerly published by Vacation-Work and distributed by Writer's Digest) lists and provides information on more than 30,000 summer jobs located outside the United States, from Australia to Yugoslavia. The employment opportunities covered are particularly suitable for high school graduates, college students, and teachers. The entries are arranged by country. Each listing specifies contact, length of employment, number of openings available, how and when to apply, rates of pay, duties, and qualifications sought. Supplemental information on visa and work permit regulations is also provided. Previously, this publication was issued under the title *Directory of Overseas Summer Jobs,* then *Directory of Summer Jobs Abroad,* and most recently as *Overseas Summer Jobs.* It is also known as *Vacation Work's Summer Jobs Abroad.* For similar but more comprehensive coverage of employment opportunities in Scotland, Wales, England, and Ireland, see *Summer Jobs Britain* (described in entry 640).

Available from: Peterson's Guides, Princeton Pike Corporate Center, 2000 Lenox Drive, P.O. Box 67005, Lawrenceville, NJ 08648. *Telephone:* (609) 896-1800; *Toll-free:* (800) 338-3282; *Fax:* (609) 896-4544; *E-mail:* sales@petersons.com
Web site: www.petersons.com

640

Summer Jobs Britain

Ed. by Andrew James and David Woodworth. Lawrenceville, NJ: Peterson's Guides, 1970- . Annual. ISSN 1064-6701. ISBN 1-85458-269-0. $17.95 (2003 ed.). Paper.

Description: More than 30,000 summer jobs (paid and volunteer) in Scotland, Wales, England, the Channel Islands, and Northern Ireland are listed in this annual directory (which was previously published by Vacation-Work and distributed by Writer's Digest). In the latest (2003) edition, these jobs range from farm hand to office worker to lorry driver. Entries cover the type of information needed to apply for each job. Also included in the volume are procedures to follow in applying for visas and work permits. This title is also known as *Vacation Work's Summer Jobs Britain.*

Available from: Peterson's Guides, Princeton Pike Corporate Center, 2000 Lenox Drive, P.O. Box 67005, Lawrenceville, NJ 08648. *Telephone:* (609) 896-1800; *Toll-free:* (800) 338-3282; *Fax:* (609) 896-4544; *E-mail:* sales@petersons.com

Web site: www.petersons.com

641

Summer Opportunities for Kids and Teenagers

Lawrenceville, NJ: Peterson's Guides, 1983- . Annual. ISSN 0894-9417. ISBN 0-7689-0844-2. $29.95. (2003 ed.). Paper.

Description: Nearly 600 of the camps and programs in the United States and abroad that are described in the latest annual edition of this directory offer employment opportunities for high school and college students in a variety of internship-like capacities. For more information on this publication, see entry 627 in the "Internships—General—United States" section of this bibliography.

Available from: Peterson's Guides, Princeton Pike Corporate Center, 2000 Lenox Drive, P.O. Box 67005, Lawrenceville, NJ 08648. *Telephone:* (609) 896-1800; *Toll-free:* (800) 338-3282; *Fax:* (609) 896-4544; *E-mail:* sales@petersons.com

Web site: www.petersons.com

SOCIAL SCIENCES

General

642

Jobs You Can Live With

http://www.spusa.org/publications/200_employers.html

Description: The web edition of this directory identifies over 200 private and public organizations that offer internships and entry-level jobs relating to global security, bioethics, energy, development, and the environment. For more information about the listing, see entry 669 in the "Internships—Sciences—Technology" section of this bibliography.

Available from: Student Pugwash, USA, 2029 P Street, N.W., Suite 301, Washington, DC 20036. *Telephone:* (202) 429-8900; *Fax:* (202) 429-8905; *E-mail:* spusa@spusa.org

Web site: www.spusa.org

Internships–Social Sciences–Political Science

643 🕸 ¢

Progressive Publications Internship Database

http://www.progressivepubs.com/internships
Description: Similar in scope to the Progressive Publications Foundation Database on ProgressivePubs.com web site (see entry 465), this free online database provides information on hundreds of internships with progressive organizations and companies. The entries can be searched by state, topic, or keyword. Brief descriptions are provided for each of the opportunities included in the database. Users are encouraged to post comments (positive or critical) about the companies and organizations listed.
Available from: ProgressivePubs.com, Inc., P.O. Box 11335, Washington, DC 20008. *E-mail:* webmaster@progressivepubs.com
Web site: www.progressivepubs.com

Political Science and International Affairs

644 📖

Human Rights Organizations and Periodicals Directory

11th ed. Berkeley, CA: Meiklejohn Civil Liberties Institute, 2003. 225p. ISSN 0098-0579. $100, individuals; $125, libraries and institutions. Looseleaf.
Description: This is a biennially-updated list of 1,200 organizations and periodicals in the United States that are concerned with human rights. In the 11th edition, entries provide contact information, indicate current activities, and identify organizational publications (including frequency and price). Because 1) each entry also indicates if internships (both paid and unpaid) are offered and 2) there is an internship index, individuals looking for on-the-job work experiences in the human rights area will find the directory useful.
Available from: Meiklejohn Civil Liberties Institute, P.O. Box 673, Berkeley, CA 94701-0673. *Telephone:* (510) 848-0599; *Toll-free:* (888) 848-0599; *Fax:* (510) 848-6008; *E-mail:* mcli@mcli.org
Web site: www.mcli.org

Psychology

645

Directory of Internship and Post-Doctoral Fellowships in Clinical Child/Pediatric Psychology

3rd ed. By Susan J. Simonian and Kenneth J. Tarnowski. Mahwah, NJ: Lawrence Erlbaum Associates, 1999. 129p. ISBN 0-8058-3595-4. $39.95. Paper.

Description: Aimed at psychology graduate students, faculty, and clinical supervisors, this directory identifies predoctoral internships and postdoctoral fellowships that are self-defined as offering training in "clinical child psychology" and "pediatric psychology." For a similar but more general listing, use the Association of Psychology Post-Doctorate and Internship Center's *Directory of Internship and Post-Doctoral Programs in Professional Psychology* (published annually since 1967).

Available from: Lawrence Erlbaum Associates, Inc., 10 Industrial Avenue, Mahwah, NJ 07430-2262. *Telephone:* (201) 236-9500; *Toll-free:* (800) 9-BOOKS-9; *Fax:* (201) 236-0072; *E-mail:* orders@erlbaum.com
Web site: www.erlbaum.com

Sociology and Social Services

646

Internships in Youth Development

http://www.nassembly.org/html/search.html

Description: Whether you are preparing for a career, looking for your first job, reentering the work force, or considering a career change, an internship can provide you with the on-the-job experience needed to get started in your career. If you are planning on a career working with or on behalf of young people and their families, you will be particularly interested in the internships described on this free web site. The listing is prepared and hosted by the National Assembly of Health and Human Service Organizations (formerly known as the National Assembly of National Voluntary Health and Social Welfare Organizations). More than 1,100 paid and unpaid internships with nonprofit human service organizations throughout the United States are described here. You can search for internships by state or city. For narrower results, you can limit the search by the type of internships you are seeking. Funding for the database is provided by the DeWitt Wallace-Reader's Digest Fund. Previously, this listing was issued in print, as the *Directory of Internships in Youth Development;* now the information is available only online.

Internships–Humanities–General

Available from: National Assembly of Health and Human Service Organizations, 1319 F Street, N.W., Suite 601, Washington, DC 20004. *Telephone:* (202) 347-2080; *Fax:* (202) 393-4517
Web site: www.nassembly.org

HUMANITIES
General

647

Art Deadlines List

Ed. by Richard Gardner. Cambridge, MA: Art Deadlines List. Monthly. $36, paper; $18, e-mailed.
Description: Every month subscribers are mailed an international list of internships, grants, fellowships, competitions, contests (primarily), call for entries/papers, scholarships, residencies, and other opportunities for individuals involved in art or other creative activities (e.g., writing, photography, music). For more information about the service, see entry 560 in the "Awards and Prizes—Humanities—General" section of this bibliography.
Available from: Art Deadlines List, Box 381067, Harvard Square Station, Cambridge, MA 02238-1067. *E-mail:* contact@artdeadlineslist.com
Web site: www.artdeadlineslist.com

Communications and Mass Media

648

ASNE Internship Search

http://www.asne.org
Description: This Internet service, which is in the "Careers" section of the American Society of Newspaper Editors' web site, lists newspapers offering summer or year-round internships. You can browse all of the listings or search by state, internship function, time of year, and/or whether or not the deadline has expired, a career is required, a driver's license is required, previous internship experience is required, and/or help with housing is available. For each newspaper listed, the following is provided: address, contact and phone number, e-mail link, timing of internships (e.g., summer, fall semester) and their deadline dates, types of internships available, salary, and various details (e.g., if a driver's

How to Find Out About Financial Aid and Funding

license is required; if help with housing is offered). In addition, some links to newspaper sites are provided.

Available from: American Society of Newspaper Editors, 11690B Sunrise Valley Drive, Reston, VA 20191-1409. *Telephone:* (703) 453-1122; *Fax:* (703) 453-1133; *E-mail:* asne@asne.org

Web site: www.asne.org

649

Gardner's Guide to Internships in New Media 2004: Computer Graphics, Animation and Multimedia

2nd ed. By Garth Gardner. Annandale, VA, Garth Gardner, 2002. 240p. ISBN 1-58965-008-5. $34.95. Paper.

Description: Finding an internship at some of the hottest studios, organizations, and companies in the United States just got easier. The second edition of this directory profiles hundreds of companies and studios that offer internships to high school and college students in the new media: computer graphics, animation, and multimedia, including graphic design, photography, television production, web design, film, and computer graphics. Information is provided on various industry magazines, international festivals, and fully-digital television production studios. The following information is given for each: company description, internships available (summer, fall, winter, spring, or year round), benefits, and contacts (often with e-mail and web addresses). Although the title would suggest that the book focuses on internships, don't be misled; instead, the focus is on organizations that may offer internships in the new media. Note: although this is titled the 2004 edition, the directory was actually issued in 2002.

Available from: Garth Gardner Company (GGC/Publishing), 4602 John Hancock Court, No. 302, Annandale, VA 22003. *Telephone:* (703) 793-8604; *Toll-free:* (866) Go-Gardner; *Fax:* (703) 793-8830; *E-mail:* info@ggcinc.com

Web site: www.gogardner.com

650

Gardner's Guide to Internships @ Multimedia and Animation Studios

By Garth Gardner. Annandale, VA, Garth Gardner, 2001. 256p. ISBN 1-58965-000-X. $29.95. Paper.

Description: This is the second internship directory prepared by Garth Gardner (for a description of the first title, see entry 649). Profiled here are hundreds of computer graphics, animation, and multimedia companies in the United States and Canada where internships are often available. For each, the following information is provided: area of specialization, number of employees, company's achievements, and contacts (including e-mail and web addresses). Entries are indexed by name of studio and geographic location. The title of this guide is somewhat misleading. This is really more of a directory to employers than a guide to available internships; little information is provided about specific internships the listed studios might offer.

Available from: Garth Gardner Company (GGC/Publishing), 4602 John Hancock Court, No. 302, Annandale, VA 22003. *Telephone:* (703) 793-8604; *Toll-free:* (866) Go-Gardner; *Fax:* (703) 793-8830; *E-mail:* info@ggcinc.com
Web site: www.gogardner.com

651

Newspapers, Diversity, & You

Princeton, NJ: Dow Jones Newspaper Fund, 1993-1999. Annual. Free (1999 ed.). Paper.

Description: One section of this free booklet deals with internships, scholarships, fellowships, and special training programs for minorities interested in journalism. For more information about the publication, see entry 149 in the "Scholarships, Fellowships & Loans—Humanities—Communications and Mass Media" section of this bibliography.

Available from: Dow Jones Newspaper Fund, P.O. Box 300, Princeton, NJ 08543-0300. *Telephone:* (609) 452-2820; *Fax:* (609) 520-5804; *E-mail:* newsfund@wsf.dowjones.com
Web site: djnewspaperfund.dowjones.com/fund/default.asp

652

PNPA Foundation Newspaper Internship Guide

http://www.pa-newspaper.org/foundation/internguide/index.htm

Description: Until 1999, this guide was issued in print. Since then, it has been updated annually and posted on the foundation's web site. The latest (2003) online Internship Guide identifies opportunities at newspapers in Pennsylvania and is divided into two sections: daily and nondaily newspapers. Both sections are alphabetized by city. Each listing provides detailed information on the internships available, including contact, duration, salary, application deadline, and special requirements. Also included, in a separate section, is a new media listing for students interested in the digital newspaper industry; it lists internships that deal with web design and other digital projects.

Available from: Pennsylvania Newspaper Association, 3899 North Front Street, Harrisburg, PA 17110. *Telephone:* (717) 703-3000; *Fax:* (717) 717-703-3001; *E-mail:* info@pa-news.org
Web site: www.pa-newspaper.org

653

SND Foundation Internship Directory

http://www.snd.org/jobs/jobsearch.qry

Description: Originally issued as an eight-page pamphlet, this information is now provided as part of the online job bank on SND's web site. There you can find more than 100 opportunities (mostly paid) to intern with news organization in the United States and a smattering of other countries. The entries provide information on: address and telephone number, contact, number of positions, duration, application procedures, and stipend (if offered). Programs open specifically to minorities are designated. Previously, the sponsor was known as the Society of Newspaper Design.

Available from: Society for News Design, 1130 Ten Rod Road, F-104, North Kingstown, RI 02852-4177. *Telephone:* (401) 294-5233; *Fax:* (401) 294-5238; *E-mail:* snd@snd.org

Web site: www.snd.org

654

Virginia Newspaper Internship Guide

http://www.vpa.net

Description: Initially, this information was printed in a small free pamphlet by the Virginia Press Association, first under the title *Journalism Internship Guide,* then as *Newspaper Internship Guide,* and last as the *Virginia Newspaper Internship Guide* (final print edition: 2000). Since then, the information has been available only at the association's web site. The programs included are designed to offer students hands-on work experience and to prepare them for a newspaper career after they complete their education. Each Virginia daily and weekly newspaper provided the information presented here. Entries indicate number of internships available, skills required to apply for the position, and skills taught in the position. Both paid and volunteer positions are covered. The listings, which are updated on an on-going basis, can be accessed by type of newspaper: daily or nondaily.

Available from: Virginia Press Association, 11529 Nuckols Road, Glen Allen, VA 23059. *Telephone:* (804) 521-7570; *Fax:* (800) 849-8717; *E-mail:* publicats@vpa.net

Web site: www.vpa.net

History

655

Grants, Fellowships, and Prizes of Interest to Historians

Ed. by Pillarisetti Sudhir, with Kim Foote and Jesse Erdheim. Washington, DC: American Historical Association, 1978-2000. Annual. ISSN 0275-830X. $10, members; $12, nonmembers (2000-2001 ed.). Paper.

Description: Last issued in 2000, this directory identifies and describes more than 450 internships, awards, prizes, fellowships, and travel grants of interest to graduate students, postdoctoral researchers, and scholars in history. For more information about the publication and its online replacement, see entry 287 in the "Grants for Individuals—Humanities—History" section of this bibliography.

Available from: American Historical Association, 400 A Street, S.E., Washington, DC 20003-3889. *Telephone:* (202) 544-2422; *Fax:* (202) 544-8307; *E-mail:* pubsales@theaha.org

Web site: www.theaha.org

Music

656

Music and Entertainment Industry Internship Guide

13th ed. Ed. by Beverly McCloud. Livingston, NJ: Entertainment Media Consultants, 2002. 670p. $110. Paper

Description: Aimed at undergraduate and graduate students, this guide is broader than its title might indicate. Identified here are internship opportunities in music, film and video, broadcasting, literary arts, publicity, management, entertainment law, television, theater, dance, performing arts, marketing, arts organizations, and news print media. Entries provide the following information: address, phone and fax numbers, and requirements. Also included are guidelines for securing and maximizing an internship experience.

Available from: Entertainment Media Consultants, P.O. Box 2395, Livingston, NJ 07039. *Telephone:* (973) 535-6186

Performing Arts

657 📖

Music and Entertainment Industry Internship Guide

13th ed. Ed. by Beverly McCloud. Livingston, NJ: Entertainment Media Consultants, 2002. 670p. $110. Paper

Description: Aimed at undergraduate and graduate students, this guide identifies internship opportunities in the performing arts and a number of other related fields. For more information on this title, see entry 656 in the "Internships—Humanities—Music" section of this bibliography

Available from: Entertainment Media Consultants, P.O. Box 2395, Livingston, NJ 07039. *Telephone:* (973) 535-6186

658 📖

National Directory of Arts Internships

Ed. by Warren Christensen and Ron Clawges. Los Angeles: National Network for Artist Placement, 1989- . Annual. ISSN 1043-092X. ISBN 0-945941-13-7. $85 (2003-2004 ed.). Paper.

Description: More than 3,000 internship and fellowship opportunities open to undergraduates, graduate students, and others in the performing and other arts are described in this directory. For more information about the publication, see entry 660 in the "Internships—Humanities—Visual Arts" section of this bibliography.

Available from: National Network for Artist Placement, 935 West Avenue 37, Los Angeles, CA 90065. *Telephone:* (323) 222-4035; *Fax:* (323) 222-4035; *E-mail:* NNAPnow@aol.com

Web site: www.artistplacement.com

Religion

659 📖 🕸 ¢

Project Book

Elgin, IL: Brethren Volunteer Service, 2000. 55p. Free. Paper and online.

Description: Brethren Volunteer Service (BVS) was started in 1948. It was one of the first organized volunteer programs of any kind, either faith-based or secular. This free booklet lists approximately 100 projects sponsored by BVS (in the United States or abroad); these projects are grouped by category, including children, farmworkers, prisoners, and refugees. Two important points: 1) some of the projects listed are secular in nature, rather than faith-based; and 2) volunteers receive substantial benefits, including travel to and from the project, room, board, monthly stipend, full medical coverage, life insurance, and an annual retreat in the United States or Europe. Last issued in print in 2000, this annually-updated list is now available on the Brethren Volunteer Service's web site; in addition to browsing the categories there, you can also access the information by geographic location.

Available from: Brethren Volunteer Service, 1451 Dundee Avenue, Elgin, IL 60120-1694. *Telephone:* (847) 742-5100; *Toll-free:* (800) 323-8039; *Fax:* (847) 742-0278; *E-mail:* bvs_gb@brethren.org
Web site: www.brethren.org

Visual Arts

660

National Directory of Arts Internships

Ed. by Warren Christensen and Ron Clawges. Los Angeles: National Network for Artist Placement, 1989- . Annual. ISSN 1043-092X. ISBN 0-945941-13-7. $85 (2003-2004 ed.). Paper.

Description: If you are interested in finding out about internships or fellowships in the visual or performing arts, this is the place to look. More than 1,250 host organizations offering approximately 3,000 internship opportunities open to undergraduates, graduate students, and others in the arts are described in the latest (2003-2004) edition. The internships are listed by sponsoring organization in 16 sections, including photography, literacy, film/video, music, dance, and the performing arts. Entries specify purpose, assignment, eligibility requirements, application procedure, and contact person. Both paid and unpaid opportunities are covered. In addition to the listings, the directory includes useful sections on how to design an individual internship as well as how to prepare resumes, cover letters, and portfolios.

Available from: National Network for Artist Placement, 935 West Avenue 37, Los Angeles, CA 90065. *Telephone:* (323) 222-4035; *Fax:* (323) 222-4035; *E-mail:* NNAPnow@aol.com
Web site: www.artistplacement.com

SCIENCES

Aviation

661 🕸 ¢

AvScholars.com Free Scholarship Database

http://www.avscholars.com
Description: In addition to covering scholarships, fellowships, and loans, there is a separate section on the web site listing internships for high school, college, and graduate students interested in preparing for a career in aviation. For more information, see entry 172 in the "Scholarships, Fellowships & Loans—Sciences—Aviation" section of this bibliography.

Available from: AvScholars Network Foundation, 8526 South Drexel Avenue, Chicago, IL 60619. *Telephone:* (708) 493-0324; *Fax:* (708) 493-0324; *E-mail:* info@avscholars.com
Web site: www.avscholars.com

Biological Sciences

662 📖

Directory of Public Garden Internships

Wilmington, DE: American Association of Botanical Gardens and Arboreta, 2003. $10, members; $18, nonmembers. Paper.
Description: Produced annually by the American Association of Botanical Gardens and Arboreta (AABGA), this directory lists 700 summer jobs and internships at approximately 119 North American botanical gardens, arboreta, and other horticultural institutions in grounds management, education, collections, curation, and more. Positions restricted to a student from a specific university or location are excluded. Each entry contains the following information: sponsoring organization, address and contact, number, duration, stipend, eligibility, and deadline date. Previously, this directory was issued under the title *Student Employment and Internships at Botanical Gardens and Arboreta* and *AABGA Internship Directory*.

Available from: American Association of Botanical Gardens and Arboreta, 100 West 10th Street, Suite 614, Wilmington, DE 19801. *Telephone:* (302) 655-7100; *Fax:* (302) 655-8100
Web site: www.aabga.org

Environmental Sciences

663

Jobs You Can Live With

http://www.spusa.org/publications/200_employers.html
Description: The web edition of this directory identifies over 200 private and public organizations that offer internships and entry-level jobs relating to global security, bioethics, energy, development, and the environment. For more information about the listing, see entry 669 in the "Internships—Sciences—Technology" section of this bibliography.
Available from: Student Pugwash, USA, 2029 P Street, N.W., Suite 301, Washington, DC 20036. *Telephone:* (202) 429-8900; *Fax:* (202) 429-8905; *E-mail:* spusa@spusa.org
Web site: www.spusa.org

Health and Medical Sciences

664

Directory of Pathology Training Programs (Residencies and Fellowships) in the United States and Canada

Bethesda, MD: Intersociety Committee on Pathology Information, 1970- . Annual. ISSN 0070-6086. $5, medical students and residents; $25, all others. Paper.
Description: This annually-issued directory identifies anatomic, clinical, and specialized pathology training programs (residencies and fellowships) in the United States and Canada. For more information about the publication, see entry 179 in the "Scholarships, Fellowships & Loans—Sciences—Health and Medical Sciences" section of this bibliography.
Available from: Intersociety Committee on Pathology Information, Inc., 9650 Rockville Pike, Bethesda, MD 20814-3993. *Telephone:* (301) 571-1880; *Fax:* (301) 571-1879; *E-mail:* ICPI@pathol.faseb.org
Web site: www.pathologytraining.org

How to Find Out About Financial Aid and Funding

665

Directory of Residencies and Fellowships

Kansas City, MO: American College of Clinical Pharmacy, 1983- . Annual. Free (2002 ed.). Paper.

Description: Issued annually since 1983 by the American College of Clinical Pharmacy, this is the only regularly published listing of clinical pharmacy fellowships and residencies. Described in the latest edition (2002) are 365 residencies ("organized, directed, postgraduate training programs in a defined area of pharmacy practice") and 99 fellowships ("directed, highly individualized postgraduate programs designed to prepare the participant to become an independent researcher") in pharmacy practice, infectious diseases, ambulatory care, and drug information. Annual stipends offered by these programs range from $22,500 through $40,000 (with a mean of $30,000). Entries average half a page and provide the following information: type of program, contact, specialties, duration, accreditation, degree required, start date, stipend, and program description. Using the indexes, it is possible to identify opportunities by geographic location and primary specialty. Much of this information is also available without charge at the American College of Clinical Pharmacy's web site (searchable by type and geographic location); within the search results, programs are designed "R" for residencies, "F" for fellowships, and "R/F" for programs that offer both residency and fellowship training.

Available from: American College of Clinical Pharmacy, 3101 Broadway, Suite 380, Kansas City, MO 64111. *Telephone:* (816) 531-2177; *Fax:* (816) 531-4990

Web site: www.accp.com

666

Graduate Medical Education Directory

Chicago: American Medical Association, 1981- . Annual. $55 (2002-2003 ed.), members, paper; $75, nonmembers, paper; $80, members, CD-ROM; $105, nonmembers, CD-ROM.

Description: This annual directory describes nearly 8,000 residency training programs at more than 1,600 teaching institutions accredited by the Accreditation Council for Graduate Medical Education. For more information about the publication, see entry 181 in the "Scholarships, Fellowships & Loans—Sciences—Health and Medical Sciences" section of this bibliography.

Available from: American Medical Association, 515 North State Street, Chicago, IL 60610. *Telephone:* (312) 464-5000; *Toll-free:* (800) AMA-3211; *Fax:* (312) 464-5837

Web site: www.ama-assn.org

667

Interorganizational Financial & Experiential Information Document: "If I'd" Only Known about That Scholarship

Prep. by the member organizations of the Interorganizational Council on Student Affairs. Washington, DC: Interorganizational Council on Student Affairs, 1999. Unpaged. Free. Paper or online.

Description: Aimed at undergraduate and graduate pharmacy students, this free listing provides (in tabular format) information on available experiential programs, awards, loans, grants, fellowships, and residencies. For more information about the listing, see entry 184 in the "Scholarships, Fellowships & Loans—Sciences—Health and Medical Sciences" section of this bibliography.

Available from: Interorganizational Council on Student Affairs, 2215 Constitution Avenue, N.W., Washington, DC 20037-2985. *Telephone:* (202) 429-7595; *Toll-free:* (800) 237-AphA, ext. 7595; *E-mail:* edt@mail.aphanet.org

Web site: www.aphanet.org/students/ifeid.html

668

Residency Directory

http://www.ashp.org/directories/residency

Description: Previously printed as part of the two-volume *Opportunities: The Source for Residency Information* (last edition: 1998. $11, students; $25, members; $31, all others), this information is now available only on the American Society of Health-System Pharmacists' web site in the "Residency Directory." This free online directory identifies pharmacy practice residency programs and specialized pharmacy practice programs (including those in oncology, pharmacotherapy, infectious disease, pediatrics, critical care, drug information, nutritional support, and psychopharmacy). Students can search for residencies several ways, including by geographic location and by program name. In addition to contact information, the residency profiles identify duration and type of residency, number of positions, starting date, application deadline, estimated stipend, and whether or not an interview is required.

Available from: American Society of Health-System Pharmacists, 7272 Wisconsin Avenue, Bethesda, MD 20814. *Telephone:* (301) 657-3000, ext. 1439; *E-mail:* students@ashp.org

Web site: www.ashp.org

Technology

669 🕸 ¢

Jobs You Can Live With

http://www.spusa.org/publications/200_employers.html
Description: Last published in print in 1996 (5th ed. ISBN 0-9639007-1-4. $12.95, students; $17.95, all others), this guide is now available only online, on the Student Pugwash USA web site. Student Pugwash USA is a national, educational, nonprofit organization run by recent graduates and young professionals interested in understanding the ways in which science, technology, and society interact. One of the purposes of the organization is to introduce socially-committed students and recent graduates to internship, volunteer, and career opportunities through which they can impact their local and global communities. The online version of *Jobs You Can Live With* identifies over 200 "ethical" organizations (mostly in the nonprofit sector) that offer internships and entry-level jobs relating to global security, bioethics, energy, food and agriculture, information technology, and the environment. The organizational profiles are listed alphabetically and link directly to the listed organizations. It is clear the listing is kept up to date; all tested links worked.

Available from: Student Pugwash, USA, 2029 P Street, N.W., Suite 301, Washington, DC 20036. *Telephone:* (202) 429-8900; *Fax:* (202) 429-8905; *E-mail:* spusa@spusa.org
Web site: www.spusa.org

SPECIAL POPULATION GROUPS
Ethnic Groups

670 📖

Financial Aid for African Americans

By Gail Ann Schlachter and R. David Weber. El Dorado Hills, CA: Reference Service Press, 1997- . Biennial. (Minority Funding Set). ISBN 1-58841-068-4. $40 (2003-2005 ed.). Hardcover.
Description: Described here are 1,500 internships, fellowships, scholarships, grants, loans, awards, and prizes—representing billions of dollars—open specifically to Black/African Americans. For more information about the publication, see entry 198 in the "Scholarships, Fellowships, & Loans—Special Population Groups—Ethnic Groups" section of this bibliography.

Internships–Special Population Groups–Ethnic Groups

Available from: Reference Service Press, 5000 Windplay Drive, Suite 4, El Dorado Hills, CA 95762. *Telephone:* (916) 939-9620; *Fax:* (916) 939-9626; *E-mail:* findaid@aol.com
Web site: www.rspfunding.com

671

Financial Aid for Asian Americans

By Gail Ann Schlachter and R. David Weber. El Dorado Hills, CA: Reference Service Press, 1997- . Biennial. (Minority Funding Set). ISBN 1-58841-069-2. $37.50 (2003-2005 ed.). Hardcover.

Description: More than 1,000 internships, awards, fellowships, scholarships, loans, and grants set aside for Asian Americans are described here. For more information about the publication, see entry 199 in the "Scholarships, Fellowships & Loans—Special Population Groups—Ethnic Groups" section of this bibliography.

Available from: Reference Service Press, 5000 Windplay Drive, Suite 4, El Dorado Hills, CA 95762. *Telephone:* (916) 939-9620; *Fax:* (916) 939-9626; *E-mail:* findaid@aol.com
Web site: www.rspfunding.com

672

Financial Aid for Hispanic Americans

By Gail Ann Schlachter and R. David Weber. El Dorado Hills, CA: Reference Service Press, 1997- . Biennial. (Minority Funding Set). ISBN 1-58841-070-6. $40 (2003-2005 ed.). Hardcover.

Description: This directory identifies nearly 1,400 internships, fellowships, scholarships, loans, grants, and awards available to Hispanic Americans, including Mexican Americans, Puerto Ricans, Cuban Americans, and others of Latin American origin. For more information about the publication, see entry 200 in the "Scholarships, Fellowships & Loans—Special Population Groups—Ethnic Groups" section of this bibliography.

Available from: Reference Service Press, 5000 Windplay Drive, Suite 4, El Dorado Hills, CA 95762. *Telephone:* (916) 939-9620; *Fax:* (916) 939-9626; *E-mail:* findaid@aol.com
Web site: www.rspfunding.com

673

Financial Aid for Native Americans

By Gail Ann Schlachter and R. David Weber. El Dorado Hills, CA: Reference Service Press, 1997- . Biennial. (Minority Funding Set). ISBN 1-58841-071-4. $40 (2003-2005 ed.). Hardcover.

Description: Detailed information on nearly 2,000 internships, awards, grants, scholarships, fellowships, and loans open to American Indians, Native Alaskans, and Native Pacific Islanders (including Native Hawaiians and Samoans) is presented in this directory. For more information about the publication, see entry 201 in the "Scholarships, Fellowships & Loans—Special Population Groups—Ethnic Groups" section of this bibliography.

Available from: Reference Service Press, 5000 Windplay Drive, Suite 4, El Dorado Hills, CA 95762. *Telephone:* (916) 939-9620; *Fax:* (916) 939-9626; *E-mail:* findaid@aol.com

Web site: www.rspfunding.com

674

National Directory of Scholarships, Internships, and Fellowships for Latino Youth

2nd ed. Washington, DC: Congressional Hispanic Caucus Institute, 2002. 136p. Free. Paper.

Description: In addition to covering scholarships and fellowships, this free publication aimed at Latino students and young professionals also identifies internships and leadership development opportunities. For more information about the publication, see entry 204 in the "Scholarships, Fellowships & Loans—Special Population Groups—Ethnic Groups" section of this bibliography.

Available from: Congressional Hispanic Caucus Institute, 504 C Street N.E., Washington, DC 20002. *Telephone:* (202) 543-1771; *Toll-free:* (800) EXCEL-DC; *Fax:* (202) 546-2143

Web site: www.chci.org

675

Newspapers, Diversity, & You

Princeton, NJ: Dow Jones Newspaper Fund, 1993-1999. Annual. Free (1999 ed.). Paper.

Description: One section of this free booklet deals with internships, scholarships, fellowships, and special training programs for minorities interested in journalism. For more information about the publication, see entry 149 in the

Internships–Special Population Groups–Disabilities

"Scholarships, Fellowships & Loans—Humanities—Communications and Mass Media" section of this bibliography.
Available from: Dow Jones Newspaper Fund, P.O. Box 300, Princeton, NJ 08543-0300. *Telephone:* (609) 452-2820; *Fax:* (609) 520-5804; *E-mail:* newsfund@wsf.dowjones.com
Web site: djnewspaperfund.dowjones.com/fund/default.asp

676

Pathways to Career Success for Minorities: A Resource Guide to Colleges, Financial Aid, and Work

Ed. by Tim Schaffert. Chicago: Ferguson, 2000. 360p. ISBN 0-89434-303-3. $29.95. Paper.
Description: One small section in this directory briefly describes internships either available to minorities or offered by minority organizations. For more information about the publication, see entry 234 in the "Scholarships, Fellowships & Loans—Special Population Groups—Ethnic Groups" section of this bibliography.
Available from: Ferguson Publishing Company, 200 West Jackson Boulevard, Chicago, IL 60606. *Toll-free:* (800) 306-9941; *Fax:* (800) 306-9942
Web site: www.fergpubco.com

Persons with Disabilities

677

Financial Aid for the Disabled and Their Families

By Gail Ann Schlachter and R. David Weber. El Dorado Hills, CA: Reference Service Press, 1988- . Biennial. ISSN 0898-9222. ISBN 1-58841-042-0. $40 (2002-2004 ed.). Hardcover.
Description: This is the only comprehensive and up-to-date listing of internships, awards, grants-in-aid, scholarships, fellowships, and loans for individuals with disabilities and their families. For more information about the publication, see entry 222 in the "Scholarships, Fellowships & Loans—Special Population Groups—Persons with Disabilities" section of this bibliography.
Available from: Reference Service Press, 5000 Windplay Drive, Suite 4, El Dorado Hills, CA 95762. *Telephone:* (916) 939-9620; *Fax:* (916) 939-9626; *E-mail:* findaid@aol.com
Web site: www.rspfunding.com

Religious Groups

678

Financial Support for Jewish College Students

http://www.thebagel.org/financial_aid/matcher.php
Description: This searchable database identifies more than 100 internships, awards, loans, scholarships, and fellowships available to Jewish students for study, research, or other activities in the United States or abroad (particularly in Israel). For more information about the publication, see entry 227 in the "Scholarships, Fellowships & Loans—Special Population Groups—Religious Groups" section of this bibliography.

Available from: Los Angeles Hillel Council, 6505 Wilshire Boulevard, Suite 450, Los Angeles, CA 90048. *Telephone:* (323) 761-8555; *Fax:* (323) 761-8566; *E-mail:* mail@lahillel.org

Web site: www.lahillel.org

Women

679

Directory of Financial Aids for Women

By Gail Ann Schlachter and R. David Weber. El Dorado Hills, CA: Reference Service Press, 1978- . Biennial. ISSN 0732-5215. ISBN 1-58841-067-6. $45 (2003-2005 ed.). Hardcover.

Description: This is the only extensive and regularly updated listing of internships, loans, grants, fellowships, scholarships, and awards/prizes available primarily or exclusively to women. For more information about the publication, see entry 232 in the "Scholarships, Fellowships & Loans—Special Population Groups—Women" section of this bibliography.

Available from: Reference Service Press, 5000 Windplay Drive, Suite 4, El Dorado Hills, CA 95762. *Telephone:* (916) 939-9620; *Fax:* (916) 939-9626; *E-mail:* findaid@aol.com

Web site: www.rspfunding.com

Internships–Special Population Groups–Women

680

Free College and Training Money for Women

1st ed. By Matthew Lesko and Mary Ann Martello. Rockville, MD: Information USA, 2000. 767p. ISBN 0-878346-52-0. $24.95. Paper.

Description: In addition to identifying random sources of college money for women, this over-hyped guide lists federal and state job training agencies and programs. For more information about the directory, see entry 233 in the "Scholarships, Fellowships & Loans—Special Population Groups—Women" section of this bibliography.

Available from: Information USA, Inc., 12079 Nebel Street, Rockville, MD 20852. *Toll-free:* (800) 955-POWER

Web site: www.lesko.com

681

Pathways to Career Success for Women: A Resource Guide to Colleges, Financial Aid, and Work

Ed. by Laurie Sabol. Chicago: Ferguson, 2000. 360p. ISBN 0-89434-281-9. $29.95. Paper.

Description: One section in the directory briefly describes internships either available to women or offered by women's organizations. For more information about the publication, see entry 234 in the "Scholarships, Fellowships & Loans—Special Population Groups—Women" section of this bibliography.

Available from: Ferguson Publishing Company, 200 West Jackson Boulevard, Chicago, IL 60606. *Toll-free:* (800) 306-9941; *Fax:* (800) 306-9942

Web site: www.fergpubco.com

Federal Government Bookmarks

Many government agencies describe their financial aid offerings or funding opportunities on their web sites. Most of these sites, however, are not identified in the first five chapters, because listings from a single sponsor are generally excluded there. Since billions of dollars in financial aid and funding are offered by the government to both individuals and organizations, this chapter identifies the URLs of the federal web sites that would be of most interest to fundseekers. The listing is divided into two sections: 12 guides to federal government sites and 52 web sites of individual government departments or agencies. Brief descriptions of the grant information provided at each site is given.

Guides to Federal Sites

682 🕸 ¢
E-Grants
http://grants.gov
This site replaces the Federal Commons Project. It is intended to be the "electronic storefront for Federal Grants." Its content is similar to the *Catalog of Federal Domestic Assistance* (see 339), except that the listings focus solely on grant opportunities offered by federal agencies in the following fields: agriculture, arts, business and commerce, community development, consumer protection, disaster prevention and relief, education, employment and labor, energy, environmental quality, food and nutrition, health, housing, humanities, information and statistics, law and justice, natural resources, regional development, science and technology, social services, and transportation. Eventually, you will also be able to apply online for any funding opportunity you see displayed here.

683 🕸 ¢
Federal Government Resources: Grants, Contracts, and Auctions
http://www.lib.umich.edu/govdocs/fedgt.html
Sponsored by the University of Michigan Document's Center, this site provides access to the *Catalog of Federal Domestic Assistance* (see entry 339), Education Department grants, *Federal Register* (see entry 357), the Small Business Administration, etc. Other areas on the site identify grants awarded (in the Federal Assistance Award Data System and the Consolidated Federal Funds Report), contracts available (particularly in FedBizOpps, described in entry 467), contracts awarded, and auctions.

684 🕸 ¢
The Federal Web Locator
http://www.infoctre.edu/fwl
This service is offered by Center for Information Law and Policy and is intended "to bring the cyber citizen to the federal government's doorstep." Its search engine can be used to locate federal Internet sources. Or, use its Quick Jumps area to find an agency or organization.

685 🕸 ¢

FedWorld Information Network
http://www.fedworld.gov
This is a comprehensive and easy-to-use subject index to government information online (particularly technical and scientific information). It is sponsored by the National Technical Information Service and is updated daily. Here, fundseekers can browse the site, search the web pages on the network, search for U.S. government reports, access more than 20 full-text government databases (e.g., Government Job Announcements), or explore U.S. government web sites.

686 🕸 ¢

FirstGov
http://firstgov.gov
Prepared by the President's Management Council, and replacing the White House Office of Public Liaison's Nonprofit Gateway, this site is intended to be "your first click to the U.S. Government." In one place, you can search more than 30 million pages of government information from 20,000 web sites, and your search results will be ranked by relevancy. In addition, you can browse FirstGov by topic area, the most relevant of which is FirstGov for Nonprofits. Covered here are: grants, loans, and other assistance for nonprofits (including access to the *Catalog of Federal Domestic Assistance* (see entry 339), state and local funding directories, and surplus property donations), fundraising and outreach, tax information for nonprofits, registration and licensing for nonprofits, management and operations, laws and regulations, online services, and agency specific non-profit resources (Departments of Agriculture, Commerce, Defense, Education, etc.).

687 🕸 ¢

Government Information Locator Service (GILS)
http://www.access.gpo.gov/su_docs/gils/index.html
Known also as GILS, this index to government information has an "advanced search facility" that fundseekers will find helpful. All listings link to detailed descriptions of available information.

688 🕸 ¢

Government Information INFOMINE
http://infomine.ucr.edu
INFOMINE, which began in January, 1994 as a project of the Library of the University of California, Riverside, is one of the first web resources of any type offered by a library. Use this comprehensive and searchable

Federal Government Bookmarks–Guides To Federal Sites

subject index to locate government Internet sites (primarily U.S. based, although some international locations are also included).

689

Government Resources
http://www.nttc.edu/resources/government/govresources.asp
Maintained by the National Technology Transfer Center, this site contains about 1,000 government links grouped into five categories: U.S. Legislative Branch, U.S. Executive Branch, U.S. Judicial Branch, Independent Government Agencies, and The 50 States. There is also a separate section that provides a comprehensive listing of current and past SBIR and STTR solicitations.

690

GovSpot
http://www.govspot.com
Produced by StartSpot Mediaworks and aimed at the novice searcher, this well-organized site offers a portal to government information online. The main pages are listed by topic (e.g., justice, money) and the Shortcuts section offers a complete list of federal agencies (as well as state sources of information). Other interesting categories include Must-See Sites, Do You Know, and You Asked for It.

691

GPO's Browse Topics
http://www.access.gpo.gov/su_docs/locators/topics/index.html
This service organizes government Internet sites by topic. The main list of topics is based on the current *Guide to U.S. Government Information*, which is also known as *The Subject Bibliography Index*. One area links to sites offering "Grants and Awards." In addition, specific federal online databases can be accessed through the "Database List," including the *Code of Federal Regulations* (see entry 326), FedBizOpps (formerly CBD*Net*, see entry 467), and the *Federal Register* (see entry 357).

692

SearchGovernment
http://www.isleuth.com/gove.html
This sophisticated search engine makes it possible to locate information within government agencies' Internet sites.

693

Yahoo—Government Directory
http://www.yahoo.com/Government/Web_Directories
This site provides a search of Yahoo's government listings only. Other search engines—for example, Google—also offer similar access.

Web Sites

694

Administration for Children and Families (ACF)
http://www.acf.dhhs.gov
Click on "Grants & Contracts to find program announcements, funding opportunities, financial reports and data, grant applications and other forms, and grant review opportunities offered by the ACF.

695

Administration on Aging (AOA)
http://www.aoa.dhhs.gov/research.html
This site provides information about grants as well as more general resources (e.g., statistical portraits and topical overviews). One area of the site offers a sub-directory of foundations supporting research and projects related to aging.

696

Agency for Healthcare Research and Quality (AHRQ)
http://www.ahcpr.gov/fund
The "Funding Opportunities" section of this site includes announcements of grants and contracts, notices, information about upcoming research agendas, and details on research training assistance.

697

AmeriCorps
http://www.americorps.org
In 1993, the National Community Service Trust Act was signed into law and established the AmeriCorps program. This program offers an opportunity for Americans over the age of 17 to perform community service at the same time that they set aside money for college. Jobs, fellowships,

Federal Government Bookmarks–Web Sites

and internship opportunities with AmeriCorps and the Corporation for National Service are listed here (although, because of current budget constraints, AmeriCorps has temporarily suspended benefits).

698 ¢

Centers for Disease Control (CDC)
http://www.cdc.gov
Check here for new funding opportunities posted by the Centers for Disease Control; current areas of funding interest include chronic disease prevention/health promotion, AIDS/HIV programs, injury and violence prevention and control, occupational safety and health; and sexually transmitted diseases.

699 ¢

Centers for Medicare & Medicaid Services (CMS)
http://www.cms.gov
The web site for CMS, formerly the Health Care Financing Administration (HCFA), contains grant and contract solicitations for research studies or demonstration projects when funding is available.

700 ¢

Department of Agriculture (USDA)
http://www.usda.gov/nonprofi.htm
The USDA's web site provides information on farms, food production, agricultural trade, and politics. In its Nonprofit Gateway area, it also identifies funding opportunities for business, community development, food security, research and education, and volunteers.

701 ¢

Department of Commerce (DOC)
http://www.commerce.gov
Click on "Grant Opportunities" to link to funding offered by various DOC units (e.g., Economic Development Administration, Minority Business Development Agency, National Oceanic and Atmospheric Administration, and National Institute of Standards and Technology). To access FedBizOpps, the Department's single point-of-entry for federal government procurement opportunities over $25,000 (which replaced CBD*Net* and *Commerce Business Daily,* entry 467), go to www.fedbizopps.gov.

How to Find Out About Financial Aid and Funding

702

Department of Defense (DOD)
http://www.defenselink.mil/pubs/almanac/osd.html
Included on the Secretary of Defense's homepage are links to military services, where information on their various funding programs can be found.

703

Department of Education (ED)
http://www.ed.gov/index.jsp
This is the first place searchers should check for information on federal financial aid. Click on the "Financial Aid" tab for materials related to federal scholarships, fellowships, loans, and student grants. Funding opportunities (grants and contracts) offered by the Department of Education are also covered on the site (click on "Grants & Contracts). Links to a directory of state higher education agencies is provided as well. To access the "student's gateway" to the U.S. government (including lists of scholarship search web sites and the Department of Education's Project EASI), go to www.students.gov.

704

Department of Energy (DOE)
http://www.energy.gov
In addition to information and links to federal energy policy, regulations, and statistics, this site describes funding offered by the agency (click on "Science & Technology").

705

Department of Health and Human Services (HHS)
http://www.hhs.gov
HHS has approximately 300 grant programs, most of which are administered in a decentralized manner by several agencies. A number of these programs are covered here (click on "Grants & Funding"). The site also includes recent listings from the *Catalog of Federal Domestic Assistance* (see entry 339); these are sorted alphabetically by program and by function or subject (and searchers can choose programs for individuals or families or only those for organizations or institutions, programs by department or independent agency, or new programs appearing for the first time).

Federal Government Bookmarks–Web Sites

706

Department of Housing and Urban Development (HUD)
http://www.hud.gov/grants/index.cfm

This site focuses on community and housing policies and programs. The "Grants" area covers grants awarded to organizations and groups for a variety of purposes. You can find the following categories of information here: available funding (notices that tell you when grant funds are available and how to apply); funding announcements (lists of those who were awarded grants); grants program inventory (a description of every grant that HUD awarded during the previous fiscal year); a link to web sites that list all federal grant programs, and information on HUD's new automated grants management system.

707

Department of Justice (DOJ)
http://www.usdoj.gov/10grants/index.html

The DOJ offers funding opportunities to conduct research, to support law enforcement activities in state and local jurisdictions, to provide training and technical assistance, and to implement programs that improve the criminal justice system. This funding is described in the "Grants" section of the web site. General financial aid for college study is not available from this agency.

708

Department of Labor (DOL)
http://www.dol.gov/oasam/grants/main.htm

This site provides access to information on salaries, working conditions, and other related topics. Its "Grant and Contract Information" page reviews funding opportunities offered by the department and other federal agencies.

709

Department of the Interior (DOI)
http://www.doi.gov/non-profit/index1.html

This site focuses on America's natural resources and cultural heritage. Its "Non-Profit Information Gateway" provides information on DOI financial assistance and grant programs, volunteer opportunities, and non-financial assistance offerings.

How to Find Out About Financial Aid and Funding

710

Department of the Treasury
http://www.treas.gov
This site supplies information on budget, taxation, money supply, and other fiscal matters. The Awards Recognition Page describes awards and grants offered by the department.

711

Department of Transportation (DOT)
http://www.dot.gov/business.html
The DOT annually funds approximately $25 billion in grants and cooperative agreements. These programs are described in the "Doing Business with DOT" section of the site.

712

Department of Veteran Affairs (DVA)
http://www.va.gov
This site covers monetary and nonmonetary assistance programs for veterans, dependents, and survivors in the following areas: burial, compensation, education, health, home loans, life insurance, and vocational rehabilitation. Online applications are provided for many of these programs.

713

Economic Development Administration (EDA)
http://www.osec.doc.gov/eda
Under the Department of Commerce, EDA provides grants to nonprofit and local governments for projects that alleviate unemployment and underemployment in economically distressed areas.

714

Environmental Protection Agency (EPA)
http://www.epa.gov/epahome/educational.htm
This is the first place to check for information on federal environmental activities and the state of the nation's environment. Click on "Students" to learn about EPA internships, fellowships, and student programs. Click on "Researchers" to find out about research funding available on the federal, regional, and state level to environmentally-oriented organizations, governmental units, and individuals.

Federal Government Bookmarks–Web Sites

715 🕸 ¢

Federal Aviation Administration (FAA)
http://www2.faa.gov/education/rlib/grant.htm
Turn here to find a lengthy list of aviation-related and other scholarships and grants.

716 🕸 ¢

Federal Information Exchange, Inc. (FEDIX)
http://www.sciencewise.com
Funding and educational opportunities sponsored by eight participating agencies were described at this site: Department of Defense, National Aeronautics and Space Administration, Department of Transportation, Office of Naval Research, National Institutes of Health, Air Force Office of Scientific Research, Agency for International Development, and Department of Agriculture. However, in mid-2002, ScienceWise's operations were suspended. Although the web site promises that "the combination of free and paid-for services" would resume as of December, 2002, the site was still not operating during the first quarter of 2003 and e-mails sent to the posted contact were returned as undeliverable.

717 🕸 ¢

Federal Trade Commission (FTC)
http://www.ftc.gov
This homepage offers consumer protection information and provides valuable tips on how to avoid scholarship search scams (click on "Consumer Protection").

718 🕸 ¢

Government Printing Office (GPO)
http://www.access.gpo.gov/su_docs
GPO Access, which is located on this web site, offers a number of government databases; of particular interest to the grantseeker are these: *Federal Register* (1994 forward, see entry 357), *Code of Federal Regulations* (see entry 326), and CBD*Net* archives.

719 🕸 ¢

Government Services Administration (GSA)
http://www.cfda.gov/default.htm
The *Catalog of Federal Domestic Assistance* (see entry 339), produced by the General Services Administration and located on this web site, is probably the most important government resource available to grant-

seekers. It describes federal programs, projects, services, and activities that provide assistance or benefits to the American public. Use terms like "money," "grants," and "assistance" to search the listings online. You can access the database by program number, keyword, a list of the top 10 percent of programs, SQL-like queries, or browsing.

720

Health Resources and Services Administration (HRSA)
http://www.hrsa.gov

HRSA's site offers information on available grants (including a Preview Online Ordering section) as well as funding opportunities open to students in the health professions (click on "Grants" in the Funding section).

721

HHS's GrantsNet
http://www.hhs.gov/grantsnet/grantinfo.htm

GrantsNet is a tool for finding and exchanging information about the Department of Health and Human Service and selected other federal grant programs. Use the "Electronic Roadway to Grants" to find the following sections: how to find information about HHS programs; how to apply for an HHS grant; HHS and other funding opportunities; and managing grants.

722

Institute of Museum and Library Services (IMLS)
http://www.imls.gov/grants/index.htm

IMLS grants and awards are identified and described on this web site.

723

Internal Revenue Service (IRS)
http://www.irs.ustreas.gov

The IRS's online site offers forms, instructions, and information on federal taxation, Of particular interest are four IRS documents that relate directly to students and/or scholarship holders: *Student's Guide to Federal Income Tax* (Publication 4); *Tax Benefits for Work-Related Education* (Publication 508); *Scholarships and Fellowships* (Publication 520); and *Tax Benefits for Higher Education* (Publication 970).

Federal Government Bookmarks–Web Sites

724 🕸 ¢

National Aeronautics and Space Administration (NASA)
http://www.nasa.gov

NASA and NASA-affiliated organizations offer billions of dollars in grants each year for research and education. Many of these programs are described here.

725 🕸 ¢

National Agricultural Library (NAL)
http://www.nal.usda.gov/ric/richs/grants.htm

Covered here are federal grant opportunities related to rural health. This list is updated periodically by the National Agricultural Library's Rural Information Center Health Services Program. For each grant, title, scope, and agency contact are indicated. Similar information is also provided for organizations.

726 🕸 ¢

National Archives and Records Administration (NARA)
http://www.archives.gov

The National Historical Publications and Records Commission is the grant-making affiliate of the National Archives. It makes grants to preserve and provide public access to photographs, records, and other materials that document American history. Access to the *Federal Register* (see entry 357) is also provided on the site.

727 🕸 ¢

National Endowment for the Arts (NEA)
http://arts.endow.gov

This site consists of three parts: "Explore," which contains arts features, interviews, new work in the Gallery, and the writer's corner; "Art Forms," where you can choose an arts discipline/field to find resources, grant listings, field reports, and archived features; and "Cultural Funding," a new online resource listing federal funding available for arts initiatives through national, state, and local funding programs.

728 🕸 ¢

National Endowment for the Humanities (NEH)
http://www.neh.fed.us

Check here for information on more than $14.5 million in grants and fellowships from NEH; grant guidelines and applications are also available online.

How to Find Out About Financial Aid and Funding

729 🕸 ¢

National Institute of Justice (NIJ)
http://www.ojp.usdoj.gov/nij/funding.htm
Included on this site are current NIJ solicitations and application forms, many of which are available to be downloaded.

730 🕸 ¢

National Institute of Standards and Technology (NIST)
http://www.nist.gov/public_affairs/grants.htm
NIST grants/awards supporting research at industry, academic, and other institutions are available on a competitive basis through several Institute offices; those programs (including NIST's Advanced Technology Program and Small Business Innovation Research Program) are described here.

731 🕸 ¢

National Institutes of Health (NIH)
http://www.nih.gov/grants/index.cfm
The "Grants Page" leads to information about NIH grants and fellowship programs, applying for a grant or fellowship, policy changes, administrative responsibilities of awardees, the CRISP database, and the numbers and characteristics of awards made by the NIH. Also available is an online version of the *NIH Guide for Grants and Contracts,* the official document announcing the availability of NIH funds for biomedical and behavioral research and research training.

732 🕸 ¢

National Library of Medicine (NLM)
http://www.nlm.nih.gov
The National Library of Medicine's web site provides program announcements, lists of grants awarded and available, fact sheets on extramural programs, and online application forms.

733 🕸 ¢

National Oceanic and Atmospheric Administration (NOAA)
http://www.ofa.noaa.gov/~grants/index1.html
Described here are NOAA's major grant programs, including NOAA's Minority Serving Institutions Initiative.

Federal Government Bookmarks–Web Sites

734 🕸 ¢

National Park Service (NPS)
http://www.cr.nps.gov/helpyou.htm
Information is provided here on grants available to preserve and protect cultural resources nationwide, including maritime history grants, historic preservation tribal grants, and recreation and museum funding. Also described are tax credits for historic rehabilitation.

735 🕸 ¢

National Science Foundation (NSF)
http://www.nsf.gov
In addition to information on the status of science and research in the United States, this site covers grants sponsored by the foundation (these account for about 20 percent of federal support to academic institutions for basic research). Online copies of NSF's E-Bulletin (which replaced the *NSF Bulletin* that ceased publication in September, 1998) are also available here; E-Bulletin provides up-to-date information on deadlines and target dates for NSF programs. If you are interested in learning about grant opportunities as soon as they become available, click on "Custom News Service" to subscribe to NSF's electronic news service.

736 🕸 ¢

National Telecommunications and Information Administration (NTIA)
http://www.ntia.doc.gov
Information is provided here on grants (click on "Grants Programs"), training, and research services in the telecommunications area.

737 🕸 ¢

Office of Minority Health Resource Center (OMH-RC)
http://www.omhrc.gov
The Office of Minority Health Resource Center maintains a database of funding and grant resources that can help support minority health projects (click on "What's New"). The database lists federal, state, and local resources, community resources, private and public foundations, and pharmaceutical and insurance organizations. A Funding Resource guide for grantseekers is also provided.

738

Office of Naval Research (ONR)
http://www.onr.navy.mil/02

The Office of Naval Research's mission is to plan, foster, and encourage basic and applied scientific research. Identified on ONR's Grant Terms page is federal funding (grants and contracts) for university research, not-for-profit institutions, selected individuals, and businesses.

739

Peace Corps
http://www.peacecorps.gov

The Peace Corps places 3,000 Americans around the world each year. Information on this program (one of the best paid volunteer opportunities) is presented on this web site.

740

Small Business Administration (SBA)
http://www.sba.gov/financing

This is the place to check for information about SBA loans, in addition to accessing instructional materials on starting and running a small business.

741

Smithsonian Institution (SI)
http://www.si.edu/ofg/start.htm

A searchable database of SI's internships, fellowships, and grants is provided here. Also available is an online version of *Smithsonian Opportunities for Research,* which describes SI's annual funding programs.

742

Social Security Administration (SSA)
http://www.ssa.gov

Turn to this homepage for full-text information on retirement and medical programs as well as on personal Social Security benefits.

743

State Departments of Education and Guaranty Agencies
http://www.ed.gov/offices/OPE/Students/other.html

Maintained by the Department of Education, this site provides a list of links, arranged alphabetically, to 1) departments of education and higher

Federal Government Bookmarks–Web Sites

education commissions (which often run assistance programs for college-bound students) and 2) to loan guaranty agencies in the 50 states and U.S. territories. These two sets of agencies are a good source of information about state-based loans and grants.

744

Substance Abuse and Mental Health Services Administration (SAMHSA)
http://www.samhsa.gov/funding/content/funding_main.html
SAMHSA has several programs that offer discretionary grant funding. The primary source of funds for these programs is the Knowledge Development and Application (KD&A) program, which aims to develop new knowledge about ways to improve the prevention and treatment of substance abuse and mental illness. Information on SAMHSA grants and contracts is provided on this site.

745

U.S. Civilian Research & Development Foundation (CRDF)
http://www.crdf.org
The U.S. Civilian Research & Development Foundation for the Independent States of the Former Soviet Union (CRDF) was founded in 1995 and is a private, nonprofit charitable organization created by the U.S. government as America's response to the declining state of science and engineering in the former Soviet Union (FSU). Information about CRDF's mission, activities, and support for collaborative projects between U.S. and FSU researchers is provided on this site (click on "Awards").

Indexes

The guide provides five indexes to make it easy to search for resources listing available financial aid and funding opportunities. Title, Name, Publisher and Producer, Geographic, and Subject Indexes follow a word-by-word arrangement and refer the user to the appropriate entry by number.

Title Index

The current, previous, and variant names of the print, electronic, and Internet resources covered in *How to Find Out About Financial Aid and Funding* (either as separate entries or as references in annotations describing other titles) are indexed here. More than 700 individual titles are listed alphabetically, word by word, except in the cases of certain prefixes, such as "A," "An," and "The." The number following each title refers to the entry that contains the fullest description of that resource.

The A's and B's of Academic Scholarships, 1
AABGA Internship Directory, 662
Absolutelyscholarships.com, 65
Academe Today, 277
Access Advisor, 53
AFL–CIO Scholarship Guide: A Source for Union Sponsored Scholarships, Awards, and Student Financial Aid, 230
African–American Yearbook, 62
After Latin American Studies: A Guide to Graduate Study and Employment for Latin Americanists, 137
Aid for Education, 355
AIDS Funding, 513
Alaska Employment Guide, 622
Alaska Funding and Resource Guide: The Directory of Foundations, Corporate Giving and Technical Assistance Programs for Alaskan–based Organizations, 385
Alaska Funding Guide, 385
Alternatives to the Peace Corps: A Directory of Third World & U.S. Volunteer Opportunities, 630
American Art Directory, 163
American Journalism Review, 569
American Theatre, 574
America's New Foundations, 337
America's Top Internships, 607
America's Top 100 Internships, 607
Annual Index Foundation Reports, 411
Annual Register of Grant Support: A Directory of Funding Sources, 235
Anuario Hispano–Hispanic Yearbook, 62
ARIS Funding Messenger: Biomedical Sciences Report, 316
ARIS Funding Messenger: Creative Arts and Humanities Report, 282
ARIS Funding Messenger: Social and Natural Sciences Report, 271
ARIS Funding Reports: Student Funding Sources, 44

Arizona Guide to Grants & Giving, 387
Arkansas Funding Directory, 388
Arkansas Student Information Service, 79
Art Deadlines List, 560
Artists and Writers Colonies: Retreats, Residencies, and Respites for the Creative Mind, 289
Artists' Communities: A Directory of Residencies in the United States That Offer Time and Space for Creativity, 303
Arts & Culture Funding Report, 493
Artweek, 565
ASIS, 79
ASNE Internship Search, 648
Assistantships and Graduate Fellowships in the Mathematical Sciences, 189
Athletic Scholarships: Thousands of Grants—and over $400 Million—for College–Bound Athletes, 192
Audio Video Market Place, 567
Audiovisual Market Place, 567
AV Market Place, 567
AvScholars.com Free Scholarship Database, 172
Awards, Competitions, and Prizes, 575
Awards, Honors and Prizes: An International Directory of Awards and Their Donors, 530

The Back Door Guide to Short–Term Job Adventures: Internships, Extraordinary Experiences, Seasonal Jobs, Volunteering, Work Abroad, 606
Beneficios Federales para los Veteranos y sus Dependientes, 327
Best Buys in College Education, 3
The Best Way to Save for College, 61
Best 106 Internships, 607
Best 109 Internships, 607
The Big Book of Library Grant Money: Profiles of Private and Corporate

385

Title Index

Foundations and Direct Corporate Givers Receptive to Library Grant Proposals, 484
Big Book of Minority Opportunities: The Directory of Special Programs for Minority Group Members, 207
Big Book of Opportunities for Women: The Directory of Women's Organizations, 234
Big Green Internship Book, 621
Black Excel African American Student's College Guide: Your One-Stop Resource for Choosing the Right College, Getting in, and Paying the Bill, 196
The Black Student's Guide to Scholarships: 700+ Private Money Sources for Black and Minority Students, 197
The Blue Book, 87
The Bowker Annual Library and Book Trade Almanac, 559
BrokeScholar, 4
The Buck Starts Here...A Guide to Assistive Technology Funding in Kentucky, 332

California Foundation DataBook, 389
Capital Assistance Funding: A Rural Health Resource Guide, 505
The CARE Book: College Aid Resources for Education, 5
Career Guide for Singers, 584
Career Guide for Young American Singers, 584
Career Guide Update, 584
Career Opportunity News, 15
Cash for College: The Ultimate Guide to College Scholarships, 6
Cash for Grad School: The Ultimate Guide to Grad School Scholarships, 6
CASHE, 13, 77
Catalog of Federal Domestic Assistance, 339
Catalog of State Assistance to Local Governments, 401
Catalog of Wyoming State Grants, 453
Catalogs I–VI: Outside Financial Resources for Theological Students, 162
Catholic Funding Guide: A Directory of Resources for Catholic Activity, 498
CBDNet, 466
Charitable Foundations Directory of Ohio, 433
Charitable Trust Directory, 448
CharityBrowser, 340
Children and Youth Funding Report, 355
Children's Books: Awards & Prizes, 571
Children's Writer's & Illustrator's Market, 572

Chronicle Financial Aid Guide: Scholarships and Loans for High School Students, College Undergraduates, Graduates, and Adult Learners, 8
Chronicle Four-Year College Databook, 8
Chronicle Guide to Grants, 341
Chronicle of Higher Education, 277
Chronicle of Philanthropy, 342
Chronicle Perspectives PLUS, 8
Chronicle Two-Year College Databook, 8
Chronicle Vocational School Manual, 8
Church Funding Resource Guide, 502
Co–op College Roster, 614
Co–op Education Undergraduate Program Directory, 614
Code of Federal Regulations, Title 38: Pensions, Bonuses, and Veterans' Relief, 326
College Aid Resources for Education, 5
College Aid Sources for Higher Education, 13, 77
College Athletic Scholarship Guide, 193
College Athletic Scholarships Database, 193
The College Blue Book, 9
The College Board College Cost & Financial Aid Handbook, 10
The College Board Scholarship Handbook, 11
College Cost Book, 10
College Costs and Financial Aid Handbook, 10
College Dollars, 12
College Edge, 58
College Financial Aid Emergency Kit, 13
College Financial Aid for Dummies, 13
College Grants from Uncle Sam, 49
College: How to Get There & Go for Free!, 14
College Loans from Uncle Sam, 49
College Quest, 56
College Spotlight, 15
College Student's Guide to Merit and Other No–Need Funding, 16
Collegeboard.com Scholarship Search, 17
CollegeJournal.com, 69
CollegeView's Scholarship Search, 18
Collegiate Aviation Scholarship Listing, 173
Colorado Collegiate Handbook, 80
Colorado Grants Guide, 391
Commerce Business Daily, 466–467
Community Foundation Locator, 343
Community Health Funding Report, 355
Community of Science Funding Alert, 237
Community of Science Funding News, 237

386

Title Index

Community of Science Funding Opportunities, 237
The Complete Directory for People with Disabilities, 220
The Complete Guide to Florida Foundations, 395
The Complete Guide to Literary Contests, 573
Complete Guide to Seasonal State Park Employment, 621
The Complete Scholarship Book, 19
COMSEARCH Printouts, 369
Congressional Internship Book, 621
Connecticut Foundation Directory, 392
Connections: A Directory of Volunteer Opportunities, 610
Corporate Foundation Profiles, 344
Corporate Giving Directory: Comprehensive Profiles of America's Major Corporate Foundations and Corporate Charitable Giving Programs, 345
Corporate Giving Yellow Pages: Guide to Corporate Giving Contacts, 346
Corporate Grantmaking for Racial and Ethnic Communities, 520
COS Funding Alert, 237
COS Funding News, 237
COS Funding Opportunities, 237
Creating Options: A Resource on Financial Aid for Students with Disabilities, 221
Criminal Justice Funding Report, 493

Dan Cassidy's Worldwide College Scholarship Directory, 21
Dan Cassidy's Worldwide Graduate Scholarship Directory, 22
Directory of Biomedical and Health Care Grants, 313
Directory of Building and Equipment Grants: A Reference Directory Identifying Building, Renovation, and Equipment Grants Available to Nonprofit Organizations, 348
Directory of Charitable Funds in New Hampshire, 257
Directory of Charitable Trusts and Foundations: A Guide for Hawai'i's Nonprofit Organizations, 398
Directory of Charitable Trusts and Foundations for Hawaii's Non–Profit Organizations, 398
Directory of Computer and High Technology Grants: A Reference Directory Identifying Computer, Software, and High–Tech Grants Available to Nonprofit Organizations, 515
Directory of Corporate and Foundation Givers, 349

Directory of Family Practice Residency Programs, 181
Directory of Financial Aids for Minorities, 198–201
Directory of Financial Aids for Women, 232
A Directory of Foundations in the State of Maine, 410
Directory of Grants for Crafts: How to Write a Winning Proposal, 285
Directory of Grants for Medical Study and Research in the U.S.A., 210
Directory of Grants for Organizations Serving People with Disabilities: A Reference Directory Identifying Grants Available to Nonprofit Organizations, 524
Directory of Grants for Study and Research in the U.S.A., 210
Directory of Grants for Study and Research Overseas, 210
Directory of Grants in the Humanities, 280
Directory of Idaho Foundations, 399
The Directory of Illinois Foundations, 402
Directory of Indiana Grantmakers, 404
Directory of Indiana & Kentucky Grantmakers, 404
Directory of Indiana & Kentucky Grantmakers Searchable Database, 404
Directory of International Corporate Giving in America and Abroad, 350
Directory of International Grants and Fellowships in the Health Sciences, 314
Directory of Internship and Post–Doctoral Fellowships in Clinical Child/Pediatric Psychology, 645
Directory of Internship and Post–Doctoral Programs in Professional Psychology, 645
Directory of Internships in Youth Development, 646
The Directory of Kansas Foundations, 406
Directory of Kentucky Grantmakers, 404
Directory of Maine Grantmakers, 410
The Directory of Missouri Foundations, 420
Directory of Missouri Grantmakers, 421
Directory of Operating Grants, 351
Directory of Overseas Summer Jobs, 639
Directory of Pathology Training Programs (Residencies and Fellowships) in the United States and Canada, 179
Directory of Pennsylvania Foundations, 439
Directory of Private Scholarships and Grants, 31
Directory of Program Grants, 352
Directory of Public Garden Internships, 662
Directory of Research Grants, 238

Title Index

Directory of Residencies and Fellowships, 184, 665
Directory of Residency Training Programs Accredited by the Accreditation Council for Graduate Medical Education, 181
Directory of Student Placements in Health Care Settings in North America, 181
Directory of Summer Jobs Abroad, 639
Directory of Texas Foundations, 444
Directory of Texas Foundations Online, 444
Directory of Virginia Foundations, 447
Disability Funding News, 355
Discounts and Deals at the Nation's 360 Best Colleges: The Parent Soup Financial Aid and College Guide, 24
Distance Learning Funding $ourcebook: A Guide to Foundation, Corporate and Government Support for Telecommunications and the New Media, 471
Don't Miss Out: The Ambitious Student's Guide to Financial Aid, 25
Dramatists Sourcebook: Complete Opportunities for Playwrights, Translators, Composers, Lyricists, and Librettists, 574

Editor & Publisher, 568
Editor & Publisher Journalism Awards and Fellowships Directory, 568
Education Funding News, 479
Education Grants Alert, 356
eduPASS: The SmartStudent Guide to Studying in the United States, 30
Embark, 58
Energywi$e Construction Funding Directory for Green Buildings, 286
EntertainmentCareers.net, 624
Environmental Grantmaking Foundations, 507
Environmental Internships, 622
eSchool News Online, 519
ExPAN, 26
ExPAN for the Home 1.0, 26
EZ/EC Notices of Funding Availability, 357

FAADS: Federal Awards Assistance Data System, 255
Faculty Grants Directory, 302
FAFSA on the Web, 73
FAME/Fleet Bank Scholarship Book, 89
Family Services Funding Report, 355
FASTaid, 27
FastWeb: Financial Aid Search Through the Web, 28

FC Scholar: The Foundation Center's Database of Education Funding for Individuals, 243
FC Search, 354
FedBizOpps, 467
Federal Assistance Monitor, 355
Federal Assistance Program Retrieval System (FAPRS), 339
Federal Benefits for Veterans, 327
Federal Benefits for Veterans and Dependents, 327
Federal Business Opportunities, 467
Federal Financial Aid Programs, 73
Federal Funding Sources for Rural Areas, 505
Federal Grant Deadline Calendar, 479
Federal Grants & Contracts Weekly: Project Opportunities in Research, Training, and Services, 356
Federal Money Retriever, 472
Federal Register, 357
Federal Register Subject Index, 357
Federal Support for Rural Health: A Compendium of Federal Programs That Support the Provision of Health Care in Rural Areas, 505
FEDIX Opportunity Alert, 240, 240
FedMoney.org, 472
Fellowship and Residency Electronic Interactive Database Access, 181
Fellowship Plus, 162
Fiction Writer's Market, 578
FinAid: The Financial Aid Information Page, 30
FinAid! The SmartStudent Guide to Financial Aid, 30
The Financial Aid Book, 31
Financial Aid for African Americans, 198
Financial Aid for Asian Americans, 199
Financial Aid for Hispanic Americans, 200
Financial Aid for Lesbian, Gay and Bisexual Students, 213
Financial Aid for Minorities: Awards Open to Students with Any Major, 207
Financial Aid for Minorities in Business and Law, 207
Financial Aid for Minorities in Education, 207
Financial Aid for Minorities in Engineering and Science, 207
Financial Aid for Minorities in Health Fields, 207
Financial Aid for Minorities in Journalism and Mass Communications, 207
Financial Aid for Native Americans, 201

Title Index

Financial Aid for Research and Creative Activities Abroad, 262
Financial Aid for Research, Study, Travel, and Other Activities Abroad, 112, 262
Financial Aid for Students with Disabilities, 221
Financial Aid for Study and Training Abroad, 112
Financial Aid for Texas Students, 99
Financial Aid for the Disabled and Their Families, 222
Financial Aid for Veterans, Military Personnel, and Their Dependents, 216
The Financial Aid Information Page, 30
Financial Aid Search, 8
Financial Aid Search Through the Web, 28
Financial Aid Tool Belt: A How–To Guide for Students, 89
Financial Assistance for Library and Information Studies, 136
Financial Assistance for Library Education, 136
Financial Assistance Resource Guide, 180
Financial Support for Jewish College Students, 227
Financing Graduate School: How to Get Money for Your Master's and Ph.D., 39
F.I.N.D., 395–396
Five Federal Financial Aid Programs, 73
Florida Funding—The Monthly Newsletter for Florida Grantseekers, 395–396
Florida Information Network Database, 395–396
Florida Scholarships: Guide to Scholarships, Loans, Grants, and Other Financial Assistance Programs, 81
Florida State Grant Programs, 396
Focus on Financial Aid, 92
For the People: 1,608 Ways to Get Your Share of the Little–Known Bargains the Government Offers, 241
Foundation Center Data Book, 377
The Foundation Center's Guide to Grantseeking on the Web, 358
Foundation & Corporate Grants Alert, 356
The Foundation Directory, 359
The Foundation Directory Online, 360
The Foundation Directory Online Plus, 361
The Foundation Directory Part 2, 361
The Foundation Directory Supplement, 362
Foundation Finder, 363
Foundation Giving Watch, 365
The Foundation Grants Index on CD–ROM, 364
Foundation Grants to Individuals, 243

Foundation Reporter: Comprehensive Profiles and Analyses of America's Major Private Foundations, 365
The Foundation 1000, 366
Foundations in Wisconsin: A Directory, 452
FoundationSource, 403
Free College and Training Money for Women, 233
Free Help from Uncle Sam to Start Your Own Business (Or Expand the One You Have), 275
Free Money and Help for Women Entrepreneurs, 233
Free Money for College: A Guide to More Than 1,000 Grants and Scholarships for Undergraduate Study, 34
Free Money for Graduate School: A Guide to More Than 1,000 Grants and Scholarships for Graduate Study, 35
Free Money for Your Retirement, 233
Free Money to Change Your Life, 233
The Free Scholarship Search Service, 36
FREIDA Online, 181
FreSch! The Free Scholarship Search Service, 36
Fulbright and Other Grants for Graduate Study Abroad, 263
Fulbright and Related Grants for Graduate Study and Research Abroad, 263
Fulbright Awards Abroad, 264
Fulbright Lecturing and Research Abroad, 264
Fulbright Scholar Program: Grants for Faculty and Professionals, 264
Fulbright Senior Scholars Awards Abroad, 264
Fulbright Teacher Exchange Program, 264
Fund Raiser's Guide to Human Service Funding, 488
Fund Raiser's Guide to Religious Philanthropy, 500
Funders of Lesbian, Gay, Bisexual and Transgender Programs: A Directory for Grantseekers, 523
FundFinder, 26
Funding for Persons with Visual Impairments, Large Print Edition, 222
Funding for Persons with Visual Impairments, PLUS Edition, 222
Funding Law Enforcement Hotline, 486
Funding Private Schools, 477
Funding Sources for Children and Youth Programs, 489
Funding Sources for Community and Economic Development: A Guide to

Title Index

Current Sources for Local Programs and Projects, 468
Funding Sources for K–12 Education, 473
Funding Sources for K–12 Schools and Adult Basic Education, 473
fundingAlert, 310
Fundsnet, 367
FundSource, 268

Gaining the Co–op Edge: A Student Guide to Cooperative Education, 614
Gardner's Guide to Internships in New Media 2004: Computer Graphics, Animation and Multimedia, 649
Gardner's Guide to Internships @ Multimedia and Animation Studios, 650
Gekkan Asia no Tomo, 120
Georgia Foundation Directory, 397
Georgia Giving, 432
German–American Scholarship Guide: Exchange Opportunities for Historians and Social Scientists, 288
Get Free Cash for College: Scholarship Secrets of Harvard Students, 38
Get Outside!, 615
Getting Money for Graduate School: More than 1,000 Scholarships, Grants, Prizes, Forgivable Loans, and Fellowships, 39
GLBT Student Scholarship Resource Guide, 213
GoCollege.com, 69
Government Assistance Almanac, 368
The Government Financial Aid Book: The Insider's Guide to State & Federal Government Grants and Loans, 40
Government Giveaways for Entrepreneurs IV, 233
Graduate Assistantship Directory in Computing, 191
Graduate Medical Education Directory, 181
Graduate Medical Education Directory on CD–ROM, 181
Graduate Scholarship Directory: The Complete Guide to Scholarships, Fellowships, Grants & Loans for Graduate & Professional Study, 22
The Graduate School Funding Handbook, 41
The Grant Advisor, 474
The Grant Advisor Plus, 474
Grant Deadline Monitor, 479
Grant Funding for Elderly Health Services, 511
The Grant Guides, 369

GrantFinder: The Complete Guide to Postgraduate Funding Worldwide: Arts and Humanities, 281
GrantFinder: The Complete Guide to Postgraduate Funding Worldwide: Medicine, 315
GrantFinder: The Complete Guide to Postgraduate Funding Worldwide: Sciences, 306
GrantFinder: The Complete Guide to Postgraduate Funding Worldwide: Social Sciences, 269
GrantLink, 270
Grantmakers Directory: A Resource for Social Change Funders & Grantseekers, 463
Grants and Awards Available to American Writers, 575
Grants and Funding for Higher Education, 475
Grants: Corporate Grantmaking for Racial and Ethnic Communities, 520
GRANTS Database, 247
Grants, Fellowships, and Prizes of Interest to Historians, 287
Grants for At–Risk Youth, 490
Grants for Cities and Town, 486
Grants for Health–Related Nonprofit Organizations: A Guide to Non–Research Funding, 512
Grants for K–12 Hotline, 477
Grants for K–12 Schools, 476
Grants for Libraries and Information Services, 487
Grants for Libraries Hotline, 486
Grants for Medical Research, 512
Grants for School Districts, 477
Grants for School Technology, 517
Grants for Schools, 476
Grants for Special Education and Rehabilitation: How to Find and Win Funds for Research, Training and Services, 478
Grants for Technology, 517
Grants on Disc, 370
The Grants Register: The Complete Guide to Postgraduate Funding Worldwide, 265
Grantsbook: A Resource Guide to Fundraising in Rhode Island, 440
GrantScape, 371
A Grantseeker's Guide to Tennessee Funders, 443
The Grantseeker's Handbook of Essential Internet Sites, 372
GrantSelect, 247
GrantsInfo.com: Biomedical Sciences, 316

390

Title Index

GrantsInfo.com: Creative Arts and Humanities, 282
GrantsInfo.com: Social and Natural Sciences, 271
GrantsInfo.com: Student Funding Sources, 44
GrantSmart, 374
GrantsNet, 169
GrantSource, 403
GrantStation, 375
Green Book, 181
Guaranteed–scholarships.com, 51
Guide to California Foundations, 390
Guide to Connecticut Grantmakers, 392
A Guide to Federal Funding for Education, 479
Guide to Federal Funding for Governments & Nonprofits, 376
A Guide to Financial Assistance for Graduate Study, Dissertation Research and Internships for Students in Latin American Studies, 137
A Guide to Financial Assistance for Latin American Studies, 137
A Guide to Florida State Programs, 396
Guide to Funding for International and Foreign Programs, 460
Guide to Greater Washington D.C. Grantmakers on CD–ROM, 393
Guide to Minnesota Foundations and Corporate Giving Programs, 417
Guide to Minnesota Grantmakers, 417
Guide to Ohio Grantmakers, 434
Guide to Oregon Foundations, 436
Guide to U.S. Foundations: Their Trustees, Officers, & Donors, 377
GuideStar, 378

Handbook of Illinois Postsecondary Institutions, 83
Handbook of United Methodist–Related Schools, Colleges, Universities, and Theological Schools, with a Guide to United Methodist Loans and Scholarships, 228
Handbook on Federal Benefits for Veterans, 327
Handicapped Funding Directory, 524
Health Funds Grants Resources Yearbook, 511
Health Grants & Contracts Weekly: Project Opportunities in Research, Training, and Services, 512
Health Grants Funding Alert, 511

Helping Out in the Outdoors: Your Source for Outdoor Volunteer Opportunities, 615
High School Senior's Guide to Merit and Other No–Need Funding, 45
Hillel/FACETS National Guide to Scholarships, Fellowships, and Financial Support for Jewish Students, 227
The Hispanic Scholarship Directory: Over 1,000 Ways to Finance Your Education, 202
History Internship Book, 621
Hooper Directory of Texas Foundations, 444
How Do I Pay for It: A Guide to Funding Assistive Technology Equipment, 332
How to Find a Scholarship Online, 46
How to Go to College Almost for Free, 66
How to Pay for Your Degree in Agriculture & Related Fields, 171
How to Pay for Your Degree in Business & Related Fields, 130
How to Pay for Your Degree in Education & Related Fields, 134
How to Pay for Your Degree in Journalism & Related Fields, 146
How to Win a Sports Scholarship, 194
Human Rights Internship Book, 621
Human Rights Organizations and Periodicals Directory, 644

Idealist.org, 635
IEFA's Scholarship Database, 118
Illinois Foundation Profile, 402
Illinois Funding Source, 403
Illinois Researcher Information Service, 249
ILMP Online, 577
Index to Private Foundation Reports, 411
Insider's Guide to Atlanta Internships & Part–Time Employment, 622
Insider's Guide to Boston Internships & Part–Time Employment, 622
Insider's Guide to Washington D.C. Internships & Part–Time Employment, 622
International Foundation Directory, 461
International Literary Market Place: The Directory of the International Book Publishing Industry, 576
International Scholarship Directory: The Complete Guide to Financial Aid for Study Anywhere in the World, 21–22
International Scholarships Online, 118
InternationalScholarships.com, 118
Internet Nonprofit Center's Nonprofit Locator, 378
InternJobs.com, 624

Title Index

The Internship Bible, 619
InternshipPrograms.com, 620
Internships in Information Technology, 622
Internships in International Affairs, 621
Internships in Youth Development, 646
Internships with America's Advertising Agencies, 621
Internships with America's Top Companies, 621
Internships: 30,000 On-the-Job Training Opportunities for Today's Job Market, 623
Internships-USA.com, 621
Intern.studyabroad.com, 118
Interorganizational Financial & Experiential Information Document: "If I'd" Only Known about That Scholarship, 184
Iowa Foundation DataBook, 405
IRIS Alert Service, 249
IRIS (Illinois Researcher Information Service), 249

Jobs You Can Live With, 669
Journalism Awards and Fellowships, 569
Journalism Career and Scholarship Guide, 148
Journalism Career Guide for Minorities, 149
Journalism Internship Guide, 654
The Journalist's Road to Success: A Career and Scholarship Guide, 148
Just the Facts about Student Financial Aid, 99
Justice Technology Monitor, 493

Kaplan Scholarships, 48

Legal Essay Contest Catalogue, 558
Legal Internships-USA, 622
Lesko Business Money Finder for Maryland, 276
Literary Market Place: The Directory of the American Book Publishing Industry, 577
LMP Online, 577
Loans and Grants from Uncle Sam: Am I Eligible and for How Much?, 49
Local/State Funding Report, 376
Louisiana Foundation DataBook, 408
Louisiana Funding Guide, 409
Louisiana's Financial Aid Handbook, 87

MACH25, 50
Making a Difference: College & Graduate Guide, 126

Making a Difference: Scholarships for a Better World, 126
The Market Guide for Young Writers, 583
Maryland Funders, 412
Maryland Grants Searchable Database, 255
Maryland/DC Foundation Directory Online, 394, 413
Massachusetts Foundation Directory, 415
Massachusetts Foundation Directory Supplement: Sources of Private Support for Individuals, 415
Massachusetts Grantmakers Directory, 415
Media Internship Guide, 621
Medical Research Funding Bulletin, 318
MeritMoney.com, 51
Michigan Foundation Directory, 416
Minnesota Foundation Directory, 418
Minnesota Foundation Directory Update Service, 418
Minnesota Grantmakers Online, 417
Minnesota Grants Directory, 419
Minnesota's List of Gay, Lesbian, Bisexual, & Transgender Scholarships, 213
Minority Funding Set, 198–201
Minority On-Line Information Service, 203
The Mitchell Guide: A Directory of New Jersey Foundations, 428
MOLIS (Minority On-Line Information Service), 203
Money for Graduate Students in the Arts & Humanities, 143
Money for Graduate Students in the Biological & Health Sciences, 174
Money for Graduate Students in the Humanities, 143
Money for Graduate Students in the Physical & Earth Sciences, 190
Money for Graduate Students in the Sciences, 174, 190
Money for Graduate Students in the Social & Behavioral Sciences, 127
Money for Graduate Students in the Social Sciences, 127
Money Magazine, 3
MonsterTRAK, 624
Montana and Wyoming Foundations Directory, 422
Montana Foundation Directory, 422
Music and Entertainment Industry Internship Guide, 656
Musical America: International Directory of the Performing Arts, 586

Title Index

NASSP National Advisory List of Contests and Activities, 543
National Data Bank, 377
National Directory of Arts Internships, 660
National Directory of Corporate Giving, 380
National Directory of Corporate Philanthropy for Native Americans, 521
National Directory of Corporate Public Affairs, 381
National Directory of Foundation Grants for Native Americans, 521
National Directory of Scholarships, Internships, and Fellowships for Latino Youth, 204
National Directory of Seed Money Grants for American Indian Projects, 522
National Guard Almanac, 329
National Guide to Funding for Children, Youth and Families, 491
National Guide to Funding for Elementary and Secondary Education, 480
National Guide to Funding for Information Technology, 518
National Guide to Funding for Libraries and Information Services, 487
National Guide to Funding for the Environment and Animal Welfare, 508
National Guide to Funding for Women and Girls, 528
National Guide to Funding in Aging, 492
National Guide to Funding in AIDS, 513
National Guide to Funding in Arts and Culture, 496
National Guide to Funding in Health, 514
National Guide to Funding in Higher Education, 481
National Guide to Funding in Religion, 501
National Internships Guide, 622
National Network of Grantmakers Membership Directory, 463
National Science Foundation Guide to Programs: A Compilation of NSF Funding Opportunities, 309
Nebraska Foundation DataBook, 424
Nebraska Foundation Directory, 425
Need a Lift? To Educational Opportunities, Careers, Loans, Scholarships & Employment, 217
Nevada Foundation Directory, 426
Nevada Funding Directory, 426
New Hampshire Directory of Foundations, 427
New Jersey Grants Guide, 429
New Jersey Internships, 629

New Jersey Mitchell Guide: Foundations, Corporations, and Their Managers, 428
The New Mexico Funding Directory, 430
New Program Updates, 479
New York State Foundations, 431
New York State Grants Guide, 429
Newspaper Internship Guide, 654
Newspapers, Diversity, & You, 149
Nonprofit Locator, 378
Nonprofit Vermont Newsletter: Real Help for People Involved in Vermont Organizations, 446
North Carolina Corporate Giving, 432
North Carolina Giving, 432
North Carolina Giving Online, 432
The Northwest Indiana Directory of Local Scholarships: A Guide for Lake, LaPorte, and Porter County Students, 85
Notices of the AMS, 189
Novel & Short Story Writer's Market: Places to Sell Your Fiction, 578
NSF Bulletin, 309
NSF E-Bulletin, 309
NYFA Source, 301
Nyquist Report on Funding for Community, Junior, and Technical Colleges, 482

Off to College, 15
Ohio Grants Guide, 429
Oklahoma Foundation DataBook, 435
On the Road to Higher Education: Guide to Hispanic Financial Aid Opportunities, 206
Online Study Abroad Directory, 119
Operating Grants for Nonprofit Organizations, 382
Opportunities in New Music, 587
Opportunities: The Source for Residency Information, 668
Opportunity Update, 587
Oregon Foundation DataBook, 437
Organizations for Composers, 587
Overseas Summer Jobs, 639
OverseasJobs.com, 624

Pacific Northwest Grantmakers Forum Member Directory, 449
Pacific Northwest Scholarship Guide, 97
Pathways to Career Success for Minorities: A Resource Guide to Colleges, Financial Aid, and Work, 207
Pathways to Career Success for Women: A Resource Guide to Colleges, Financial Aid, and Work, 234

Title Index

Paying Less for College: The Complete Guide to $36 Billion in Financial Aid, 53
P.E.N. American Center Newsletter, 575
Pennsylvania Grants Guide, 429
Pepsi–Cola Tuition Funding Sources, 74
Peterson's College Money Handbook, 53
Peterson's Complete Guide to Financial Aid, 54
Peterson's Guide to Four–Year Colleges, 57
Peterson's Guide to Two–Year Colleges, 57
Peterson's Internships: More than 50,000 Opportunities to Get an Edge in Today's Competitive Job Market, 623
Peterson's Internships: The Largest Source of Internships Available, 623
Peterson's Scholarship Almanac: A Compact Guide to Financial Aid, 55
Peterson's Scholarship Almanac: Key Facts You Need to Know about Scholarships, 55
Peterson's Scholarship Search, 56
Peterson's Scholarships and Loans for Adult Students, 224
Peterson's Scholarships for Study in the USA & Canada: The Money You Need for the Education You Want, 211
Peterson's Scholarships, Grants & Prizes: Sources of Financial Aid That Anyone Can Apply For, 57
Peterson's Scholarships, Grants & Prizes: The Most Complete Guide to College Financial Aid from Private Sources, 57
Peterson's Sports Scholarships & College Athletic Programs, 195
Peterson's Top Private Sources of Financial Aid: A Guide to Scholarships, Loans, and Grants, 57
Philanthropic Foundations of Utah Directory, 445
Philanthropy Northwest Member Directory, 449
Photographer's Market: Places to Sell Your Photographs, 566
The Playwright's Companion: A Practical Guide to Script Opportunities in the U.S.A., 294
PNPA Foundation Newspaper Internship Guide, 652
Poet's Market, 579
Poets & Writers Magazine, 295
Postgraduate Orthopaedic Fellowships, 187
The PRI Directory: Charitable Loans and Other Program–Related Investments by Foundations, 469
Princeton Review Scholarship Search, 58

Princeton Theological Seminary Scholarship Guide, 229
Profiles of American Colleges, 3
Progressive Publications Foundation Database, 465
Progressive Publications Internship Database, 643
Project Book, 659
Prospector's Choice, 383
Public and Safety Funding Hotline, 486
Public Schools Grants and Funding Opportunities, 477

Queertheory.com, 213

The Red Book: Catalog of State Assistance Programs, 255
Religious Funding Resource Guide, 502
Research and Funding: A German–American Guide for Historians and Social Scientists, 288
Reserve Forces Almanac, 329
Residency Directory, 184, 668
Resident Matching Program, 184
Resort Internship and Seasonal Employment Guide, 621
ResortJobs.com, 624
Resources for People with Disabilities: A National Directory, 333
Retired Military Almanac, 329
Rhode Island Grantsbook: A Resource for Grant Seekers in Rhode Island, 440
RI Grantsbook, 440
Rising Star Internships, 624
RSP Funding for Engineering Students, 176
RSP Funding for Graduate Students, 59
RSP Funding for Nursing Students and Nurses, 188
RSP Funding for Postdoctorates and Professionals, 251
RSP Funding for Undergraduates, 60
RSP Graduate Funding Set, 127, 143, 174, 190
Rural Health Services Funding: A Resource Guide, 505

Saint Louis University School of Law's Writing Competitions, 558
SavingforCollege, 61
Scholar$earch, 62
Scholar$ite, 62

Title Index

The Scholarship Advisor: Hundreds of Thousands of Scholarships Worth More Than $1 Billion, 63
The Scholarship Book: The Complete Guide to Private–Sector Scholarships, Fellowships, Grants, and Loans for the Undergraduate, 64
Scholarship & Grant Guide, 65
The Scholarship Handbook, 11
Scholarship Resource Network Express, 72
Scholarship Resource Network/PC, 72
The Scholarship Scouting Report: An Insider's Guide to America's Best Scholarships, 66
ScholarshipExperts, 67
Scholarships Available to Vermonters, 100
Scholarships, Fellowships and Financial Support for Jewish Students, 227
Scholarships, Fellowships and Loans, 68
Scholarships for Foreign Students in Japan (Japanese & English), 120
Scholarships for International Students in Japan, 121
Scholarships for Re–entry Students: Grants and Retraining Assistance for Adults Returning to College, 225
Scholarships 101, 69
Scholarships–Ar–Us, 79
Scholarships.com, 70
School Administrator's Title I Hotline, 477
School Technology Funding Directory, 519
School Technology OneBook, 519
ScienceWise, 310
Scijobs.org, 310
A Singer's Guide to the Professional Opera Companies, 584
SMARTS, 252
SND Foundation Internship Directory, 653
Social Science Research Council Fellowships and Grants for Training and Research, 129
Songwriter's Market, 588
Source Book Profiles, 366
Sources of Financial Aid Available to American Indian Students, 208
Sources of Operating Grants, 384
South Carolina Foundation Directory, 441
South Dakota Grant Directory, 442
SPIN Matching and Researcher Transmittal System, 252
SPIN (Sponsored Programs Information Network), 252
Sponsored Programs Information Network, 252
Sports Internship Book, 621
SRN Express Scholarship Search, 72

State & Homeland Security Funding Report, 355
Student Employment and Internships at Botanical Gardens and Arboreta, 662
Student Expenses at Postsecondary Institutions, 10
Student Financial Aid and Scholarships at Wyoming Colleges, 102
Student Financial Aid for American Indians, 208
Student Financial Aid for North Carolinians, 96
Student Funding Sources, 44
The Student Guide: Financial Aid from the U.S. Department of Education, 73
Student Guide to Higher Education and Financial Aid in Maryland, 91
Student's Guide to Chicago Internships & Part–Time Employment, 622
Student's Guide to Denver Internships & Part–Time Employment, 622
Student's Guide to Florida Internships & Part–Time Employment, 622
Student's Guide to New Jersey Internships & Part–Time Employment, 622
Student's Guide to New York City Internships & Part–Time Employment, 622
Student's Guide to North Carolina Internships & Part–Time Employment, 622
Student's Guide to Northern California Internships & Part–Time Employment, 622
Student's Guide to Ohio Internships & Part–Time Employment, 622
Student's Guide to Philadelphia Internships & Part–Time Employment, 622
Student's Guide to Seattle Internships & Part–Time Employment, 622
Student's Guide to Southern California Internships & Part–Time Employment, 622
Student's Guide to Texas Internships & Part–Time Employment, 622
Study Abroad: International Scholarships, International Courses, 123
Studyabroad.com, 118
Substance Abuse Funding News, 355
SumemrJobs.com, 624
A Summary of Department of Veterans Affairs Benefits, 327
Summary of Educational Benefits, 327
Summer Employment Directory of the United States, 626
Summer Jobs, 626
Summer Jobs Abroad, 639
Summer Jobs Britain, 640

Title Index

Summer Jobs for Students: Where the Jobs Are and How to Get Them, 626
Summer Opportunities for Kids and Teenagers, 627

Taft Foundation Reporter: Comprehensive Profiles and Analysis of America's Private Foundations, 365
Technology Law Moot Court and Writing Competitions, 558
TFS, 74
Tuition Funding Sources (TFS), 74

Ultimate College Money Guide, 18
Undergraduate Programs of Cooperative Education, 614
Uniformed Services Almanac, 329
Union–Sponsored Scholarships and Aid, 230
University of Richmond School of Law Legal Essay Contest Catalogue, 558
U.S. Student Fulbright Grants & Other Grants for Graduate Study and Research Abroad, 263
USnews.com, 69

Vacation Work's Summer Jobs Abroad, 639
Vacation Work's Summer Jobs Britain, 640
Vermont Directory of Foundations, 446
Veterans' Benefits: A Guide to State Programs, 219
Virginia Corporate Giving, 432
Virginia Giving, 432
Virginia Newspaper Internship Guide, 654, 654
VISTA Scholarship Guide for Hispanics, 206, 209

Washington Foundation DataBook, 450
Washington Foundation Directory: How to Get Your Slice of the Pie, 451
Washington Internships in Law and Policy, 621
The Welfare Reporter, 493
Where's the Money?, 209
Winning Scholarships for College: An Insider's Guide, 75
Wintergreen/Orchard House Scholarship Finder, 76
Wiredscholar, 77
Women's Collegiate Sports Scholarship Guide, 193
Women's Rights Internship Book, 621

World Guide to Foundations, 462
The Writer, 581
The Writer's Handbook, 581
Writer's Market Online, 582
Writer's Market: Places to Sell What You Write, 582
Wyoming Foundations Directory: A Guide to Private Foundations, 454

Yale Daily News Guide to Fellowships and Grants, 78
Yale Daily News Guide to Internships, 628
The Young Writer's Guide to Getting Published, 583
Your Guide to Florida Scholarships and Other Financial Assistance Programs, 81

529 College Savings Plans, 61
75 Scholarships Every Black High School Student Should Know About, 197

Name Index

Indexed here are the authors, editors, and compilers listed on the title pages of the specific resources cited in *How to Find Out About Financial Aid and Funding*. Since not all sources credit individual authors, a number of publications described in the guide (particularly those that are serial in nature, published by an organization, or offered on the Internet) are not represented here. Indexed names are arranged alphabetically, word by word. The numbers following each name refer to the entries that contain the fullest annotations of the individual's work.

Abbe, Elfrieda, 581
Adams, Cynthia M., 375, 385
Adams, John L., 396
Adjemian, Katherine, 381
Alarid, William, 275
Alliance of Artists' Communities, 303
American Library Association. Office for Human Resource Development and Recruitment, 136
American Psychological Association, 268
Armstrong, R.E., 219

Bares, Joan, 422
Batten, Donna, 530
Beckham, Barry, 197
Bessler, Ian C., 588
Black Excel, 196
Black, Issac, 196
Blum, Laurie, 34–35
Borman, Anne, 420
Bowling, Anne, 578
Breen, Nancy, 578–579
Breithaupt, Douglas J., 97

Cassidy, Daniel J., 21–22, 64
Caven, Todd D., 194
Christensen, Warren, 660
Cisneros, Jose A., 81
Clark, Amy, 192
Clark, Andy, 192
Clawges, Ron, 660
CollegeView, 18
Council of Michigan Foundations, 416

Davis, Herm, 5, 13
DeFiore, Laura, 36
Dillehay, James, 285

Disability Law Project, 332
Dumouchel, J. Robert, 368

Eckstein, Richard M., 348, 351–352, 515, 524
Elder, Amy, 430
Erdheim, Jesse, 287

Fabio, William F., 573
Fitzpatrick, Mary, 332
Flores, Andrea, 502
Foote, Kim, 287
Foundation Center, 416
Freidus–Flagg, Alberta, 398
Frenn, Mary C., 452

Gardner, Daniel, 221
Gardner, Garth, 649–650
Gardner, Richard, 560
Graham, Christine, 427, 446
Graham, Michael, 629
Greene, Justin, 96
Guide Line, Inc., 436

Hackwood, Sara, 265
Hamadeh, Samer, 619
Hamel, April Vahle, 41
Hammon, Bruce G., 24
Hastings, Penny, 194
Healy, Samantha R., 574
Heiberger, Mary Morris, 41
Henderson, Kathy, 583
Hines, Sedgwick, 172
Hispanic Association of Colleges and Universities, 206, 209
Holm, Kirsten C., 582
Hurley, Joseph, 61

Name Index

Ireland, Kevin, 241

James, Andrew, 639–640
Jankowski, Katherine E., 349–350

Kaplan, Ben, 66
Kennedy, Joyce Lain, 13
Klein, Charna, 451
Kletzie, S. Damon, 439
Krebs, Arlene, 471
Kregar, Shirley A., 137

Landes, Michael, 606
Leider, Anna, 1, 25, 49
Leider, Robert, 25
Leonard, Natacha, 381
Leppert, Elaine C., 399
Lesko, Matthew, 233, 276
Lucia Solórzano, 3

Madramootoo, Jerome, 573
Marsh, Jane, 391
Martello, Mary Ann, 233
Mauch, Christof, 288
McAdams, Jan, 286
McCloud, Beverly, 656
McDuffie, Elizabeth, 96
McKee, Cynthia Ruiz, 6
McKee, Phillip C., Jr., 6
McPherson, Craig, 437, 450
Meiners, Phyllis A., 521–522
Merchant, Jan, 208
Meserve, Mollie Ann, 294
Middleton, Robyn, 289
Miller, M. Ann, 454
Miller, Priscilla, 410
Miller, Shanan Y., 429
Mitchell, Janet A., 428
Moore, Mardell, 451
Moore, Maxine, 136
Moore, Pamela, 356, 512
Morkes, Andrew, 15
Morton, David, 61
Mudd, Mollie, 372, 384, 476, 488
Murphy, Diane R., 381

Nallim, Jorge, 137
Naprawa, Andrew, 233

National Assembly of Health and Human Service Organizations, 646
National Committee for Responsive Philanthropy, 520
National Science Foundation, 268

Offerman, Susan, 210
Oldman, Mark, 619

Passannante, Frances S., 396
Paul, Mary Eileen, 502
Pearson, Ford T., 389, 405, 408, 424, 435
Plagianos, James M., 573
Plothow, Roger Henry, 445
Poehner, Donna, 566
Pope, Alice, 572
Powell, Joan, 630

Ragins, Marianne, 75
Reed, Ellen B., 426
Reference Service Press, 48, 78
Reynnells, M. Louise, 505
Rice, Frances L., 410
Rigg, Mandy M., 429
Rizzauti, Terry P., 219
Robinson, Kerry A., 498

Sabol, Laurie, 234
Schaffert, Tim, 207
Schlachter, Gail Ann, 16, 45, 48, 78, 112, 127, 130, 134, 143, 146, 171, 174, 176, 188, 190, 198–201, 216, 222, 232, 262
Schladweiler, Kief, 358
Schultz, Robbie, 96
Scott, Tanya, 221
Sheridan, Valerie S., 381
Simonian, Susan J., 645
Sokolov, Jennifer, 574
Sova, Kathy, 574
Srinivasan, Kalpana, 628
Student Financial Services, 31, 40
Student Services, Inc., 19, 28
Sudhir, Pillarisetti, 287
Surratt, Melinda L., 505

Taft Group, 484
Tanabe, Gen S., 38
Tanabe, Kelly Y., 38
Tarnowski, Kenneth J., 645
Trombley, Nicole, 463

Name Index

Turlington, Shannon R., 46

United Way Columbia–Willamette, 436
U.S. General Services Administration, 339
U.S. Internal Revenue Service, 378
U.S. Office of Federal Register, 357

Vick, Julia Miller, 41
von Lossberg, Ann, 412
Vuturo, Christopher, 63

Wala, Michael, 288
Walker, Ronald E., 195
Wallen, Denise A., 430
Weber, R. David, 16, 45, 48, 78, 112, 127, 130, 134, 143, 146, 171, 174, 176, 188, 190, 198–201, 216, 222, 232, 262
Weinstein, Miriam, 126
Wilson, Susan R., 404
Womack, Idalah D., 14
Woodworth, David, 639–640

Yale Daily News, 628

Zils, Michael, 462
Zischke, Birgit, 288

Publisher and Producer Index

More than 250 publishers and producers are responsible for the 700+ print, electronic, and Internet resources that have been issued since 1999 and are described in this guide. These organizations and companies constitute a virtual "who's who" in the area of financial aid publishing. They are listed here alphabetically, word by word. Use the numbers following each publisher/producer name to 1) identify the publications they've issued in the field, 2) read a summary about the content of each of these publications, or 3) get their most recent contact information, including (when available) address, telephone number, toll–free number, fax number, e–mail address, and web site.

Academic Research Information System, Inc., 44, 271, 282, 316
Action Without Borders, Inc., 635
AFL–CIO, 230
Alaska Funding Exchange, Inc., 385
Allworth Press, 303
American Academy of Orthopaedic Surgeons, 187
American Association for the Advancement of Science, 169
American Association of Botanical Gardens and Arboreta, 662
American College of Clinical Pharmacy, 665
American Hiking Association, 615
American Historical Association, 287
American Journalism Review, 569
American Legion, 217
American Library Association, 136, 484
American Mathematical Society, 189
American Medical Association, 181
American Music Center, 587
American Physical Therapy Association, 180
American Psychological Association, 268
American Society of Health–System Pharmacists, 668
American Society of Newspaper Editors, 648
Arkansas Single Parent Scholarship Fund, 79
Art Deadlines List, 560
Artweek, 565
Asian Students' Cultural Association, 120
Aspen Publishers, Inc., 356, 371–372, 384, 476, 478, 490, 512, 517
Associated Grantmakers of Massachusetts, 415
Association for Computing Machinery, 191
Association of International Education, Japan, 121

Association of Theological Schools in the United States and Canada, 302
AvScholars Network Foundation, 172

Barron's Educational Series, Inc., 3
Bernan Associates/UNIPUB, 123
Blue Heron Publishers, 289
Brethren Volunteer Service, 659
BrokeScholar, 4, 70

Caldwell Public Library, 399
Canyon Research, 374
Capital Development Services, Inc., 432
Capitol City Publishers, 493
Career Education Institutes, 621
Career Press, 21–22
Carolyn Looff & Associates, 270
CD Publications, 355
C&D Publishing, 340, 389, 405, 408, 424, 435, 437, 450
Center for Non–Profit Corporations, 429
Center for Non–Profit Management, 443
Children's Book Council, Inc., 571
Chronicle Guidance Publications, 8
Chronicle of Higher Education, 277
Chronicle of Philanthropy, 341–342
College Board Publications, 10–11, 17, 26
College & Career Press, 15
College Planning Network, 97
CollegeNET, Inc., 50
Colorado Council on High School/College Relations, 80
Columbia Books, Inc., 381
Commonwealth Business Media, Inc., 586
Community of Science, Inc., 237
Community Resource Center, 391

Publisher and Producer Index

Congressional Hispanic Caucus Institute, 204
Connecticut Council for Philanthropy, 392
Consultant Services Northwest, Inc., 451
Council for International Exchange of Scholars, 264
Council of Michigan Foundations, 416
Council on Foundations, 343
CPG Enterprises, 427, 446
CRC Publishing Company, 521–522

DaimlerChrysler Corporation, 206, 209
Directory of Missouri Foundations, 420
Donors Forum of Chicago, 402–403
Dow Jones Newspaper Fund, 148–149

Editor & Publisher, 568
Education Funding Research Council, 479
eFinancialAid.com, Inc., 65
Entertainment Media Consultants, 656
eSchool News, 519

Facts On File, 34–35, 192
FADICA, Inc., 498
Falcon Management Group, Inc., 74
FastWeb Inc., 28
Feedback Theatrebooks, 294
Ferguson Publishing Company, 207, 234, 333
FinAid Page, LLC, 30
Finance Authority of Maine, 89
First Base Sports, Inc., 194
Florida Funding Publications, Inc., 81, 395–396
Food First Books, 630
Foundation Center, 243, 344, 354, 358–364, 366, 369, 377, 380, 393, 421, 431, 434, 460, 469, 480–481, 487, 491–492, 496, 501, 508, 513–514, 518, 528
Foundation Data Center, Inc., 418
FreSch! Information Services, LLC, 36
Fund for Theological Education, Inc., 162
Funders for Lesbian and Gay Issues, 523
Fundsnet Online Services, 367

The Gale Group, 68, 461–462, 530
Garth Gardner Company (GGC/Publishing), 649–650
German Historical Institute, 288
Government Information Services, 376
The Grant Advisor, 474
Grants Connection, Inc., 447
GrantStation.com, Inc., 375

Greenwood Publishing Group, Inc., 219
Guide Line, Inc., 436

HarperCollins Publishers, 6, 66
Health Resources Publishing, 511
HEATH Resource Center, 221
Helping Hands Hawai'i, 398
Henry Dean Publishing, Inc., 445
Henry Holt and Company, Inc., 75
Hieu Press, 412
Hobsons Publishing Company, 18

IDI Magic Tech Corp., 472
Illinois Commission on Intergovernmental Cooperation, 401
Illinois Researcher Information Service (IRIS), 249
Illinois Student Assistance Commission, 83
Indian Resource Development, 208
Indiana Grantmakers Alliance, Inc., 404
Infinity Publishing.com, 14
InfoEd International, Inc., 252
Information Today, Inc., 235, 559, 567, 576–577
Information USA, Inc., 233, 276
Institute of International Education, 263
International Education Finance Corporation, 118
Interorganizational Council on Student Affairs, 184
Intersociety Committee on Pathology Information, Inc., 179
iUniverse.com, Inc., 85

Jankowski Associates, Inc., 394, 413
John E. Fogarty International Center for Advanced Study in the Health Sciences, 314
John Wiley & Sons, Inc., 13, 196
Junior League of Omaha, 425
JUST GRANTS! Arizona, 387

Kalmbach Publishing Company, 581
Kansas Non Profit Association, 406
Kendall/Hunt Publishing Company, 471

Laramie County Community College, 454
Las Vegas–Clark County Library District, 426
Lawrence Erlbaum Associates, Inc., 645
Los Angeles Hillel Council, 227

Publisher and Producer Index

Louisiana Association of Nonprofit Organizations, 409
Louisiana Office of Student Financial Assistance, 87

Macmillan Reference USA, 9
Madison Books, 197
Maine Philanthropy Center, 410
Marquette University Memorial Library, 452
Maryland Attorney General Office, 411
Maryland Department of Planning, 255
Maryland Higher Education Commission, 91
McAdams Group, 286
McGraw–Hill, 46
Meiklejohn Civil Liberties Institute, 644
MeritMoney.com, 51
Minnesota Council of Nonprofits, 419
Minnesota Council on Foundations, 417
Minnesota Gay/Lesbian/Bisexual/Transgender Education Fund, 213
Minnesota Higher Education Services Office, 92
Mitchell Guide, 428
Montana State University at Billings, 422
Moyer Bell, Ltd., 520

National Agricultural Library, 505
National Assembly of Health and Human Service Organizations, 646
National Association of Secondary School Principals, 543
National College Scholarship Foundation, 5
National Commission for Cooperative Education, 614
National Internships Online/American Campus Company, 622
National Network for Artist Placement, 660
National Network of Grantmakers, 463
National Register Publishing, 163
National Scholarship Research Service, 27
National Science Foundation, 309
New Hampshire Department of Justice, 257
New York Foundation for the Arts, 301
Nonprofit Resource Center of Texas, 444
Nonprofit Resources, 388
Nonprofit Resources of Southern New England, 440
North Carolina State Education Assistance Authority, 96
Northern California Grantmakers, 390
Nyquist Associates, 482

Octameron Associates, 1, 25, 49
Ohio Attorney General's Office, 433
Omnigraphics, Inc., 368
Opera America, 584
Oryx Press, 238, 247, 280, 313, 382, 468, 473, 489
Overseas Academic Opportunities, 210
Ovid Technologies, 59–60, 251

Palgrave, 265, 269, 281, 306, 315
P.E.N. American Center, 575
Pennsylvania Newspaper Association, 652
Perpetual Press, 31, 40
Peterson's Guides, 39, 53–57, 195, 211, 224, 623, 626–627, 639–640
Philanthropic Research, Inc., 378
Philanthropy Northwest, 449
Pinnacle Peak Solutions, Inc., 69
Poets & Writers Inc., 295
Prentice Hall, 64
Princeton Review, 58
Princeton Theological Seminary, 229
ProgressivePubs.com, Inc., 465, 643
Prometheus Books, 573
Puma Publishing, 275

Quinlan Publishing Group, 475, 477, 486

Random House, 63, 607, 619
Reference Service Press, 16, 45, 112, 127, 130, 134, 143, 146, 171, 174, 176, 188, 190, 198–201, 216, 222, 232, 262
Research Communications, Inc., 629
Research Grant Guides, Inc., 348, 351–352, 515, 524
Resources for Global Sustainability, Inc., 507
ResourceWomen, 502
Rising Star Internships, 624
Rodale, Inc., 241

SageWorks Press, 126
Sallie Mae Servicing L.P., 77
Savingforcollege.com LLC, 61
Scholarship Experts, 67
Scholarship Resource Network, Inc., 72
Science Support Center, 318
ScienceWise, 203, 240, 310
Sedgwick Press/Grey House Publishing, 220
Simon & Schuster, 48, 78, 628
Sinclair, Townes and Co., 397
Social Science Research Council, 129

403

Publisher and Producer Index

Society for News Design, 653
Sourcebooks, Inc., 19
South Carolina State Library, 441
South Dakota State Library, 442
St. Martin's Press, 24
St. Vincent Pallotti Center for Apostolic Development, 610
State Farm Insurance, 12
Student Pugwash, USA, 669
SuperCollege, LLC, 38

Taft Group, 337, 345–346, 349–350, 365, 370, 383, 488, 500
Ten Speed Press, 606
Texas Higher Education Coordinating Board, 99
Theatre Communications Group, 574
TIYM Publishing Company, Inc., 62
Triadvocates Press, 439

Uniformed Services Almanac, Inc., 329
United Methodist Church, 228
University Aviation Association, 173
University of Minnesota, 119
University of New Mexico, 430
University of Pennsylvania Press, 41
University of Pittsburgh, 137
University of Richmond, 558
University of Wyoming, 102
U.S. Department of Commerce, 466–467
U.S. Department of Education, 73
U.S. Government Printing Office, 326–327, 339, 357

Vermont Assistive Technology Project, 332
Vermont Student Assistance Corporation, 100
Virginia Press Association, 654

Warm Snow Publishers, 285
Washington Secretary of State, 448
WD Communications LLC, 225
WetFeet, 620
Wintergreen/Orchard House, 76
Women's Sports Foundation, 193
WPR Publishing, 202
Writer's Digest Books, 566, 572, 578–579, 582–583, 588
Wyoming State Library, 453

Geographic Index

This index identifies the geographic coverage provided by the print, electronic, and Internet resources listed in *How to Find Out About Financial Aid and Funding*. Country, region, state, and other geographic terms are used. These terms are arranged in alphabetical order (word by word) and subdivided by type of funding covered in the sources: scholarships, fellowships & loans, grants for individuals, grants for organizations, awards, and/or internships. The numbers included in the index identify the entries where the resources are cited and/or described. Liberal cross–references provide access to broader or more specific geographic index terms.

Alaska: **Grants for Organizations,** 375, 385–386, 449. *See also* United States; names of specific cities

Arizona: **Grants for Organizations,** 387. *See also* United States; names of specific cities and counties

Arkansas: **Scholarships, Fellowships & Loans,** 79; **Grants for Organizations,** 388. *See also* United States; names of specific cities and counties

Australia: **Scholarships, Fellowships & Loans,** 116, 124, 141, 167, 182; **Grants for Individuals,** 265, 269, 281, 306, 315; **Awards & Prizes,** 554, 556, 562, 591, 595. *See also* Foreign countries

Britain. *See* United Kingdom

California: **Grants for Organizations,** 375, 389–390. *See also* United States; names of specific cities and counties

Canada: **Scholarships, Fellowships & Loans,** 68, 109, 116–117, 124, 132, 136, 140–141, 148, 163, 167, 179, 181–182, 189, 211, 234; **Grants for Individuals,** 238, 247, 261, 265–266, 269, 280–281, 292, 297, 302, 306, 315, 334; **Grants for Organizations,** 458–459, 473, 494, 499, 507; **Awards & Prizes,** 530, 552–556, 561–562, 567, 573, 575, 579, 584, 591, 595; **Internships,** 633–634, 650, 662, 664, 666, 681. *See also* Foreign countries

Colorado: **Scholarships, Fellowships & Loans,** 80; **Grants for Organizations,** 375, 391. *See also* United States; names of specific cities and counties

Connecticut: **Grants for Organizations,** 392. *See also* United States; names of specific cities and counties

District of Columbia. *See* Washington, D.C.

East Germany. *See* Germany

England: **Internships,** 640. *See also* Foreign countries; United Kingdom

Federal Republic of Germany. *See* Germany

Florida: **Scholarships, Fellowships & Loans,** 81; **Grants for Organizations,** 395–396. *See also* United States; names of specific cities and counties

Foreign countries: **Scholarships, Fellowships & Loans,** 9, 20–22, 27, 35, 37, 41, 104–115, 117–119, 122–123, 129, 137, 139, 142, 144–145, 152, 163–164, 177–178, 187, 189, 234; **Grants for Individuals,** 235, 237–238, 244, 247, 252, 259–264, 266–267, 274, 279, 282, 284, 287, 289, 292, 297, 299, 302, 304, 313–314, 334; **Grants for Organizations,** 350, 367, 455–463, 495, 499, 509; **Awards & Prizes,** 530, 551–553, 555, 560, 563, 565–566, 568, 571, 575–576, 584, 587, 590, 594; **Internships,** 606, 610, 621–623, 627, 630–639, 641, 647, 659, 681. *See also* names of specific continents; names of specific countries

Georgia: **Grants for Organizations,** 397. *See also* United States; names of specific cities and counties

German Democratic Republic. *See* Germany

Germany: **Scholarships, Fellowships & Loans,** 128, 151; **Grants for Individuals,** 273, 288. *See also* Foreign countries

Great Britain. *See* United Kingdom

405

Geographic Index

Hawaii: **Grants for Individuals,** 254; **Grants for Organizations,** 375, 398. *See also* United States; names of specific cities and counties

Idaho: **Scholarships, Fellowships & Loans,** 82; **Grants for Organizations,** 375, 399–400, 449. *See also* United States; names of specific cities and counties

Illinois: **Scholarships, Fellowships & Loans,** 83; **Grants for Organizations,** 401–403. *See also* United States; names of specific cities and counties

Indiana: **Scholarships, Fellowships & Loans,** 84–85; **Grants for Organizations,** 404. *See also* United States; names of specific cities and counties

Iowa: **Grants for Organizations,** 405. *See also* United States; names of specific cities and counties

Ireland: **Scholarships, Fellowships & Loans,** 116, 124, 141, 167, 182; **Grants for Individuals,** 265, 269, 281, 306, 315; **Awards & Prizes,** 554, 556, 562, 591, 595; **Internships,** 640. *See also* Foreign countries

Israel: **Scholarships, Fellowships & Loans,** 227; **Awards & Prizes,** 604; **Internships,** 678. *See also* Foreign countries

Japan: **Scholarships, Fellowships & Loans,** 120–121. *See also* Foreign countries

Kansas: **Grants for Organizations,** 406. *See also* United States; names of specific cities and counties

Kentucky: **Scholarships, Fellowships & Loans,** 86; **Grants for Individuals,** 332; **Grants for Organizations,** 404, 407. *See also* United States; names of specific cities and counties

Latin America. *See* South America

Louisiana: **Scholarships, Fellowships & Loans,** 87; **Grants for Organizations,** 408–409. *See also* United States; names of specific cities and parishes

Maine: **Scholarships, Fellowships & Loans,** 88–89; **Grants for Organizations,** 410. *See also* United States; names of specific cities and counties

Maryland: **Scholarships, Fellowships & Loans,** 90–91; **Grants for Individuals,** 255, 276; **Grants for Organizations,** 394, 411–414. *See also* United States; names of specific cities and counties

Massachusetts: **Grants for Individuals,** 256; **Grants for Organizations,** 415. *See also* United States; names of specific cities and counties

Michigan: **Grants for Organizations,** 416. *See also* United States; names of specific cities and counties

Minnesota: **Scholarships, Fellowships & Loans,** 92; **Grants for Organizations,** 417–419. *See also* United States; names of specific cities and counties

Missouri: **Scholarships, Fellowships & Loans,** 93; **Grants for Organizations,** 420–421. *See also* United States; names of specific cities and counties

Montana: **Scholarships, Fellowships & Loans,** 94; **Grants for Organizations,** 375, 422–423, 449. *See also* United States; names of specific cities and counties

Nebraska: **Grants for Organizations,** 424. *See also* United States; names of specific cities and counties

Nevada: **Grants for Organizations,** 426. *See also* United States; names of specific cities

New Hampshire: **Scholarships, Fellowships & Loans,** 95; **Grants for Individuals,** 257; **Grants for Organizations,** 427. *See also* United States; names of specific cities and counties

New Jersey: **Grants for Organizations,** 428–429; **Internships,** 629. *See also* United States; names of specific cities and counties

New Mexico: **Grants for Organizations,** 375, 430. *See also* United States; names of specific cities and counties

New York: **Grants for Organizations,** 431. *See also* United States; names of specific cities and counties

New Zealand: **Scholarships, Fellowships & Loans,** 116, 124, 141, 167, 182; **Grants for Individuals,** 265, 269, 281, 306, 315; **Awards & Prizes,** 554, 556, 562, 591, 595. *See also* Foreign countries

North Carolina: **Scholarships, Fellowships & Loans,** 96; **Grants for Organizations,** 432. *See also* United States; names of specific cities and counties

Ohio: **Grants for Individuals,** 258; **Grants for Organizations,** 375, 433–434. *See also* United States; names of specific cities and counties

406

Geographic Index

Oklahoma: **Grants for Organizations**, 435. *See also* United States; names of specific cities and counties

Oregon: **Scholarships, Fellowships & Loans**, 97; **Grants for Organizations**, 375, 436–438, 449. *See also* United States; names of specific cities and counties

Pennsylvania: **Grants for Organizations**, 439; **Internships**, 652. *See also* United States; names of specific cities and counties

Rhode Island: **Grants for Organizations**, 440. *See also* United States; names of specific cities

Scotland: **Internships**, 640. *See also* Foreign countries; United Kingdom

South Africa: **Scholarships, Fellowships & Loans**, 116, 124, 141, 167, 182; **Grants for Individuals**, 265, 269, 281, 306, 315; **Awards & Prizes**, 554, 556, 562, 591, 595. *See also* Foreign countries

South America: **Scholarships, Fellowships & Loans**, 137. *See also* Foreign countries; names of specific countries

South Carolina: **Grants for Organizations**, 441. *See also* United States; names of specific cities and counties

South Dakota: **Scholarships, Fellowships & Loans**, 98; **Grants for Organizations**, 442. *See also* United States; names of specific cities and counties

Tennessee: **Grants for Organizations**, 443. *See also* United States; names of specific cities and counties

Texas: **Scholarships, Fellowships & Loans**, 99; **Grants for Organizations**, 444. *See also* United States; names of specific cities and counties

United Kingdom: **Scholarships, Fellowships & Loans**, 116, 124, 141, 167, 182; **Grants for Individuals**, 265, 269, 281, 306, 315; **Awards & Prizes**, 554, 556, 562, 591, 595. *See also* Foreign countries; names of specific countries

United States: **Scholarships, Fellowships & Loans**, 1–78, 81, 96–97, 124–234; **Grants for Individuals**, 235–240, 242–253, 265, 268–275, 277–296, 298–331, 333–336; **Grants for Organizations**, 337–374, 376–384, 425, 460–528; **Awards & Prizes**, 529–550, 556–575, 577–605; **Internships**, 606–628, 630, 635, 642–651, 653, 655–681. *See also* names of specific cities, counties, states, and regions

Utah: **Grants for Organizations**, 445. *See also* United States; names of specific cities and counties

Vermont: **Scholarships, Fellowships & Loans**, 100; **Grants for Individuals**, 332; **Grants for Organizations**, 446. *See also* United States; names of specific cities and counties

Virginia: **Grants for Organizations**, 447; **Internships**, 654. *See also* United States; names of specific cities and counties

Wales: **Internships**, 640. *See also* Foreign countries; United Kingdom

Washington: **Scholarships, Fellowships & Loans**, 97, 101; **Grants for Organizations**, 375, 448–451. *See also* United States; names of specific cities and counties

Washington, D.C.: **Grants for Organizations**, 393. *See also* United States

West Germany. *See* Germany

Wisconsin: **Grants for Organizations**, 452. *See also* United States; names of specific cities and counties

Wyoming: **Scholarships, Fellowships & Loans**, 102–103; **Grants for Organizations**, 375, 453–454. *See also* United States; names of specific cities and counties

407

Subject Index

This index identifies the subject emphasis of the hundreds of print, electronic, and Internet resources covered in *How to Find Out About Financial Aid and Funding*. Nearly 300 subject areas are represented. Index terms are arranged in alphabetical order, ranging from "Accounting" to "Writers and writing," and are subdivided by type of program described in the sources: scholarships, fellowships & loans, grants for individuals, grants for organizations, awards, and/or internships. The numbers included in the index identify the entries where the resources are cited and/or described. Liberal cross–references provide access to broader, more specific, or variant subject terms.

Accounting: **Scholarships, Fellowships & Loans,** 130. *See also* Finance; General programs

Acquired Immunodeficiency Syndrome. *See* AIDS

Acting. *See* Performing arts

Addiction. *See* Alcohol use and abuse; Drug use and abuse

Administration. *See* Business administration; Management; Personnel administration; Public administration

Adolescents: **Grants for Individuals,** 247; **Grants for Organizations,** 355, 489–491, 528. *See also* General programs

Adult education. *See* Education, adult

Advertising: **Scholarships, Fellowships & Loans,** 146. *See also* Communications; General programs; Marketing; Public relations

Aeronautics: **Scholarships, Fellowships & Loans,** 172; **Internships,** 661. *See also* Aviation; General programs; Physical sciences

Aerospace sciences. *See* Space sciences

African American affairs: **Scholarships, Fellowships & Loans,** 198; **Grants for Individuals,** 322; **Awards & Prizes,** 598; **Internships,** 670. *See also* General programs; Minority affairs

Aged and aging: **Grants for Organizations,** 492, 511. *See also* General programs; Social sciences

Agribusiness: **Scholarships, Fellowships & Loans,** 171. *See also* Agriculture and agricultural sciences; Business administration; General programs

Agricultural economics. *See* Economics, agricultural

Agricultural engineering. *See* Engineering, agricultural

Agriculture and agricultural sciences: **Scholarships, Fellowships & Loans,** 168, 171;

Grants for Individuals, 271, 307; **Grants for Organizations,** 503. *See also* Biological sciences; General programs

Agrimarketing and sales. *See* Agribusiness

AIDS: **Grants for Organizations,** 513. *See also* Disabilities; General programs; Medical sciences

Alcohol use and abuse: **Grants for Organizations,** 355. *See also* General programs; Health and health care

American history. *See* History, American

American Indian affairs. *See* Native American affairs

American literature. *See* Literature, American

Animal rights: **Grants for Organizations,** 506, 508. *See also* General programs; Veterinary sciences

Animation: **Internships,** 649–650. *See also* Cartoonists and cartoons; Filmmaking; General programs

Anthropology: **Scholarships, Fellowships & Loans,** 140; **Grants for Individuals,** 270, 280; **Grants for Organizations,** 494; **Awards & Prizes,** 561. *See also* General programs; Social sciences

Applied arts. *See* Arts and crafts

Architecture: **Grants for Individuals,** 286. *See also* Fine arts; General programs; Historical preservation

Arithmetic. *See* Mathematics

Armed services. *See* Military affairs

Art: **Scholarships, Fellowships & Loans,** 139–140, 142, 163–166; **Grants for Individuals,** 247, 279–280, 282, 289, 303–305; **Grants for Organizations,** 494–495; **Awards & Prizes,** 560–561, 563, 565, 590; **Internships,** 647, 660. *See also* Education, art; General programs; Illustrators and illustrations; names of specific art forms

Art education. *See* Education, art

409

Subject Index

Arts and crafts: **Scholarships, Fellowships & Loans,** 140; **Grants for Individuals,** 280, 285; **Grants for Organizations,** 494, 497; **Awards & Prizes,** 561, 565, 590. *See also* Art; General programs; names of specific crafts

Asian American affairs: **Scholarships, Fellowships & Loans,** 199; **Grants for Individuals,** 323; **Awards & Prizes,** 599; **Internships,** 671. *See also* General programs; Minority affairs

Athletics: **Scholarships, Fellowships & Loans,** 192–195, 231; **Internships,** 621, 636. *See also* General programs; names of specific sports

Attorneys. *See* Legal studies and services

Audiovisual materials and equipment: **Grants for Organizations,** 496; **Awards & Prizes,** 567. *See also* General programs; specific types of media

Automation. *See* Computer sciences; Information science; Technology

A.V. *See* Audiovisual materials and equipment

Aviation: **Scholarships, Fellowships & Loans,** 172–173; **Internships,** 661. *See also* General programs; Space sciences

Ballet. *See* Dance

Banking: **Scholarships, Fellowships & Loans,** 130. *See also* Finance; General programs

Behavioral sciences: **Scholarships, Fellowships & Loans,** 125, 127; **Grants for Individuals,** 268, 271; **Grants for Organizations,** 464, 512. *See also* General programs; Social sciences; names of special behavioral sciences

Biological sciences: **Scholarships, Fellowships & Loans,** 169, 174, 183; **Grants for Individuals,** 247, 308, 311, 313, 316; **Grants for Organizations,** 512; **Awards & Prizes,** 592. *See also* General programs; Sciences; names of specific biological sciences

Birth control. *See* Family planning

Black American affairs. *See* African American affairs

Botany: **Internships,** 662. *See also* Biological sciences; General programs

Broadcasting: **Scholarships, Fellowships & Loans,** 146. *See also* Communications; Radio; Television

Business administration: **Scholarships, Fellowships & Loans,** 125, 130; **Grants for Individuals,** 241, 270–271, 275–276; **Grants for Organizations,** 464, 466–467; **Internships,** 621, 636. *See also* Entrepreneurship; General programs; Management

Business enterprises. *See* Entrepreneurship

Business reporting: **Scholarships, Fellowships & Loans,** 146. *See also* Business administration; General programs; Journalism

Cartoonists and cartoons: **Scholarships, Fellowships & Loans,** 139, 145; **Grants for Individuals,** 279; **Awards & Prizes,** 560, 568; **Internships,** 647. *See also* Art; General programs; Illustrators and illustrations

Chicano affairs. *See* Hispanic American affairs

Child care. *See* Day care

Child development: **Grants for Individuals,** 247; **Grants for Organizations,** 355, 489, 491. *See also* Adolescents; General programs

Children's literature. *See* Literature, children's

Choruses. *See* Voice

Civil liberties: **Internships,** 644. *See also* General programs; Political science and politics

Civil rights: **Grants for Organizations,** 528; **Internships,** 621, 636, 644. *See also* General programs; Political science and politics

Colleges and universities. *See* Education, higher

Commerce. *See* Business administration

Communications: **Scholarships, Fellowships & Loans,** 146–148; **Grants for Organizations,** 518; **Awards & Prizes,** 569; **Internships,** 621, 636, 649–650, 652. *See also* General programs; Humanities

Community colleges. *See* Education, higher

Community development: **Grants for Individuals,** 247; **Grants for Organizations,** 468–469. *See also* General programs; Rural affairs

Community services. *See* Social services

Composers and compositions: **Scholarships, Fellowships & Loans,** 158–160; **Grants for Individuals,** 296, 298, 300, 303; **Awards & Prizes,** 574, 585, 588. *See also* General programs; Music

Computer sciences: **Scholarships, Fellowships & Loans,** 125, 168, 189, 191; **Grants for Individuals,** 271, 307; **Grants for Organizations,** 503, 518. *See also* General programs; Information science; Libraries and librarianship; Mathematics; Technology

Computers. *See* Computer sciences

Conflict resolution. *See* Peace studies

Conservation. *See* Environmental sciences

Crafts. *See* Arts and crafts

Criminal justice: **Grants for Organizations,** 493; **Internships,** 621, 636. *See also* General programs; Legal studies and services

410

Subject Index

Dairy science: **Scholarships, Fellowships & Loans,** 171. *See also* Agriculture and agricultural sciences; General programs

Dance: **Scholarships, Fellowships & Loans,** 139–140, 161, 166; **Grants for Individuals,** 279–280, 301; **Grants for Organizations,** 494, 496; **Awards & Prizes,** 560–561; **Internships,** 647, 656–658, 660. *See also* General programs; Performing arts

Data entry. *See* Computer sciences

Day care: **Grants for Organizations,** 528. *See also* General programs

Defense. *See* Military affairs

Demography. *See* Population studies

Disabilities: **Grants for Organizations,** 355, 524. *See also* General programs; Rehabilitation; names of specific disabilities

Documentaries. *See* Filmmaking

Drama. *See* Plays

Drug use and abuse: **Grants for Organizations,** 355. *See also* General programs; Health and health care

Earth sciences: **Scholarships, Fellowships & Loans,** 175, 190; **Grants for Individuals,** 312; **Awards & Prizes,** 593. *See also* General programs; Natural sciences; names of specific earth sciences

Ecology. *See* Environmental sciences

Economic development: **Grants for Individuals,** 247; **Grants for Organizations,** 468–469. *See also* Economics; General programs

Economic planning. *See* Economics

Economics: **Scholarships, Fellowships & Loans,** 130; **Grants for Individuals,** 270; **Grants for Organizations,** 463. *See also* General programs; Social sciences

Economics, agricultural: **Scholarships, Fellowships & Loans,** 171. *See also* Agriculture and agricultural sciences; Economics; General programs

Editors and editing: **Scholarships, Fellowships & Loans,** 145; **Awards & Prizes,** 568. *See also* General programs; Writers and writing

Education: **Scholarships, Fellowships & Loans,** 125, 134; **Grants for Individuals,** 247, 271; **Grants for Organizations,** 352, 355, 464, 471–472, 477, 479, 483, 519, 528. *See also* General programs; specific types and levels of education

Education, adult: **Scholarships, Fellowships & Loans,** 132; **Grants for Organizations,** 473. *See also* Education; General programs

Education, art: **Grants for Organizations,** 528. *See also* Art; Education; General programs

Education, elementary: **Scholarships, Fellowships & Loans,** 132; **Grants for Organizations,** 473, 476, 480. *See also* Education; General programs

Education, higher: **Scholarships, Fellowships & Loans,** 131, 133; **Grants for Individuals,** 277–278; **Grants for Organizations,** 341, 470, 474–475, 481–482. *See also* Education; General programs

Education, secondary: **Scholarships, Fellowships & Loans,** 132; **Grants for Organizations,** 473, 476, 480. *See also* Education; General programs

Education, special: **Grants for Organizations,** 478. *See also* Disabilities; Education; General programs

Elementary education. *See* Education, elementary

Energy: **Grants for Organizations,** 508; **Internships,** 642, 663, 669. *See also* Environmental sciences; General programs

Engineering: **Scholarships, Fellowships & Loans,** 168, 170, 176; **Grants for Individuals,** 271, 307, 309–310; **Grants for Organizations,** 503–504, 518. *See also* General programs; Physical sciences; names of specific types of engineering

Engineering, agricultural: **Scholarships, Fellowships & Loans,** 171. *See also* Agriculture and agricultural sciences; Engineering; General programs

Enology and viticulture: **Scholarships, Fellowships & Loans,** 171. *See also* Agriculture and agricultural sciences; General programs

Entrepreneurship: **Scholarships, Fellowships & Loans,** 233; **Grants for Individuals,** 241, 275–276. *See also* Business administration; General programs

Environmental sciences: **Scholarships, Fellowships & Loans,** 125–126, 168; **Grants for Individuals,** 271, 307; **Grants for Organizations,** 463–464, 503, 506–508; **Internships,** 621–622, 636, 642, 663, 669. *See also* General programs; Sciences

Equipment: **Grants for Organizations,** 348, 515. *See also* General programs

Ethics: **Scholarships, Fellowships & Loans,** 140; **Grants for Individuals,** 280; **Grants for Organizations,** 494; **Awards & Prizes,** 561; **Internships,** 642, 663, 669. *See also* General programs; Humanities

Ethnic affairs. *See* Minority affairs

Family planning: **Grants for Organizations,** 491, 528. *See also* General programs; Population studies

411

Subject Index

Farming. *See* Agriculture and agricultural sciences

Feminist movement. *See* Women's studies and programs

Fertility. *See* Family planning

Fiction: **Scholarships, Fellowships & Loans,** 157; **Grants for Individuals,** 292, 295; **Awards & Prizes,** 573, 575, 578, 580, 582. *See also* General programs; Writers and writing

Filmmaking: **Scholarships, Fellowships & Loans,** 139, 161, 166; **Grants for Individuals,** 279; **Grants for Organizations,** 496; **Awards & Prizes,** 560; **Internships,** 647, 656–658, 660. *See also* Audiovisual materials and equipment; General programs

Finance: **Scholarships, Fellowships & Loans,** 130; **Grants for Individuals,** 270. *See also* Economics; General programs

Fine arts: **Scholarships, Fellowships & Loans,** 139–141, 165–166; **Grants for Individuals,** 279–281, 296, 300, 303; **Grants for Organizations,** 493–494; **Awards & Prizes,** 560–562, 565, 590; **Internships,** 647, 660. *See also* General programs; Humanities; names of specific fine arts

Flight science. *See* Aviation

Floriculture. *See* Horticulture

Flying. *See* Aviation

Folklore: **Scholarships, Fellowships & Loans,** 140; **Grants for Individuals,** 280; **Grants for Organizations,** 494; **Awards & Prizes,** 561. *See also* General programs; Literature

Foreign affairs. *See* International affairs

Foreign language. *See* Language and linguistics

Forestry management: **Grants for Organizations,** 506, 508. *See also* General programs; Management

Gardening. *See* Horticulture

Gender. *See* Women's studies and programs

General programs: **Scholarships, Fellowships & Loans,** 1–123, 133, 137, 196–204, 206–225, 227, 230, 233–234; **Grants for Individuals,** 235–267, 277–278, 322–333; **Grants for Organizations,** 337–351, 353–459, 461–462, 474, 521–523, 525; **Awards & Prizes,** 529–555, 598–604; **Internships,** 606–614, 616–620, 622–629, 631, 633–635, 637–641, 670–674, 676–678, 680–681

Geography: **Grants for Individuals,** 270. *See also* General programs; Social sciences

Geosciences. *See* Earth sciences

Geriatrics. *See* Aged and aging

Gerontology. *See* Aged and aging

Government. *See* Political science and politics; Public administration

Grade school. *See* Education, elementary

Graphic arts: **Internships,** 621, 636, 649–650. *See also* Art; Arts and crafts; General programs

Graphic design: **Scholarships, Fellowships & Loans,** 146. *See also* General programs; Graphic arts

Handicapped. *See* Disabilities

Health and health care: **Scholarships, Fellowships & Loans,** 174, 177–178, 185–186; **Grants for Individuals,** 247, 270, 313–314, 316, 318–319; **Grants for Organizations,** 505, 509–512, 514, 528; **Awards & Prizes,** 594, 596. *See also* General programs; Medical sciences

High schools. *See* Education, secondary

Higher education. *See* Education, higher

Hispanic American affairs: **Scholarships, Fellowships & Loans,** 200; **Grants for Individuals,** 324; **Awards & Prizes,** 600; **Internships,** 672. *See also* General programs; Minority affairs

Historical preservation: **Grants for Organizations,** 496; **Internships,** 621, 636. *See also* General programs; History

History: **Scholarships, Fellowships & Loans,** 140, 150–151; **Grants for Individuals,** 270, 280, 287–288; **Grants for Organizations,** 494; **Awards & Prizes,** 561, 570; **Internships,** 655. *See also* General programs; Humanities; Social sciences; specific types of history

History, American: **Internships,** 621, 636. *See also* General programs; History

Homeland security. *See* Security, national

Horticulture: **Scholarships, Fellowships & Loans,** 171; **Internships,** 662. *See also* Agriculture and agricultural sciences; General programs; Sciences

Hospitals. *See* Health and health care

Human resources. *See* Personnel administration

Human rights. *See* Civil rights

Human services. *See* Social services

Humanities: **Scholarships, Fellowships & Loans,** 129, 141–144; **Grants for Individuals,** 281–284; **Grants for Organizations,** 493, 495; **Awards & Prizes,** 562–564. *See also* General programs; names of specific humanities

Subject Index

Illustrators and illustrations: **Awards & Prizes,** 571–572. *See also* Art; General programs; Graphic arts

Industrial relations: **Scholarships, Fellowships & Loans,** 126, 130. *See also* General programs

Information science: **Grants for Organizations,** 487, 518; **Internships,** 622. *See also* Computer sciences; General programs; Libraries and librarianship

International affairs: **Grants for Individuals,** 270; **Grants for Organizations,** 460; **Internships,** 621, 630, 636, 642, 663, 669. *See also* General programs; Political science and politics

International relations. *See* International affairs

Internet journalism. *See* Journalism, online

Journalism: **Scholarships, Fellowships & Loans,** 139, 145–149, 205; **Grants for Individuals,** 279, 292; **Awards & Prizes,** 560, 568–569, 575, 582; **Internships,** 621, 636, 647–649, 651–654, 656–657, 675. *See also* Communications; General programs; Writers and writing; names of specific types of journalism

Journalism, business. *See* Business reporting

Journalism, medical. *See* Science reporting

Journalism, online: **Scholarships, Fellowships & Loans,** 146. *See also* General programs; Journalism

Journalism, science. *See* Science reporting

Journalism, sports. *See* Sports reporting

Junior colleges. *See* Education, higher

Jurisprudence. *See* Legal studies and services

Labor unions and members: **Scholarships, Fellowships & Loans,** 126. *See also* General programs; Industrial relations

Language and linguistics: **Scholarships, Fellowships & Loans,** 140; **Grants for Individuals,** 280; **Grants for Organizations,** 494; **Awards & Prizes,** 561. *See also* General programs; Humanities; names of specific languages

Latino affairs. *See* Hispanic American affairs

Law. *See* Legal studies and services

Law enforcement. *See* Criminal justice

Lawyers. *See* Legal studies and services

Legal studies and services: **Scholarships, Fellowships & Loans,** 125; **Grants for Individuals,** 270–271; **Grants for Organizations,** 464, 528; **Awards & Prizes,** 558; **Internships,** 621–622, 636, 656–657. *See also* Criminal justice; General programs; Social sciences

Librarians. *See* Libraries and librarianship

Libraries and librarianship: **Scholarships, Fellowships & Loans,** 132, 135–136, 155; **Grants for Organizations,** 473, 484–487; **Awards & Prizes,** 559, 577. *See also* General programs; Information science; Social sciences

Life sciences. *See* Biological sciences

Linguistics. *See* Language and linguistics

Literature: **Scholarships, Fellowships & Loans,** 140, 154, 157; **Grants for Individuals,** 280, 291–292, 295, 301; **Grants for Organizations,** 494, 496; **Awards & Prizes,** 561, 574–575, 580, 583. *See also* General programs; Humanities; Writers and writing; specific types of literature

Literature, American: **Awards & Prizes,** 582. *See also* General programs; Literature

Literature, children's: **Awards & Prizes,** 571–572, 582–583. *See also* General programs; Literature

Magazines. *See* Journalism; Literature

Management: **Grants for Individuals,** 270; **Internships,** 656–657. *See also* General programs; Social sciences

Marketing: **Scholarships, Fellowships & Loans,** 130; **Internships,** 621, 636, 656–657. *See also* Advertising; General programs; Public relations

Mass communications. *See* Communications

Mathematics: **Scholarships, Fellowships & Loans,** 168, 170, 189; **Grants for Individuals,** 271, 307, 309; **Grants for Organizations,** 503–504. *See also* Computer sciences; General programs; Physical sciences; Statistics

Media. *See* Broadcasting; Communications; names of specific media

Media specialists. *See* Libraries and librarianship

Medical journalism. *See* Science reporting

Medical sciences: **Scholarships, Fellowships & Loans,** 169, 177–179, 181–182, 185, 210; **Grants for Individuals,** 247, 308, 313–316, 318; **Grants for Organizations,** 509–510, 512; **Awards & Prizes,** 594–595; **Internships,** 664, 666. *See also* General programs; Health and health care; Sciences; names of specific diseases; names of medical specialties

Merchandising. *See* Sales

Mexican American affairs. *See* Hispanic American affairs

413

Subject Index

Microcomputers. *See* Computer sciences

Military affairs: **Scholarships, Fellowships & Loans,** 215; **Grants for Individuals,** 327. *See also* General programs

Minority affairs: **Scholarships, Fellowships & Loans,** 149, 205; **Grants for Organizations,** 520; **Internships,** 651, 675. *See also* General programs; names of specific ethnic minority groups

Missionary work. *See* Religion and religious activities

Museums: **Scholarships, Fellowships & Loans,** 132; **Grants for Organizations,** 473, 496; **Internships,** 621, 636. *See also* General programs; Libraries and librarianship

Music: **Scholarships, Fellowships & Loans,** 139–140, 158–161, 166; **Grants for Individuals,** 279–280, 296–301, 303; **Grants for Organizations,** 494, 496; **Awards & Prizes,** 560–561, 574, 584–589; **Internships,** 647, 656–658, 660. *See also* Fine arts; General programs; Humanities; Performing arts

Narcotics. *See* Drug use and abuse

National security. *See* Security, national

Native American affairs: **Scholarships, Fellowships & Loans,** 201; **Grants for Individuals,** 325; **Awards & Prizes,** 601; **Internships,** 673. *See also* General programs; Minority affairs

Natural sciences: **Scholarships, Fellowships & Loans,** 168; **Grants for Individuals,** 271, 307; **Grants for Organizations,** 503. *See also* General programs; Sciences; names of specific sciences

Newspapers. *See* Journalism

Nurses and nursing, general: **Scholarships, Fellowships & Loans,** 188; **Grants for Individuals,** 320. *See also* General programs; Health and health care; Medical sciences; names of specific nursing specialties

Online journalism. *See* Journalism, online

Opera. *See* Music; Voice

Orchestras. *See* Music

Orthopedics: **Scholarships, Fellowships & Loans,** 187. *See also* General programs; Medical sciences

Painting. *See* Art

Pathology: **Scholarships, Fellowships & Loans,** 179; **Internships,** 664. *See also* General programs; Medical sciences

Peace studies: **Scholarships, Fellowships & Loans,** 126. *See also* General programs; Political science and politics

Pediatrics: **Internships,** 645. *See also* General programs; Medical sciences

Performing arts: **Scholarships, Fellowships & Loans,** 140, 142, 158, 160–161, 166; **Grants for Individuals,** 280, 282, 296, 300–301, 303; **Grants for Organizations,** 494–496; **Awards & Prizes,** 561, 563, 586, 589; **Internships,** 656–658, 660. *See also* General programs; names of specific performing arts

Personnel administration: **Scholarships, Fellowships & Loans,** 130. *See also* General programs; Management

Pharmaceutical sciences: **Scholarships, Fellowships & Loans,** 184; **Grants for Individuals,** 317; **Internships,** 665, 667–668. *See also* General programs; Medical sciences

Philology. *See* Language and linguistics

Philosophy: **Scholarships, Fellowships & Loans,** 140; **Grants for Individuals,** 280; **Grants for Organizations,** 494; **Awards & Prizes,** 561. *See also* General programs; Humanities

Photography: **Scholarships, Fellowships & Loans,** 139–140, 145, 166; **Grants for Individuals,** 279–280; **Grants for Organizations,** 494; **Awards & Prizes,** 560–561, 566, 568; **Internships,** 647, 649, 660. *See also* Fine arts; General programs

Photojournalism: **Scholarships, Fellowships & Loans,** 146. *See also* General programs; Journalism; Photography

Physical sciences: **Scholarships, Fellowships & Loans,** 190; **Grants for Individuals,** 321; **Awards & Prizes,** 597. *See also* General programs; Sciences; names of specific physical sciences

Physical therapy: **Scholarships, Fellowships & Loans,** 180. *See also* Disabilities; General programs; Health and health care; Rehabilitation

Plays: **Scholarships, Fellowships & Loans,** 154, 156, 159; **Grants for Individuals,** 291, 294, 298; **Awards & Prizes,** 573–575, 582, 585. *See also* General programs; Literature; Performing arts; Writers and writing

Poetry: **Scholarships, Fellowships & Loans,** 139, 157; **Grants for Individuals,** 279, 295; **Awards & Prizes,** 560, 573, 575, 579–580, 582; **Internships,** 647. *See also* General programs; Literature; Writers and writing

Police science. *See* Criminal justice

Political science and politics: **Grants for Individuals,** 270, 288; **Grants for Organiza-**

Subject Index

tions, 463. *See also* General programs; Public administration; Social sciences

Population studies: **Grants for Individuals,** 270. *See also* Family planning; General programs; Social sciences

Posters. *See* Graphic arts

Preservation, historical. *See* Historical preservation

Presidents, U.S. *See* History, American

Press. *See* Journalism

Print journalism. *See* Journalism

Prints. *See* Art; Graphic arts

Psychology: **Scholarships, Fellowships & Loans,** 138; **Grants for Individuals,** 270; **Internships,** 645. *See also* Behavioral sciences; General programs; Social sciences

Public administration: **Scholarships, Fellowships & Loans,** 90; **Grants for Individuals,** 255, 270; **Grants for Organizations,** 414; **Internships,** 621, 630, 636. *See also* General programs; Management; Political science and politics; Social sciences

Public affairs. *See* Public administration

Public policy. *See* Public administration

Public relations: **Scholarships, Fellowships & Loans,** 146; **Internships,** 621, 636, 656–657. *See also* General programs; Marketing

Public sector. *See* Public administration

Publicity. *See* Public relations

Publishers and publishing: **Scholarships, Fellowships & Loans,** 155; **Awards & Prizes,** 576–577. *See also* General programs

Radio: **Scholarships, Fellowships & Loans,** 147; **Grants for Organizations,** 496; **Awards & Prizes,** 569. *See also* Communications; General programs

Rape: **Grants for Organizations,** 528. *See also* General programs; Women's studies and programs

Recreation: **Internships,** 615, 621, 636. *See also* General programs; names of specific recreational activities

Rehabilitation: **Grants for Organizations,** 478. *See also* General programs; Health and health care; specific types of therapy

Religion and religious activities: **Scholarships, Fellowships & Loans,** 140, 162, 226, 228–229; **Grants for Individuals,** 280, 302, 334–335; **Grants for Organizations,** 494, 498–502, 526; **Awards & Prizes,** 561; **Internships,** 659. *See also* General programs; Humanities

Reproduction. *See* Family planning

Retailing. *See* Sales

Rural affairs: **Grants for Organizations,** 505. *See also* Agriculture and agricultural sciences; General programs; Sociology

Sales: **Scholarships, Fellowships & Loans,** 130. *See also* General programs; Marketing

Schools. *See* Education

Science reporting: **Scholarships, Fellowships & Loans,** 146. *See also* General programs; Journalism; Sciences; Writers and writing

Sciences: **Scholarships, Fellowships & Loans,** 167, 169–170; **Grants for Individuals,** 306, 308–310; **Grants for Organizations,** 504; **Awards & Prizes,** 591. *See also* General programs; names of specific sciences

Sculpture: **Scholarships, Fellowships & Loans,** 139–140; **Grants for Individuals,** 279–280; **Grants for Organizations,** 494; **Awards & Prizes,** 560–561; **Internships,** 647. *See also* Fine arts; General programs

Secondary education. *See* Education, secondary

Security, national: **Grants for Organizations,** 355. *See also* General programs; Military affairs

Sexual abuse. *See* Rape

Singing. *See* Voice

Social sciences: **Scholarships, Fellowships & Loans,** 124–129; **Grants for Individuals,** 268–274, 288; **Grants for Organizations,** 463–465, 512; **Awards & Prizes,** 556–557; **Internships,** 642–643, 663, 669. *See also* General programs; names of specific social sciences

Social services: **Grants for Organizations,** 355, 488, 490, 492; **Internships,** 610, 632, 646, 659. *See also* General programs; Social welfare

Social welfare: **Grants for Organizations,** 491, 493; **Internships,** 646. *See also* General programs; Social services

Sociology: **Grants for Individuals,** 270; **Grants for Organizations,** 488, 490. *See also* General programs; Social sciences

Songs. *See* Music

Space sciences: **Scholarships, Fellowships & Loans,** 168, 172; **Grants for Individuals,** 271, 307; **Grants for Organizations,** 503; **Internships,** 661. *See also* General programs; Physical sciences

Special education. *See* Education, special

Sports. *See* Athletics

Sports reporting: **Scholarships, Fellowships & Loans,** 146. *See also* General programs; Journalism; Writers and writing

Stage design. *See* Performing arts

Subject Index

Statistics: **Scholarships, Fellowships & Loans,** 189; **Grants for Individuals,** 270. *See also* General programs; Mathematics

Substance abuse. *See* Alcohol use and abuse; Drug use and abuse

Teaching. *See* Education

Technology: **Grants for Organizations,** 471, 483, 515–519; **Internships,** 622, 642, 663, 669. *See also* Computer sciences; General programs; Sciences

Teenagers. *See* Adolescents

Telecommunications: **Grants for Organizations,** 471, 516, 518. *See also* Communications; General programs; Radio; Television

Television: **Grants for Organizations,** 496; **Internships,** 656–657. *See also* Communications; Filmmaking; General programs

Theater. *See* Performing arts; Plays

Theology. *See* Religion and religious activities

Trade unions. *See* Labor unions and members

Translators and translations: **Scholarships, Fellowships & Loans,** 154, 159; **Grants for Individuals,** 291; **Awards & Prizes,** 574, 585. *See also* General programs; Language and linguistics; Writers and writing

TV. *See* Television

Unions and unionization. *See* Industrial relations; Labor unions and members

Universities. *See* Education, higher

Unrestricted programs. *See* General programs

Urban development. *See* Community development

Veterans. *See* Military affairs

Veterinary sciences: **Scholarships, Fellowships & Loans,** 171. *See also* General programs; Sciences

Video. *See* Filmmaking; Television

Violence: **Grants for Organizations,** 528. *See also* General programs

Visual arts. *See* Art

Viticulture. *See* Enology and viticulture

Voice: **Grants for Individuals,** 297; **Awards & Prizes,** 584. *See also* General programs; Music; Performing arts

Water resources: **Grants for Organizations,** 506, 508. *See also* Environmental sciences; General programs

Web journalism. *See* Journalism, online

Welfare. *See* Social services; Social welfare

Wine making. *See* Enology and viticulture

Women's studies and programs: **Scholarships, Fellowships & Loans,** 232; **Grants for Individuals,** 336; **Grants for Organizations,** 527–528; **Awards & Prizes,** 605; **Internships,** 621, 636, 679. *See also* General programs

World literature. *See* Literature

Writers and writing: **Scholarships, Fellowships & Loans,** 139, 152–153, 155–157; **Grants for Individuals,** 279, 289–290, 292–295, 301, 303; **Grants for Organizations,** 496; **Awards & Prizes,** 558, 560, 571–573, 575–583; **Internships,** 647, 656–657. *See also* General programs; Literature; specific types of writing

Youth. *See* Adolescents; Child development